THE
BIBLE
BOOK

THE
BIBLE
BOOK

DK LONDON

PROJECT EDITOR
Sam Kennedy

SENIOR ART EDITOR
Gillian Andrews

SENIOR EDITOR
Victoria Heyworth-Dunne

ILLUSTRATIONS
James Graham

JACKET EDITOR
Claire Gell

SENIOR JACKET DESIGNER
Mark Cavanagh

JACKET DESIGN
DEVELOPMENT MANAGER
Sophia MTT

PRODUCER, PRE-PRODUCTION
Gillian Reid

PRODUCER
Mandy Inness

MANAGING EDITOR
Gareth Jones

SENIOR MANAGING ART EDITOR
Lee Griffiths

ASSOCIATE PUBLISHING DIRECTOR
Liz Wheeler

ART DIRECTOR
Karen Self

DESIGN DIRECTOR
Philip Ormerod

PUBLISHING DIRECTOR
Jonathan Metcalf

DK DELHI

SENIOR ART EDITOR
Ira Sharma

PROJECT ART EDITORS
Vikas Sachdeva, Vikas Chauhan

ART EDITORS
Sourabh Challariya, Revati Anand

ASSISTANT EDITOR
Smita Mathur

ASSISTANT ART EDITORS
Monam Nishat, Simran Saini

ILLUSTRATORS
Arun Pottirayil, Mohd Zishan

JACKET DESIGNER
Suhita Dharamjit

JACKETS EDITORIAL COORDINATOR
Priyanka Sharma

SENIOR DTP DESIGNERS
Shanker Prasad, Harish Aggarwal

DTP DESIGNER
Nand Kishor Acharya

PICTURE RESEARCHER
Aditya Katyal

MANAGING JACKETS EDITOR
Saloni Singh

PICTURE RESEARCH MANAGER
Taiyaba Khatoon

PRE-PRODUCTION MANAGER
Balwant Singh

PRODUCTION MANAGER
Pankaj Sharma

MANAGING EDITOR
Kingshuk Ghoshal

SENIOR MANAGING ART EDITOR
Arunesh Talapatra

TOUCAN BOOKS

EDITORIAL DIRECTOR
Ellen Dupont

SENIOR DESIGNER
Thomas Keenes

SENIOR EDITOR
Dorothy Stannard

EDITOR
Abigail Mitchell

ADDITIONAL EDITING
John Andrews, Guy Croton, Larry Porges,
Vicky Richards, Rachel Warren Chadd

EDITORIAL ASSISTANT
Michael Clark

EDITORIAL INTERN
Zara Mandel

INDEXER
Marie Lorimer

PROOFREADER
Marion Dent

ADDITIONAL TEXT
Autumn Green, Jeremy Harwood,
Vicky Hales-Dutton

original styling by
STUDIO 8

First American Edition, 2018
Published in the United States by DK Publishing
345 Hudson Street, New York, New York 10014

Copyright © 2018 Dorling Kindersley Limited
DK, a Division of Penguin Random House LLC
18 19 20 21 22 10 9 8 7 6 5 4 3 2 1
001–305929–Feb/2018

A catalog record for this book
is available from the Library of Congress.
ISBN: 978-1-4654-6864-2

DK books are available at special discounts
when purchased in bulk for sales promotions,
premiums, fund-raising, or educational use. For
details, contact: DK Publishing Special Markets,
345 Hudson Street, New York, New York 10014
SpecialSales@dk.com

Printed and bound in Hong Kong

A WORLD OF IDEAS:
SEE ALL THERE IS TO KNOW

www.dk.com

CONTRIBUTORS

TAMMI J. SCHNEIDER, PHD, CONSULTANT

Dr. Tammi J. Schneider is a Professor of Religion at Claremont Graduate University, having received a doctorate in Ancient History from the University of Pennsylvania. Her books include: *Sarah: Mother of Nations; Judges; Mothers of Promise: Women in the Book of Genesis;* and *An Introduction to Ancient Mesopotamian Religion.* She excavates in Israel.

SHELLEY L. BIRDSONG, PHD

Dr. Shelley L. Birdsong is a member of the Religious Studies faculty at North Central College, Naperville, Illinois. Her interests range from topics such as women in the Bible to specific text-critical issues in ancient Jeremiah manuscripts.

ANDREW KERR-JARRETT

Andrew Kerr-Jarrett read English at Trinity College, Cambridge. He is a writer and editor of more than 25 years' standing. He facilitates seminars and workshops at the Mount Street Jesuit Centre in London, UK.

REV. DR. ANDREW STOBART

Rev. Dr. Andrew Stobart is a Methodist Minister in Darlington, UK, and commissioning editor of *Holiness*, an online theological journal published by Wesley House, Cambridge. He studied theology at the London School of Theology, Aberdeen University, and Durham University, and has contributed to a number of reference works, including DK's *The Illustrated Bible* and *The Religions Book.*

BENJAMIN PHILLIPS, PHD, CONSULTANT AND CONTRIBUTOR

Dr. Benjamin Phillips is Associate Dean and Associate Professor of Systematic Theology at Southwestern Baptist Theological Seminary's Houston Campus, where he teaches courses in Christian doctrine and preaching. He is also Director of Southwestern's Darrington Extension, which offers a bachelor's degree in Biblical Studies to offenders in the Texas prison system.

GUY CROTON

Guy Croton is an author and editor who has written, co-written, or edited books and articles on a variety of subjects in a career spanning more than 30 years. A Christian Humanist by religious and moral inclination, he studied theology and biblical history as part of his degree at the University of Sussex.

NICHOLAUS PUMPHREY, PHD

Dr. Nicholaus Pumphrey is the Assistant Professor of Religious Studies and Curator of the Quayle Bible Collection at Baker University, Baldwin City, Kansas. He specializes in Biblical Studies, Ancient Near Eastern history and literature, and Islamic Studies. He is currently a senior staff member on the Tel Akko Total Archaeology Project in Akko, Israel.

CONTENTS

WISDOM AND PROPHETS
JOB 1:1–MALACHI 4:6

THE GOSPELS
MATTHEW 1:1–JOHN 21:25

ACTS, EPISTLES, AND REVELATION
ACTS 1:1– REVELATION 22:21

INTRODU

CTION

The Bible is the world's most famous book and a keystone text of Western civilization. It has been translated into more languages than any other text in history, and it remains the most prolifically published book since the invention of the printing press. Christians worldwide look to it as sacred scripture—the written word of God, given by divine inspiration. It has influenced art, language, music, and literature for more than 2,000 years: in fact, the history of Western art cannot be fully understood without at least some knowledge of the Bible.

The Bible's teachings have also shaped social, economic, and political developments, contributing to Western civilization's emphasis on the value of the individual rather than the state. It is the subject of academic study by believers and skeptics, and its words are the source of comfort and challenge from pulpits on every continent.

Moved by God

The Bible is a collection of 66 books, written by some 40 authors, living on three continents (Africa, Asia, and Europe), over 1,400 years (c.1200 BCE–c.100 CE). These authors understood themselves to be "moved by God" to write "the word of the Lord." By the 1st century BCE, most Jews had come to recognize the 39 books of the Hebrew Bible, written in Hebrew and Aramaic, as God's written word—the scriptures (from *scriptura*, Latin for "writings"). Later, the Christian churches of the 1st and 2nd centuries CE similarly acknowledged the four Gospels and a range of apostolic letters, written in Greek, as the word of God, alongside the earlier Hebrew scriptures.

These texts communicate to the modern reader through a system of transmission and translation that began with the ancient Israelites. As early as the 3rd century CE, scholars were comparing copies

We did not follow cleverly devised stories … but we were eyewitnesses of His majesty.
2 Peter 1:16

and translations of the Hebrew Bible. This process continues among scholars today, who collect and compare newly discovered copies of biblical texts in order to establish a "critical text" from which translations are then made.

The most famous English translation is the Authorized Version, also called the King James Version, published in 1611. *The Bible Book* refers to the New International Version, an English translation from 1978 that aims to make the text understandable to modern readers.

Book of books

The 66 books of the Bible are divided into two major sections. The first in the Christian Bible is the Old Testament (the Hebrew scriptures of Judaism, known as the Tanakh), comprising 39 books, which were written for the ancient nation of Israel. It begins with the five books of the Law (the Torah: Genesis to Deuteronomy), and proceeds through the Historical Books (Joshua to Esther). Although these books are arranged in roughly chronological order, the writing of the books occurred at various points along the timeline. For example, Psalms was probably written quite early, while Isaiah

and Amos were contemporaries. The third group of books are the Poetical Books (Job to Song of Solomon), followed by the Major Prophets (meaning "large books": Isaiah to Daniel) and the Minor Prophets (meaning "small books": Hosea to Malachi). These books are considered sacred texts by both Christians and Jews.

A small set of books, often referred to as the Apocrypha (from the Latin *apocryphus*, meaning "hidden") are considered by Roman Catholic and Eastern Orthodox Christians to be part of the Old Testament. These seven books, plus additions to the Books of Daniel and Esther, were primarily written in Greek from 400–300 BCE. They are not regarded as scripture by either Protestant Christians or Jews, who argue that these books deny that there was any prophetic word from God (the characteristic of scripture) during the period in which they were written.

The New Testament comprises the Christian scriptures, 27 books that are accepted by all Christian denominations as the complete list of New Testament books. The title "New Testament" arises from the prophecy of a new covenant ("testament") that God would give to His people (Jeremiah 31:31–34).

Most of the 27 books of the New Testament were written in the 1st century CE by Jesus's apostles, although some books, such as Hebrews, are anonymous. They were written for Christian churches and individuals scattered across the eastern half of the Roman Empire. The first group of books are the four Gospels (Matthew, Mark, Luke, and John), which present the life and ministry of Jesus Christ as the fulfillment of the Old Testament prophecies heralding a savior for Israel and the nations.

The Book of Acts describes the spread of the message about Jesus in the 30 years after His death, resurrection, and ascension into heaven, while the New Testament letters, known as "epistles," are divided into the Pauline Epistles (Romans to Philemon) and the General Epistles (Hebrews to Jude). The final New Testament text is the Book of Revelation.

Literary genres

There are many different types of literature in the 66 books of the Bible. Historical accounts, genealogies, and legal texts comprise most of the Law and Historical books of the Old Testament. The Poetical books contain proverbs, laments, praises, and even prayers for judgment on the wicked. The longest chapter in the Bible is a poem (Psalm 119), in which each of the 22 stanzas comprises 16 lines beginning with one of the 22 letters of the ancient Hebrew alphabet. The prophetic books contain parables, historical accounts, songs, and visions.

The Gospels are a unique literary genre, containing speeches, sermons, arguments, visions, and miracles, often interpreting events in Jesus's life as the fulfillment of the Old Testament prophecies. The letters of the New Testament contain teaching, encouragement, and even rebuke. Many use literary devices common in Greco-Roman literature of the 1st century CE »

Man shall not live on bread alone, but on every word that comes from the mouth of God.
Matthew 4:4

such as lists of vices and virtues, household codes (instructions about family relationships), and topical treatments of moral questions. Finally, the most difficult form of literature in the Bible is the apocalyptic texts. Found in the Old Testament books of Daniel and Ezekiel, and in the New Testament Book of Revelation, these highly symbolic texts describe God's triumph over the wicked and vindication of the righteous.

Key themes

The Bible begins with the creation of the world and humanity. This original paradise indicates God's intent for humanity—to live in a rich and joyful relationship with God and others, exercising stewardship over God's world. This goal is challenged, however, when Adam and Eve disobey God, bringing ruin and decay upon themselves and creation. This "Fall" introduces the central tension in the biblical narrative; the holiness of God demands the judgment of sinful humanity, yet the love of God calls for the restoration of humanity and the fulfillment of God's purpose for creation. The rest of the Bible is taken up with resolving this tension, culminating, in the New Testament, with the fulfillment of

the prophecy in Genesis (3:17) of one who will "crush the head of the serpent" and lift the curse of God's judgment on humanity and the Earth. Often, God pursues His purpose by making covenants with humankind, such as those made with Abraham, Moses, and David. God promised Abraham that his descendants would become a great nation (Israel) and that one particular descendant would bless the whole world. The Mosaic Covenant, also called the Law of Moses, was given through Moses to the nation of Israel, setting the terms of their relationship with God. The covenant with David promised that one of David's descendants would sit on the throne of Israel forever. Christians

Within the covers of the Bible are all the answers for all the problems men face.
Ronald Reagan

believe these covenants converge in the life of Jesus, who claimed that "[the Scriptures] speak of Me" (John 5:39) and explained how Moses and all the prophets pointed to Him (Luke 24:27).

Human weakness is a recurring theme in the Bible. Even the greatest leaders are shown to be flawed. Jacob was a manipulative liar, Samson fornicated with Delilah, David committed adultery with Bathsheba and murdered her husband to cover it up, and even the prophets Elijah and Jeremiah wanted to give up their calling. God uses the weak to confound the strong. He makes a slave nation into His Chosen People (Israel), a murderer into a liberator (Moses), barren women into mothers (Sarah and Hannah), and a shepherd into a king (David). In the New Testament, God uses murderers (Paul) and flawed leaders (Peter) to spread the teaching of Jesus.

Early analysis

Traditionally, Jewish scholars, or rabbi, focused on memorization of the Hebrew scriptures as well as debates over their interpretation and application to Jewish life. By contrast, early Christian scholars, mostly pastors, analyzed the way in which the scriptures

 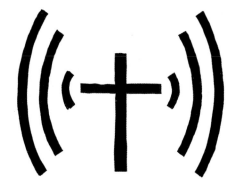 

spoke of Christ. Many tools used by these scholars are still popular today. They included examinations of grammar and analysis of word choice, such as the links between the words "Passover" and "passion." Some, such as Clement (c.150–215 CE) and Augustine (354–430 CE), adapted pagan philosophy to aid their reading of scripture.

Christian scholars tended to see difficulties and differences within scripture as fruitful sources of knowledge for those with enough faith to ponder them deeply. In the 2nd and 3rd centuries CE, such scholars struggled to understand how there could be only one God,

The Bible has been the Magna Carta of the poor and oppressed. The human race is not in a position to dispense with it.
Thomas Huxley

while the Father, Son, and Holy Spirit are each fully God, yet also distinct. The 200-year debate, which took account of the full range of biblical statements on these points, without undercutting any, eventually led to the Christian doctrine of the Trinity.

Modern perspectives

Modern-day biblical scholars utilize many of the same tools as their ancient counterparts, analyzing, for example, the range of meaning in *agape* (love) across the Bible and contemporary Greek literature. Some scholars affirm the ancient Christian conclusions about scripture, while others operate with a skeptical mindset and rely on external confirmation—physical evidence or historical records—before accepting biblical accounts of events. For example, some scholars rejected the biblical account of David as the founder of a royal dynasty until the discovery of the Tel Dan stele in northern Israel in 1993–1994. This battle monument, raised about 200 years after David would have lived, tells of an Aramean king celebrating a victory over "the house of David." In cases such as this, some Christian scholars, through their employment of

skepticism and the scientific method, use historical evidence to inform their theology, and in order to develop conclusions as to the legitimacy of biblical scripture. Those who possess a naturalistic worldview (insisting that things are the result of natural causes) generally reject claims of divine intervention in history. As a result, skeptical modern scholarship often employs an archaeological approach to the Bible, in which perceived errors must first be sorted through in order to expose underlying truths.

Lay study

Study of the Bible is not the sole domain of scholars and clerics, but their work can enlighten the understanding of the average reader. Today, a number of readable Bible translations place the sacred books of Judaism and Christianity into the hands of any interested reader. While certain books are more difficult to read than others, and history and the Gospels are more engaging than the lineages and law codes, those who read carefully can find wisdom, inspiration, and hope in its pages. *The Bible Book* is intended to help readers to understand more of this most significant of books. ■

GENESIS

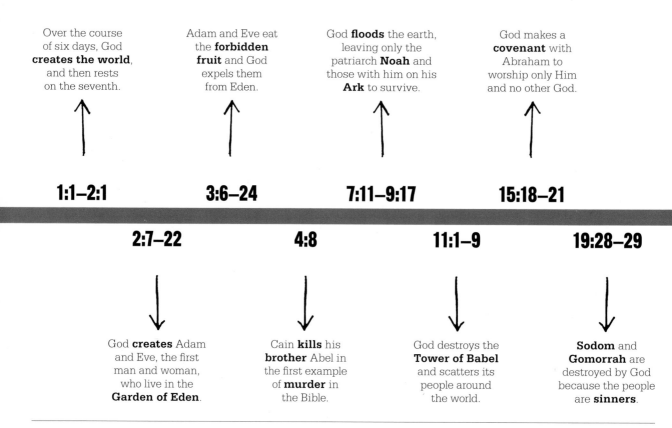

Over the course of six days, God **creates the world**, and then rests on the seventh.

1:1–2:1

Adam and Eve eat the **forbidden fruit** and God expels them from Eden.

3:6–24

God **floods** the earth, leaving only the patriarch **Noah** and those with him on his **Ark** to survive.

7:11–9:17

God makes a **covenant** with Abraham to worship only Him and no other God.

15:18–21

2:7–22

God **creates** Adam and Eve, the first man and woman, who live in the **Garden of Eden**.

4:8

Cain **kills** his **brother** Abel in the first example of **murder** in the Bible.

11:1–9

God destroys the **Tower of Babel** and scatters its people around the world.

19:28–29

Sodom and **Gomorrah** are destroyed by God because the people are **sinners**.

Genesis (*Beresht* in Hebrew) means the origin of everything. For Jews, Genesis is the first of the five books of the Torah (the Pentateuch in Greek) that open the Hebrew Bible. It not only relates the origin of humankind but also how the Jews' ancestors, the Israelites, were chosen by God to be monotheists. For Christians, the origin story of Genesis is the first in a pair of bookends, the second of these being Revelation, the last book of the Bible, which describes the apocalypse.

Themes and authors

Genesis divides into two sections, the first concerning the primeval period, and the second the historical, or patriarchal, period, although some scholars view the story of Joseph as a third section. The primeval period is concerned with creation, disobedience (the Fall, Cain and Abel), uncreation and punishment (the Flood, Tower of Babel), and recreation. In the patriarchal period, God chooses two descendants of Noah— Abraham and Sarah—to travel to the Promised Land and "be fruitful and multiply." The narratives then follow the exploits of their offspring, especially of Abraham's grandson Jacob, whose sons found the 12 tribes of Israel. In the final story, Jacob's son Joseph brings the family to Egypt, preparing the ground for the transition to the Book of Exodus.

According to Jewish and Christian traditions, Moses, inspired by God, penned the entire Torah, including his death in Deuteronomy, a belief still held by traditionalists. However, in the 17th century, Protestant reformers began to doubt the Mosaic authorship. In 1878, the German biblical scholar Julius Wellhausen published his theory that the Torah was written by four authors, whom he labeled J, E, P, and D—J for the Jahwist who used the name YHWH for God; E for the author who used Elohim; P for the Priestly class who wrote about genealogies and rituals and created the structure for the narratives of J and E; and D for the author of Deuteronomy.

Many scholars see repetitions and contradictions in Genesis as a sign of this composite authorship. Genesis 1 and 2, for example, tell different creation stories, with God creating humans at separate points in the narrative. Abraham tells two

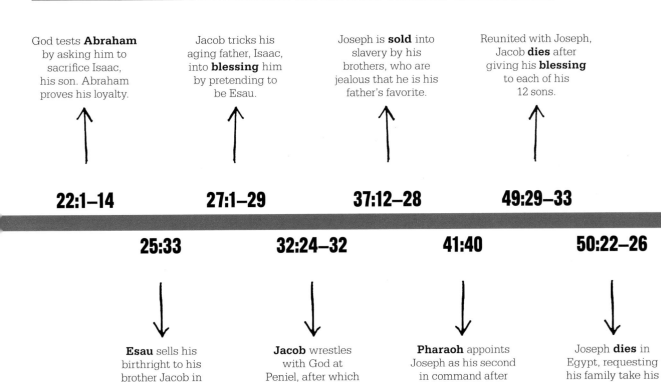

God tests **Abraham** by asking him to sacrifice Isaac, his son. Abraham proves his loyalty.

22:1–14

Jacob tricks his aging father, Isaac, into **blessing** him by pretending to be Esau.

27:1–29

Joseph is **sold** into slavery by his brothers, who are jealous that he is his father's favorite.

37:12–28

Reunited with Joseph, Jacob **dies** after giving his **blessing** to each of his 12 sons.

49:29–33

25:33

Esau sells his birthright to his brother Jacob in exchange for food.

32:24–32

Jacob wrestles with God at Peniel, after which he is given a new name: **Israel**.

41:40

Pharaoh appoints Joseph as his second in command after Joseph **interprets** his dreams.

50:22–26

Joseph **dies** in Egypt, requesting his family take his bones with them when they **leave**.

different kings that Sarah is his sister, not his wife (Genesis 12 and 20), and Jacob is renamed Israel twice (Genesis 32 and 35). The acceptance of these multiple truths is a fundamental aspect of rabbinic Judaism. For Christian traditionalists, however, there can be no contradictions: Genesis 2 is a further explanation of 1; Genesis 12 and 20 are two separate stories; and Jacob's name is only officially changed in Genesis 35 after his covenant with God.

Political purpose
Wellhausen and other scholars also believed the identity of the Genesis authors could be contextualized from theological and political implications present in the text. One theory dates the authors to the reigns of David and Solomon (c.900 BCE), with the "J" author compiling stories from Judah and the "E" author compiling stories from the northern tribes, creating political narratives to unite the divided Israelites.

Schools of interpretation
In the 1960s, scholars led by Robert Alter turned to literary criticism to unlock Genesis, examining its "final form" in Hebrew. They looked at literary devices, such as wordplay (often lost in translation), and repetition, and the different genres (which might indicate the merging of multiple texts).

In the latter half of the 20th century, scholars shifted criticism from the text itself to the personal agendas of its interpreters and claimed there was no "right" way to read the Bible. Most interesting to nonscholarly readers of the Bible, perhaps, is the tension between Genesis and science. Translation of *Gilgamesh*, the Babylonian creation story, in 1872 revealed a flood story similar to the biblical one. For some, this confirmed that Genesis was accurate, but for others, it indicated the influence of Babylonian mythology. This translation came only 13 years after Darwin published his theory of evolution in *The Origin of Species* (1859). In 1925, the Scopes trial to determine whether Darwin or Genesis should be taught in Tennessee schools pushed the issue to the top of US politics. Debate continues in the US today, as a new wave of creationist museums seek to demonstrate that science and Genesis are not necessarily incompatible. ■

AND GOD SAID, "LET THERE BE LIGHT"

GENESIS 1:3, CREATION

IN BRIEF

PASSAGE
Genesis 1:1–2:2

THEME
The creation of the universe

SETTING
Primeval period Inside the Garden of Eden, during the time covered by the first 11 chapters of Genesis.

KEY FIGURE
God Creator of the universe.

T he first few words of the Bible—"In the beginning God created the heavens and the earth"—introduce us to its central character, God. They also reveal the universal scope of the Bible's narrative, from the heavens to the Earth, and present its overarching theme—the relationship between God and everything else. With so much covered in so few words, it is not surprising that the start of Genesis is considered to be one of the Bible's most eloquent yet difficult passages.

These opening verses were most likely written down sometime in the 6th century BCE, while the Israelites were being held in exile by Babylon, the most powerful state in the region. The story provided a hopeful message about God's purposes for his people and for the entire world. In contrast to the Babylonians' own origin story, Genesis attributes the existence of the universe to the goodwill of one God. It served to reassure the Israelites that even on foreign soil, they were not out of the reach of God's care, since God had created all land. God did not stand at a distance, but was intimately involved in the story of the world.

A world in seven days
Genesis 1:1–2:2 tells a single story about the beginning of everything. The origin of the universe starts with darkness and emptiness (1:2). As God's actions over the course of seven days unfold, life springs into existence. First, God calls out, "Let there be light," and light appears. Then God makes the sky. On the third day, God calls the water to gather into seas, creating dry land, on which plants and trees flourish. On day four, the sun and the moon are put in place, along with a host of stars. Next, God fills the sky with birds, and the seas with all their creatures. On the sixth day, God populates the land with all kinds of animals, and finally creates humanity "in his own image" (1:27). At this point in the story, the pinnacle of God's creative work, God entrusts creation into humanity's stewardship. On the seventh day, God rests.

Rhythms of life
The story of creation has its own structural beauty. Each account of God's activity is punctuated with "and God said," "and there was evening and there was morning," "and God saw that it was good." This rhythm helps to emphasize three key messages of the creation story. The first of these is that God creates simply by speaking. Throughout the rest of the Bible,

---

The Babylonians' creation story

Believed to have been written down during the Israelites' captivity in Babylon, Genesis provides a significant contrast to the Babylonians' own creation story known as the Enuma Elish ("When on High"). While the God of Genesis has a loving relationship with humans and regards them as stewards of His creation, the Babylonian god Marduk enslaves humanity.

Enuma Elish is essentially an explanation for the supremacy of Marduk in the Babylonian pantheon. After a power struggle between the gods, Marduk defeats his rival Tiamat, ripping open her body and fashioning the two halves into the earth and the skies. Marduk then destroys another rival and uses his blood to create humankind to perform the work that the lesser gods have done until then. Marduk also imposes order on the universe by regulating the moon and the stars and takes control of the weather and calendar.

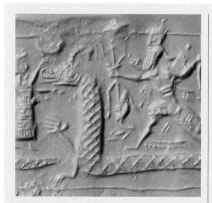

This impression on a Neo-Assyrian cylinder seal used to create imprints on wet clay shows the battle between Marduk and Tiamat.

> The heavens declare the Glory of God; the skies proclaim the work of his hands.
> **Psalm 19:1**

the word of God is understood to be powerful and dynamic, able to pronounce blessing, judgment, and forgiveness. If God's word can speak the whole universe into existence, then God's word can bring hope to exiles in Babylon or provide wise advice for ordinary life. The creation of the world by God's word stands behind the repeated invitation throughout the Bible to "hear the word of the Lord."

The second message is that, while Genesis speaks about the creation of the physical world and all living things, it is also about creating a rhythm to life. Along with the daily rhythm of night and day, there is a weekly pattern of six days of work followed by one day of rest and a seasonal cycle marked by the creation of sun, moon, and stars. Throughout the Old Testament, these daily, weekly, and yearly rhythms are enshrined in Jewish religious practice, with daily prayer, the weekly rest on the Sabbath, and an annual cycle of religious festivals. While it would later become theological orthodoxy to speak about creation *ex nihilo* (out of nothing), here in Genesis

God's act of creation is understood as the giving of order and purpose to the chaos of "the deep."

The third message of the story is that God's creation is "good," even "very good" (Genesis 1:31). »

The Creation is one of 117 woodcut illustrations by Lucas Cranach the Elder in Martin Luther's Bible of 1534. It shows a benevolent God looking down on his creation, with Adam and Eve at the center of the Garden of Eden.

Contrary to many ancient philosophies, which saw the physical world as a cumbersome drag on the human spirit, Jewish and Christian thinking begins with an affirmation of the goodness of the created world. Despite humanity's later departure from God's intentions, a belief in creation's innate goodness means that Judaism and Christianity have an earthly character. They expect the spiritual life to have an impact on the physical world, whether through the rhythms of worship and prayer, or through acts of service and love that promote the original goodness of God's world.

The opening of Genesis is a vision of the entire creation. This stands behind many of the Psalms—songs or hymns—later in the Bible, which delight in the beauty and variety of the created world, and find that creation is a signpost to the existence and character of God. It is a concept developed in "natural theology," which uses the beauty and complexity of the world as proof of God's existence.

Natural theology is sometimes explained using the "watchmaker analogy," in which the skill that brought a watch into existence is "proof" that a watchmaker exists. Those who have faith see the complexity, order, and purpose of the natural world as an indication that the Earth is no accident, but rather designed and made by God.

Modern response

This creationist view was challenged in the 19th century, when scientific discoveries led to new theories of the universe's origins. Charles Darwin's *On the Origin of Species* (1859) put forth the theory of evolution, which stood in stark contradiction to the Genesis account of a seven-day creation.

For some people, the theory of evolution is a reason to reject not only the Genesis account of creation, but the whole Bible. Among Christians, there is a spectrum of responses to the creation story. Some believe it is absolutely true and a reason for rejecting theories of evolution and geological evidence; others view the biblical account as allegorical rather

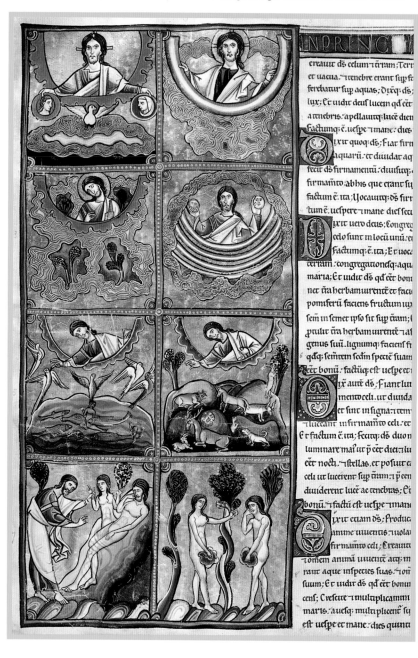

This illuminated illustration of the Creation is from the Bible of Souvigny, produced in Cluny Abbey, France, in the 12th century. In the Middle Ages, even non-religious books often opened with an image of the Creation.

According to the first book of Genesis, God created the world, all that is in the world, as well as the entire universe in seven days.

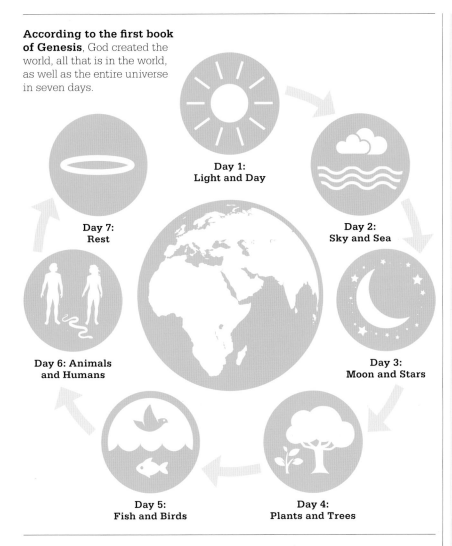

Day 1:
Light and Day

Day 2:
Sky and Sea

Day 3:
Moon and Stars

Day 4:
Plants and Trees

Day 5:
Fish and Birds

Day 6: Animals
and Humans

Day 7:
Rest

than literal; a third camp seeks to combine the two by promoting the idea of intelligent design that set the process of evolution in motion.

Current biblical scholarship also considers the Creation story in the context of the period in which it was written down—during the exile of the Israelites in Babylon in the 6th century BCE. Faced with a threat to their identity by King Nebuchadnezzar II of Babylon, God's people are encouraged by the poetic affirmation in Genesis that the world is a result of God's good and creative purposes, which will ultimately triumph over chaos. ∎

In the beginning was the Word, and the Word was with God, and the Word was God ... Through Him all things were made.
John 1:1–3

The symbolism of seven

In Genesis, the world is created in six days, followed by a seventh day of rest. This is the origin of the understanding of the number seven as a perfect, or complete, number throughout the rest of the Bible. Seven— or its multiples—are used to draw the reader's attention to something that is complete, in the sense that it is all that God wants it to be. For instance, in the Hebrew Bible, God has seven different names. In the New Testament (Matthew 18:22), Jesus tells his disciples to forgive 70 times seven, meaning completely and repeatedly. In the book of Revelation, there is a series of sevens—seven letters, seven lampstands, seven judgments, seven trumpets—that represents the completeness of God's plan. The seven churches that the apostle John addresses at the start of Revelation represent the universal church.

The menorah, the candlestick used in Jewish rituals, has seven branches. The design of the lamp was revealed to Moses on the top of Mount Sinai (Exodus 25:31).

LET US MAKE MAN IN OUR IMAGE, IN OUR LIKENESS

GENESIS 1:26, THE GARDEN OF EDEN

I n chapter 2 of Genesis, God creates the Garden of Eden, an earthly paradise. We cannot know Eden's exact location, but scholars have proposed several possibilities, including Mesopotamia (now Iraq), Syria, Turkey, Iran, and Armenia. Genesis 2:8 mentions the Euphrates and the Tigris rivers, which both flow into the Persian Gulf via Turkey, Syria, and Iraq.

God creates the garden by bringing streams up from the earth and filling the ground with plants that are "pleasing to the eye and good for food." There are two trees in the middle of the garden—the Tree of Life and the Tree of the Knowledge of Good and Evil.

The making of man

Genesis depicts the creation of humankind in two separate passages. The first of these (1:27),

See also: The Fall 30–35 ▪ Covenants 44–47 ▪ Entering the Promised Land 96–97 ▪ The New Jerusalem 322–29

Adam is made in God's image in Michelangelo's *God creates Adam* (c.1512), one of nine scenes from the book of Genesis painted on the ceiling of the Sistine Chapel in the Vatican.

believed to have been written in the 6th century BCE by the Jewish priestly writer referred to as "P," is cursory. It implies that both sexes are formed at the same time, on the sixth day of creation: "So God created mankind in his own image," "male and female he created them."

The second passage, chapter 2:7, attributed to the oldest source of the Pentateuch (the first five books of the Bible), known as Jahwist (or "J"), provides more detail and describes God in human terms. In this account, God forms the man out of dust and "breathes into his nostrils the breath of life." God goes on to create Eve when He sees that it is not good for *Adam* (Hebrew for man) to be alone. Putting Adam into a deep sleep, God removes a rib from his side and creates a woman from it (2:21). Seeing that this new being closely resembles him, Adam composes a poem: "This is now bone of my bones and flesh of my flesh; she shall be called 'woman,' for she was taken out of man" (2:23). She is not referred to as

Eve until Genesis 3:20, after eating the fruit from the Tree of the Knowledge of Good and Evil (see pp. 30–35).

Biblical references to God's image, in which humankind is made, are contradictory. Some passages ascribe human features, such as arms, eyes, hands, and a beard to God and refer to Him as "walking in the garden" (3:8). Others depict him as a type of angel, sheltering humans "under his wings." More significant are the spiritual attributes shared by God and humankind, which include intellect, the capacity for rational thought, morality, free will, creativity, and compassion.

Divine spark

Inherent in God giving Adam life through His divine breath is the implication that humans themselves—unlike animals—»

Paradise

According to the Bible, the Garden of Eden is perfection itself—a place of beauty and abundance, free of disease, death, and evil, into which God sets Adam, the pinnacle of His creation. After around 500 BCE, this wondrous place becomes synonymous with the Hebrew term *pardes* (orchard), stemming from the Persian word *paridayda* (walled enclosure).

The concept of paradise is important within Christianity, Judaism, and Islam. Even as He is dying on the cross, Jesus says to a thief hanging beside him, "Truly, I tell you, today you will be with me in Paradise" (Luke 23:43). The Jewish Talmud (the written version of oral law) associates paradise with the Garden of Eden, and within Islam, the concept of *jannah* or "garden" describes the destination of the righteous after death.

Strange and familiar beasts populate the Garden of Eden portrayed in the left-hand panel of Hieronymus Bosch's *The Garden of Earthly Delights*, c.1510.

> Adam was placed in Paradise in perfect estate ... God walked and did talk with him.
>
> **John Jewel (1522–1571)**
> *Bishop of Salisbury*

are blessed with the essence of divinity. Mankind's capacity for rationality and morality is the reason why no suitable companion could be found for Adam among the animals and why God gave Adam and Eve responsibility to look after the Earth and rule over the animals (1:26–28). In Judeo-Christian philosophy, these passages have been cited to justify humans using animals to serve their own needs.

Yet, despite having divine spark and being created in God's image, Adam and Eve are flawed (Matthew 19:26). God is everywhere (Proverbs 5:21) and is superior to everything else in the universe (Psalms 115:3), while Adam and Eve are limited. In the 13th century, the theologian Thomas Aquinas defined God as perfect (lacking nothing), immutable, and infinite, unlike humans, whom he described as spiritually, intellectually, and emotionally limited.

Original innocence

Although their flaws are revealed by subsequent events, Adam and Eve are created without sin and in complete innocence. Genesis 2:25 tells us that they are naked and unashamed. As they are alone with God, some readers assume that their days are centered around worshipping and communing with Him; their relationship with God is unlike any other creatures'.

In addition to managing the animals and tending the garden ("to work it and take care of it"), the pair are instructed to reproduce ("be fruitful and increase in number"). For now, at least, Adam and Eve are content with their bountiful lives and observe God's one prohibition: while they are free to eat the fruit from the Tree of Life, which grants them immortality, to eat the fruit from the mysterious Tree of the Knowledge of Good and Evil will be on pain of certain death (2:17).

One man, one woman

Adam and Eve are the first couple (2:24–25 says the pair become "one flesh") and their union has traditionally been the yardstick for God's perfect intention for marriage—one man and one woman united in matrimony for life. Crucially, the affirmation in Genesis that both sexes are made in the image of God is often used to support the concept that God created all humans as equal, regardless of gender, race, or any other characteristics.

Yet the Bible is sometimes cited in support of claims that women are inferior to men. Genesis 2:18 refers to Eve's creation as Adam's "helper" (Hebrew *ezer*) and therefore potentially subordinate to him. However, some scholars suggest that *ezer* should have been translated as "companion," implying greater equality.

The divine "We"

In Genesis and throughout the Old Testament, God is often talked about in the plural—for example, "our" likeness (Genesis 1:26). This has triggered much debate and many theories. Possible explanations include polytheism (meaning that God himself is referring to more than one god), although this is soundly refuted in passages such as Isaiah 45:6 where God states, "I am the LORD, and there is no other."

God pulls Eve from the rib of the sleeping Adam in an image from a manuscript of 1480 based on St. Jerome's 4th-century Latin translation of the Hebrew Bible.

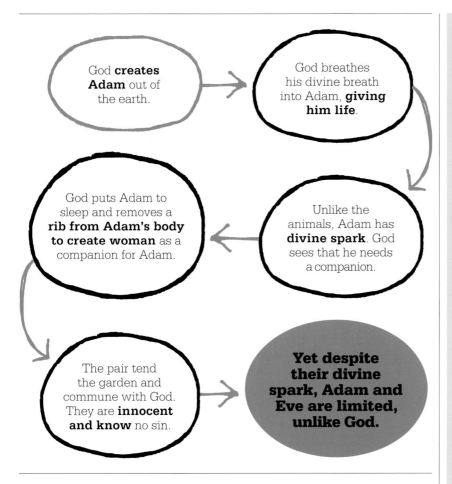

God **creates Adam** out of the earth.

God breathes his divine breath into Adam, **giving him life**.

Unlike the animals, Adam has **divine spark**. God sees that he needs a companion.

God puts Adam to sleep and removes a **rib from Adam's body to create woman** as a companion for Adam.

The pair tend the garden and commune with God. They are **innocent and know** no sin.

Yet despite their divine spark, Adam and Eve are limited, unlike God.

Adam and Eve

The first human couple, Adam and Eve were created—as adults—in the image of God. As they were not born in the same way as their descendants, they would not have needed umbilical cords. Despite this, navels are still present in many artistic representations of the pair.

Genesis 2:7 says that Adam is created out of dust. *Adamah* is Hebrew for "ground" or "earth," a reference to both Adam's origins and his fate after the Fall (see pp. 30–35). The word Eve means "life." She and the man are inseparable, made from one flesh, as they come from the same body (Adam's) and are brought together, both in marital union with each other and in full communion with God. Humankind's remarkable journey begins with Adam and Eve. Without them there is no fall from grace or sin, and thereby no need for suffering, mortality, redemption, atonement, or Jesus Christ.

Other explanations are that God is including his attendant angels in the "us" of Genesis 1:26. Another explanation is that the plurals here and in Genesis 3:22 ("the man has now become like one of us") describe a conversation that God the Father is having with God the Son and God the Holy Spirit, the Trinity, a concept developed in the New Testament.

Human origins

The creation of Adam and Eve and the events unfolding in the Garden of Eden are also described in the Islamic Qur'an. While many Christians reject a literal interpretation of Genesis in favor of a more allegorical approach that also encompasses evolutionary theories of creation, recent surveys in the United States have revealed a widespread belief in the existence of Adam and Eve. (They are partly supported by a group of scientists who have traced human genetic history back many thousands of years, potentially to the first men and women.)

The Bible is clear—in Genesis and elsewhere—that Adam is the first man and not descended from other humans. Adam is referred to in Luke 3:38 as "the son of God," just as angels in the Old Testament are made by God (for example, Job 1:6, 38:7 and Daniel 3:25). The Bible depicts Adam as a living entity with many descendants who, according to Genesis 5:5, lives until he is 930 years old. ■

THEY REALIZED THAT THEY WERE NAKED

GENESIS 3:7, THE FALL

IN BRIEF

PASSAGE
Genesis 3:1–24

THEME
Original sin

SETTING
Primeval period The Garden of Eden during the time covered by the first 11 chapters of Genesis.

KEY FIGURES
Serpent In the Christian view, the embodiment of Satan, the archenemy of God.

Adam The first man, created by God in His own image on the sixth day of creation.

Eve The first woman, created as a companion for Adam, with whom he would populate the Earth.

For God knows that when you eat from it your eyes will be opened, and you will be like God, knowing good and evil.
Genesis 3:5

In the third chapter of Genesis, Adam and Eve's disobedience, punishment, and alienation from God pave the way for the emergence of evil, bringing suffering, discord, and death into a sinless world. Until then, Adam and Eve live and work in paradise, enjoying a close relationship with each other and with God. They are forbidden only one thing—fruit from the Tree of the Knowledge of Good and Evil, which grows in the center of the garden. Eating this, warns God, will result in death. He gives no reasons or details for His command, but Adam obeys and avoids the Tree.

The forbidden fruit from the Tree of the Knowledge of Good and Evil passes from Eve to Adam in a detail from Cornelus van Haarlem's *The Fall of Man*, c.1592.

It is the serpent, identified in Genesis 3:1 as an extremely crafty animal, that questions God's motives in forbidding the fruit. It slyly implies that God is deliberately withholding something desirable—the means by which Adam and Eve can obtain wisdom and be like God. Eve needs little persuasion. The fruit looks good and she is tempted, so she eats

See also: Sodom and Gomorrah 48–49 ▪ David and Bathsheba 118–19 ▪ The Crucifixion 258–65 ▪ Salvation through Faith 301

By the sweat of your brow you will eat your food until you return to the ground.
Genesis 3:19

it and gives some to Adam. Immediately, the couple see that they are naked. Ashamed, they sew fig leaves together to cover themselves and hide. Later, Adam admits to eating the fruit but blames Eve: "She gave me some fruit from the tree, and I ate it" (3:12). Eve passes on responsibility too: "The snake deceived me, and I ate" (3:13).

God's punishments are swift and severe. He condemns the serpent to crawl and eat dust for the rest of its life. Eve is told she will suffer excruciating pain in childbirth and be ruled by her husband. Cursing the ground from which Adam was made, God tells Adam he must forever toil before he can eat. Finally, God expels Adam from the garden—Eve leaves with him—and places cherubim (angelic hybrid creatures) and a flaming sword on the east side of Eden to keep them out.

The creation of death

It soon becomes clear that there is a price for gaining wisdom—pain, toil, scarcity, fear, and suffering. Denied access to fruit from the Tree of Life, humans are now mortal and will die. As God informs Adam, "For dust you are and to dust you will return" (3:19). Cast adrift, humankind is now in constant danger from the evil within themselves and from others.

Humankind and free will

In Christian thought, a sinful act is a deliberate action, attitude, or thought against God. This includes things that are done but should not be (sins of commission) and those that are not done but should be (sins of omission). The fact that all choices are open to sin takes humankind down a path of perpetual wrongdoing, frequently referred to in the Bible as "slavery."

For Christians, the exercise of free will is central to the story of the Fall. Adam and Eve's actions show that human beings have the freedom to make poor choices, but there is a price to pay. Up to this point, Adam and Eve have chosen to obey God. In the face of temptation, they make unwise choices that have catastrophic results. God insists that the couple face up to what they have done—with every exercise of free will comes a consequence (desirable or not) for which responsibility must be taken.

Theologians have long been occupied by the matter of theological fatalism, or the incompatibility between the concepts of free will and God's omniscience. If people can choose, how can God foresee their choices? Judaism accepts this as a paradox beyond human understanding, believing that God exists outside of time. His knowledge of the past, present, and future does »

The role of the serpent

No one knows why the crafty serpent is chosen to tempt Eve into disobedience. Unlike most animals in the Bible, it is able to talk, implying that it is more intelligent than other animals. Whispering into Eve's ear in Genesis 3:5, it causes her to doubt God. The Genesis account does not mention Satan, although the wily serpent is seen within Christianity (but not Judaism) as the devil or his mouthpiece. Satan is later specifically alluded to in Revelation 20:2 as "that ancient snake, who is the devil, or Satan …"

Snakes are not always represented as evil entities in the Bible. They are also seen as strong, courageous creatures. For example, Moses's staff turns into a snake on his command (Exodus 4:3) and God asks him to make a statue of a serpent with the power to heal snake bites (Numbers 21:8).

The serpent descends from the Tree of the Knowledge of Good and Evil to tempt Eve in the defining moment of the Fall. For its part in the catastrophe, the serpent is cursed above all livestock and all wild animals.

A cherub drives Adam and Eve from the Garden of Eden with "a flaming sword flashing back and forth to guard the way to the Tree of Life" (Genesis 3:24).

not interfere with free will. Some Christians reconcile this conundrum by believing that God limits his omniscience to preserve humankind's dignity and freedom.

Original sin

According to Christian doctrine, the consequence of Adam and Eve's disobedience is that all humans are born sinful, with an inborn tendency to succumb to temptation and disobey God. While God is blameless, people are damned, deserve to suffer, and require salvation. Known as Original Sin (or ancestral sin), this doctrine was set out by Paul the Apostle, in Romans 5:12: "Sin came into the world through one man

[Adam], and death through sin, and so death spread to all men because all sinned." In the 5th century, St. Augustine (354–430 CE) developed Paul's doctrine further, saying that spiritual weakness was inherited via "concupiscence," or sexual intercourse, which deprives people of self-control.

The Augustinian view of Original Sin was formally adopted by the Roman Catholic Church during the 16th century. The doctrine was also popular among Protestant reformers, such as Martin Luther and John Calvin. They equated it with perpetual human longing for fleshly pursuits that persist even

Judaism and sin

The doctrine of Original Sin became a central tenet of Christianity but this concept is rejected by Judaism. Instead, Jews believe that we are born pure rather than tainted by the sins of our ancestors. They think Adam is not to blame for the wrongdoing of his descendants. We commit sin (*het* in Hebrew, meaning "something that goes astray") because we are not perfect beings. We must accept that we all transgress at some

point in our lives. Because we have free will (*behirah*), we are naturally frail and likely to give way to our sinful inclinations (*yetzer*). Not all sins are committed deliberately, but those that are will be punished, either here on Earth or later, after death.

The many Old Testament stories concerning the nation of Israel and its sins look at the nature of human beings, the meaning of sin, and the potential for the forgiveness of those sins.

The serpent

The woman

Adam

God punishes the wrongdoers. The serpent is forced to crawl on its belly and eat dust; Eve and her daughters are destined to endure pain in childbirth; and Adam and his sons will always toil in order to eat.

after baptism (the rebirth and the washing away of hereditary sin). Calvin went further, rejecting the concept of free will in favor of predestination—the idea that all events are willed by God.

Both Judaism and Islam reject the idea of Original Sin. According to the Qur'an, Adam and Eve are *equally* responsible for the Fall. After their expulsion from the Garden of Eden, they are forgiven by God and become His representatives on Earth.

The wages of sin
Original Sin helps to explain why God allows innocent people to suffer. Personal innocence is no immunity against God's wrath; everyone is a sinner by nature and (eventually) by choice. "All have sinned and come short of the glory of God," says Romans 3:23.

Christian doctrine maintains that because of humankind's Original Sin, every person is born separated from God. When Paul states in Romans 6:23 that "the wages of sin are death," he is referring to Adam's original sin and death as a condemnation by and separation from God rather than a physical death. The inability to have a relationship with God is described in Ephesians 2:1 as a form

of spiritual death: "You were dead in your transgressions and sins …"

For Christians, it is only through faith in Jesus Christ, who was sent by God to die for humankind's sins, that someone can be born again and reawaken spiritually. This is a central theme of redemption (the act of cleansing away Original Sin). Redemption is achieved by receiving God's grace, through baptism, and accepting that Jesus Christ died for the sins that enslave humankind.

In his letter to the Galatians (5:1), Paul proclaims, "It is for freedom that Christ has set us free. Stand firm, then, and do not let

Nor can the Apostle mean that Eve only sinned … for if Adam sinned willfully and knowingly, he became the greater transgressor.
Mary Astell (1666–1731)
English feminist

yourselves be burdened again by a yoke of slavery." Christians sometimes refer to Christ as the "Second Adam." The first Adam sins and causes the fall of humanity; the second (Christ) dies and redeems humanity.

Blame falls on Eve
Christianity has traditionally blamed Eve—and all womankind—for the Fall from God's grace, and seen her as degenerate, morally weak, and subordinate to man. Paul contributed to this view. In 1 Timothy 2:14, he absolves Adam and blames Eve, saying, "Adam was not deceived, but the woman was deceived and became a transgressor." Many medieval theologians echoed Paul's views, and Christian art reinforced this interpretation. Michelangelo's fresco of the Fall (c.1510) in the Sistine Chapel in the Vatican shows a serpent with the upper body and long blonde hair of a woman, an image that was prevalent during the Renaissance.

However, Genesis itself does not attribute blame for the Fall. On the contrary, it indicates that Adam is present when the serpent speaks to Eve and receives equal punishment, suggesting that they are both culpable. ∎

AM I MY BROTHER'S KEEPER?

GENESIS 4:9, CAIN AND ABEL

The story of Cain and Abel is the second installment of the Fall narrative, describing the first manifestation of evil in humankind. Genesis 4 tells how Adam and Eve's elder son, Cain, murders his brother, Abel. It follows a similar pattern to the previous chapter: ignoring divine warnings and committing a sin is punished, in this case with exile. While Adam and Eve disobey God's specific command, Cain's sin is violent: his anger at God and jealousy of Abel lead him to commit an act of fratricide.

Sibling rivalry

Genesis 4 begins with the birth of the two brothers to Adam and Eve. When the boys reach adulthood, they pursue different occupations. The elder brother, Cain, becomes an agriculturalist, a tiller of the soil, like his father; Abel, the second son, becomes a pastoralist, a keeper of sheep and goats. These were the chief occupations during the time in which the authors of Genesis were writing, and tensions sometimes flared up between agriculturalists and pastoralists over the use of the land. However, there is no

Death of Abel by Andrea Schiavone (c.1510–1563) shows Cain committing the first murder in the Bible. The dying sheep depicted in the background foreshadows the death of Abel.

suggestion that disputes over land use—or any inherent conflict between the occupations—was the source of the animosity between Cain and Abel.

In the passage, both brothers bring sacrificial offerings to God. Abel takes "fat portions from some of the firstborn of his flock," while Cain brings "some of the fruits of the soil" (4:3). God responds favorably to Abel's offering, but

See also: Joseph the Dreamer 58–61 ▪ The Ten Commandments 78–83 ▪ The Prodigal Son 218–21 ▪ The Final Judgment 316–21

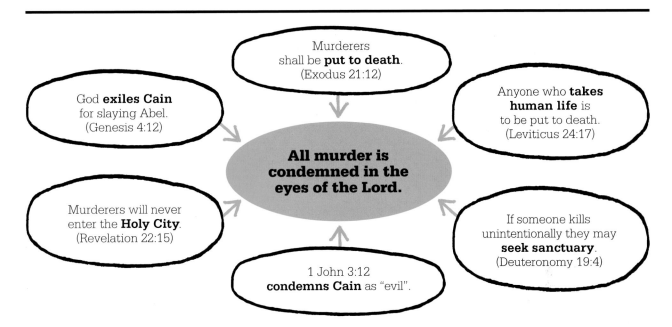

God **exiles Cain** for slaying Abel. (Genesis 4:12)

Murderers shall be **put to death**. (Exodus 21:12)

Anyone who **takes human life** is to be put to death. (Leviticus 24:17)

Murderers will never enter the **Holy City**. (Revelation 22:15)

All murder is condemned in the eyes of the Lord.

1 John 3:12 **condemns Cain** as "evil".

If someone kills unintentionally they may **seek sanctuary**. (Deuteronomy 19:4)

not to Cain's, which is less valuable. Cain is jealous of Abel. Noticing Cain's anger (4:7), God warns him that if he does not do what is right, sin will "crouch" at the door (the Hebrew word for "crouching" being the same as the Babylonian word for a demon that waits in doorways, a play on words by the authors of Genesis, who were writing during the Jews' captivity in Babylon in the sixth century BCE). God tells Cain to master the demonic temptation of sin. Cain, however, does not temper his impulses. Instead, he lures his brother out into the fields and murders him.

Cain's punishment

When God asks Cain where Abel is, Cain says that he does not know. "Am I my brother's keeper?" he asks (4:9). In another play on words, he is insolently asking, "Am I, the agriculturalist, the shepherd of my shepherd brother?" God knows

what Cain has done and banishes Cain from the land onto which he spilled his brother's blood. "You will be a restless wanderer on the earth," God says (4:12).

Unrepentant, Cain says his punishment is more than he can bear. Before exiling him to the land

of Nod ("east of Eden"), God puts a mark on Cain. Contrary to popular wisdom, this "mark of Cain" is a sign of God's continued protection, not a brand of shame. God says that anyone who kills Cain "will suffer vengeance seven times over." Cain then leaves for the land of Nod. ▪

The sanctity of life

The Ten Commandments that God gives to Moses on Mount Sinai in Exodus are clear: "You shall not murder" (Exodus 20:13). Cain's punishment for murder was exile. God punished him, but also showed mercy by extending Cain his protection.

In this way, God sought to avert a potential cycle of violence and retaliation. By marking Cain (Genesis 4:15), He stopped others from taking the law into their own hands by killing Cain. God's plan seemed to work, for a time, as the next

murder to be recorded by the Bible happens five generations later in Genesis 4:26. This time the murderer is Cain's descendant Lamech, who kills a man for wounding him. Lamech says: "If Cain is avenged seven times, then Lamech seventy-seven times" (4:24).

In Israel during biblical times, "Anyone who takes the life of a human being is put to death" (Leviticus 24:17), but places of refuge were also created for anyone who killed someone "accidentally and unintentionally" (Joshua 20:3).

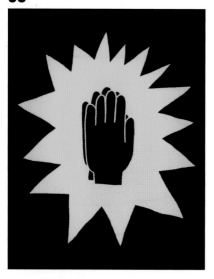

AT THAT TIME PEOPLE BEGAN TO CALL ON THE NAME OF THE LORD

GENESIS 4:26, THE ORIGIN OF PRAYER

The first extended prayer in the Bible arises from the anguish of a couple longing for children. It bursts forth during a conversation initiated by God with Abraham. After the King of Sodom tries to strike a deal that will obligate Abraham, God tells Abraham not to be afraid. God himself will be Abraham's shield and "very great reward." To this Abraham retorts: "What can you give me since I remain childless?" (Genesis 15:2). God's answer to this outburst, or prayer, is to take Abraham outside and point to the night sky: "Look up at the heavens and count the stars—if indeed you can count them." God pauses, then adds: "So shall your offspring be."

A God who cares

Abraham's encounter says much about prayer in the Bible. First, it takes place within the context of a dialogue between God and humankind, initiated by God. It assumes there is a God who cares and can be pleaded with. The person praying expresses themself with honesty and vigor, the prayer often taking the form of a lament about a painful situation. A common pattern involves a crisis, leading to prayer in which the person praying complains about, or laments, the situation and petitions God to intervene. This leads to resolution following divine intervention, which may take the form of a promise.

Petitioning God

According to Genesis, the cult of Israel's God, Yahweh, begins during the third generation of human life on Earth, when Adam

Prayer beads, used to count prayers, are clasped by members of the congregation at a Catholic church in Baghdad, following the death of Pope John Paul II in 2005.

See also: Esau and Jacob 54–55 ▪ The Exodus 74–77 ▪
The Prophet Samuel 110–15 ▪ The Crucifixion 258–65

The evolution of prayer

Petitionary prayer. Abraham **prays for an heir** and is rewarded with one. Genesis 15:5

A prayer in peril. Moses **prays for help** when his people turn against him. Exodus 17:4

A conviction that prayer of all kinds reaches God.

Silent prayer. Hannah **prays in her heart**. Samuel 1:13

Prayer as confession. Ezra **prays and confesses**. Ezra 9:5–10:4

and Eve's third son Seth has a son called Enosh. At this time, Genesis tells us, people begin to invoke the name of Yahweh.

Many of the earliest prayers are petitions for the birth or protection of children. Isaac's prayer to Yahweh on behalf of his wife Rebekah leads to her becoming pregnant with the twins Esau and Jacob. The passion of such petitions is sometimes expressed in the names given to longed-for sons. For example, Leah, the first wife of Jacob, names her first son Reuben ("See, a son"), because, she explains, "the Lord has seen my misery" (Genesis 29:32).

Another particularly poignant prayer involves Hagar, the Egyptian concubine of Abraham, Isaac's father. The jealousy of Abraham's wife, Sarah, leads to Hagar and her son Ishmael being banished to the wilderness, where they run out of water. Hagar places Ishmael in the shade of a bush, then sits a short distance away because she cannot bear to watch her child die. Her prayer brings a response from the angel of God, who calls out to reassure her of God's protection. She opens her eyes to see a well.

Prayers of thanksgiving
Another great strand of prayer, praise and thanksgiving, occurs when Abraham sends his servant to Mesopotamia to find a wife for Isaac. The servant petitions God for success in his mission. When his prayer is answered, he bows down and worships Yahweh, saying: "Praise be to the Lord, the God of

The names of God

Names in biblical times were more than just a label: they stood for a person's being and status. Even more significant were the names of God. The three names for God most frequently used in the Hebrew Bible are El (more than 200 times), Elohim (2,570 times), and Yahweh (6,800 times). El was both a generic word for "god" and the name of the chief god of the Canaanites— a benevolent deity portrayed as an old man with a beard. El is often used in compounds: Everlasting God, God Almighty, Most High God. Elohim is another generic word for "god," emphasizing God's universality. It is used in the first verse of Genesis: "In the beginning God created the heavens and the earth." Yahweh (or YHWH, since ancient Hebrew script lacked vowels) is the personal name of the God of Israel. The name is explained in Exodus, during Moses's encounter at the burning bush, where God's words are translated: "I am who I am."

my master Abraham, who has not abandoned his kindness and faithfulness to my master." The addition of such praise becomes more common later in the Bible. For believers, biblical examples of prayer show that humans can communicate with God and that God listens and responds. In the New Testament, prayer is usually communicated to God in the name of Jesus Christ, through the Holy Spirit. Prayer relies on promises of the Spirit's aid in prayer and God's favorable reception of prayers offered under Jesus's authority (Romans 8:26 and John 14:13–14). ▪

ONLY NOAH WAS LEFT, AND THOSE WHO WERE WITH HIM IN THE ARK
GENESIS 7:23, THE FLOOD

IN BRIEF

PASSAGE
Genesis 6:1–8:14

THEME
Obedience and trust in God

SETTING
Primeval period The floodwaters sent by God to cover the Earth; Mount Ararat, Mesopotamia.

KEY FIGURE
Noah Son of Lamech, who is a descendant of Seth, the third son of Adam and Eve. A righteous man, Noah becomes father to Shem at 500 years old, and then to Japheth and Ham.

Genesis establishes humans as **stewards of the Earth**.

→

But after several generations, humanity has **grown corrupt**.

↓

But he **preserves Noah and the animals** to begin a new life after the Flood.

←

God resolves to **remake the world**.

↓

God **makes a covenant** with Noah that he will not destroy the earth again.

→

God tells Noah all creatures are given into his hands. Humanity must now care for the Earth and behave well.

Human stewardship is **affirmed** in Psalm 8.

←

A t the end of the first chapter of Genesis, God surveys His creation. "God saw what he had made," Genesis tells us, "and it was very good" (1:31). By the sixth chapter, the mood has darkened. "God saw how corrupt the earth had become, for all the people of the earth had corrupted their ways" (6:12). His heart "filled with pain," He resolves to "wipe mankind … from the face of the earth—men and animals, and creatures that move along the ground, and birds of the air—for I am grieved that I have made them."

Noah's family and the animals leave the Ark when it comes to rest in the Ararat region of Mesopotamia. Simon de Myle's painting (c.1570) shows aggression and chaos soon returning.

One thing makes Him modify His intention, however: the existence of one "righteous man," Noah.

Remaking the world

The writers of Genesis used the story of Noah to reflect upon what scholars have called creation, un-creation, and re-creation. God makes creation good; humanity spoils it. Patiently, God un-creates in order to re-create. Like other stories in Genesis, The Flood shows that God will judge and punish sin but also offer salvation to the faithful and penitent.

To deal with human depravity, God sends a flood to wipe out "all life under the heavens" apart from "righteous" Noah, his family, and a full sampling of animal life. God tells Noah to build an ark, or ship, to contain him, his family, and "two of all living creatures, male and female, to keep them alive" (6:19). Noah does as God bids. When they enter the ark, God shuts them in.

As the waters rise, God remembers Noah, and all the animals and livestock. In the Bible, remembering often involves the fulfillment of an obligation or promise. Here, God sends a wind, and the waters recede. In a famous passage, Noah sends out a raven to test how far the waters have withdrawn. It flies back and forth until the land is dry again. The second time, Noah sends out a dove—it returns with an olive leaf in its bill. The next time, the dove does not return. Noah now knows that it is safe to leave the ark.

The first covenant

Cleansed by water, the world emerges anew. Noah, effectively a second Adam, makes a sacrifice to God, who repeats to Noah and his family the blessing made in Genesis 1: "Be fruitful and increase in number and fill the earth." God also enters into a covenant with Noah, the first of a series of covenants between God and humankind. "Never again will all life be cut off by the waters of a flood; never again will there be a flood to destroy the earth." The sign of this pact is the rainbow. ▪

Flood stories

Cultures worldwide have sagas of cataclysmic floods. In the case of ancient Mesopotamia and the surrounding region, there are at least three other versions of the Great Flood story, possibly inspired by a devastating flooding of the Tigris and Euphrates rivers known to have taken place in 2900 BCE. In the Sumerian flood story, the equivalent of Noah is Ziusudra, a man known for his humility. In a version of the flood narrative found on one of the tablets recording the Babylonian epic of Gilgamesh, which may have been written down as early as the 22nd century BCE and was probably based on an older oral tradition, the sole human survivor of the flood is called Utnapishtim. The third account is the Akkadian epic of Atrahasis, written down in around 1700 BCE, whose eponymous hero is "exceedingly wise."

These stories later found their way into Greek and Roman mythology—the Roman poet Ovid tells a version of the flood story in his *Metamorphoses*.

COME, LET US BUILD OURSELVES A CITY, WITH A TOWER THAT REACHES TO THE HEAVENS
GENESIS 11:4, THE TOWER OF BABEL

IN BRIEF

PASSAGE
Genesis 11:1–9

THEME
The power of humanity

SETTING
After the Great Flood
Shinar, Mesopotamia.

KEY FIGURE
People of the world
Descendants of Noah,
who speak one language.

Genesis 11 describes a large people journeying westward in a mass migration. They decide to settle in the land of Shinar, another name for Babylonia, after finding the Mesopotamian floodplain fertile. Although there is no stone with which to build a city, the people are technologically innovative and learn to create imposing structures using bricks, with bitumen for mortar. They establish a great city and begin to build a ziggurat, a temple tower in the shape of a pyramid that reaches toward the heavens. Not surprisingly, they are proud of this achievement.

High ambitions

The story of the Tower of Babel comes at the end of the first section of Genesis, before moving on from the creation of the universe to a more particular account of the ancestral origins of the nation of Israel. The Babel narrative draws on historical realities—people did migrate and Babel was an early name for Babylon—in order to tell a universal story about humankind's tendency to behave against God's wishes. It is not just the Babylonians who are depicted here, but the whole world, all speaking the same language.

After settling in Shinar, the people spur themselves on with two emphatic statements: "Come, let's make bricks and bake them thoroughly. … Come, let us build ourselves a city, with a tower that reaches to the heavens, so that we may make a name for ourselves and not be scattered over the face of the whole earth" (Genesis 11:4).

Wary of what is happening among the people of Shinar, God visits the city and its tower. He sees that if the citizens of Babel continue to progress at this rate, nothing will be beyond them. Part of their power, He decides, lies in the fact that they all speak the same language.

The sin of arrogance

Genesis does not explicitly state the reasons for God's disapproval, but among the options suggested by scholars is that the tower is an outward expression of the sin of human arrogance. In a statement of His own, God says, "Come, let us go down and confuse their language so they will not understand each other" (11:7).

If … they have begun to do this, then nothing that they propose to do will now be impossible for them.
Genesis 11:6

He separates the people of Babel by language so that they are unable to complete the tower. God then scatters them across the world, in accordance with His previous command in Genesis 1:22 to be "fruitful and increase in number and fill the earth."

Political purpose

The story also has a satirical undercurrent. In the last verse, for example—"That is why it was called Babel—because there the Lord confused the language of the whole world" (11:9)—play is made of a similarity between the name

Babel and the Hebrew *balal*, meaning "confuse." The intention may be to poke fun at Babylon, whose name meant "Gate of God." A more appropriate name, the Genesis writers may be suggesting, would be confusion.

Hostility toward Babylon is not surprising given that the book of Genesis probably took its final form in the 5th century BCE, not long after the Judeans had returned to Judah from their enforced exile in Babylon following the Babylonian capture of Judah. That experience, along with the Israelites' sufferings at the hands of other regional powers, may help explain the author's seeming preference for smaller scattered nations, each with its own language and territory, over the consolidation of power in a single imperial city. ▪

Cloud obscures the soaring tip of the Tower of Babel in a painting by an unknown 16th-century Flemish artist, who set the tower in a busy river port with basilicas and mosques.

Gateways to heaven

Most Mesopotamian cities, including Babylon, had ziggurats, which rose from the surrounding plain like artificial mountains reaching up to the heavens. These temples were seen as gateways between the world of humans and the gods—an act of pride disliked by the God of the Israelites. They were built with brick—there was little or no stone in the Mesopotamian floodplain—with solid mud-brick cores and exteriors of fired brick. Sometimes their sides were landscaped, as is commonly depicted in images of the Hanging Gardens of Babylon.

The inspiration for the story of the Tower of Babel is thought to be the Etemenanki ("House of the Foundation of Heaven and Earth"), a seven-story ziggurat topped by a sanctuary dedicated to the god Marduk. The chief temple of Babylon, the Etemenanki was destroyed by the Assyrian King Sennacherib in 689 BCE.

Ziggurats have not survived as well as the stone-built pyramids of Egypt but their remains still exist, including those of the Great Ziggurat of Ur in southern Iraq.

Partially restored, the Great Ziggurat of Ur, in modern-day Iraq, was built during the Third Sumerian Dynasty, c.2100 BCE. Like other ziggurats, it was climbed by sloping ramps.

I WILL MAKE OF YOU A GREAT NATION

GENESIS 12:2, COVENANTS

The conversion of Abraham by God is one of the most remarkable in the Bible. God's decision to reveal Himself to this ordinary man resulted in the emergence of three of the world's major religions—Judaism, Christianity, and Islam.

In Genesis 12:2, God appears to Abraham and urges him to leave his home and go to Canaan. In this critical narrative of posterity, introducing the concept of a people chosen to deliver God's message of salvation, God tells Abraham: "I will make you into a great nation, and I will bless you; I will make your name great, and you will be a blessing. I will bless those who bless you, and whoever curses you I will curse; and all peoples on earth will be blessed through you."

See also: The Fall 30–35 ▪ The Flood 40–41 ▪ The Testing of Abraham 50–53 ▪ The Ten Commandments 78–83

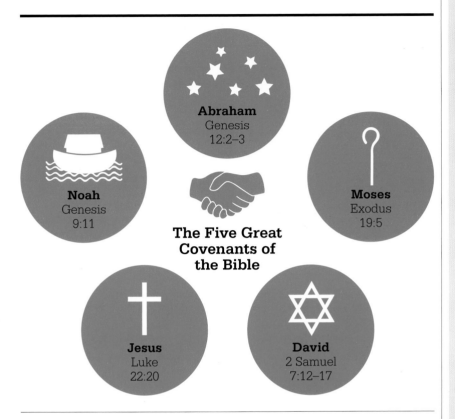

Abraham
Genesis
12:2–3

Noah
Genesis
9:11

Moses
Exodus
19:5

The Five Great Covenants of the Bible

Jesus
Luke
22:20

David
2 Samuel
7:12–17

The Abrahamic Faiths

Abraham is one of the most important figures in the religions of the Middle East and the Western world. He is universally recognized as the father of the three great monotheistic faiths: Judaism, Christianity, and Islam. To the Jewish people, Abraham was the founder of Israel and their first patriarch. He taught them that there is only one God and inspired their faith with his unquestioning obedience and unwavering loyalty to God.

Christians view Abraham as possibly the greatest exponent of a human relationship with God. They believe that it is through Abraham's descendant, Jesus, that all God's promises are fulfilled. In Islam, where he is known as "Ibrahim," Abraham is regarded as a great prophet whose son Ishmael, by Hagar, became the father of the Arab peoples and the ancestor of the Prophet Muhammad, the founder of Islam. Muslims celebrate Abraham on the festival of Eid-al-Adha, held in memory of Abraham's willingness to obey God's command to sacrifice his son (see pp. 50–53).

God reiterates his promise on several occasions. The basic components always remain the same: that Abraham's descendants will become a great nation, live in a fruitful land, be blessed, and be a blessing to all the peoples of the Earth. The nation God promises is one of generations of worshippers in their own land. This is the "covenant"—binding contract—that God and Abraham make. God offers divine promises in return for the continued faith of Abraham and his descendants. The covenant is part of God's plan of establishing a nation of people free from sin.

A momentous journey

In a clear demonstration of his faith, Abraham obeys God's call to leave his homeland. He is **»**

A 16th-century Brussels tapestry dramatizes the calling of Abraham and his journey. In fact, the biblical passage mentions neither the setting nor circumstances of the calling.

Punished by God, the repentant Pharaoh returns Sarah to Abraham and sends them out of Egypt. Pharaoh permits Abraham to retain the riches he has amassed during his stay.

(meaning "exalted father") to Abraham ("father of many") in Genesis 17. In this same chapter, God promises Abraham a son—Isaac—whose descendants will found a nation named Israel. The significance of Sarai's name change to Sarah is less clear. Both names mean "princess," but "Sarah" may also mean "queen."

Journey to Egypt

Abraham, Sarah, and Lot's initial stay in the Promised Land is brief due to a famine. Along with all the other people of Canaan, they are forced to flee to Egypt in search of food. Concerned that Sarah's great beauty may attract the Egyptians' attention, and that he may be murdered in order to clear the way for a marriage, Abraham instructs Sarah to tell the Egyptians that she is his sister.

The ruse backfires when Pharaoh takes Sarah into his harem. In turn, Pharaoh rewards Abraham for having a beautiful "sister" and showers him with

Blessed is the nation whose God is the Lord, the people whom He has chosen for His own inheritance.
Psalm 33:12

Covenants in Judaism and Christianity

In religion, a "covenant" denotes a formal alliance or agreement between God and humankind, either a religious group such as the Israelites or humanity in general. The covenant God makes with Abraham is fundamental to Judaism, as it forms the basis for the Jews being the "chosen people." God promises to make Abraham the father of a great nation and commands that his descendants must obey Him. To this day, Jewish males are circumcised when they are eight days old as a symbol of this covenant.

In Christianity, a covenant has a different significance. Christians believe that the New Covenant was instituted by Christ at the Last Supper as part of the Eucharist. They believe it represents an ongoing relationship between God and his followers that will only come to full fruition with the Second Coming of Christ.

accompanied on his great journey through the Fertile Crescent by his wife Sarah, their nephew Lot, and servants. They travel along a well-trodden trade route from Harran in Mesopotamia to Egypt.

Following God's instructions, they eventually stop at the Great Tree of Moreh near a place named Shechem in the heart of Canaan. Here, God appears to Abraham once more and tells him that his descendants will inherit this new "Promised Land"—the chosen land for God's people. Seeing in advance the rewards God has promised him, Abraham builds the first of many altars to his Lord (12:7).

Father of many

At the time of their departure, Abraham and Sarah are 75 and 65 years old respectively. Although these might appear to be very advanced ages at which to establish a new nation, let alone have children, the patriarchs were long-lived. Abraham dies at the age of 175 and Sarah at 127.

At this stage, Abraham and Sarah are referred to as Abram and Sarai. God changes Abram's name

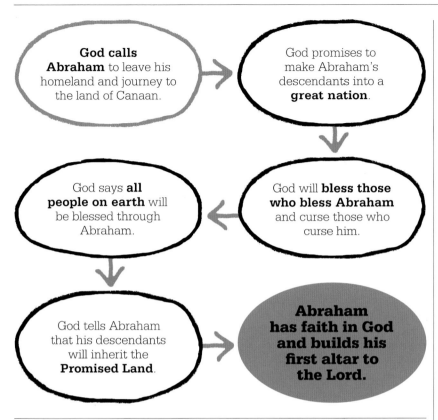

God calls **Abraham** to leave his homeland and journey to the land of Canaan.

God promises to make Abraham's descendants into a **great nation**.

God will **bless those who bless Abraham** and curse those who curse him.

God says **all people on earth** will be blessed through Abraham.

God tells Abraham that his descendants will inherit the **Promised Land**.

Abraham has faith in God and builds his first altar to the Lord.

wealth, servants, and livestock. When God hears that Pharaoh has taken Abraham's wife as his own, he inflicts plague on Pharaoh and his household. Realizing he has been lied to, Pharaoh summons Abraham and asks him why he pretended Sarah was his sister. After an angry exchange, Pharaoh commands Abraham and Sarah to leave Egypt, yet he allows Abraham to retain the riches he has accumulated. Leaving Egypt, Abraham, Sarah, and Lot head toward the Negev.

Traditions and meanings
The biblical account of Abraham's life is rooted in oral traditions rather than historical records, so no true biography of Abraham can be written. However, the story of Abraham's life is so central to the fabric of the Bible that scholars have long debated when Abraham lived and what were the precise circumstances of his existence.

One commonly held view is that the story of Abraham's journey to Canaan was first related in the early Persian period (late 6th century BCE) by Jewish landowners defending their property in the face of Jews returning to Judah from their captivity in Babylon (see pp. 128–31). They were keen to trace the ownership of their lands back to their "father Abraham" to counter the land claims of the returning exiles.

Many readers of Abraham's narrative are struck by the moral ambiguity at its heart—Abraham's lie that Sarah is his sister instead of his wife, which he tells in order to preserve his own life. As if to soften the blow of this deception, the story later reveals that Sarah

is Abraham's half-sister, as well as his wife: "Besides, she really is my sister, the daughter of my father" (20:12). This means that Abraham's statement to the Egyptians can be construed not only as a practical measure to ensure his survival, but also as a half-lie, or half-truth.

A merciful God
The ambiguities in the story also serve to show God as a benevolent, forgiving Lord. Later in the Bible, all kinds of noble acts are ascribed to Abraham (see pp. 50–53), but here he is an ordinary man, an example of how God's work can be carried out through anyone. God allows Abraham to lie to the Egyptians in order to save his life, but punishes Pharaoh for taking another man's wife as his own. Abraham is allowed to retain the riches he has accumulated because God is gracious and lenient. Although God does not approve of Abraham's actions, He will not rescind His promise or His blessing.

In order to understand the full impact of God's choice of Abraham as such an important representative on Earth, the reader must look beyond his deception in Egypt in the broader context of the subsequent events in his life. ■

Nation will not lift up sword against nation, and never again will they learn war.
Isaiah 2:4

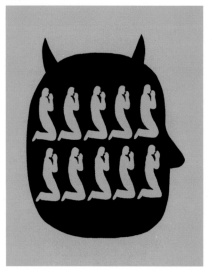

FOR THE SAKE OF TEN MEN I WILL NOT DESTROY IT

GENESIS 18:32, SODOM AND GOMORRAH

IN BRIEF

PASSAGE
Genesis 18:1–19:29

THEME
Divine punishment

SETTING
Around 1900 BCE In Sodom and Gomorrah, two towns in the Valley of Siddim, possibly near the Dead Sea.

KEY FIGURES
Abraham Son of Terah and the future father of all nations.

The angels God's messengers on Earth.

Lot Abraham's nephew, who has settled with his family in Sodom.

Lot's wife A woman who may have enjoyed living in the sinful city of Sodom.

The men of Sodom Depicted as a sinful and unfaithful people.

L ike the Great Flood, in which God destroyed and remade creation, the destruction of Sodom and Gomorrah is one of the most dramatic examples of divine punishment in the Bible. It illustrates the need for human beings both to fear God's power and trust in His judgment.

In Genesis 18, Abraham is visited by three angels in human form. One of them, speaking as if he is God, tells Abraham that He has come to investigate reports of sinful behavior in the towns of Sodom and Gomorrah. The angel—or God himself—indicates that if the "outcry against Sodom and Gomorrah is so great and their sin so grievous" as He has heard, He will destroy the cities.

The writers of Genesis then reveal the close relationship between Abraham and God. Abraham challenges God's plan and humbly asks, though he is "nothing but dust and ashes," whether it is right to take such drastic action. While he is not prepared to resist God's wishes, Abraham bargains with Him, confident that the "judge of all earth" (18:25) will do right. Eventually, God agrees that He

Other biblical references to Sodom and Gomorrah

In Deuteronomy 29:22–23, **Moses** refers to the **destruction** of Sodom and Gomorrah.

In Isaiah 13:19–22, **Isaiah warns Babylon** that it may end like Sodom and Gomorrah.

In Ezekiel 16:48–50, God compares **Jerusalem** to Sodom.

In Luke 10:12–13, **Jesus** cites places that are **more damnable**.

See also: The Fall 30–35 ▪ The Flood 40–41 ▪ The Ten Plagues 70–71 ▪ The Fall of Jericho 98–99

will not destroy the cities if He finds at least ten good people within them.

God's wrath

The story moves to the city of Sodom, where Lot, Abraham's nephew, invites two angel-strangers to stay at his home rather than in the town's square. Lot prepares a meal for the angels, "baking bread without yeast," foreshadowing the hasty meal the Israelites prepare when they flee Egypt (Exodus 12:8).

Later that night, the men of Sodom arrive at Lot's door and ask: "Where are the men who came to you tonight? Bring them out to us so that we can have sex with them" (19:5). Refusing the men's request, Lot offers his two virgin daughters to the crowd instead, but the men refuse Lot's offer and try to break down the door. The angels strike the crowd with blindness. They warn Lot and his family that God is about to destroy the city.

Lot flees from Sodom with only his wife, two daughters, and the angels. God rains down fire and brimstone to destroy the two cities.

> The day Lot left Sodom, fire and sulfur rained down from heaven and destroyed them all.
> **Luke 17:29**

Fire engulfs the sinful while Lot, a "righteous" man, makes his escape with his wife and two daughters in *The Destruction of Sodom and Gomorrah*, by John Martin, 1852.

The angels warn Lot not to look back, but Lot's wife glances behind her and is turned to a pillar of salt.

Saving the penitent

The sin of Sodom and Gomorrah is traditionally considered to be homosexuality, giving rise to the word "sodomy." However, passages about the cities' sins focus on the abandonment of justice and neglect of the poor (Isaiah 3:8–15 and Ezekiel 16:48–50). More significant is what the story reveals about God's judgments and His relationship with Abraham. God considers the evidence before making judgment and allows Abraham to bargain with Him. God is prepared to reward the righteous and save the penitent. Nonetheless, His judgment is final: the cities of sin are not spared. ▪

Cities of sin

Sodom and Gomorrah are not the only sinful cities in the Bible. Other debauched or lawless settlements include the other three cities of the "Valley of Siddim" (Admah, Zeboiim, and Zoar), Edom, and Jerusalem. States such as Egypt and Assyria are also censured for their lack of morality and disregard for God's laws.

These cities of sin were held up as dramatic warnings about the terrifying power of God's wrath. The book of Revelation describes the destruction of the city of Babylon at the end of time, noting that "the smoke from her goes up for ever and ever" (19:3). This is a direct reference to the smoke from fire and brimstone (sulfur) that rose up from the cities of Sodom and Gomorrah during their destruction.

NOW I KNOW THAT YOU FEAR GOD

GENESIS 22:12, THE TESTING OF ABRAHAM

IN BRIEF

PASSAGE
Genesis 16:1–22:19

THEME
Sacrifice

SETTING
Early 2nd millennium BCE
Beersheba and the region
of Moriah, a three-day donkey
ride from Beersheba.

KEY FIGURES
Abraham Son of Terah,
"an ordinary man," who
becomes father of Ishmael
and Isaac.

Sarah Abraham's wife,
mother of Isaac.

Hagar Sarah's maidservant
and mother of Abraham's
first-born son Ishmael.

Isaac Son of Abraham
and Sarah.

The demand God makes of Abraham—to sacrifice his own son—is one of the most extreme tests of faith in the Bible. The fact that Abraham's son Isaac is the long-awaited child of promise makes the sacrifice even harder to fulfill.

At the start of Abraham's story, when God first tells him to set out into the unknown, he promises to make of him "a great nation," implying Abraham will have many descendants. He later promises Abraham offspring as numerous as the "dust of the earth." Despite God's promises, after many years of marriage Abraham and his wife Sarah remain childless. When Abraham complains to God about his plight, God's reply is to tell him

See also: Origin of Prayer 38–39 ▪ The Raising of Lazarus 226–27 ▪ The Nature of Faith 236–41 ▪
The Crucifixion 258–65 ▪ Salvation through Faith 301

Sarah presents Hagar, her Egyptian maidservant, to Abraham, in a 1743 painting of the event by Louis-Joseph Le Lorrain. Sarah hopes Hagar will conceive a child by Abraham.

to look up at the night sky: his descendants would be as numerous as the stars. Abraham's belief in God is firm, but when there is no child, in desperation, Sarah proposes her maidservant Hagar as a surrogate. Through this union, Abraham gains a son—Ishmael—but Sarah remains childless.

Then, at long last, with Sarah well past normal childbearing age, the miracle happens: Isaac is born. This is the child through whom the whole world would be blessed.

The child Isaac

When Isaac is old enough to carry heavy loads and ask questions, God makes an astonishing demand of Abraham. God calls Abraham, who replies, "Here I am," the usual reply to a divine call in the Bible. God says, "Take your son, your only son,

whom you love—Isaac—and go to the region of Moriah. Sacrifice him there as a burnt offering on a mountain I will show you" (Genesis 22:2). The description of Isaac as Abraham's "only son," even though he has another son, Ishmael, underlines Isaac's role as the inheritor of Abraham's covenant with God. For Christians, God asking Abraham to kill his "only son" mirrors God's later sacrifice of His own son, Jesus.

God's use of the imperative "go" occurs in only one other place in the Bible: when God tells Abraham to "go" from his father's house and country to the land of Canaan (12:1)—a huge personal sacrifice. The now elderly Abraham (according to Genesis, he is 100 years old when Isaac is born) is being asked to perform another

act of faith and set out on another journey into the unknown by making this second sacrifice.

As before, Abraham is prompt to obey God. Rising early the next morning, he saddles his donkey, cuts some wood to make a fire for the burnt offering, chooses two young followers to accompany him and Isaac, and sets off from Beersheba. After three days' traveling, they see in the distance the place chosen by God for the sacrifice. Father and son bid farewell to the two followers and set out on the last lap of their journey alone. The two of them "went on together" (22:6).

In a touching gesture of fatherly care, Abraham gives Isaac the wood to carry, while he himself takes the more dangerous flame torch (or perhaps firestone) and knife. The silence as they walk is »

By faith Abraham, when God tested him, offered Isaac as a sacrifice. He who had received the promises was about to sacrifice his one and only son.
Hebrews 11:17

easy to imagine. After a while, however, Isaac speaks. "Father?" he asks. "Here I am," replies Abraham for the second time in the story. "The fire and wood are here," says Isaac, "but where is the lamb for the burnt offering?" Abraham replies, "God himself will provide the lamb for the burnt offering, my son" (22:8). Abraham's speech here

shows that despite the enormity God asks, he still trusts God to provide for him.

When father and son reach the designated place, Abraham builds an altar from stones, takes the wood his son has been carrying, and places it on top of the altar. He binds Isaac—hence the Jewish name for the story, the *Akedah*,

A 6th-century mosaic in the Basilica of San Vitale in Ravenna, Italy, depicts Abraham preparing to sacrifice Isaac. Three angels are in attendance and Sarah hovers in the background.

from the Hebrew *Akedat Yizhak*, "binding of Isaac"—and places him on top of the wood ready for the sacrifice.

Abraham reaches out his hand and takes the knife to start the process. At this moment, a voice cries urgently to him from heaven: "Abraham! Abraham!" For the third time in the story, Abraham replies, "Here I am," the repetition highlighting his unwavering faithfulness. "Do not lay a hand on the boy," says the voice. "Do not do anything to him. Now I know that you fear God, because you have not withheld from me your son, your only son" (22:12). To fear God in the Bible is not so much an emotion of terror, but rather a profound respect for God, implying obedience and trust. Many Hebrew words for fear

Offerings to the Lord

Burnt offerings were common to most ancient religions in the Middle East. The meat was burned on an altar, its smoke rising as a pleasing odor to the deity or deities. Once religious rituals had become established among the Israelites, such offerings were made morning and evening in the Jerusalem Temple, along with offerings of grain and drink. The Israelites also believed that firstborn males should be offered to God: "The first offspring to open the

womb among the Israelites belongs to me, whether human or animal," the Lord tells Moses in Exodus 13:1. Scholars believe the ancient Israelites, in common with neighboring peoples, such as the Phoenicians and Egyptians, practiced child sacrifice, though it had ceased among the Israelites by the 7th or 6th century BCE. Instead, parents made burnt offerings of animals to "redeem" their firstborn sons. There is an echo of the abolition of child sacrifice among the Israelites in the story of Abraham and Isaac.

> Through your offspring all nations on earth will be blessed, because you have obeyed me.
> **Genesis 22:18**

also mean reverence and respect. Abraham's trust and obedience shows he respects God's will.

Earlier, Abraham told Isaac that God would provide a lamb for their burnt offering. The Hebrew for "provide" is the same as the word for "see." When Abraham looks up, he sees a ram in a nearby thicket. Abraham takes the ram and offers it in place of his son. Genesis tells us that he named the place "The Lord will provide" (22:14)—suggesting a place where God revealed himself, or let himself be seen.

Multitude of blessings

So far, God has blessed Abraham six times in Genesis. The voice from heaven now pronounces God's seventh and final blessing upon him: "I swear by myself, declares the Lord, that because you have done this and have not withheld your son, your only son, I will surely bless you." The covenant contained in the blessing is threefold. Yet again, God swears to make Abraham's offspring numerous, "as numerous as the stars in the sky and as the sand on the seashore" (22:17). God promises to give Abraham's descendants victory in the face of their enemies. In addition, God promises to bless the entire world through them. After receiving the blessing, Abraham rejoins his followers and they make their way home.

A symbolic death

Some commentators view the ordeal of Isaac as an initiation rite involving a symbolic process of death and rebirth. In many cultures across the world, young men are put through an ordeal in which it seems, for a while, they will die. The purpose of the shock and terror of this experience is to prepare them for real death when it comes. It also creates a rupture with childhood. Through their symbolic death and rebirth, the young men leave their parents and infancy behind to take on the responsibilities of adulthood.

In many ways, the story of Isaac's near-sacrifice fits this pattern. Father and son both undergo an ordeal. For Abraham it is the last test in a life of faith and obedience to God, leading to a culminating blessing or covenant. After this, his life's journey is nearly done. The blessing passes to Isaac, the next link in the patriarchal and covenantal chain. ∎

> And the scripture was fulfilled that says, "Abraham believed God, and it was credited to him as righteousness," and he was called God's friend.
> **James 2:23**

Festivals of remembrance

Both Jews and Muslims celebrate annual festivals that remember Abraham's willingness to sacrifice his son: for Jews, it is Rosh Hashanah, the Jewish New Year, and for Muslims, the festival of Eid al-Adha. At Rosh Hashanah, the Akedah, or Binding of Isaac, in Genesis 22, is one of the key Torah readings for the feast. It is also invoked in one of the feast's special prayers. In this, God is asked to remember the "merciful promise" he made to Abraham on Mount Moriah where Abraham "suppressed his fatherly love in order to do Your will." The ritual blowing of the shofar, or ram's-horn trumpet, is linked to the ram.

For Muslims, Eid al-Adha ("Festival of the Sacrifice") commemorates Abraham's unconditional submission to God, but in Islam it is Ishmael, ancestor of the Arabs, rather than Isaac whom Abraham must sacrifice.

Hands decorated with henna bid people Eid Mubarak (blessed Eid) on Eid al-Adha in India. On this day, Muslims sacrifice a lamb to commemorate Abraham's willingness to obey God's command and sacrifice his son.

54

MAY NATIONS SERVE YOU AND PEOPLES BOW DOWN TO YOU
GENESIS 27:29, ESAU AND JACOB

IN BRIEF

PASSAGE
Genesis 25:25–29:28

THEME
The power of blessing

SETTING
Second millennium BCE
Beersheba and Haran.

KEY FIGURES
Isaac Son of Abraham and Sarah.

Rebekah The wife of Isaac.

Esau The older twin brother of Jacob.

Jacob The younger twin of Esau.

Laban Rebekah's brother.

T he story of Esau and Jacob involves sibling rivalry, favoritism, and deceit. The twin sons of Isaac and Rebekah have been fighting since they were in the womb. "Two nations are in your womb," God tells the pregnant Rebekah, "and

two peoples from within you will be separated, one people will be stronger than the other, and the older will serve the younger."

According to Genesis 25:25, Esau was the firstborn ("the first to come out was red, and his whole body was like a hairy garment"), but Jacob followed promptly, his hand clinging to his brother's heel. The boys grow up to be different characters: Esau is a hunter; Jacob is quieter. Once, when Esau returns from hunting, he finds his brother cooking a stew. When Esau asks for some, Jacob agrees on the condition that Esau surrenders his birthright— an elder son's entitlement to a double portion of any inheritance. Too hungry to care, Esau agrees.

The favorite son

Esau is Isaac's favorite son, Jacob his mother's. When Isaac is old, almost blind, and near death, he tells Esau to go out and hunt some game. Esau must then cook the meat and take the dish to Isaac so that he may bless his favorite son, a deathbed ritual believed to confer God's presence and protection on the recipient. Overhearing this exchange, Rebekah wants Jacob to receive the blessing. Her reasons

are not stated, though some scholars suggest she is the instrument of God, whose plan for Jacob was revealed to her during her pregnancy. She tells Jacob to slaughter two kids from their flock, which she will cook. Jacob should then take the dish to his near-blind father, pretending to be Esau. Before he does this, she covers his hands and neck with goatskin to make him feel hairy like Esau. The deceit works: Jacob receives his father's blessing.

Shortly after this, Esau returns and discovers he has been cheated, but the blessing has already been

I am with you and will watch over you wherever you go … I will not leave you until I have done what I have promised to you.
Genesis 28:15

See also: The Testing of Abraham 50–53 ▪ Jacob Wrestles with God 56–57 ▪ The Psalms 138–43 ▪ Sermon on the Mount 204–09 ▪ The Trinity 298–99

given, so cannot be revoked. In his fury, Esau vows to murder Jacob once their father is dead.

Jacob's ladder

Warned by his mother, Jacob flees under the guise of finding a wife among their own people. He heads for Haran, where Rebekah's brother Laban lives. One night on the journey, he has a dream in which he sees angels ascending and descending a stairway between Earth and heaven. God is present in this symbolic bond of the divine and the human. He assures Jacob of protection and promises that the covenant made with Jacob's grandfather, Abraham, and father,

Isaac, will extend to him and his offspring. They will be as numerous as the "dust of the earth," a blessing to the whole world. Jacob, a younger son who has deceived his brother, receives God's favor.

Laban tricks Jacob

However, Jacob's behavior is punished, and also by a trick. When Jacob arrives at his uncle Laban's house, he falls in love with his cousin Rachel. Laban promises him her hand in marriage after seven years. However, at the end of this time, Laban substitutes his eldest daughter Leah at the ceremony. Jacob must work another seven years to marry Rachel. ▪

Women in Genesis

The four Jewish matriarchs in Genesis—Sarah, Rebekah, Rachel, and Leah—are noted for their faith and dedication to God. Even though they struggle to conceive children, they keep faith in God's plan and acknowledge His role in continuing Abraham's lineage by granting them miraculous pregnancies, even well past normal childbearing age.

Yet the women of Genesis are not passive. They are catalysts. Eve sets the history of humankind in motion when she defies God's command not to eat from the Tree of the Knowledge of Good and Evil, and women continually determine who will inherit God's promise to Abraham: Sarah secures the succession of her son Isaac when she persuades Abraham to expel Hagar and her son Ishmael, and Rebekah engineers for Jacob to receive his father's blessing instead of his older brother Esau.

JACOB . AND . ESAU .

Esau sells his birthright to Jacob, an impetuous act depicted in one of a series of biblical paintings, c.1860–80, by Lady Waterford for Waterford Hall, near Berwick-upon-Tweed, England.

YOUR NAME WILL NO LONGER BE JACOB

GENESIS 32:28, JACOB WRESTLES WITH GOD

IN BRIEF

PASSAGE
Genesis 31:1–33:7

THEME
The birth of Israel

SETTING
Second millennium BCE
Haran and Peniel.

KEY FIGURES
Jacob Son of Isaac and
Rebekah and younger
brother of Esau.

Laban Uncle of Jacob and
Esau and father of Jacob's
wives Leah and Rachel.

Leah The eldest daughter
of Laban and Jacob's first wife.

Rachel The second daughter
of Laban and Jacob's second
and favorite wife.

The unknown stranger
A mysterious figure believed
to be an angel or God himself.

Esau The elder brother
of Jacob.

W hen Jacob's growing
wealth as a herdsman
incurs the jealousy of
Laban's sons, who think it is at
their father's expense, God tells
Jacob to go back to Canaan, "the
land of your fathers" (Genesis 31:3).
Jacob calls his wives Leah and
Rachel (Laban's daughters) to tell
them they must leave. He says how
God has always been with him,
enabled him to prosper, and never
allowed Laban to do him harm.
Leah and Rachel support Jacob
and tell him that "all the wealth
that God took away from our father
belongs to us and our children"
(31:16). They tell Jacob to do
everything that God has told him.

Return to Canaan
Together with his wives and
servants, Jacob prepares to escape
and sends his livestock on ahead.
Unbeknownst to Jacob, his second
wife Rachel steals Laban's precious
heirloom idols, known as teraphim,
and packs them for their journey.
Three days after Jacob's escape,
Laban discovers that the teraphim
are missing and that Jacob has
fled. Furious, he pursues Jacob for
seven days before catching up with
them in the hill country of Gilead.

However, a dream in which God
warns Laban not to "say anything
to Jacob" tempers his response.
When Laban asks for the return of
his teraphim, Jacob allows his
uncle to search their tents.

Hearing this, Rachel hides the
teraphim in her camel saddle and
sits on it. When Laban searches her
tent, she excuses herself for not
standing, on the pretense that she
is menstruating. Jacob chastises
Laban for his lack of trust, and the

Jacob Wrestles with an Angel
by Edward Jakob von Steinle, 1837,
shows Jacob evenly matched with
the mysterious stranger in the place
Jacob called Peniel—"the face of God."

See also: Covenants 44–47 ▪ The Ten Commandments 78–83 ▪
Entering the Promised Land 96–97 ▪ The Fall of Jerusalem 128–31

two form a covenant before God,
making a sacrifice. Jacob promises
never to treat his wives poorly, or
take another wife besides Laban's
two daughters.

The wrestling match

As Jacob approaches Canaan, he
receives word that his estranged
brother Esau is advancing to meet
him with 400 men. Shaken by the
news, Jacob sends gifts of camels,
sheep, goats, and cattle to pacify
his brother. He then has his wives
and sons escorted across the ford
of the Jabbok, while he ruminates
on the situation on the sands.

What follows is one of the most
mysterious passages in the Old
Testament. A stranger challenges
Jacob to wrestle. The ensuing
struggle lasts the night, with
neither party prevailing. Eventually,
at daybreak, Jacob's opponent
realizes that he cannot defeat Jacob.
To bring the wrestling match to
a close, he touches the socket of
Jacob's hip, dislocating the bone.
Despite the pain, Jacob refuses to
release his hold until the stranger
blesses him. In reply, the stranger
tells Jacob that his name will no
longer be Jacob, but Israel ("He
struggles with God") because he
has struggled with both God and
man and prevailed. The stranger
blesses Jacob and vanishes.

The next day, Jacob meets his
brother Esau and bows down before
him to signal that he means no
harm. The two men are reconciled.

Scholars dispute the identity of
the stranger. Some say, following
Hosea 12:3–4, that it was the Angel
of the Lord; others that it was the
spirit of Jesus Christ taking the
form of a man. Still more say it
was God Himself. ▪

God tells Jacob to
return to Canaan.

↓

Laban pursues Jacob but
**God tells him not to
harm him**.

↓

Nearing Canaan, **Jacob
asks God for protection**
from Esau.

↓

**A stranger wrestles
all night with Jacob,
who eventually
triumphs.**

↓

The stranger **blesses Jacob**
and names him Israel,
"struggles with God."

↓

Having received God's
blessing, Jacob **enters
the land of Canaan**.

↓

Jacob's sons will found the
12 tribes of Israel.

Twelve Tribes of Israel

During his years of self-
imposed exile, Jacob prospers
both in terms of wealth and in
the number of children born
to his wives and concubines.
His first wife, Leah, bears
six sons—Reuben, Simeon,
Levi, Judah, Issachar, and
Zebulun—while Rachel, his
favorite wife, who struggles
to conceive, gives birth to
Joseph and Benjamin, the last
child causing her to die in
childbirth. In addition, Bilhah,
Rachel's handmaiden, and
Zilpah, Leah's servant, each
give birth to two sons by
Jacob—Dan, Naphtali, Gad,
and Asher.

Biblical tradition holds that
these 12 sons, along with two
of Jacob's grandsons through
Joseph, would form the 12
tribes of Israel, or Israelites
after the name given to Jacob
by the stranger on the sands
at Peniel.

A mosaic represents the
12 tribes of Israel descended from
Jacob. The 12 tribes will eventually
populate Canaan, the Promised
Land, from the Wadi of Egypt to
the Euphrates (Genesis 15:18).

WE WILL SEE WHAT WILL BECOME OF HIS DREAMS

GENESIS 37:20, JOSEPH THE DREAMER

The second youngest of Jacob's 12 sons, and the patriarch's favorite, Joseph is celebrated in Genesis as a dreamer. Through keeping faith with the messages of his divinely inspired dreams, Joseph rises to become chief adviser to the Egyptian Pharaoh and brings his family, destined to found the 12 tribes of Israel, into Egypt.

Joseph's story is a continuation of the history of the Israelites' ancestry, with divine calls and promises, but God is less obviously present than in earlier stories. Here, the emphasis is on the importance of forgiveness and reconciliation.

The meaning of dreams

From a young age, Joseph believes that his dreams contain messages about future events. However, his

See also: Covenants 44–47 ▪ Esau and Jacob 54–55 ▪ Jacob Wrestles with God 56–57 ▪ The Wisdom of Solomon 120–23 ▪ Daniel in Babylon 164–65

A composite illustration from a 13th-century illuminated manuscript shows Joseph being lowered into a cistern, being traded for 20 shekels of silver, and traveling to Egypt.

Prophetic dreams in the Bible

God employs dreams and visions throughout the Bible as a way of revealing and furthering his divine plan. These dreams act as a bridge between God and man. In Genesis 15:1, as Abraham falls into a deep sleep, God uses a vision to restate His covenant with Abraham. Later on in the Old Testament, Samuel, Solomon, and Daniel are all noted dreamers. Samuel has his first vision as a young boy in 1 Samuel: 3, when "the Word of the Lord was rare; there were not many visions," and in 1 Kings: 3:5, Solomon dreams that God invites him to choose a gift (Solomon asks for a discerning heart to help him "distinguish between right and wrong.") In Daniel 7, Daniel is terrified by a vision of four great beasts that represent four future kingdoms, which will only give way to the Son of Man.

brothers see Joseph's narration of his dreams as boastful. In his first dream, Joseph sees himself and his brothers binding sheaves of wheat in the fields. While his sheaf stands upright, the sheaves of his brothers bow down before his sheaf. The unwelcome message of Joseph's dream—at least to his brothers—is that Joseph is destined to rule over them. Their unease is reinforced when Joseph dreams that the sun and moon, representing his father and mother, and 11 stars (his brothers) pay homage to him. Even Jacob is bemused by this and scolds Joseph: "What is this dream you had? Will your mother and I and your brothers actually come and bow down to the ground before you?" (Genesis 37:10).

Plot against Joseph
In Genesis 37:13, when Joseph's older brothers are out grazing their flocks, Jacob sends Joseph to check on them. The brothers decide to take advantage of Joseph's visit to the remote location to murder him and thus prevent his dreams from coming true. However, Reuben, Jacob's firstborn, opposes this proposal and argues against killing Joseph outright. He recommends that they strip Joseph of his ornate coat, which is a gift from their father, and throw him into a cistern to die naturally. (Reuben secretly plans to rescue Joseph when his brothers' backs are turned.) However, another brother, Judah, also troubled by the idea of killing »

Joseph's dream An upright sheaf of wheat is surrounded by 11 others, which bow down before it. (Genesis 37:7)

The cupbearer's dream A hand squeezes one of three bunches of grapes into a goblet. (40:9–11)

Pharaoh's Egypt

Ancient Egypt was a sharply segregated society. At the top stood the pharaoh, not just as a king, but as an incarnation of divine power. Below the pharaoh came the nobles and then the priests; at the bottom were the farmers and slaves, the largest group.

Although the country was mainly desert, agriculture along the Nile valley created enormous wealth for ancient Egypt. The unusual fertility of the Nile valley was due to the *akhet* (the annual inundation), when the Nile floods. The silt left behind enriched the soil, leading to abundant harvests. Tax on this bounty created immense wealth for Pharaoh and the nobles.

Hapi, the Nile god, and Osiris, god of life, received hymns and offerings to ensure the inundation. These gods were among more than 2,000 in ancient Egypt, including Anubis, god of the underworld, Isis, goddess of love, and the sun god Ra. It is not known to what extent the Israelites in Egypt embraced these gods or stayed true to their one God.

their own flesh and blood, suggests selling Joseph to a passing group of Midianite traders for 20 silver shekels. The brothers follow Judah's plan and also dip Joseph's robe in goat's blood to pretend to their father that their brother has been killed by a wild animal.

Fortunes in Egypt

The Midianites sell Joseph on to Ishmaelites traveling to Egypt, who, in turn, sell him into slavery in the house of Potiphar, the captain of Pharaoh's guard. Joseph serves his master well and is soon in charge of the entire household. However, when Potpihar's wife falsely accuses Joseph of seducing her, Potiphar throws him in prison.

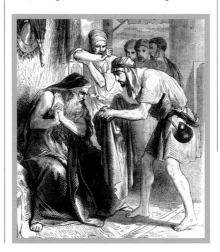

As Joseph stays true to his faith by resisting sexual temptation, God does not desert him in his suffering. He is put in charge of the other prisoners, and interprets the dreams of two of them—Pharaoh's chief cupbearer and head baker. He tells them that in three days the baker will be put to death, while the cupbearer will be pardoned. When his predictions come true, Joseph asks the cupbearer to put in a good word for him with Pharaoh, which he promises to do.

However, the cupbearer, unlike God, is fallible and forgets his promise until two years later, when Pharaoh begins to have strange dreams. In the first dream, seven sickly cows devour seven healthy ones as they graze beside the Nile. In the second, seven sickly ears of grain swallow seven fat ones. At this point, the cupbearer remembers Joseph. Hearing the cupbearer's story, Pharaoh has Joseph brought before him.

Joseph is quick to explain the meaning of Pharaoh's dream, while also being careful to stress that he

Jacob is shown examining Joseph's blood-stained coat in a 19th-century engraving. Refusing to be comforted, Jacob says: "I will continue to mourn until I join my son in the grave" (37:35).

The baker's dream The baker has three baskets of bread on his head. Birds eat from the top one. (40:16–17)

Pharaoh's dream Seven skinny cows devour seven sleek, fat cows on the banks of the Nile. (41:4)

is simply an instrument of God and that the dreams are a sign of God's purpose. He tells Pharaoh that his dreams signify seven years of plenty followed by seven years of famine. He advises Pharaoh to store supplies of grain during the years of plenty in order to use them later. Pharaoh takes Joseph's advice and appoints him as his chief adviser.

The legacy of Joseph

Joseph's tale does not end here. Eventually, he is reconciled with his brothers, who, during the years of famine, are sent to Egypt by Jacob to buy grain. Joseph forgives his brothers, believing it is thanks to their earlier wrongdoings that he is able to feed them in their time of need. "God sent me before you to preserve life," he pronounces in Genesis 45:5. Pharaoh allows Joseph to bring Jacob and his people to Egypt, where they prosper. They remain there until, generations later, a new pharaoh, "to whom Joseph meant nothing" (Exodus 1:8), comes to the throne.

Joseph devotes his life to serving others. He always credits God for his achievements and remains faithful to Him. His story, which is also chronicled in the Qur'an, which regards him as a prophet, illustrates the power of forgiveness. Crucially for the next book in the Bible, the story also explains how the Israelites came to be in Egypt. ∎

Joseph's success at interpreting Pharaoh's dream, shown in this 1894 painting by British artist Reginald Arthur, leads to his appointment as Pharaoh's chief adviser.

The dreams of Pharaoh are one and the same. God has revealed to Pharaoh what he is about to do.
Genesis 41:25

EXODUS
DEUTER

TO
ONOMY

Moses is born and set adrift in a basket on the River Nile.

God sends **ten plagues** to Egypt in order to free the Israelites from slavery.

Moses parts the **Red Sea** and the Israelites escape Pharaoh's army.

God gives the Israelites instructions for building the **Ark** and the **Tabernacle**.

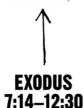

EXODUS 2:1–3

EXODUS 7:14–12:30

EXODUS 14:1–31

EXODUS 25:10–27:20

EXODUS 3:1–22

EXODUS 12:31–42

EXODUS 19:17–20:26

EXODUS 32:1–20

A vision of God appears to Moses in a **burning bush**.

Moses leads the **Exodus** of the Israelites through the desert.

God delivers the **Ten Commandments** to Moses, who inscribes them on stone tablets.

The Israelites fashion and worship a **golden calf**, causing Moses to destroy the stone tablets in anger.

Resuming the story of the Israelites from Genesis, the books of Exodus, Leviticus, Numbers, and Deuteronomy follow the liberation of the Israelites from slavery in Egypt under the guidance of Moses, their receipt of the Ten Commandments and other laws, and their journey to the Promised Land. The central message is one of deliverance through God's covenant with Moses, a continuation of the divine promise begun in Genesis and picked up through the Bible. In Christianity, Jesus is seen as a second Moses, who offers salvation from death.

The Bible as history
Scholars have long attempted to link events in Exodus to historical sources in order to verify and date the Israelites' flight from Egypt. No archaeological evidence has so far been found and there is no historical record. The Bible does not identify the pharaoh at the time of the Exodus. This lack of corroboration has led to a hunt for circumstantial evidence, such as the widespread migrations that are known to have occurred in the eastern Mediterranean during the transition from the Bronze Age to the Iron Age in around 1200 BCE, a period when trade routes changed and civilizations collapsed.

Some scholars link the Israelites with the Hyksos, Semitic peoples who ruled parts of Egypt in the 1600s BCE but were driven out by Thutmose III in the 1400s. The 1st-century historian Josephus Flavius, keen to stress the antiquity of the Jews, supported this idea.

Other theories draw on the Amarna Letters, a correspondence on clay tablets sent by Pharaoh Akhenaten (1350s–1330s BCE) in Amarna, Upper Egypt, to the rest of the Ancient Near East. They point to mentions of a group of bandits called *haipiru/haibiru,* words similar to "Hebrew," that are to be driven from the land.

In 1939, Sigmund Freud, in his book *Moses and Monotheism*, proposed that Moses was a priest of Akhenaten's god, who introduced monotheism to Egypt. Despite this, attempts to link the Book of Exodus to historical events have proved futile.

Monotheism is all
Central to the Book of Exodus is the doctrine of monotheism, developed from the Book of Genesis. However, the first of the Ten Commandments

Moses
records the Ten Commandments on stone tablets for the second time.

The Israelites leave the desert of **Sinai**.

Balaam and his donkey encounter the **angel of the Lord** in the road.

Moses **gathers** all of Israel and **recites** the Ten Commandments.

EXODUS 34:1–27

NUMBERS 10:11–36

NUMBERS 22:21–41

DEUTERONOMY 5:1–8:20

LEVITICUS 8:1–36

NUMBERS 14:33–35

DEUTERONOMY 4:39

DETEURONOMY 31:1–34:12

Moses's brother Aaron and his sons are **ordained as priests**.

God sentences the Israelites to **40 years of wandering** in the desert.

Moses reminds the **Israelites** that there are no gods except God Himself.

Moses introduces **Joshua** as his successor, blesses the **tribes of Israel**, and dies.

given to Moses on Mount Sinai, "You shall have no other gods before me," is ambiguous. Early biblical scholars, convinced that monotheism was not present from the start of the Bible but developed over time, believed that this suggested henotheism, effectively a middle stage between polytheism and monotheism in which one god is paramount among multiple gods.

However, the text of the Book of Deuteronomy (the "second law"), which follows Exodus, is clear. Not only does it proclaim that there is only one deity, but it establishes a creed, the *Shema* ("hear"), to reinforce the idea: "Hear, O Israel, the Lord your God" (Deuteronomy 6:4), a daily declaration of belief.

Deuteronomy is a retelling of the Law, which sets out to reestablish the Mosaic covenant. According to Jewish tradition, the Book of Deuteronomy was found in a dusty corner of the Temple in the 7th century BCE.

Building a religion

Whenever the Israelites ignore God's laws, disaster ensues. When they worship a false god in the form of the golden calf soon after receiving the Ten Commandments, they are condemned to wander aimlessly through the desert for 40 years. During this time, they formalize their religion, establishing its structure and liturgy. The Tabernacle, built according to God's instructions, is a moveable version of the Temple that will later be built by Solomon in Jerusalem, and Moses's brother Aaron founds a hereditary priesthood through his bloodline

(the Levites). The text of the Pentateuch, or Torah, ends with Moses dying on the threshold of the Promised Land of Canaan. After his death, the Israelites, led by Joshua, Moses's appointed successor, are ready to retake the land promised to them by God from the polytheistic Canaanites.

As religious scripture, the Torah is significant to Judaism, Christianity, and Islam, and is highly influential on Western culture. For Jews, the Torah is the most important of the biblical texts because it establishes God's relationship with His Chosen People, while for Christians, Moses foreshadows the coming Messiah. In the Qur'an, the Torah is referred to as *al-kitab* ("the book") and Moses (Musa) is mentioned more times than any other prophet. ■

THOUGH THE BUSH WAS ON FIRE IT DID NOT BURN UP

EXODUS 3:3, MOSES AND THE BURNING BUSH

IN BRIEF

PASSAGE
Exodus 3:1–4:17

THEME
Human inadequacy in the face of God

SETTING
14th–13th century BCE
The foothills of Mount Horeb (also called Mount Sinai).

KEY FIGURES
Moses A descendant of Jacob through his son Levi, tasked by God with liberating the Israelites. He later becomes one of the greatest prophets.

Aaron Brother of Moses. Initially more articulate and confident than his brother, he assists Moses in carrying out God's plan.

The story of God appearing to Moses as a burning bush illustrates not only His compassion toward His initially reluctant prophet, but also His ability to enact His will through ordinary individuals. Although Moses would become one of the most famous figures in the Old Testament by freeing the Israelites from 400 years of slavery in Egypt, at this point in the Bible's narrative he is an outcast. An Israelite raised in Egypt's royal court after an Egyptian princess found him floating in a basket, he fled to Midian (possibly in Sinai) after killing an Egyptian he found beating a Hebrew slave.

See also: The Exodus 74–77 ▪ The Ten Commandments 78–83 ▪
The Twelve Spies 88 ▪ Entering the Promised Land 96–97

Moses removes his shoes before
speaking with God in this 15th-century
painting by Dieric Bouts the Elder. God
commanded him to remove his sandals
before entering holy ground.

In Midian, Moses marries a local
woman and becomes a shepherd.
It is while he is tending his flock
beneath Horeb, the mountain of
God (also known as Mount Sinai),
that God first speaks to Moses.
Spying a bush that is burning
without being consumed by the
fire, Moses approaches the bush to
investigate the phenomenon. When
God appears to Moses from within

the flames, his first reaction is one
of dread: he hides his face, afraid
to witness God. God, however, has
a mission for Moses: He tells him
that He has heard the crying of the
Israelites in bondage and that He
has chosen Moses to lead His
people out of Egypt.

Uncertain prophet

Moses demonstrates his human
frailty by demurring in the face
of God's request. He tells God that
he is not the right person for the
mission, fearing that neither
the Israelites nor the Egyptians
will listen to his entreaties. Moses
further complains that the Israelites
will not believe that God has shown
Himself to him, because he does
not know God's personal name.

God is patient with Moses,
mirroring the intimacy He has
previously shown to the individuals
He chooses to carry out His will,
such as Abraham (see pp. 44–47).
He tells Moses "I am who I am"
(Exodus 3:14), indicating His
perpetual omnipresence. To provide
further evidence of His almighty
nature to both the Israelites and
to the Egyptians, He gives Moses
the power to perform three »

The prophet Moses

Moses is one of the greatest
figures of the Bible—a leader
and lawgiver who is brought
up as an Egyptian prince,
becomes a social outcast,
and ultimately goes on to
become a leading prophet.
After avoiding Pharaoh's
slaughter of the Israelite
firstborn sons when his
mother hides him in a basket
on the Nile, he returns to his
people as an adult to lead
them out of slavery. After his
initial reluctance, Moses not
only becomes the liberator of
the Israelites, but shepherds
them across the desert for
40 years as their spiritual and
military leader. A figure of
authority and justice, he
adopts and enforces God's
Ten Commandments.

The symbolism behind Moses's journey

The adoption of Moses
by an Egyptian princess
echoes Pharaoh's
promotion of Joseph
in Genesis (41:41).

Moses murders
an Egyptian who is
mistreating a Hebrew
slave, foreshadowing the
punishment of Egypt.

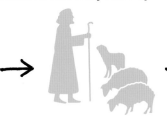

**Moses becomes a
shepherd**, anticipating
his role as a shepherd
of the Israelites in their
exodus from Egypt.

**God speaks
to Moses** from
a burning bush, a
symbol of God's
everlasting presence.

miraculous acts. First, when Moses throws his staff (probably a shepherd's crook) to the ground, it becomes a snake. Second, when Moses puts his hand into his cloak and then withdraws it, his hand appears leprous and white. When he repeats the action, the hand is restored to health. Third, God tells Moses that if he takes water from the Nile and pours it on the ground, it will turn to blood.

In spite of these miracles, Moses remains reluctant. He blames his lack of eloquence, saying "I am slow of speech and tongue" (4:10). God encourages Moses, telling him that He will be with him and will give him the right words to say. He entreats Moses to leave, but again, Moses refuses, and pleads: "Lord, please send somebody else to do it" (4:13). As in many Old Testament stories, the servant God chooses to enact His will is not at first particularly worthy or even willing. Moses's equivocation, indicative of human weakness, contrasts with the strength he later finds when he puts his trust in God.

God eventually loses patience with Moses. His anger "burns bright" against him, yet He also

shows His compassion by allowing Moses's brother, Aaron, a confident speaker, to assist him on his mission and make up for Moses's shortcomings as an orator. God tells Moses: "I will help both of you speak and teach you what to do" (4:15). He then gives Moses another staff with which to perform miraculous signs.

Moses must eventually agree to God's election of him to lead the Israelites, because in verse 18, he is

St. Catherine's Monastery in Egypt claims to be the place where Moses saw the burning bush. Founded in the 6th century at the foot of Mount Sinai, it is a UNESCO world heritage site.

preparing to return to Egypt with his wife and sons, taking the "staff of God in his hand" (4:20).

A holy site

The likely location of the episode of the burning bush has been greatly debated by biblical scholars. The Hebrew word for bush—and used in the narrative—is *seneh*, which is remarkably close to "Sinai" and may be a pun, a common feature in ancient Hebrew texts. *Seneh* is also widely believed to be another name for Horeb ("God's mountain"). The word "Horeb" is often interpreted as "heat," although others translate it to mean "desert" or "desolation," fitting the isolated locations in which God often communicates with His chosen instrument.

Although Mount Sinai is widely accepted as the location of the bush, some modern scholars insist that evidence points to other sites

The Kenites

Moses is linked through his father-in-law Jethro to a tribe known as the Kenites. This nomadic clan of coppersmiths and metalworkers played a key role in the establishment of ancient Israel. Believed to be descendants of Cain, many members of the tribe settled among the Israelite peoples and influenced their development.

Jethro, a shepherd and priest, lived in the land of Midian, where "Yahweh" was historically a deity. The "Kenite

hypothesis," first proposed by the 19th-century German theologian Friedrich Wilhelm Ghillany, suggests that the Hebrews adopted the cult of Yahweh from the Midianites, who had previously learned it from the Kenites. In the story of the burning bush, when God tells Moses "I am what I am," this is translated from the Hebrew *hayah*, which in turn gives rise to the word *yahweh*. God's clarification to Moses is a statement of his identity as the God of the patriarchs and thus the God of the Israelites.

as far away as Hijaz (a region in the northwest of modern Saudi Arabia) or northern Arabah (west Jordan). The monks of the Sacred Monastery of the God-Trodden Mount Sinai (also known as St. Catherine's Monastery) are adamant that their complex, in a narrow valley at the foot of Mount Sinai, in Egypt, was built on the site of the burning bush. However, while this part of Egypt, which includes mountainous desert, is called the Sinai Peninsula due to this claim, there is little consensus about which mountain is the Mount Sinai of the Bible.

The burning bush

Some scholars believe that the inflammable plant *Dictamnus* might have inspired the biblical account of Moses's election by God. This flowering shrub, native to warm, open woodland habitats and found throughout the Middle East, is covered with isoprene-based, volatile oils that can catch fire easily in hot weather. It is these natural oils that burn—enveloping the exterior of the entire plant—and not the bush itself, which is generally unharmed once the

Earth's crammed with heaven, And every common bush afire with God.
Elizabeth Barrett Browning
Poet (1806–1861)

There the angel of the Lord appeared to him in flames of fire from within a bush.
Exodus 3:2

flames extinguish themselves. It is possible that this natural phenomenon occurred regularly on the plains of the ancient Holy Land and would have been known to the oral storytellers and early scripture writers who shaped the Old Testament.

Whatever the explanations for the burning bush, it serves as a potent and highly visual symbol of God's omnipresence. In the early books of the Bible, God appears in a number of dramatic forms (known as theophany), underlining His unique ability to appear in different guises and circumstances. The declaratory marvel of the burning bush is juxtaposed with Moses's ambivalent attitude, reflecting the difference between the divine and the human. While God's reputation as the Almighty is emphasized through the spectacle, Moses's uncertainty demonstrates human weakness in the face of the divine.

The burning bush is one of the most dramatic symbols in the Bible and has come to represent many

Dictamnus albus, shown here in a 16th-century manuscript dedicated to St. Mark, may have been the burning bush of Exodus. The plant is covered in a flammable oil used to heal snake bites.

different things for religious institutions across the world. The motto adopted by the Reformed Church of France, *"Flagror non consumor"* (I am burned, I am not consumed), best exemplifies the significance that the burning bush has acquired in modern times. God is referred to elsewhere in the Bible as a "consuming fire" (Deuteronomy 4:24 and Hebrews 12:29), but the fact that the bush remains intact despite the fire can be interpreted as representing God's infinite capacity for mercy.

In Scotland, Ireland, Canada, Australia, the Netherlands, and a number of other countries, the bush has become the adopted symbol of Presbyterian churches. In the United States, the Jewish Theological Seminary has adopted the symbol with the accompanying phrase "and the bush was not consumed." In all cases, the symbolism associated with the image suggests that the Church suffers yet lives on. ∎

ALL THE WATER WAS CHANGED INTO BLOOD

EXODUS 7:20, THE TEN PLAGUES

IN BRIEF

PASSAGE
Exodus 7–10

THEME
Divine intervention

SETTING
14th–13th century BCE
Egypt.

KEY FIGURES
The Israelites Followers of
the patriarch Jacob, who are
enslaved in Egypt.

Moses A future prophet,
chosen by God to lead the
Israelites out of captivity into
the Promised Land.

Aaron Moses's older brother,
a Levite and skilled orator.

Pharaoh Egyptian leader and
enslaver of the Israelites.

The ten plagues of Egypt occur at a time when the Israelites have been enslaved in Egypt for around 400 years. With their trust in God wavering, the plagues act as a sign from God that reaffirms the Israelites as His chosen people and shows His superior power over the many gods worshipped by the Egyptians.

On the instructions of God, Moses and Aaron confront Pharaoh and ask him to free the Israelites. Although Moses is respected by Pharaoh's advisers, God hardens Pharaoh's heart and he refuses Moses's request.

The identity of this Pharaoh is a matter of conjecture among scholars, since Exodus does not name him and there is no firm agreement about the date of the Israelites' eventual escape from

The Fifth Plague of Egypt by J.M.W. Turner actually depicts the hailstorm of the seventh plague. The mistitled painting was Turner's first major work to be shown at the Royal Academy.

See also: Moses and the Burning Bush 66–69 ▪ The Passover 72–73 ▪ The Exodus 74–77 ▪ The Twelve Spies 88 ▪ The Final Judgment 316–21

Evidence for the plagues

Over the years, scientists have made many attempts to discover evidence for the ten plagues and explain what caused them. Working in the 1950s, Danish academic Greta Hort was the first to argue that the plagues were the result of a chain of natural catastrophes in Egypt. Later, in the 1990s, Hort's theory was given further credibility by American epidemiologists John S. Marr and Curtis Malloy, who suggested that the tenth plague could be attributed to poisonous mycotoxins (fungal toxins) infecting the grain supply in Egypt.

In 2010, new theories of how the plagues could have resulted from natural causes emerged. These included ideas that a shift in the Egyptian climate from wet to dry was the trigger for the first plague, and that the penultimate three plagues were the result of a volcanic eruption on the island of Santorini in Greece, causing a large ash cloud to spread across Egypt.

Egypt. No record exists of this in Egyptian sources. Some scholars date the Exodus to around 1446 BCE, which would place it during the reign of Thutmose III, while others say it may have happened as late as 1275 BCE, during the reign of Ramesses II. Several other pharaohs have also been proposed.

Plague follows plague

God's response to Pharaoh's refusal to free the Israelites is to have Moses summon a series of plagues to afflict the Egyptian people, culminating in the tenth and most calamitous: the slaying in a single night of all the firstborn male children and animals of the Egyptians (see pp. 72–73). Excluding this final plague, the plagues come in sets of three, a number often associated with divinity and used by the writers of Exodus as a device to build narrative tension and expectation. The first two plagues in each set are preceded by a warning; the last is not. The gravity of the plagues increases with each set.

The plagues not only convince Pharaoh to free the Israelites, but they also rekindle the Israelites' faith in the Lord. These powerful acts demonstrate that the God of their fathers is worthy of worship and superior to the host of pagan gods in Egypt, the most powerful country in the region at that time. Plagues reappear as a symbol of God's wrath and judgment later in the Bible. They include the Seven Last Plagues that complete God's wrath at the Final Judgment, described in Revelation by the Apostle John.

God's purpose

There is little historical evidence for the plagues. The one surviving document that may provide evidence, the Ipuwer Papyrus, describes scenes that could match the Exodus story—including a reference to a river of blood (the first plague)—but scholars believe that it was written between 1850 and 1600 BCE, preceding any of the proposed dates for the Exodus by several centuries. ▪

The Ten Plagues

1. Blood The Nile River turns to blood, so it is undrinkable.

2. Frogs Land, houses, and people are covered in frogs.

3. Gnats The dust throughout Egypt turns into gnats.

4. Flies Swarms of flies cover Pharaoh's officials.

5. Livestock All the livestock of the Egyptians dies.

6. Boils People and animals break out in boils.

7. Hail A severe hailstorm falls on Egypt.

8. Locusts All the trees and plants are devoured by locusts.

9. Darkness The sky turns dark for three days.

10. Firstborn All the firstborn sons of the Egyptians die.

WHEN YOU ENTER THE LAND THAT THE LORD WILL GIVE YOU AS HE PROMISED, OBSERVE THIS CEREMONY
EXODUS 12:25, THE PASSOVER

IN BRIEF

PASSAGE
Exodus 12:25

THEME
Passover

SETTING
14th–13th century BCE
Nile Delta.

KEY FIGURES
Moses Leader of the Israelite people, who ensures that God's instructions are carried out to the letter.

Aaron Moses's older brother, who assists him in carrying out God's orders.

Pharaoh Leader of the Egyptians, who refuses to heed Moses's warnings of God's intentions.

The Jewish holiday of Passover commemorates the Israelites' deliverance from their Egyptian slavery. It also celebrates specifically how God makes a distinction between the Israelites and the Egyptians, sparing the Israelites from the last—and worst—of the plagues.

God's tenth plague against the Egyptian people kills all of the firstborn sons. In order not to harm the Israelites during this plague, God instructs His Angel of Death, a destructive figure, to *pass over* (hence the name of the holiday) the Israelites as it carries out His work. God tells Moses and Aaron to instruct the Israelites to sacrifice

When I see
the blood, I will
pass over you.
Exodus 12:13

lambs and smear their blood over the door frames of their houses, in order to distinguish their homes from those of the Egyptians.

The angel kills the oldest son of every family in Egypt, including Pharaoh's own offspring, the crown prince. It is this event that forms the basis of the Passover holiday—Pesach—celebrated annually by Jewish families today, more than 3,000 years later.

Origins and significance

Scholars are generally in agreement that, in line with standard biblical chronology, the Passover would have occurred around 1300 BCE. Most also believe that the event derives from a protection rite employed by nomadic shepherds as they moved in search of pasture.

The blood of a lamb, sacrificed in a protective ritual, symbolized the life-giving power of God and protected the shepherds against any evil forces. The roasting and consumption of the lamb's meat—part of God's very detailed instructions to the Israelites at the time of the first Passover—would further seal the links between God and His people. The dramatic escape from Egypt gave this

See also: The Exodus 74–77 ▪ The Ten Commandments 78–83 ▪ Entering the Promised Land 96–97

ancient rite a whole new meaning, as it came to commemorate the victory of the Israelites' God over Egyptian gods and God's ongoing covenant with His chosen people.

God tells the Israelites to take part in the ritual of the Passover when they enter the land He has promised to them, and to carry this out for generations to come. As God has protected the firstborns of the Israelites, their lives now belong to God, and this ritual observance honors that. Passover can also be seen to represent the idea that Israel is God's firstborn, whom He will continually protect.

The bread of the Israelites

As well as eating the meat of the sacrificed lambs, according to God's instructions the Israelites ate unleavened bread. This meant that it contained no yeast and therefore had not "risen." Such was the rush accompanying the Israelites' departure from Egypt that there was no time to bake the bread with leavening yeast. Consequently, the

Passover is also known as the Feast of Unleavened Bread, and during this time Jews discard all traces of yeast from their homes and eat entirely unleavened foods. God also prescribes the eating of bitter herbs during Passover as a symbol of the Israelites' bitter lives as slaves in Egypt.

Over the centuries, a number of other elements were added to the ritual of Passover, including special wines, foods, prayers, and blessings. Its significance in Jewish culture is inestimable: all subsequent acts of deliverance in the Israelites' history were seen as consequences of the Exodus (see pp. 74–77) and celebrated as extensions of the Passover. The holiday serves as a reminder of the drama and significance of the Exodus for God's chosen people. ▪

The Israelites prepare for the tenth plague of Egypt in this 1639 engraving by Johann Sadler. By marking their homes with animal blood, they show God which houses to avoid.

Pesach and Judaism

The Hebrew name for Passover, "Pesach" is one of the most important Jewish holidays. As with two other major holidays, Shavuot and Sukkot, Pesach originally required Jews to make a pilgrimage to the Jerusalem Temple to sacrifice an animal. When the Romans destroyed the Temple in 70 CE—most scholars believe it stood on the site of the Dome of the Rock, the Muslim shrine in the heart of Jerusalem—the original stipulations of Pesach had to be altered. These days, most Jewish families celebrate the holiday at home, an arrangement similar to the original biblical tradition of holding the Passover in individual homes.

The term "pesach" may also refer to the lamb or goat that was designated for sacrifice during the holiday (in recognition of God's original orders). Known as the Korban Pesach, today this ritual sacrifice remains a central symbol of Passover. It is commemorated in a set of scriptural and Rabbinic passages and the presentation of *zeroa*, a symbolic meat-based food placed on the ceremonial Passover "seder plate" but not eaten. The seder plate also contains an egg to symbolize sacrifice.

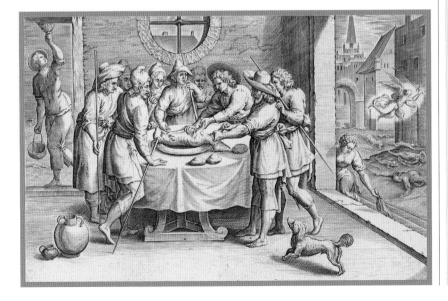

STRETCH OUT YOUR HAND OVER THE SEA TO DIVIDE THE WATER

EXODUS 14:16, THE EXODUS

IN BRIEF

PASSAGE
Exodus 14–17

THEME
Divine deliverance

SETTING
14th–13th century BCE
Northeastern Egypt.

KEY FIGURES
Moses God's appointed leader
of the Israelites, who follows
God's instructions to lead
them out of bondage.

Aaron Moses's brother, who
assists him in guiding the
Israelites out of Egypt.

Miriam Sister to Moses and
Aaron, later a prophetess.

Pharaoh Ruler of the
Egyptians, who chases after
the Israelites, despite having
released them from slavery
after the plagues of Egypt.

Central to Judaism, the Exodus (from a Greek word meaning "exit") narrative is the account of the founding of the nation of Israel. The tale also features one of the most famous episodes in the Old Testament— Moses parting the Red Sea.

Following a barrage of plagues sent by God, Pharaoh summons Moses and Aaron and tells them that their people can leave. The Israelites—more than 600,000 of them—hastily gather their belongings and make their way out of Egypt and into the wilderness. They are at last free of bondage, but their troubles are not over.

Moses leads the Israelites through the Red Sea in this 1849 painting by Vasilii (Wilhelm) Alexandrovich Kotarbinsky. With the waters parted, they are able to walk across the seabed.

God leads the Israelites toward the Promised Land, manifesting Himself as a pillar of cloud by day and a pillar of fire by night, in order to light their way and make the exit from Egypt as swift as possible. He leads the people southeast, in the direction of the land He has promised to them. The Israelites, however, are confused by the directions they are given and complain to Moses, who consults God at every sign of trouble.

Pharaoh's reaction

God then does something that is surprising. He "hardens" the heart of Pharaoh (Exodus 14:4), prompting the Egyptian ruler to decide to pursue the Israelites. This serves two purposes: it tests the faith of His chosen people by making the situation even more perilous while at the same time defending them by luring the Egyptians into a trap.

Pharaoh dispatches an army of chariot-borne soldiers, which catches up with the Israelites on the shores of a sea near a place called Pi Hahiroth (Exodus 14:9). (The Hebrew translation of Exodus calls the area *yam suf*—sea of reeds—whereas the Greek translation refers to it as *thalassa erythra*, red sea.) As the Israelites realize they are trapped between the water and Pharaoh's army, they panic and cry out to Moses. Transformed by God, Moses has lost his former reluctance to lead. He calms his followers by telling them simply to be still and that God will deliver them. God then instructs Moses to raise his staff »

The Red Sea

A 1,400-mile (2,250-km) long seawater inlet of the Indian Ocean, the Red Sea lies between Africa and Asia. At 16–18 miles (26–29km) wide at its narrowest point and about 165 feet (50m) deep at its shallowest, it would have been a significant hurdle for the Israelites to cross.

The name Red Sea has two possible derivations. First, the word "red" was used in some ancient Asiatic languages to denote the direction "south," just as "black" was used for north and other colors for east and west. Alternatively, the name may derive from the presence of large blooms of cyanobacteria, or "sea sawdust," called *Trichodesmium erythraeum*, which turns reddish-brown as it dies off.

The ubiquity of this weed on the surface of the Red Sea may also explain the Hebrew name *yam suf*, "sea of reeds." Although some scholars believe *yam suf* might refer to a reed-strewn freshwater lake that existed in ancient times on the site of the Suez Canal, it is also possible that *yam suf* refers to the same weed that turns the sea red.

They said to Moses, "Was it because there were no graves in Egypt that you brought us to the desert to die?"
Exodus 14:11

and stretch out his hand across the water. He assures him that the waters will part and the Israelites will be able to move on across dry land. He further explains to Moses that He will "harden the hearts" of the Egyptians so that they will follow the Israelites onto the seabed. The repetition of this phrase underlines the dual purpose that God had in mind from the start.

When Moses raises his staff, everything comes to pass just as God promised. The Israelites cross dry ground between two enormous walls of water, while God holds the Egyptians back with His pillar of fire. Once the Israelites are safely across the river, God allows the Egyptians to give chase. When the army reaches the seabed, Moses lowers his arms, and the waters sweep over the Egyptian soldiers and drown them. This divine act is one of several instances in Exodus in which God demonstrates His supreme power.

Song of the Sea
Once they have been safely delivered from Pharaoh's army, the Israelites celebrate by singing a song in worship of God. Known as the "Song of the Sea" (Exodus 15), the hymn is led by Moses and his sister Miriam (see box). Moses then leads the Israelites toward his old homeland of Midian

in Sinai, where he is destined to receive God's commandments for their new nation.

The Israelites' high spirits do not last long, and Moses is soon tested by his people once more. They complain again that they might have been better off as slaves than risking starvation in the wilderness. However, every time the Israelites complain, God provides. When the people ask for more food, God rains a sticky, breadlike substance from the sky. This is *manna* and becomes part of the Israelites' diet during their 40 years of wandering. When they complain of not having enough meat, God makes a flock of quail land in their camp every day. For water, God instructs Moses to

A fresco on the wall of the Kalamíou monastery in the Peloponnese in Greece shows the Egyptians drowning as the waters of the Red Sea fall back in the wake of the Israelites' passage.

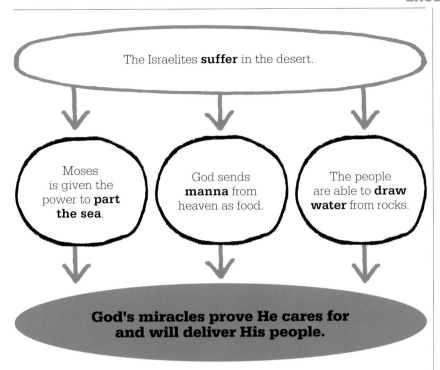

The Israelites **suffer** in the desert.

Moses is given the power to **part the sea**.

God sends **manna** from heaven as food.

The people are able to **draw water** from rocks.

God's miracles prove He cares for and will deliver His people.

Miriam

After the crossing of the Red Sea, Miriam, an older sister of Aaron and Moses—by three and six years respectively—leads the Israelite women in celebrating, shaking timbrels (tambourines), singing, and dancing (15:20). Referred to as a prophetess in this episode in Exodus, she plays a crucial role in Moses's life and is also mentioned in Numbers 12, Numbers 20:1, Deuteronomy 24:9, and Micah 6:4.

When Pharaoh orders the murder of all firstborn male Israelite children, it is Miriam who watches over Moses in the basket hidden in the reed beds of the Nile River. When Pharaoh's daughter discovers the baby, Miriam offers to find a nurse for him and secretly enlists the help of his mother and her own mother. Later in the Bible, however, Aaron and Miriam rebel against Moses. God punishes Miriam with leprosy, but then heals her after seven days. True to her story, the name Miriam means either "beloved" or "bitter."

strike a rock with his staff, from which fresh water gushes. This continued divine intervention saves the Israelites, and shows the benevolence of God.

Significance of the Exodus
The Exodus is at the very heart of Judaism, but its message of freedom has also inspired many non-Jewish groups, from early

The Lord looked down from the pillar of fire and cloud at the Egyptian army and threw it into confusion.
Exodus 14:24

Protestant settlers fleeing persecution in post-Reformation Europe to 20th-century African Americans striving for civil rights.

There is little archaeological evidence to support the Exodus as historical fact, but the largely accepted wisdom is that the event occurred sometime around the mid-1300s BCE and that Moses himself wrote the book that records it. In Exodus 34:27, God tells Moses "Write down these words …" and Jesus, in Mark 12:26, quotes from Exodus as the "Book of Moses."

God uses Moses as His instrument to rescue His chosen people not just from slavery but from a polytheistic society. The Exodus story shows God's power, His love for His people, and how He encourages and rewards trust and faith. Preceding events anticipate it and subsequent events refer back to it. Matthew 2:15 in the New Testament alludes to Jesus as the new Israel, come out of Egypt. ∎

YOU SHALL NOT MURDER

EXODUS 20:13, THE TEN COMMANDMENTS

IN BRIEF

PASSAGE
Exodus 16:1–20:17

THEME
Protecting the Israelites

SETTING
14th–13th century BCE
Mount Sinai, also called Mount Horeb, on the Sinai Peninsula, three months after the Exodus.

KEY FIGURES
Moses The leader chosen by God to challenge the Egyptian Pharaoh and lead the Israelites out of slavery.

God Appears to Moses in physical form as a thick, thunderous cloud.

The Israelites The 12 tribes descended from Jacob, recently liberated from Egypt.

Three months after leaving Egypt, the Israelites arrive at the foot of Mount Sinai in the desert of Sinai, free from the rule of Pharaoh for the first time in living memory. However, after the initial euphoria of rescue, the Israelites struggle to know what to do with their newfound freedom. God summons Moses to the top of the mountain and tells him to make an offer to the people of Israel.

Having rescued them from the tyranny of Pharaoh and provided for their daily needs in the desert, God is prepared to enter into a covenant with them, just as He entered into a covenant with their forefather Abraham. Although all the earth belongs to God, if the Israelites commit to obeying Him, they will become God's "treasured possession" out of all nations and a "kingdom of priests and a holy nation" (19:5–6). When Moses relays God's message to the elders, they respond enthusiastically to the proposition: "We will do everything the Lord has said" (19:8). Moses takes their answer back to God.

Through Moses, God then instructs the Israelites to gather at a respectful distance from the bottom of the mountain, while Moses returns to the top to receive the terms of their covenant. A thick cloud then descends over Mount Sinai, and the people hear thunder and loud trumpet blasts and see flashes of lightning, fire, and smoke. The people tremble in fear. It is a clear indication of the gravity of the relationship that they are to share with God.

A new covenant

On the mountain, God gives Moses His terms, or laws—the ten foundational rules known as the Ten Commandments, or the Decalogue (from the Greek, "ten words"). The first three concern the Israelites' relationship with God.

Moses is shown with horns in this 15th-century woodcut. These are the result of a mistranslation of the Hebrew for "rays of light" in Exodus 34:29. The error was repeated by many artists.

First, they are to worship Him alone, rather than merging their obedience to God with reverence for the deities of other people. Next, they are forbidden from making any image or idol of God, because God is not to be viewed in comparison to any earthly or heavenly creature. Thirdly, God's name is to be used with care and respect—never taken in vain. The Israelites must never forget that they owe their lives to God and not any other human or divine leader.

The fourth commandment instructs the people to keep a Sabbath day, which they could never have done as slaves working without a Sabbath rest. Just as God created the world in six days and then rested, so the Israelites should work for six days and then spend a day resting and relishing God's presence.

The last six commandments regulate the relationships between God's own people. They are to honor their parents, and refrain

See also: The Testing of Abraham 50–53 ▪ Jacob Wrestles with God 56–57 ▪ Entering the Promised Land 96–97 ▪ Call for Repentance 172

from murder, adultery, stealing, lying, and coveting things that do not belong to them.

After his encounter, Moses comes down the mountain and tells the Israelites the terms of the covenant. They respond enthusiastically: "Everything the Lord has said we will do." (24:3). Having agreed to the terms, the Israelites wait at the bottom of Mount Sinai while Moses goes back up into the thick cloud of God's presence.

Moses stays at the top of Mount Sinai for 40 days and 40 nights, during which time God provides him with tablets of stone, inscribed with the terms of the covenant. The tablets are to be a lasting reminder of the agreement between God and His newly rescued people.

Obedience slips

Subsequent events in the Bible prove that it does not take long for the Israelites to break more of the commandments – or to forget them entirely. Towards the end of his life, Moses must reiterate God's commandments for the generation born and raised during the 40 years in which the Israelites wander the desert (Deuteronomy 5). Centuries later, during the reign of King Josiah, the high priest "discovers" the Book of the Law languishing in a dusty corner of a storeroom at the Temple (2 Kings 22), and King Josiah tears his robe after the word of God is read to him, mortified that he has failed to uphold His laws. The Bible shows time and again that when the Israelites obey the law, they prosper, but when they forget it or actively disobey it, disaster ensues.

God's holy nation

The Ten Commandments are often misunderstood. Many people see them simply as a list of "dos and don'ts," but this misses their true significance. Although eight of God's commandments contain the admonition "do not," the purpose of the commandments is not primarily to prohibit, but rather to protect and promote God's "holy nation." The key to understanding the

> Now if you obey me fully and keep my covenant, then out of all nations you will be my treasured possession.
> **Exodus 19:5–6**

commandments is found in the opening words of the covenant: "I am the Lord your God, who brought you out of Egypt, out of the land of slavery." God has already given the Israelites a new sense of identity when He rescued them from the oppressive rule of Pharaoh in Egypt, turning them from slaves into "priests" (Exodus 19:6)—God's representatives on earth. The Israelites' life together had been made possible by God's dramatic »

King Hammurabi, ruler of Babylon from 1792 to 1750 BCE, produced one of the earliest known codes of law, known as the Code of Hammurabi.

Ancient law codes

Other ancient Near Eastern societies also had laws to regulate relationships between people and rights relating to property. Some of these laws were recorded in cuneiform script, inscribed in stone, giving scholars an insight into the people who lived around the Israelites in their formative years as a nation, such as the Sumerians, Babylonians, and Assyrians. Typically, a king imposed a rule of law on communities living under his protection, including those that had been conquered. Many take the form of a treaty, in which the ruler offers protection in return for obedience. Such treaties could be described as case law, in which the law dictates what would be done in certain circumstances. Punishments were sometimes specified. In Babylon's Code of Hammurabi, for example, theft was punished by death, while herdsmen found guilty of fraud received a fine.

The Mosaic Law resonates with these codes, although it is based on the authority of God rather than a human leader.

The Torah

Hebrew for "instruction" or "teaching," *torah* refers to the Ten Commandments and the other instructions given to Moses on the top of Mount Sinai. The Israelites understand that God's torah has rescued them from the restrictive and vindictive rule of Pharaoh and see it as a gift and a blessing.

Throughout the Bible, torah is recognized as God's good commandments: following the torah will enable humankind to flourish within appropriate boundaries. Torah is also used as a collective term for the first five books of the Bible: Genesis, Exodus, Leviticus, Numbers, and Deuteronomy. These books, often called the books of Moses, are of foundational importance to Jews because they tell the story of how the Israelites came to exist as a nation and contain God's rule for life. In every synagogue, the Torah is handwritten on parchment scrolls that are kept in the Ark of the Law, symbolizing the Holy of Holies in the ancient Temple of Jerusalem.

regard for them, and now God gives them commandments to protect this new identity, recognizing that it would be too easy for them to fall back into godless ways.

More than ten
The Ten Commandments form the backbone of God's relationship with Israel. There are many other instructions that Moses receives from God to pass on to the Israelites, including instructions for constructing the Tabernacle, and these additional rules are necessary for the application of the Ten Commandments in everyday life. Over time, this larger body of commands and teaching become known as *torah*, which is still the fundamental set of laws governing Judaism today.

In this episode in the Bible, Moses is presented as God's great lawgiver, and the law is often called Mosaic Law. Today, however, the ten laws have a less prominent position within Judaism than they did in Moses's time. According to the Babylonian Talmud, a collection of interpretations of the torah and Jewish law compiled in the 4th century CE, priests ceased their

recitation of these commandments, due to assertions by opponents, possibly early Christians, that they were the only laws imparted to Moses on Mount Sinai. This had led to the neglect of more than 600 other commands.

Open to interpretation
As with many verses in the Bible, the Ten Commandments are seen differently by various groups. Not only do interpretations of the laws themselves differ—does, for example, adultery refer to sexual acts outside of marriage, or only to the infidelity of married couples?—but different denominations place emphasis on different laws.

The Catholic Church, for example, following the medieval Roman tradition, does not include the commandment concerning the creation of images of God and also specifies as its own commandment that you must not covet your neighbor's wife. The prohibition

The rocky heights of Mount Sinai, where Moses is said to have received the Ten Commandments. Holy places are often also high places, where the human is nearer to the divine.

against creating images and idols is considered by Catholics to be part of the first commandment to worship no other gods. However, Greek Orthodox and Protestant denominations retain the Ten Commandments as recorded in the Book of Exodus.

Guide to life

One of the enduring legacies of the Ten Commandments is their combination of what we often see as religious and secular life. Throughout the Bible, there is no clear distinction made between the spiritual life of God's people and their practical life, or between public and private spheres. God's law covered all aspects of their lives, including politics and economics, friendships and family.

The Ten Commandments instructed the Israelites to live out their lives as God's people, showing to other people the justice and generosity that God had first given to them. Because of this positive role of law in the Israelites' lives, songs were even composed in praise of it. Psalm 17 says: "The law of the Lord is perfect, refreshing the soul." ∎

The Ten Commandments (Exodus 20)

1. You shall have no other gods before me.

2. You shall not make for yourself an idol and worship it.

3. You shall not misuse the name of the Lord your God.

4. Remember the Sabbath day and keep it holy.

5. Honor your father and your mother.

6. You shall not murder.

7. You shall not commit adultery.

8. You shall not steal.

9. You shall not give false testimony against your neighbor.

10. You shall not covet anything that belongs to your neighbor.

THEY HAVE MADE FOR THEMSELVES A GOLDEN CALF AND HAVE WORSHIPPED IT
EXODUS 32:8, THE GOLDEN CALF

IN BRIEF

PASSAGE
Exodus 32

THEME
Idolatry

SETTING
14th–13th century BCE Six weeks after Moses received the Ten Commandments, near Mount Sinai.

KEY FIGURES
The Israelites Descendants of the patriarch Jacob.

Aaron Moses's brother and the first high priest of the Israelites. He is left in charge while Moses goes to talk to God atop Mount Sinai.

Moses Leader of the Israelites, and their communicator with God.

It is remarkable that the Israelites' fall into idolatry ever took place at all. Moses had only just received God's Ten Commandments, in which it was made clear that the Israelites were to worship only one God, and that idolatry was forbidden. Speaking through Moses, God had warned of dire consequences should the Israelites break these laws.

Yet, just 40 days after Moses had left his people to continue his meeting with God on Mount Sinai, the Israelites fall into sin by deciding to worship a golden calf, an idol that Aaron, the high priest and Moses's brother, had forged for them out of the jewelry and other gold trinkets they had brought with them from Egypt.

Israelite intentions
The reasons why the Israelites are quick to forget—or deliberately break—the commandments are not made clear. All that is said is that they believed Moses's failure to return to them meant that he had died. Three traditional explanations

The Israelites celebrate a bull-calf idol in this painting by Filippino Lippi, c.1500. The golden calf Aaron makes is thought to be an image of the Egyptian bull god Apis.

See also: The Ten Commandments 78–83 ▪ Balaam's Donkey 89 ▪
Elijah and the Prophets of Baal 125

Exodus	**Deuteronomy**
According to Exodus, the Israelites **create idols** in their panic because Moses is so long returning from the mountain.	Deuteronomy makes no mention of **Moses's** delay in **returning** from Mount Sinai.
Exodus places **blame on Aaron** for building the golden calf and letting the people run amok. His pardoning is not explained.	Deuteronomy says that **Moses intervenes** for Aaron with God, but not what Aaron has done to require this intervention.
Aaron orders the people to **melt down gold** earrings to make the calf.	The metal is **not mentioned**—instead, the idol is a "molten" calf.
The sons of Levi rally when Moses calls them. They **kill 3,000** people in the camp and are appointed for sacred duty due to their zeal.	Deuteronomy 10:8–9 notes only that the sons of Levi are appointed as **God's priests** "at that time."

The role of the Levites

Descended from Levi, the son of Jacob and Leah, the Levites include Moses, Aaron, and their sister Miriam. Following the incident with the golden calf, the entire tribe is set apart by God because their actions showed their loyalty to the Covenant. The Levites' special role is confirmed in Numbers 1, when God tells Moses not to number them among the other tribes.

All of the priests in the Old Testament are descendants of Aaron, and are sometimes called the Aaronide priests. Some of the most important include Ezra, Eli, and Zechariah, the father of John the Baptist. Those Levites who are not priests are assigned specific duties to do with the Tabernacle. They also interpret the law.

Deuteronomy 9–10 also records the golden calf story. However, many of the details of Exodus 32–34 are absent and the account does not dwell on the role of Aaron.

---

for the Israelites' actions are offered in the works of medieval Jewish commentators Rashi, Nahmanides, and Abraham Ibn Ezra. Rashi argues that the golden calf was intended as an alternative god. Without Moses, the Israelites had lost their link with God and wanted a physical deity to worship.

Nahmanides, however, suggests the calf was supposed to replace Moses as the Israelites' conduit to God, whereas Ibn Ezra contends that the golden calf acted as nothing more than a pedestal, on which God was invisibly present. Whatever the reasoning behind them, the Israelites' idolatrous actions anger Moses. He persuades God not to punish them as severely as He had first intended, and climbs down Mount Sinai to confront them. To illustrate the betrayal their actions have constituted, Moses smashes the tablets bearing the commandments, then destroys the golden calf.

The prophet returns

Moses is determined to punish the Israelites himself for their transgression. The tribe of the Levites responds to his rallying call for those faithful to the Lord, and he orders them to "go back and forth through the camp," slaughtering the idolaters. Some 3,000 perish at their hands. This, however, is not their only punishment: God also strikes them with a plague "because of what they did with the calf Aaron had made" (Exodus 32:35). In a recurring theme in the Old Testament, disobedience brings disaster for the Israelites.

It might be thought that the Israelites would learn from their mistake, but this is not the case. Baal, Ashtoreth, and Molech are among three of the false gods they later choose to worship. ▪

THE PLACE WILL BE CONSECRATED BY MY GLORY

EXODUS 29:43, THE ARK AND THE TABERNACLE

IN BRIEF

PASSAGE
Exodus 25–27

THEME
Creating a sacred dwelling place for God

SETTING
14th–13th century BCE
The wilderness in which the Israelites wander for 40 years.

KEY FIGURES
Moses Prophet and leader of the Israelites who was chosen by God to receive the Ten Commandments on top of Mount Sinai.

Aaron The older brother of Moses and the Israelites' first high priest.

The Tabernacle is a portable temple where God meets with His people. It is placed at the western end of an oblong courtyard with a single gateway on its eastern side.

God takes 40 verses of Exodus to explain to Moses the Tabernacle's purpose and how it must be built. A portable sanctuary, where the Israelites could commune with God, it accompanies them during their 40 years in the wilderness. It is the focus of their worship until Solomon's Temple is built in around 960 BCE.

Portable temple
At each place they camp, the Israelites erect a linen tent with acacia wood poles to create a courtyard around the Tabernacle. This courtyard contains the altar of sacrifice, on which offerings are made, and the laver, a bronze basin filled with water in which the priests purify themselves.

The Tabernacle itself is a tent with acacia wood poles set in silver bases and a roof with four layers. The outermost layer is made of porpoise skins, the next rams' skins dyed red, the third goats' hair, and the innermost layer is made of linen embroidered with depictions of cherubim—hybrid creatures with human faces.

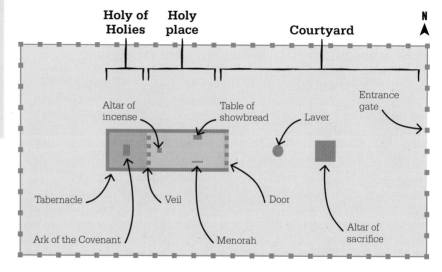

Holy of Holies · Holy place · Courtyard · N

Altar of incense · Table of showbread · Laver · Entrance gate

Tabernacle · Veil · Door

Ark of the Covenant · Menorah · Altar of sacrifice

See also: The Exodus 74–77 ▪ The Ten Commandments 78–83 ▪ The Wisdom of Solomon 120–23 ▪
The Fall of Jerusalem 128–31

God appears as a cloud over the Ark by day and as a fireball by night. Whenever the cloud lifts, it is a sign for the Israelites to move on.

Inside the Tabernacle are two inner rooms. The first is the Holy Place, containing the golden menorah (the seven-armed lampstand); the table of showbread, containing 12 loaves of unleavened bread, each representing a tribe of Israel and laid in two rows each week as specified in Exodus 25:23–30 and later confirmed by Leviticus 24:5–9; and the altar of incense, also plated in gold. Beyond this, separated by a veil, stands the Holy of Holies containing the Ark of the Covenant itself, a wooden chest overlaid inside and out with gold. Four gold rings are attached to the bottom of the chest, through which two poles can be passed to carry the Ark.

The Ark contains the two stone tablets inscribed with the Ten Commandments and a pot of manna, the food God provides for the starving Israelites in the wilderness. According to some traditions, it also contains Aaron's rod, which had miraculously produced blossoms to indicate that

Have them make a sanctuary for me, and I will dwell among them.
Exodus 25:8

Aaron was God's choice as high priest. The lid of the Ark, in Hebrew the *kapporet*, but in English known as the mercy seat, is solid gold.

Day of Atonement
Only the high priest was allowed to enter the Holy of Holies and then only once a year on the day now known as Yom Kippur, when the Israelites atoned for their sins. Burning incense to shield his eyes from the divine presence, the high priest would sprinkle blood from a newly sacrificed bull onto the mercy seat to atone for his and his family's sins and then blood from a goat to atone for the sins of the Israelites in general.

A second goat was then brought into the Holy of Holies. Placing his hands on its head, the priest then confessed the Israelites' sins before releasing the goat into the wild. This ritual is the root of the word scapegoat, as the second goat now carries all the sins of the Israelites. ▪

The fate of the Ark

The last time the whereabouts of the Ark of the Covenant is mentioned in the Bible is in 2 Chronicles 2:35. It details how King Josiah ordered the Levites to return it to the Temple of Jerusalem.

The Ark then vanishes from Bible history. One theory is that it was removed from the temple—probably by Jeremiah—before the fall of Jerusalem. It is said he hid the Ark in a cave on Mount Nebu. Other scholars suggest King Josiah buried it under a storehouse on the Temple Mount where the Dome of the Rock now stands. A more fanciful theory claims that Menelik I, the son of Solomon and the Queen of Sheba, took the Ark to Axum in Ethiopia, where it is still housed in the Church of St. Mary of Zion.

IT DOES FLOW WITH MILK AND HONEY

NUMBERS 13:27, THE TWELVE SPIES

IN BRIEF

PASSAGE
Numbers 13–14

THEME
Lack of faith

SETTING
14th–13th century BCE
Kadesh-barnea, Sinai, south of the Promised Land.

KEY FIGURES
Caleb Son of Jephunneh, of the tribe of Judah. One of the scouts sent into Canaan, he urges the Israelites to take possession of the land.

Joshua Also known as Hoshea, Son of Nun, from the tribe of Ephraim. Another scout, he supports the view of Caleb, that the Israelites should take possession of the land. Later he will succeed Moses as leader of Israel.

Moses Israelite leader, who intercedes with God for the rebellious Israelites.

Following their departure from Egypt, the Israelites approach Canaan, the Promised Land. Before going further, Moses sends 12 spies, one from each of the 12 tribes, to scout out the land for 40 days.

A land of plenty

On their return, the scouts report a land that is good, flowing with the proverbial "milk and honey" God promised. As evidence, they bring a bunch of grapes so huge they have to carry it on a pole between two of them. However, they say, the people of Canaan are intimidating and live in large, well-fortified cities.

Undaunted, one of the scouts, Caleb, believes that God will be with them to give them this new home. Supported by another of the scouts, Joshua, he urges his fellow Israelites to go and occupy it. However, the remaining ten exclaim that they cannot attack such formidable foes. The bulk of the Israelites side with the ten and begin to lament that they ever left Egypt. Angry at their faithlessness, God threatens to destroy the people, but Moses intercedes on their behalf.

God's resolution marks a watershed in the book of Numbers. Israel will still enter Canaan but not for another 40 years, due to the people's lack of faith. In the meantime, they will return to the wilderness. Among the older generation, only Caleb and Joshua will possess the Promised Land. ■

> Your children will be shepherds here for forty years, suffering for your unfaithfulness, until the last of your bodies lies in the desert.
> **Numbers 14:33**

See also: Covenants 44–47 ■ The Exodus 74–77 ■ Balaam's Donkey 89 ■ The Fall of Jericho 98–99

THE LORD OPENED THE DONKEY'S MOUTH
NUMBERS 22:28, BALAAM'S DONKEY

IN BRIEF

PASSAGE
Numbers 22–23

THEME
Spiritual blindness

SETTING
14th–13th century BCE
Banks of the Jordan River.

KEY FIGURES
Balaam A prophet thought
to come from Mesopotamia,
who is hired by Balak, king
of the Moabites, to curse
the Israelites.

Balak The ruler of the
Moabites who formed an
alliance with the Midianites
in a bid to stop the Israelites
entering and settling the
Promised Land.

Donkey Balaam's transport
on his journey to visit Balak.

Balaam's faithful donkey falls down
as an angel bars the way in this 1626
painting by Rembrandt van Rijn. The
donkey's quick actions save Balaam
from certain destruction.

The story of Balaam and
his donkey demonstrates
how God can use even
a dumb beast to carry out His
purpose. Balak, the ruler of Moab,
a land east of the Jordan River, is
concerned about the spread of the
Israelites and summons the prophet
Balaam to curse them. Mounted on
his donkey, Balaam sets off to meet
Balak. God sends an angel, armed
with a sword, to intercept him.
Neither Balaam nor other people
can see the angel, but the donkey
can. When the donkey veers off the
road, Balaam beats her. On the
third time this happens, God gives
the donkey the power to ask Balaam
why he is beating her. Then God
opens Balaam's eyes so that he
can also see the angel. Balaam falls
facedown and apologizes, as he did
not know it was God that had
blocked his path.

The angel tells Balaam that he
is free to go, providing he speaks
only what God tells him. When
Balaam meets Balak, the king
orders him to curse the Israelites.
Balaam tries seven times. Each
time, instead of cursing them, he
blesses them, underlining the
message that God will protect the
Israelites if they keep faith. ∎

See also: The Fall 30–35 ▪ The Exodus 74–77 ▪ The Twelve Spies 88 ▪
Elijah and the Prophets of Baal 125 ▪ Daniel in Babylon 164–65

THERE IS NO OTHER
DEUTERONOMY 4:39, ONLY ONE GOD

IN BRIEF

PASSAGE
**Deuteronomy 4:39;
Isaiah 44:6**

THEME
Monotheism

SETTING
14th–6th centuries BCE
Moab and Babylon.

KEY FIGURES
Moses Prophet who passed on God's laws to the Israelites, including that they should worship no other god.

Second Isaiah Prophet who gave the first indisputable edict of monotheism in the Bible. Sometimes known as "Deutero-Isaiah."

Nobody knows for certain how monotheism, the worship of one single god, emerged in ancient Israel at a time when polytheism, the worship of many gods or divine beings, was the norm not only in the Near East, but throughout the world. What is certain, however, is that the Israelites' idea of monotheism would have developed gradually. They may have started by recognizing their god Yahweh as superior to all other gods, before going on to deny the existence of any others.

One supreme god
Although the majority of religions in the region at this time were polytheistic, most of them recognized one specific god as superior to all the others in their pantheons. Examples included Marduk for the Babylonians and Ashur for Assyrians, who both believed their rulers were divinely ordained (although not divine themselves). Almost certainly, the first Israelites saw their God, Yahweh, in a similar light. Yahweh (God) was Israel's national deity, having delivered the Israelites from Egypt as His chosen people.

In Deuteronomy, Moses asks the Israelites: "Has any god ever tried to take for himself one nation out of another nation?" He reminds them of the "miraculous signs and wonders" and "great and awesome deeds" that they witnessed in Egypt. His question does not rule

Gideon and his men destroy the altar of Baal in his father's house, as described in Judges 6:27. Worshipping any other god was forbidden in the Ten Commandments.

See also: The Golden Calf 84–85 ▪ The Nature of God 144–47 ▪ The Divinity of Jesus 190–93 ▪ The Trinity 298–99

out the existence of other gods; it simply points to the uniqueness of Israel's God. The Bible is not yet proclaiming overt monotheism, although Moses's assertion may amount to much the same thing. The Israelites were only capable of thinking and expressing themselves in the terms available in their own time, and it is possible that this was the only way they could describe monotheism.

The journey to monotheism
Even though the Israelites were moving toward monotheism, the Bible tells us that they definitely did not think of God as existing completely alone in heaven. He had divine messengers, angels, to do His bidding, and the biblical writers show Him surrounded by the "host of heaven," a whole heavenly court. One of the prophet Micah's visions in Kings even reveals Him taking counsel from attendant spirits. This almost polytheistic idea of God as the supreme deity over a whole host of other divine beings could, over

time, have developed into the entirely monotheistic belief that he was, in fact, the one and only god—the belief which exists today across the Abrahamic religions.

Monotheism in the Bible
Just as the Israelites' belief in monotheism developed over time, so did the Bible's stance on the matter. In Deuteronomy, Moses says that "the Lord is God in heaven above and on the earth below. There is no other." At first glance, this seems like a definite statement of monotheism, but it could also be read to mean merely that there is no other god like Him.

It would take generations of reflection before a prophet—the so-called Second Isaiah, or Deutero-Isaiah, living during the Babylonian Exile in the 6th century BCE—was able to formulate the Bible's first explicitly monotheistic statements. This is recorded in Isaiah 44:6: "This is what the Lord says—Israel's King and Redeemer, the Lord Almighty: I am the first and I am the last; apart from me there is no God." ▪

In Deuteronomy, Moses tells the Israelites there is no other God but theirs.

↓

This could mean there are **no gods on the same level**.

↓

But as God is separate and above all others, worshipping other gods is **pointless idolatry**.

↓

This is enshrined in God's law as the Ten Commandments, which **forbid making idols** or placing other gods ahead of the Lord.

↓

Deutero-Isaiah goes further, stating explicitly that **no Gods exist beside the Israelite God**.

Deuteronomy: a new voice

Something new enters the Bible in Deuteronomy. The Israelites are on the brink of the Jordan, about to cross into Canaan, the Promised Land. Here, on the plains of Moab, Moses, now close to death, recalls God's tender care for the Israelites, urges them to live faithfully, and seeks to prepare them for their new life.

Leviticus and Numbers have an abundance of Mosaic law-giving, but the emphasis is on matters such as purity and

liturgy. In Deuteronomy, more than in the earlier books, the law is put in the context of the passionate relationship between God and His people. Because He loves them, God teaches the people His laws and by keeping those laws, the people are able to gratefully respond to that love. Relationships between the people themselves are also important. Deuteronomy's law code features statutes that favor the disadvantaged and encourage generosity.

THE HIST
BOOKS

ORICAL

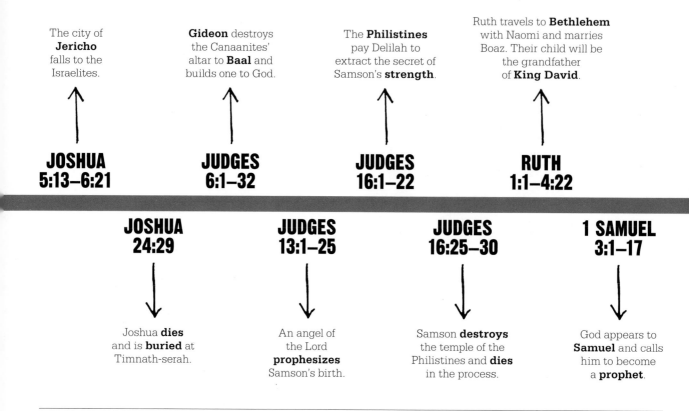

The city of **Jericho** falls to the Israelites.

Gideon destroys the Canaanites' altar to **Baal** and builds one to God.

The **Philistines** pay Delilah to extract the secret of Samson's **strength**.

Ruth travels to **Bethlehem** with Naomi and marries Boaz. Their child will be the grandfather of **King David**.

JOSHUA 5:13–6:21

JUDGES 6:1–32

JUDGES 16:1–22

RUTH 1:1–4:22

JOSHUA 24:29

JUDGES 13:1–25

JUDGES 16:25–30

1 SAMUEL 3:1–17

Joshua **dies** and is **buried** at Timnath-serah.

An angel of the Lord **prophesizes** Samson's birth.

Samson **destroys** the temple of the Philistines and **dies** in the process.

God appears to **Samuel** and calls him to become a **prophet**.

The Historical Books, which follow the books of the Torah, describe how the Israelites conquer the land of Canaan, their experiments with finding a leader, the rise of King David and the monarchy, their fall at the hands of the Babylonians, and the rebuilding of Jerusalem under Nehemiah.

The designation "historical" does not mean that the text is more historical than other parts of the Bible. It is more to do with the style of writing and the reporting of specific events, and the inclusion of dating systems. The texts that are included depend on the canon being used. For instance, the Samuel–Kings texts are found in the Prophets section (Nevi'im) of the Hebrew Bible because of the prominence of Samuel, Nathan,

Elijah, and Elisha. However, Esther and Ruth, which most Christian canons include in the Historical Books (the equivalent of the Hebrew Bible's Prophets), are considered part of the "Writings" (Ketuvim) section of the Hebrew canon. For Christians, the inclusion of the Book of Ruth is important in establishing the line of David that eventually leads to Jesus.

Like the Exodus, the account of the conquest of Canaan is fraught with historical anomalies. Many of the sites mentioned in the conquest have not been located or their dating does not align with that given by the Bible. Most likely, the authors were drawing on stories of destruction that had been woven into the Israelites' oral history. Some scholars doubt that the conquest occurred at all and

believe that the Israelites slowly settled the area, increasing in number over time. This theory is bolstered by the Book of Judges, which suggests the people of the land were never driven out. Efforts to find signs of the conquest continue today, with archaeologists looking for evidence of destruction embedded in the earth below broken pieces of Israelite pottery.

A monarchy emerges

German Bible scholar Martin Noth (1902–1968), who specialized in the early history of the Israelites, believed that the theologies of the Historical Books were similar to Deuteronomy, indicating a common date and source: the people are corrupt and need to return to the Mosaic covenant, and emphasis on the line of David underlines

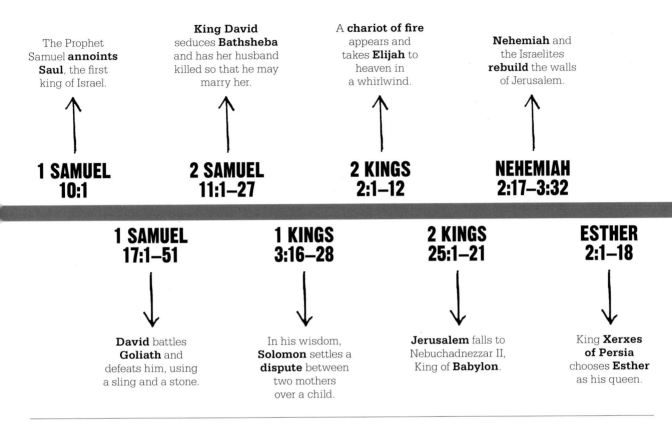

The Prophet Samuel **annoints Saul**, the first king of Israel.

King David seduces **Bathsheba** and has her husband killed so that he may marry her.

A **chariot of fire** appears and takes **Elijah** to heaven in a whirlwind.

Nehemiah and the Israelites **rebuild** the walls of Jerusalem.

1 SAMUEL 10:1

2 SAMUEL 11:1–27

2 KINGS 2:1–12

NEHEMIAH 2:17–3:32

1 SAMUEL 17:1–51

1 KINGS 3:16–28

2 KINGS 25:1–21

ESTHER 2:1–18

David battles **Goliath** and defeats him, using a sling and a stone.

In his wisdom, **Solomon** settles a **dispute** between two mothers over a child.

Jerusalem falls to Nebuchadnezzar II, King of **Babylon**.

King **Xerxes of Persia** chooses **Esther** as his queen.

the importance of the kingdom of Israel. The text follows a similar format to the Book of Genesis: people are blessed, then fail God, are punished, and then blessed again. Noth cited Judges as an example of this pattern. As the judges (leaders appointed by God to deliver the Israelites) arise, they then fail, and the Israelites' situation worsens. The story of the last judge, Samson (Judges 13–16), ends in civil war.

Throughout Judges, it is said that the people do what is right in their own eyes as there is no king in Israel to lead them. Noth believed the author was compiling both Deuteronomy and the Historical Books immediately after the Temple was destroyed by the Babylonians in 586 BCE, to offer an explanation for the fall of Jerusalem.

After the events in the Book of Judges, the Israelites cry out for a king to deliver strong government. In the Book of Samuel, God grants their request in the form of Saul, whose successor, King David, consolidates the 12 tribes of Israel as the United Monarchy of Judah and Israel. Given that the Bible is written mostly from the perspective of Judah, the central concern of the Historical Books is the rise of David in Judah, as the prophets later say that a Messiah will come from David's line.

Material evidence of King David's reign and his unification of the tribes is scant, although an elaborate stone structure that may have been David's palace has been discovered in Jerusalem. There is, however, conclusive evidence that his son, Solomon, built the

Jerusalem Temple, thereby establishing the way ancient Jews would worship for almost 1,000 years. The destruction of the Temple by the Babylonians in 586 BCE would shape the theology of the Jews and have lasting effects on Judaism through the centuries.

Hopes for a Messiah

After the dissolution of the United Monarchy following the death of Solomon, the idea of a Messiah, which originally simply meant "anointed one," began to change from someone who would revive the monarchy to someone who would establish the everlasting Kingdom of God. For Christians, this would mean Jesus, whose Davidic ancestry is documented in the genealogy of Jesus given at the start of Matthew's Gospel. ■

TAKE UP THE ARK OF THE COVENANT
JOSHUA 3:6, ENTERING THE PROMISED LAND

IN BRIEF

PASSAGE
Joshua 3–4

THEME
Entering the Promised Land

SETTING
14th–13th century BCE
Banks of the Jordan River.

KEY FIGURES
Moses Leader of the Israelites, who has brought them to the edge of the Promised Land.

Joshua Moses's lieutenant, whom God appoints to lead the Israelites after the death of Moses. God gives Joshua the gift of invincibility in battle.

Caleb Assists Joshua in leading the Israelites into the Promised Land.

W hen Moses dies just one step away from Canaan, the land promised to Abraham and his descendants as an "everlasting possession" (Genesis 17:8), there is an obvious successor: Joshua, his faithful lieutenant. God tells Joshua to prepare to cross the Jordan River: "As I was with Moses, so I will be with you; I will never leave you nor forsake you" (Joshua 1:5).

Relatively little is known about Joshua's background. He is an Ephraimite (descended from Jacob's son Joseph) who had been born in Egypt. Like the other Israelites, he had followed Moses out of the country when the Exodus began. Joshua was unquestionably Moses's most faithful disciple—as Exodus 33 puts it, he "did not leave the tent." He was chosen to go with Moses to Mount Sinai, where God issued the Ten Commandments, and, along with Caleb, was one of the 12 spies sent to scout out Canaan. The first mention of him

in the Bible is in Exodus 17:9–16, which tells how Moses chooses Joshua to lead the Israelites into battle against the Amalekites at Rephidim, most likely a broad valley, now called Wadi Feiran, about 25 miles (40km) from Mount Sinai. Joshua was to win many more victories for the Israelites.

Crossing the Jordan
When the time comes for the Israelites to enter the Promised Land, Joshua and Caleb are ready. The Israelites, now camping by the banks of the Jordan River, are more

Moses appoints Joshua to lead the Israelites to the Promised Land. This 19th-century engraving highlights Joshua's role as a military leader by depicting him in a helmet and boots.

See also: Covenants 44–47 ▪ The Exodus 74–77 ▪ The Ark and the Tabernacle 86–87 ▪ The Twelve Spies 88

For the Lord your God
is bringing you into
a good land … a land
with wheat and barley,
vines and fig trees … where
you will lack nothing.
Deuteronomy 8:7–9

hesitant. It is spring and the Jordan River, swollen by the rains and the snowmelt from Mount Hermon, is in flood. It is easy for two spies to make their way across the river, as detailed in Joshua 2:23, but now an entire nation must ford it.

For three days, they wait, and then God gives Joshua orders for the Israelites to cross the river. The people follow God's commands, and as God promised, a miracle occurs. Just as the Red Sea had parted for Moses when he led the Israelites out of Egypt, the swollen river ceases to flow. At Adam, a place 19 miles (30km) upriver, the Jordan's waters "piled up in a heap" (3:16) and the riverbed is soon dry. While the priests stand with the Ark of the Covenant in the middle of the riverbed, the Israelites cross over on dry ground. When the crossing has been completed, Joshua orders one man from each tribe to pick up the large stones from the middle of the riverbed and carry them to the far bank. Once they have done this, the priests carry the Ark of the Covenant to the other side.

The parallels with Moses's parting of the Red Sea 40 years previously clearly shows that Joshua has taken up Moses's mantle as God's instrument. It also shows the Amorite and Canaanite kings the power of the Israelites' God.

Keeping the covenant
Even though the Israelites are in enemy territory, and therefore in peril, the first thing Joshua does once they have set up camp at Gilgal, 1 mile (1.5km) east of Jericho, is to use the stones collected from the Jordan River to commemorate their miraculous crossing and remind the Israelites that God keeps His promises when they keep His law. Joshua then follows God's command to "make flint knives" (5:2) and circumcises all the men who have not fulfilled this everlasting sign of God's covenant with Abraham during the 40 years in the wilderness. Joshua knows that a promise may be deferred by God, as it was after the Exodus (see pp. 84–85), if the Israelites disobey God's Law. ▪

That day, the Lord
exalted Joshua in the sight
of all Israel, and they
revered him all the days
of his life just as they
had revered Moses.
Joshua 4:14

The significance of the camp at Gilgal

Located "on the eastern border of Jericho" (Joshua 4:19), Gilgal is the name the Israelites give to the camp they set up after crossing the Jordan River. It remains an important base for them during their conquest of Canaan: they set out from and return to Gilgal after a number of key victories, including the fall of Jericho, the destruction of the royal city of Ai, and the defeat of the Amorites at Gibeon.

In Gilgal, God orders the circumcision of all men born since the Exodus, after which He says to Joshua, "Today I have rolled away the reproach of Egypt from you" (5:9). After this, it is the site of the first Passover celebration in the Promised Land.

The Tabernacle stays in Gilgal until the conclusion of Joshua's conquest of Canaan, at which point the Israelites move west to Shiloh (18:1) and "the tent of meeting" is set up there. Later in the Bible, Saul is crowned king at a place called Gilgal (1 Samuel 11:15). This is widely believed to be the same location as the Israelites' camp, although agreement is not unanimous among biblical scholars.

NONE WENT OUT, AND NONE CAME IN

JOSHUA 6:1, THE FALL OF JERICHO

IN BRIEF

PASSAGE
Joshua 2, 6

THEME
God in war and conquest

SETTING
14th–13th century BCE
Jericho. The date is disputed
by some archaeologists.

KEY FIGURES
Joshua Moses's successor
as leader of the Israelites and
commander of their army.

Rahab A prostitute or innkeeper living in Jericho,
who shelters Joshua's spies
and helps them to elude
their pursuers.

Joshua's conquest of the city of Jericho is the beginning of God's fulfillment of His covenant with the Israelites—their settlement of Canaan, the Promised Land. Drawing on oral traditions and written sources, the authors of Joshua probably wrote the account during the Babylonian captivity of around 560 BCE in order to raise the spirits of the exiles. The story encourages the Israelites to believe that they can prevail, however poor their chances, if they put their trust in God.

Having crossed the Jordan River, Joshua plans to take Jericho, a seemingly impregnable structure. Archaeological evidence reveals that the city was built on a mound surrounded by a massive earthen embankment, with a 12–15 foot (3.6–4.6m) high retaining wall around its base. Two mudbrick walls augmented this: one on top of the base and the other at the crest of the embankment. In addition, the Bible tells us, Jericho is well provisioned for a siege. A spring inside the city walls

The Israelites have been transported
to a Renaissance-style cityscape in
this 17th-century engraving of a work
by Maarten van Heemskerck.

See also: Sodom and Gomorrah 48–49 ▪ Covenants 44–47 ▪ Entering the Promised Land 96–97 ▪ The Nature of Faith 236–41

provides fresh water, while the city's granaries are full to bursting with freshly harvested grain.

The faith of Rahab

To find out as much as he can about the city's defenses, Joshua sends two followers—Caleb and the high priest Eleazar—to spy on the city. Once inside Jericho, the men rest for the night in the house of a woman named Rahab near the city gates. Rahab, either a prostitute or innkeeper according to different translations, is soon faced with a dilemma. The Israelites have been spotted and the king's guards are in pursuit. Rahab hides the spies under stalks of flax drying on her roof and tells the guards that the men left at dusk.

When the coast is clear, Rahab helps the Israelites escape. She says, "The Lord your God is God in heaven above and on the earth below" (Joshua 2:11). They promise that she and her family will be spared when the Israelites attack. She is told to hang a scarlet thread, or cord, out of her window as a signal to keep her home safe. The spies report back to Joshua that, although Jericho's defenses are strong, its people are demoralized by the Israelite threat.

While Joshua considers his best strategy, a man carrying a drawn sword appears before him. Some biblical scholars say this is the angel of the Lord, but others argue that it is God himself. The figure tells Joshua exactly what he must do. He is to march his soldiers in silence around Jericho once a day for six days, bearing the Ark of the Covenant and preceded by the priests blowing rams' horns. On the seventh day, the Israelites are to

Cursed before the Lord is the one who undertakes, to rebuild this city, Jericho.
Joshua 6:26

march around the city seven times. The priests must then blow a last blast on the trumpets while the people raise a mighty shout.

Joshua does what God has ordered. After the final trumpet blast and the shout, the walls of the city crumble and fall down flat. Joshua's soldiers storm into Jericho, slaughtering its inhabitants and then burning it to the ground. Rahab and her family are spared.

God's triumph

The Israelite victory is complete. God has shown the Israelites He is on their side and Joshua's unwavering obedience to God has allowed them to prosper under his leadership. However, the story of a city razed to the ground, its women and children slaughtered, unsettles many modern readers, to whom indiscriminate destruction is incompatible with the concept of an ethical God. The explanation, perhaps, lies in the conquest being a metaphor for the power of faith and obedience. The character of Rahab is key. Although she is a foreigner, and possibly a prostitute, she is redeemed through her faith and good works. ▪

Archaeological finds at Jericho

One of the oldest continually inhabited cities in the world, ancient Jericho is a site of considerable archaeological importance. Excavations show that the first settlements appeared about 8000 BCE and were repeatedly destroyed and rebuilt over the following millennia. However, while it is clear that the city was invaded at some point in its history, most archaeologists dispute the biblical account.

British archaeologist Kathleen Kenyon, who worked at Jericho in the 1950s, concluded that Jericho did not exist at the time Joshua is said to have conquered it. Jericho, Kenyon postulated, was destroyed, but it was by the Hyksos of northern Egypt in around 1550 BCE, about 150 years earlier than the biblical account. Kenyon's findings also suggest that the city wall, which previously had been dated to the time of the Israelites, actually dates from the early Bronze Age, 1,000 years before. However, the story of the Israelite conquest may have some credence. It is possible that the Israelites conquered a town that had sprung up on the ruins of an earlier settlement.

HAS NOT THE LORD GONE AHEAD OF YOU?

JUDGES 4:14, GIDEON AND THE JUDGES

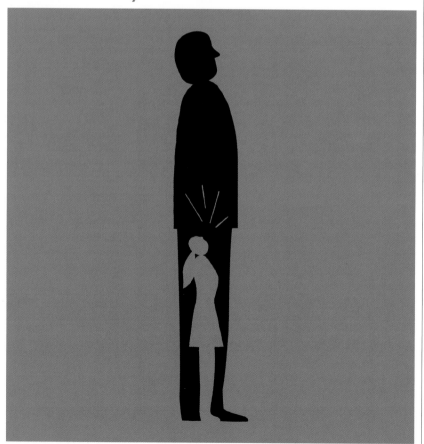

IN BRIEF

PASSAGE
Judges 4–8

THEME
Deliverance by the judges

SETTING
13th century BCE During the settlement of Canaan, the Promised Land.

KEY FIGURES
Gideon One of the 12 judges. Chosen by God to help the Israelites seize victory over the Midianites.

Abimelech Gideon's son who proclaims himself king against God's will and sets in motion the next cycle of decline for the Israelites.

The Midianites A semi-nomadic people from east of the Jordan, who fight against Israel.

The story of Gideon is typical of the events of the Book of Judges. It follows a familiar cycle of disobedience, punishment, repentance, and deliverance, as the Israelites yet again struggle to remain faithful to their God. Gideon becomes the instrument of God's intervention, and his miraculous military victory serves to set the people back on the right path, if only temporarily.

Fractious tribes

The Book of Judges began as a cycle of sagas about tribal heroes. These were pulled together into a single book probably in the late 7th century BCE, with additions

See also: Moses and the Burning Bush 66–69 ▪ The Fall of Jericho 98–99 ▪ The Exodus 74–77 ▪ The Fall of Jerusalem 128–31

and revisions made after the fall of Jerusalem in 586 BCE. The book covers the troubled period in Israel's history between the arrival of the tribes in Canaan between the 14th to 13th century BCE and the establishment of the monarchy in 1050 BCE. Judges depicts the Israelites as living in fractious tribes; it is a messier but almost certainly more accurate picture than the preceding Book of Joshua.

The book proposes to follow the fortunes of 12 judge-deliverers, perhaps to match the 12 tribes. In fact, four of these receive only minimal mention. Along with Gideon, the major stories are those of Deborah and her general Barak, Jephthah, and Samson.

The people suffer

Gideon gets the fullest treatment, his story starting, in a familiar way, with Israel's disobedience: "Again the Israelites did evil in the eyes of the Lord, and for seven years He gave them into the hands of the

Midianites" (Judges 6:1). The effect of the Midianites and their allies the Amalekites is compared to a swarm of locusts in its devastation (Judges 6:5). The land is ravaged and the Israelites are forced to seek refuge in caves and valleys. From a historical perspective, this sounds like a description of the sufferings of settled farmers at the hands of herder overlords who exact brutal harvest-time tributes. The desperate Israelites finally remember God and cry out to Him, but His initial response is to send an anonymous prophet to remind them of His record of saving them and rebuke their ingratitude (6:7–8).

Following this, God (or His angel) appears to a young man, Gideon, who is secretly threshing wheat inside a winepress, hoping to escape the attention of marauding Midianites. The exchange that follows has parallels with the calling of Moses at the burning bush. The angel greets Gideon, perhaps ironically, as a "mighty warrior" (6:12) and tells him that God is with him. However, Gideon's response is bitter, and he says God appears to have abandoned the Israelites. The angel replies: "Go in the strength you have and save Israel out of Midian's hand. Am I not sending you?" (6:14). An alarmed Gideon, like Moses before him, protests his weakness and insignificance. The angel simply reasserts that Gideon is the one who is going to strike down the Midianites. »

Gideon's fleece is covered in dew by God's angel in this painting (*c.* 1490s) from the school of Avignon, France. This is one of several signs from God that convinces Gideon He is with him.

Deborah

As well as being the only female judge, Deborah is the only one shown exercising a judicial role. She lives in the hills of Ephraim by a landmark palm tree, where people come to have their disputes settled. The wife of a man called Lappidoth, she is described as a charismatic prophet.

In her time, Israel suffers under the Canaanite king of Hazor and his general Sisera. When God tells Deborah to call up the army of the general Barak, she rides with it into battle. A sudden rainstorm helps Barak's army defeat the Canaanites, but Deborah warns that honor of the victory will go to a woman. This becomes true, when Sisera is killed by a woman called Jael with just a tent peg. Judges tells the story of this victory twice, first in prose, then in poetry, in the Song of Deborah. This is believed to be one of the oldest Bible fragments, if not the oldest: a victory song composed possibly as early as the 12th century BCE.

The Israelites use loud trumpets to shock the men in the Midianite camps in this engraving. Alarmed by the noise, and the Israelites' faith in their God, the Midianites are forced to flee.

As in other Old Testament stories, the divine promise is followed by a sign: the angel touches with the tip of his staff some meat and bread that Gideon has prepared for Him and fire rises from the ground to consume the offerings. Terrified, Gideon realizes that he has been face to face with his true God.

Tackling idolatry

God's first command to Gideon is to tear down an altar to the Canaanite god Baal that stands on Gideon's father's land. He is to build a new altar to God in its place and then sacrifice one of his father's bulls as a burnt offering. Gideon fulfills this command by night, provoking a furious but ultimately futile backlash from his townspeople the following day.

A more serious challenge comes when a huge army of Midianites and their allies marches across the Jordan and into the Valley of Jezreel. The spirit of God comes upon Gideon, who blows a horn to summon an army from among the tribes of Israel. As the troops begin to rally, Gideon is nervous and seeks reassurance from God.

He takes a woollen fleece and places it on a threshing floor. The next morning, if there is dew only on the fleece and not on the ground around it, he will know that God does indeed intend to save Israel by his hand. As dawn rises the next morning, Gideon wrings a bowlful of water out of the fleece; the ground all around is dry. Still not content, Gideon reverses the test, and when, the following morning, dew is on the ground and not on the fleece, he knows that God is truly with him.

Preparing for battle

Gideon now heads an army of 32,000 men. But this is too many for God, who is determined that Israel should know that He, God, is the one who saves them, not their own military strength. God tells Gideon to ask anyone trembling with fear to quit now. Many men do—22,000 of them—but the fighting force is still too large in God's eyes. He tells Gideon to cut the forces further.

Gideon takes his army to the waterside. God has told him to note the men who go down on their knees to drink water, and those who stay standing and lap the water up to their mouths with their

Role of the judges

The 12 judges were sent by God to deliver his chosen people from oppression. Unlike leaders such as Moses, the judges were intended to provide only temporary leadership, and scholars believe that some of these judges ruled in different regions simultaneously.

Before Israel had kings, the judges were sent by God to act as both prophets and warriors— combining the spirits of both Moses and Joshua. The judges were skilled military leaders: Deborah and her general Barak, for example, led two Israelite tribes to a grand military victory in the late 13th century BCE.

The Book of Judges emphasizes a connection between military and spiritual matters. Without a judge, the Israelites often forgot God's commands and slipped into sin. He consequently made their enemies strong to punish them. When Israel was led by a judge, however, the people were brought back into God's service, and able to defeat their oppressors.

hands. In the event, most go down on their knees; only a small number use their hands. These few will constitute Gideon's army—a mere 300 men against a much larger Midianite force. The battle lines are now set. The Midianites are encamped in a valley near Moreh in central Israel. Gideon and his guerrillalike band are stationed on the hillside above.

On the eve of battle, God gives Gideon one last reassurance. During the night, he tells Gideon and his servant to creep down to the Midianite camp and listen to what they hear. Gideon obeys. He hears a Midianite recounting a dream in which a barley cake came rolling down the hill from the Israelite camp and upset a Midianite tent. Another Midianite replies that this must be a sign of the sword of the Israelite leader Gideon and that God has put their fate in Gideon's hands.

Seeing the low morale of the Midianites, Gideon returns to his men with renewed boldness. "The Lord has given the Midianite camp into your hands" (7:15) he cries, and the men prepare for battle. His tactics are psychological. He

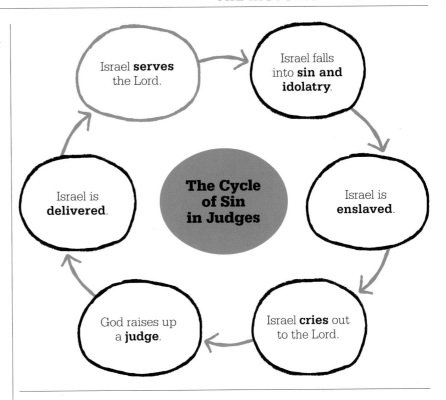

The Cycle of Sin in Judges

- Israel **serves** the Lord.
- Israel falls into **sin and idolatry**.
- Israel is **enslaved**.
- Israel **cries** out to the Lord.
- God raises up a **judge**.
- Israel is **delivered**.

The anger of the Lord burned against Israel … But when they cried out to [Him], He raised up for them a deliverer … who saved them.
Judges 3:8–9

divides his men into three groups of a hundred, issuing each of them with a horn or trumpet, an empty jar, and a torch. They are to creep down on the Midianites from three sides, and when Gideon gives the word, they are to blow their trumpets and smash their jars to reveal the blazing torches. At the same time, they will shout: "A sword for the Lord and for Gideon!" (7:20)

The plan works to perfection. The Midianites are caught by surprise and stampede in their panic, turning their swords against each other. The mighty Midianite army flees in confusion and disarray.

The cycle continues
Behind this story lie two key biblical themes: God's justice and God's mercy. According to divine justice, disobedience brings punishment. However, divine mercy also ensures that the cry of human suffering reaches God, who intervenes on the part of the supplicant. The benevolent Lord continues to protect His chosen people despite their misdeeds.

God's deliverance temporarily restores peace and the grateful Israelites ask Gideon to become their king. Although he declines, he still accepts a lion's share of the gold taken from the Midianites, and uses some of this to make an ephod (thought to be a vestment for covering an idol). Judges records how "Israel prostituted themselves by worshipping it there" (8:27), and idolatrous actions begin yet again.

Despite this lapse, the peace lasts 40 years, until Gideon's death. It is broken when his son Abimelech does what his father refused to do, by proclaiming himself king. Other judge-deliverers are raised up, but when the people turn against the king, Israel spirals into violence, as Abimelech turns his army against them. ■

THE SPIRIT OF THE LORD CAME UPON HIM

JUDGES 14:6, SAMSON

IN BRIEF

PASSAGE
Judges 13:1–16:31

THEME
Human weakness

SETTING
c. 12th–11th century BCE The low country of Judah.

KEY FIGURES
Samson Selected by God to free the Israelite people from the oppression of the Philistines. He is immensely strong, yet deeply flawed.

Samson's wife Woman whose Philistine blood displeases both Samson's parents and God.

Delilah Temptress with whom Samson falls in love. Working for the Philistines, she learns the secrets of Samson's strength.

Philistines Oppressors of the Israelites, and Samson's greatest foe. They capture, blind, and enslave him.

Samson is the ultimate strong man of the Bible, but in some respects, he is also one of its weakest subjects. In classic allegorical style, the story of Samson's rise and fall exemplifies the magnitude of human weakness and the consequent need to heed the Lord's commands.

In Judges 13:3, an angel of the Lord visits Samson's mother-to-be and informs her that, although she is barren, she will have a son, who will deliver the Israelites from the

See also: The Prophet Samuel 110–15 ▪ David and Goliath 116–17 ▪ Daniel in Babylon 164–65

Philistine oppression. Samson's mother is warned not to drink any wine or other fermented substance, nor eat anything "unclean" during her pregnancy, as her son will be a "Nazirite" from the womb.

Nazirites, whose name derived from the Hebrew word *nazir*, meaning "dedicated to God," were Israelites who took a voluntary vow to follow Nazirite law for a designated period of time in service to the Lord. By contrast, Samson's oath, made on his behalf by his mother, lasts his whole life. Two key stipulations for Nazirites were that they must not cut their hair, nor come into contact with dead bodies. However, during the course of his life, Samson breaks all of these rules and more.

Samson's strength

In Judges 14:6, Samson encounters a young lion as he is on the way to visit the vineyards of Timnah—now called Tell Batesh—in the Sorek Valley. As the lion charges, Samson is endowed by the Holy Spirit and tears the lion apart with his bare hands.

Samson later returns to the scene of the carnage. As he passes the lion's carcass, he sees that bees have made a nest in it and gathers some of the fermented honey in his hands. Samson then eats some of the honey as he goes along his way. Here, Samson breaks two key Nazirite laws in swift succession: he touches a corpse and consumes a fermented substance.

Endowed by God with superhuman strength, Samson becomes a leader and judge of the Israelites; he rules the people for 20 years. However, he continues to break his Nazirite vows and

provoke the Philistines in a series of conflicts. This culminates in Samson burning their crops and murdering large numbers of them on behalf of the oppressed Israelites. Visiting the cities of Philistia, he also spends time in the house of a harlot, indicating his weakness for women.

Yet Samson receives God's support in spite of his misdeeds. God provides the strength Samson requires to fulfill his divinely ordained mission of breaking the Philistine yoke.

Imprisonment

Matters come to a head when the Philistines confront Samson about his rampages. When Samson replies that he is only doing to the Philistines what had been done to his own people, the Philistines take Samson prisoner. However, God once more comes to Samson's aid and he breaks free. Seizing the jawbone of a freshly killed donkey »

Samson battles the lion with his bare hands in this 18th-century icon painting from Kargopol, Russia. Many famous depictions of Samson show him bravely reaching into the lion's mouth to tear it apart by the jaws.

The Philistines

This ancient group fought constantly with the Israelites throughout the 12th and 11th centuries BCE. One of the Sea Peoples who raided the eastern Mediterranean in around 1170 BCE, they were based in the five city states of Ashkelon, Ashdod, and Gaza, situated on the coast of southwestern Canaan, and Ekron and Gath inland. Their origins are unconfirmed. It was once thought the Philistines originated from Asia Minor, but recent evidence supports a theory that they came from the Aegean island of Crete and settled in Canaan around the same time as the Israelites in the 12th century BCE. In the lead-up to the founding of the Northern Kingdom of Israel in around 930 BCE, the Philistines constituted one of the country's greatest threats.

There has been much debate about the meaning of the name "Philistine," which translates from the Hebrew *Pelesheth*, as "sojourners." The area they occupied was known as Philistia, believed to be the origin of Palestine, the name given to the area by the Greeks.

Samson's Revenge and Death is a wood engraving from *Die Bible in Bildern* (The Bible in Pictures) by the German artist Julius Schnorr von Carolsfeld. Published in 30 parts between 1852 and 1860, the work contained 240 woodcut illustrations.

The Spirit of the Lord came powerfully upon him. The ropes on his arms became like charred flax and the bindings dropped.
Judges 15:14

Samson lays waste to 1,000 Philistine men with it. He then mocks the Philistines as donkeys themselves. After this victory, God rewards Samson with a drink from the spring of Lehi—a place named for the great victory, as "Lehi" means "jawbone."

Delilah's treachery

Samson's fortunes change when he encounters a woman named Delilah in the Valley of Sorek. She is working for the Philistines, who are determined to find a way of capturing Samson. Delilah seduces Samson in order to persuade him to

reveal the secret of his great strength, and how to take it from him. After several abortive attempts—and some creative lying from Samson—Delilah finally learns that if Samson's hair is shaved off, he will lose his strength. With the Philistines' help, Delilah cuts off Samson's hair while he is sleeping. The Philistines then rip out his eyes—a punishment to dissuade prisoners from rebelling—and tie him to a heavy grinding mill that he must heave in circles in order to make flour.

Meanwhile, Samson's hair steadily begins to grow back, and Samson realizes that his strength is returning. This fact is lost on his Philistine captors, who parade him in triumph at a temple festival in honor of their god Dagon. Three thousand Philistines are gathered in the temple when Samson positions himself between two great pillars supporting the roof. He prays to God for revenge on the Philistines for the loss of his two eyes, asking to die with his captors. God grants Samson the strength he requests. With a mighty heave, Samson pushes over the pillars, the roof collapses, and everyone inside the temple, including Samson, is consigned to a gory end.

Vessel of God

Biblical scholars have long debated the meaning of the tale of Samson. Some see him as a legendary hero, in the mold of Hercules or the Mesopotamian mythological figure Enkidu, or as an archetypal folk

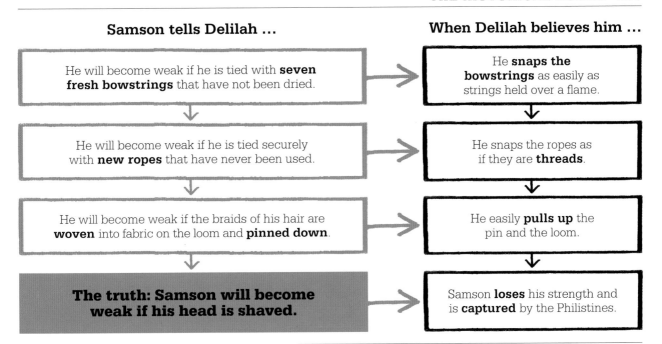

Samson tells Delilah …

He will become weak if he is tied with **seven fresh bowstrings** that have not been dried.

He will become weak if he is tied securely with **new ropes** that have never been used.

He will become weak if the braids of his hair are **woven** into fabric on the loom and **pinned down**.

The truth: Samson will become weak if his head is shaved.

When Delilah believes him …

He **snaps the bowstrings** as easily as strings held over a flame.

He snaps the ropes as if they are **threads**.

He easily **pulls up** the pin and the loom.

Samson **loses** his strength and is **captured** by the Philistines.

hero. Others see him as a real historical figure. The biblical tale of Samson sheds light on how individuals can derive strength from God's spirit, and illustrates the fundamental nature of human weakness. The contrast between divine strength and mortal frailty is shown by Samson's story. Through God he is physically strong, but he yearns for and seeks out the company of women and breaks his Nazirite vows. This ultimately brings about his downfall; he fulfills the mission he has been given by God, but he is continually diverted by selfish impulses along the way.

Two important lessons can be taken from this story. First, it makes clear that God has the power to take a human being's selfish impulses, such as Samson's lust, and use them to accomplish His will. Although Samson's life ends in tragedy, he does achieve the goal he has been set. The story also illustrates the dangers of ceaseless retaliation. Samson and the Philistines attack each other back and forth, until all parties involved are destroyed by the endless cycle of vengeance. ∎

Delilah, played by Hedy Lamarr, prepares to cut Samson's hair in the 1949 film, which cast Delilah as the vengeful sister of Samson's first wife.

Samson and Delilah in popular culture

The story of Samson—and particularly of his relationship with the woman from the Valley of Sorek, Delilah—is one of the most riveting tales in the Bible. The couple's love affair and her quest to uncover the secret of his strength have inspired artists, writers, and screenwriters. Delilah has been portrayed as a heartless seductress and a lover torn between loyalties.

Numerous artists, including Michelangelo and Rembrandt, have painted scenes from the lovers' lives. Popular literature, from *The Canterbury Tales* to Thackeray's *Vanity Fair*, is replete with references to the pair. One of the most lavish representations of the lovers is Cecil B. DeMille's 1949 Hollywood classic *Samson and Delilah*, starring Victor Mature as Samson and Hedy Lamarr as Delilah. DeMille created an action-packed drama, casting Lamarr as a minx and Mature as a handsome but simple-minded hulk.

YOUR PEOPLE SHALL BE MY PEOPLE AND YOUR GOD MY GOD
RUTH 1:16, RUTH AND NAOMI

IN BRIEF

PASSAGE
Ruth 1–4

THEME
God's care for outsiders

SETTING
1250–1050 BCE In the Kingdoms of Moab and Judah.

KEY FIGURES
Naomi Jewish woman whose husband and sons have perished abroad.

Ruth The foreign daughter-in-law of Naomi who converts to Judaism.

Boaz Relation of Naomi's husband who becomes Ruth's second husband.

In the Old Testament, the story of Ruth and Naomi appears between the stories of the judges—military as well as judicial leaders—and the establishment of the monarchy through the prophet Samuel. Neatly divided into scenes that build to a climax, the book resembles a play, suggesting a single author intent on showing God's (and the Israelites') care for those on the fringes of society, even when one is a Moabite, a foreigner.

The first scene is set in Moab, a country on the east side of the Dead Sea, to which Naomi, her

Ruth in Boaz's Field, 1828, by Julius Schnorr von Carolsfeld, depicts Ruth's first encounter with her redeemer, the landowner Boaz (left), a descendant of Abraham via Isaac.

husband, and their two sons have fled to escape a famine in the kingdom of Judah. The sons marry Moabite women called Ruth and Orpah. However, within ten years of living in Moab, Naomi's husband and sons have all died, leaving her alone with her daughters-in-law. There are no grandchildren.

Women alone
In the second scene, the famine in Judah has ended and Naomi decides to move home. She encourages her daughters-in-law to return to their homes and find new husbands. Naomi cannot offer her daughters-in-law levirate marriage, by which a widow marries the oldest surviving brother of her husband, as she has no sons. Naomi cares for Ruth and Orpah, who have both shown kindness to her: "May the Lord grant that each of you will find rest in the home of another husband," she says (Ruth 1:8–9).

Orpah returns home, but Ruth stays with Naomi. In a celebrated speech marking her conversion to Judaism, Ruth says to Naomi, "Your people shall be my people and your God my God" (1:16), confirming her loyalty to her mother-in-law, her

See also: Joseph the Dreamer 58–61 ▪ Queen Esther 132 ▪ The Golden Rule 210–11 ▪ The Good Samaritan 216–17

The story of Ruth

> Ruth, a **widow, who is also a Gentile**, has no one to care for her.

> She **converts to Judaism** and marries Boaz, a "guardian-redeemer."

> God **gives Ruth and Boaz a son**, Obed, from whom King David will descend.

> **God even provides for and works His purpose through Gentiles, such as Ruth.**

people, and their God. Naomi and Ruth proceed to Bethlehem, where they live as widows.

In the next scene, it is harvest time and Ruth takes the initiative to "glean," a form of charity that permits the poor to pick up grain left behind by the harvesters. Ruth chooses fields belonging to Boaz, a relative of her late husband, and a potential *go'el*, "one with the right to redeem." In Hebrew society, a *go'el* is a near relative who can protect a family in the absence of a head of household. This could mean buying their land to provide income (while still keeping it in the wider family), freeing slaves, or even avenging murder. Boaz is impressed with Ruth's hard work and loyalty to Naomi. Although his foreman emphasizes that Ruth is a Moabite, Boaz encourages her to stay in his fields, where he can ensure she is not harassed.

Ruth reports this to Naomi, who recognizes Boaz's status as a *go'el*. Naomi tells her to approach Boaz as he falls asleep, after the hard work of winnowing the grain. Ruth follows Naomi's advice, and when Boaz wakes, asks for the protection of marriage: "Spread the corner of your garment over me" (Ruth 3:9). Boaz agrees; but first, he must speak to her nearest male relation.

David's line

In the final scene, tension mounts before all is resolved. Boaz invites Ruth's nearest relative to buy land belonging to Naomi, on the condition that he marries Ruth. The man refuses, clearing the way for Boaz and Ruth to marry. The Lord then enables Ruth to conceive a son (4:13), who will join the line of King David. The story showed the Israelites that even Gentiles can play a part in God's purpose. ▪

Why have I found such favor in your eyes that you notice me—a foreigner?
Ruth 2:10

Shavuot

Falling anytime between May 14 and June 15, which is also harvest time in the Holy Land, "Shavuot" celebrates the gift of Torah to the ancient Israelites. It is associated with the Book of Ruth, both because of its connection to the harvest and because Ruth receives the gift of Torah upon her conversion to Judaism.

Shavuot, which translates as "weeks," a reference to the seven-week period between Passover and Shavuot, is celebrated with a feast. The Apostles were observing Shavuot when the Holy Spirit descended among them and gave spiritual gifts (Luke 22:12–13). Customs associated with the feast include the reading of a celebratory poem, the consumption of dairy products such as cheese blintzes, cheesecake, and cheese ravioli, and the decoration of homes with greenery. People stay up all night reading the Torah and there are synagogue readings of the Book of Ruth.

Members of the Samaritan faith, an ancient offshoot of Judaism, celebrate Shavuot at their holy site of Mount Gerizim near the West Bank town of Nablus.

SPEAK, FOR YOUR SERVANT IS LISTENING

1 SAMUEL 3:9, THE PROPHET SAMUEL

IN BRIEF

PASSAGE
1 Samuel 1:1–25:1

THEME
Obedience to God

SETTING
c. 1150 BCE The Tabernacle, which is at Shiloh at the beginning of Samuel's story, and then moved to Samuel's hometown, Ramah.

KEY FIGURES
Samuel Begins as Eli's prodigy in the Tabernacle, and quickly becomes God's mouthpiece to the Israelites.

Eli Priest at the Tabernacle recognized as a judge by the Israelites. Eli's two sons are known troublemakers.

Saul Israel's first king, who turns away from God's ways.

David Israel's second king, whose legacy as Israel's greatest national leader remains to this day.

F or nearly 300 years, the tribes of Israel had been loosely governed by a series of leaders, called "judges," sent by God. It had been a chaotic period, as the Israelites found themselves in repeated skirmishes with the other clans vying for control in the region. Time after time, God had raised up a judge to restore order and bring military success.

Over the lifetime of Samuel, this tumultuous situation changed. Samuel was no mere bystander to this great transition; he was God's prophet, who was entrusted with the messages and actions that would lead to the greatest king Israel ever knew: King David.

God answers Hannah

Even before his birth, Samuel is promised into God's service. His father Elkanah has two wives, Hannah and Peninnah. While Peninnah has given birth to many children, Hannah, his favorite wife, has none, which causes her great distress. Each year, when the family goes to Shiloh, where the Ark and the Tabernacle are kept, Hannah cries out to God to enable

Elkanah and his wives Hannah (left) and Peninnah (right) portrayed in a miniature from an illustrated manuscript produced in Utrecht in approximately 1467.

her to bear a child. One year, Hannah prays with great fervor and weeping, vowing that if God hears her prayer, she will dedicate the child to the service of God.

The priest, Eli, notices Hannah praying as he stands in the doorway of the sanctuary. When she tells him she has been praying because of her "great anguish and

See also: David and Goliath 116–17 ▪ The Wisdom of Solomon 120–23 ▪ The Suffering Servant 154–55 ▪ The Prophet Jeremiah 156–59 ▪ The Prophet Ezekiel 162–63 ▪ The Prophet Micah 168–71

grief," Eli blesses her: "Go in peace, and may the God of Israel grant you what you have asked of him" (1 Samuel 1). God does respond to Hannah's prayer, and when she gives birth to a son, she calls him Samuel —"heard of God."

When Samuel is around the age of 4, Hannah takes him back to the priest Eli at Shiloh and dedicates him to God's service as she has promised. She leaves him to be educated and trained by Eli.

Samuel and Eli
The early verses of Samuel's story describe how he grows both in stature and favor with God and His people. Samuel's exemplary behavior is in marked contrast to that of Eli's own sons, who steal the offerings worshippers bring to God at Shiloh.

God plans to use Samuel to bring the old leadership of Eli and his sons to an end and establish a new period of devotion to God. One night, while Samuel is asleep in the Tabernacle, he is woken by a voice calling his name. Thinking it must

The Lord was with Samuel as he grew up … all Israel from Dan to Beersheba recognized that Samuel was attested as a prophet of the Lord.
1 Samuel 3:19–20

History of the Books of Samuel

Telling the Israelites' story from the end of the era of the judges to the final days of King David's reign, Samuel is split into two books. Although Samuel 1 and 2 both bear his name, the prophet only appears as a key character in the first 16 chapters of 1 Samuel. After Samuel anoints Saul as king, Saul's story takes up the rest of 1 Samuel. The only subsequent mentions of Samuel are before his death in 1 Samuel 25:1 and as a ghost summoned by a medium on behalf of King

Saul in 1 Samuel 28. David's reign takes up all of 2 Samuel and continues in 1 Kings.

In the original Hebrew Bible, 1 and 2 Samuel were one book, but this was split into two in Greek and Latin versions due to the book's length. It is likely that the account was compiled from a variety of sources in the time of Israel's later kings, after around 600 BCE, to remind Israel's rulers that they must remain faithful to God if they want to rule well.

have been Eli, Samuel runs to Eli's bedside, ready to serve his master, but Eli says he has not called out. Back in bed, Samuel hears his name called again, so once again runs to Eli. A second time, Eli sends him back to bed; he had not called.

After a third call summons Samuel to Eli's bedside, Eli realizes that the voice Samuel is hearing must be God's. He instructs Samuel to respond with the words "Speak, Lord, for your servant is listening" if the voice calls again. Samuel's life had begun by God responding to Hannah calling out to him for a child; now God is calling that child to become a prophet. When God calls again, Samuel answers exactly as Eli has advised.

Eli's rule ends
God tells Samuel that the time for Eli and his sons to lead is coming to a close. Sure enough, during the next clash with the Philistines, Eli's sons Hophni and Phinehas are killed, and the Ark of the Covenant, which the Israelites had taken with them to the battlefield as a symbol

of God's presence and protection, is captured by the Philistines. On hearing of these calamities, the aging Eli falls off his chair, breaks his neck, and dies.

By this time, the Israelites recognize Samuel not merely as Eli's successor, but as someone even more important—a prophet, through whom God spoke to »

Eli questions Samuel after one of the boy's visions in this 19th-century illustration. Most depictions of the two highlight Samuel's youth and vision in contrast to the blind and elderly Eli.

the Israelites (1 Samuel 3:19–21). After the capture of the Ark of the Covenant, the people come to Samuel in great distress as they look for a solution. Samuel tells the people to get rid of the idols they are worshipping and return to the true worship of God. The people listen to Samuel, and the next time the Israelites face the Philistines in battle, the Israelites are victorious.

Samuel is hailed as Israel's new "judge," to whom the people look for leadership. However, while Samuel is recognized as a prophet and a judge, his sons, Joel and Abijah, just like the sons of Eli, prove to be impious and unsuitable to lead God's chosen people.

Samuel the kingmaker

As Samuel grows older, the tribal leaders of Israel come to him and ask him to appoint a king to lead them, rather than passing the mantle of leadership to his sons, whom they see as weak. Samuel is displeased with the request. However, when he speaks with God, He tells Samuel to listen to the people, saying "it is not you they have rejected, but they have rejected me as their king" (8:7). If the Israelites want to be just like all the other nations, He is willing to let them try. Samuel relays God's response to the people, solemnly warning them that a king is no substitute for following God, but they are adamant.

Samuel anoints Saul as Israel's first king, but Saul's period of good favor is short-lived. No sooner has Samuel handed over the leadership of Israel to King Saul, than Saul fails to keep God's commands, and Samuel comes to him with a rebuke: just like Eli and Samuel himself, Saul's own son would not become ruler after his death. Samuel's last and greatest act as prophet of God is to anoint a new king, a "man after God's own heart" (1 Samuel 13:14). This new king is David, the youngest son of a sheep farmer.

Samuel anoints Saul as the first king of Israel by pouring oil over Saul's head in this undated engraving. The ritual, described in 1 Samuel 10:1, marked Saul's receipt of God's spirit.

"Does the Lord delight in burnt offerings and sacrifices as much as in obeying the Lord?" To obey is better than sacrifice.
1 Samuel 15:22

The Israelites **suffered** in Egypt.

The Israelites **abandoned** God to serve the Baals and the Ashtoreths. They were **punished** by being sold into the hands of Sisera and the Philistines.

The Israelites **asked** for a king, although God was their true king.

The Israelites prayed to God for guidance and forgiveness. Each time He answered their prayers.

God sent Moses and Aaron to **lead** them out of Egypt.

God sent Gideon, Barak, Jephthah, and Samuel to **deliver the Israelites** from their enemies.

God sent the Israelites an **anointed king**.

Samuel is a central character throughout this transitional time for the Israelites. He has the unique position of being the last of the judges of Israel and the first of Israel's prophets. As a prophet of God, he is first and foremost a spiritual leader, and throughout his ministry he repeatedly has to call the Israelites back to the true worship of God.

God's mouthpiece

The role of the prophet will become more important in the Israelites' history, now that they have a royal line. As Samuel himself has done, the prophets will speak for God directly to the people, and at times even bring messages of judgment on the kings. Although the Israelites were now "like the other nations" with a royal line, prophets remind the people that they are still different from these other nations: they are the treasured possession of God, who had rescued them from slavery in Egypt and led them to the Promised Land.

Samuel is God's mouthpiece. However, from his birth and early years, he also demonstrates the importance of listening for and recognizing God's voice. In the Bible, God's voice is often ignored, or misheard, and the Israelites' inability to stay faithful to the laws given to Moses on Mount Sinai is a constant theme. When this happens, they inevitably pass through difficult times. When God's words are recognized and obeyed, God blesses the people.

Bringing the words of God to Israel will never be an easy task, since God often asks His people to change the direction of their lives. Samuel establishes the role of the prophet as someone who listens for God and who speaks what they hear, regardless of the consequences to themselves. ∎

Theocracy to monarchy

At the beginning of Samuel's story, Israel could be properly called a "theocracy," which means it was a family of tribes ruled (*cratos*) by God (*theos*). God had taken the Israelites out of Egypt and given them laws to live by. Whenever they needed His intervention, God would raise up an authoritative figure, or "judge," to unite them. In theory, this meant the people still viewed God as their king.

By the time of Samuel, many Israelites wanted a more stable leadership, and they asked for a king to lead them. However, they still faced problems under a monarchy—some kings led them well (like David) while others led them astray (like Ahab).

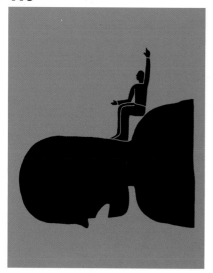

THERE WAS NO SWORD IN THE HAND OF DAVID

1 SAMUEL 17:50, DAVID AND GOLIATH

IN BRIEF

PASSAGE
1 Samuel 17

THEME
God's anointing is greater than earthly powers

SETTING
Around 1020 BCE
Valley of Elah, Judah.

KEY FIGURES
David The youngest son of Jesse of Bethlehem. He starts off as a shepherd and rises to become a mighty warrior and second king of the Israelites after the death of Saul.

Goliath A giant from Gath who is the champion of the Philistines.

Saul Israel's first king, who proves to be a weak ruler.

Samuel The last of the judges and an important prophet who anoints Saul and David as Israel's first and second kings.

The heroic victory of a simple farm boy over a giant warrior is one of the most inspiring tales in the Bible. As the king of the Israelites, Saul, wavers uncertainly on the edge of battle, David's firm actions and his enduring faith in God grant the Israelites a decisive victory.

For 40 days, the Israelites have been locked in a stalemate with the Philistines, about 15 miles (24 km) southwest of Jerusalem. Each morning on the battlefield, a warrior named Goliath emerges from the Philistine ranks and bellows out a challenge to the Israelites, daring one of them to come out and fight him. Although sources differ on his exact height, Goliath is described as a giant, and any man foolish enough to fight him looks certain to be defeated.

David is tending sheep when his father tells him to take some food to his older brothers, who are serving in Saul's army. Although he is the youngest of his brothers,

David raises his sword to cut off the head of Goliath in this 17th-century painting by Guillaime Courtois. David's against-the-odds victory has inspired artists throughout history.

See also: Samson 104–07 ▪ David and Bathsheba 118–19 ▪ The Wisdom of Solomon 120–23 ▪ The Psalms 138–43

David's potential has already been recognized by God. As related in 1 Samuel 16, he has been secretly anointed by Samuel to be Israel's next king, although David is unaware of this at the time.

The arrival of David

When he arrives at the battlefield and sees Goliath's challenge going unanswered, David is determined to fight him. Although Saul has offered rich rewards for anyone brave enough to take on Goliath, at first he tries to deter David, telling the shepherd that Goliath "has been a warrior from his youth" (1 Samuel 17:33). David responds by telling Saul how, when tending his father's sheep, he fought off and killed a lion and a bear. David has faith that, with God on his side, taking on Goliath will not be a problem. Armed only with his staff, a slingshot, and five pebbles from the bed of a stream, he goes off to fight the Philistines' champion.

The duel starts with Goliath hurling curses at David, while the latter tells the giant he is fighting him in the name of God—whom

> You come against me with sword and spear and javelin, but I come against you in the name of the Lord Almighty.
> **1 Samuel 17:45**

Goliath's size varies according to the source, but it is likely that it was within human range and the result of a hereditary disorder of the pituitary gland.

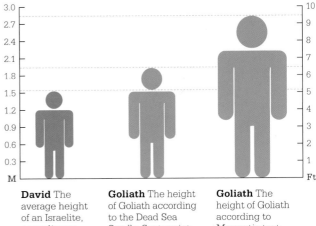

Sizing up David and Goliath

David The average height of an Israelite, according to archaeology.

Goliath The height of Goliath according to the Dead Sea Scrolls, Septuagint, and Josephus.

Goliath The height of Goliath according to Masoretic text.

Goliath and the Philistines have foolishly defied. "This day," he says, "the Lord will deliver you into my hands and I'll strike you down and cut off your head" (17:46). As the heavily armored Goliath advances, David seizes his chance. Reaching into his bag, he takes out one of the pebbles, slips it into his slingshot, and shoots it, striking Goliath on the forehead. The giant falls to the ground, and David uses Goliath's own sword to chop off the giant's head. The Philistines flee—pursued by the Israelites, who chase them to Gath and Ekron before returning to plunder the Philistines' camp.

Saul's failings

David's faith in God allows him to defeat Goliath, and this story can also be seen as evidence of Saul's moral deficiencies as king, as he does not trust in God enough to have faith in victory. Although Saul rewards David by promoting him to a high rank in his army, he soon becomes jealous and begins to plot David's downfall. ▪

Clash of champions

David and Goliath's duel was not the only clash of champions in the ancient world, although it is the only one recorded in the Bible. In classical Greece, champions from Sparta and Argos fought the so-called Battle of the Champions in 546 BCE. It ended with both sides claiming victory. Much later, in around 133 BCE, Scipio Aemilianus accepted a challenge from an Iberian warrior parading in front of the Roman ranks, daring someone to fight him. Sources say the Iberian was a giant, while Scipio was a much smaller man. Nevertheless, like David, he prevailed.

In medieval times, the notion of champions became embedded in law. Trial by combat was used to determine God's favor and thus a person's guilt or innocence.

THE MAN WHO DID THIS MUST DIE

2 SAMUEL 12:5, DAVID AND BATHSHEBA

IN BRIEF

PASSAGE
2 Samuel 11–12

THEME
Sins of the righteous

SETTING
Around 1000 BCE Jerusalem.

KEY FIGURES
David Israel's well-respected second king, who ascends to the throne after Saul's death. He sins against God by sleeping with Bathsheba.

Bathsheba The wife of Uriah the Hittite, who commits adultery with David and later marries him.

Joab The commander of David's army.

Nathan A prophet and one of David's closest advisers.

Uriah the Hittite A high-ranking officer in David's army who is married to Bathsheba.

Initially revered as a wise king, David is in the 11th year of his reign when he breaks God's laws. The events that then unfold warn of the dangers of monarchy if the king does not obey God—a theme explored elsewhere in the Book of Samuel.

David's transgression occurs during a time of war. Having secured the kingdom, he stays behind in Jerusalem rather than leading his army into another battle. While resting in his palace, the king spots a beautiful woman bathing on the roof of a nearby house. He immediately sends one of his servants to discover her identity. The servant tells him her name is Bathsheba and that she is the wife of Uriah the Hittite, a warrior serving in David's current campaign against the Ammonites.

Succumbs to sin

Despite his strength in battle, David gives in to desire. He sends for Bathsheba and sleeps with her. This seemingly uncharacteristic action by David shows us that even great men can struggle against sin. However, David's actions soon catch up with him when Bathsheba sends word that she is pregnant.

Adultery and polygamy

One of the most frequently and severely condemned sins in the Bible is adultery. It is mentioned 52 times, including in the Ten Commandments, where it is specifically prohibited; all four New Testament Gospels; and in ten other books of the Bible. Only the sins of idolatry, self-righteousness, and murder are mentioned more often. Leviticus 20:10 makes it clear how sternly God judged the crime, saying that "both the adulterer and adulteress are to be put to death." The method of execution was by stoning.

While God hates adultery, polygamy seems to be both accepted and commonplace. According to Genesis 4, Cain's descendant, Lamech, had two wives, while Abraham, Jacob, and possibly Moses are also polygamous. Scholars believe David may have had as many as 12 wives; Solomon, who "loved many foreign women" (1 Kings 11:1), had 700 wives and 300 concubines.

Bathsheba inhabits a 16th-century world in this painting by Hans Sebald (1500–1550). She may have been taking a *mikveh*, a ritual bath performed after menstruation, when David spies her.

As both Bathsheba's husband and many other members of her family hold important positions in court, David wishes to avoid a scandal at all costs.

David plots

The king's first move is to recall Uriah from the battlefront on the pretext of wanting to hear a first-hand account of the war's progress. Once Uriah is back in Jerusalem, it would be only natural for him to sleep with his wife, who could then claim her unborn child as his.

However, Uriah decides to sleep on a mat in the palace rather than go home. Demonstrating a stricter ethical code than King David, he protests that it would be unfair for him to feast and make love to his wife while his fellow soldiers are away fighting.

David invites Uriah to dine with him and plies him with alcohol, hoping this will make him forget his scruples. However, once again, Uriah does not return home. As David gets more desperate, one sin leads to another, and his thoughts turn to murder. He feels desire for Bathsheba and wants to marry her himself.

When Uriah returns to the battlefield, the king gives him a letter for his commander Joab in which he tells Joab to order Uriah "out in front where the fighting is fiercest. Then withdraw from him so he will be struck down and die" (2 Samuel 11:14). Joab carries out David's orders and sends word that Uriah has been killed. Once Bathsheba's period of mourning is over, David promptly marries her.

God's anger

The Lord is displeased by David's actions and sends Nathan the prophet to confront the king. Nathan tells David a parable about a rich man who, despite his wealth, takes and kills a poor man's only lamb. When David condemns the injustice, saying "the man who did this must die!" (2 Samuel 12:5), Nathan replies tersely "You are the man!" (12:7) and denounces the enormity of David's sins. David repents, but God still punishes him. When Bathsheba bears their son, the child dies within days of the birth.

As well as showing how even the most righteous can fall into sin, this story is a cautionary tale about the dangers of power. Through committing the heinous sins of both adultery and murder, King David acts as though he considers himself above the laws of God. Only his true repentance for the harm he has done allows him to recover God's favor and even then, he and his family will continue to suffer the consequences of his actions. ▪

Why did you despise the word of the Lord by doing what is evil in His eyes? You struck down Uriah the Hittite with the sword and took his wife to be your own.
2 Samuel 12:9

CUT THE LIVING CHILD IN TWO, AND GIVE HALF TO ONE AND HALF TO THE OTHER

1 KINGS 3:25, THE WISDOM OF SOLOMON

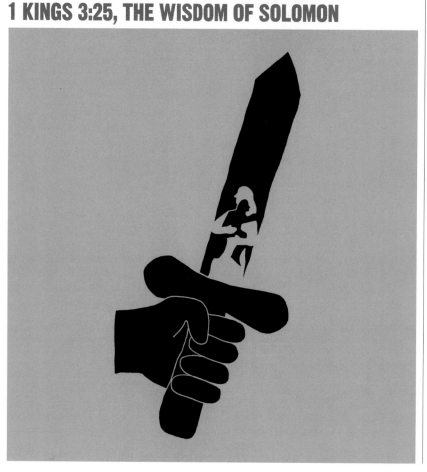

IN BRIEF

PASSAGE
1 Kings 3

THEME
God's wisdom through Solomon

SETTING
c.962–922 BCE
Jerusalem, the capital
city of Israel.

KEY FIGURES
King Solomon The son
of David and Bathsheba,
Solomon rules Israel from
around 962 to 922 BCE. He
is wise, just, and devout.

King David The father of
Solomon and the second
king of Israel.

Two unknown women
Described as prostitutes,
the women ask Solomon to
decide which of them is the
rightful mother of a baby.

Queen of Sheba Her visit
to Solomon is described in
one brief biblical passage
(1 Kings 10:1–13) but has
intrigued readers of the
Bible for centuries.

Zadok The first high priest
to serve in the Temple.

S olomon is one of the Bible's
most charismatic figures.
His 40-year reign is widely
regarded as a golden age, but
it is during the first 20 years,
when he builds the First Temple,
that he proves himself as a glorious
monarch and faithful servant
of God. He fulfills his father King

See also: The Ark and the Tabernacle 86–87 ▪ David and Bathsheba 118–19 ▪ The Fall of Jerusalem 128–31 ▪ Rebuilding Jerusalem 133

David's dream of building God's First Temple and he turns Israel into one of the wealthiest and most powerful nations in the world by expanding trade and executing a program of construction.

From father to son
In around 970 BCE, King David passes the throne of a unified Israel to Solomon, his surviving son by Bathsheba. David exhorts his son to love and obey God so that the kingdom will prosper and their descendants will always be kings (1 Kings 2:2–4). Solomon follows his father's advice.

A little later (3:5), God appears to Solomon in a dream and says He will give the young king anything he desires. Modestly, Solomon asks only for a discerning heart and wisdom to distinguish between right and wrong. Pleased by this response, God grants the wish, and also bestows long life, wealth, and power "so that in your lifetime you will have no equal among kings" (3:13).

The wisdom of Solomon
As God has promised, Solomon is all-powerful and famously wise. He puts his wisdom to good use when two women claim to be the mother of the same baby. The women, both prostitutes, come before Solomon to plead their case. Their story is that they live in the same house and recently gave birth within days of each other. One woman claims the other has accidentally smothered her child by lying on it and then swapped the dead child for her living infant. Legally, the case is highly contentious. There are no witnesses nor any evidence, other

than the word of one woman against the other. Both women are vehement in their protestations of affection for the child.

After listening to both women, Solomon devises a judgment that is simple but effective. He calls for a sword and gives orders to divide the child so that each woman can have half. One woman readily agrees while the other, horrified, pleads for the child's life. If only

The Judgment of Solomon (1649) by Nicolas Poussin depicts the moment Solomon delivers his ruling. The balance of colour and form in the composition mirrors the justice of God and Solomon.

the baby can live, she will willingly give him up to her rival, who does not realize that she has exposed the emptiness of her claim by agreeing to the grisly solution. Solomon orders that the baby be handed to the woman who has given him up, saying, "Do not kill him; she is his mother" (1 Kings 3:27).

Building God's Temple
Solomon achieves much during his reign—he fortifies the kingdom, builds a palace, and constructs a fleet of ships to boost maritime trade. His crowning achievement is the construction of God's First Temple, which takes seven years to complete. This Temple will be the dwelling of God and a safe home for the Ark of the Covenant. It supersedes the Tabernacle, built during the time of Moses and »

God gave Solomon wisdom and very great insight, and a breadth of understanding as measureless as the sand on the seashore.
1 Kings 4:29

> During Solomon's lifetime Judah and Israel ... lived in safety, everyone under their own vine and ... own fig tree.
> **1 Kings 4:25**

used by the Israelites in the wilderness. Many detailed plans and preparations have already been drawn up by King David, who had wanted to undertake the project himself. God had told David (through the prophet Nathan) that he could not build the Temple because he was a warrior and had shed blood.

The responsibility and plans for building the Temple therefore pass to Solomon. David tells his son that these are divinely inspired, "All this ... I have in writing as a result of the Lord's hand on me" (1 Chronicles 28:19).

Solomon builds the Temple, which, with pillars and courtyards, reflects the style familiar to the Phoenician craftsmen who worked on it, next to the royal palace to allow access between the two most important buildings in Jerusalem. This proximity symbolizes the king's status as God's appointed ruler.

Specifications

Although ornate and beautiful, the Temple itself is not particularly large. The specifications given in the Bible are expressed in cubits, an ancient unit of length, estimated at about 18 inches (45 cm). The Temple building is described as being 60 cubits long, 20 cubits wide, and 30 high, or three stories high, with a towering porch 120 cubits high. Modern estimates give the dimensions as 120–150 feet (35–40m) long by 45–60 feet (15–20m) wide. At the entrance are two bronze pillars known as Jachin and Boaz, symbolizing God's greatness.

The complex consists of three main areas: the great court (1 Kings 7:9), where people assemble to worship, the inner court or court of the priests (2 Chronicles 4:9), with a large sacrificial altar, and the inner sanctuary (1 Kings 6:5), comprising the Holy Place (*hekal*), in which there are ten gold menorah, a table of showbread (for offerings), and a golden incense altar (1 Chronicles 28:18). Around the inner sanctuary are chambers for the priests.

Behind the incense altar lies the Holy of Holies, the resting place of the Ark of the Covenant and the tablets of the Ten Commandments. These are guarded by two huge statues of olive-wood cherubim overlaid with gold. One of the most striking features is the "bronze sea," a huge bronze basin that provides water for the priests to purify themselves, with ten wheeled basins for carrying water.

No expense is spared for either the construction or the furnishing of the Temple. Solomon conscripts 30,000 Israelites to build it, with a further 80,000 to quarry stone, 70,000 to carry stone, and 3,300 managers to oversee the work (1 Kings 5:13 and 2 Chronicles 2:2). Large, expensive stones are cut for the foundations, and the finest materials, including gold, silver, bronze, cedarwood, and precious stones, are used throughout. The

The Queen of Sheba

A visit to Jerusalem by the Queen of Sheba is mentioned in the Hebrew Bible, the Qur'an, and the Ethiopian holy book, the Kebra Nagast. The Bible passage is brief but ambiguous. It states that the unnamed queen hears of Solomon's fame and wishes to test his wisdom. Traveling from the land of Sheba (believed to be modern-day Yemen or possibly Ethiopia), she arrives with gifts of gold, precious stones, spices, and incense. Solomon answers all her questions and she is impressed, praising God for placing Solomon on the throne. She leaves after

Solomon gives her "all she desired and asked for" (1 Kings 10:13). Open to interpretation, this phrase could simply mean that she is satisfied with Solomon's answers or that she is carrying his child. Ethiopians believe that the Sheban queen bore Solomon a son, Menelik I, from whom all Ethiopian kings are descended. They also believe that when Menelik later traveled to Jerusalem to visit his father, he smuggled the Ark of the Covenant back to Axum in northern Ethiopia, where it still resides.

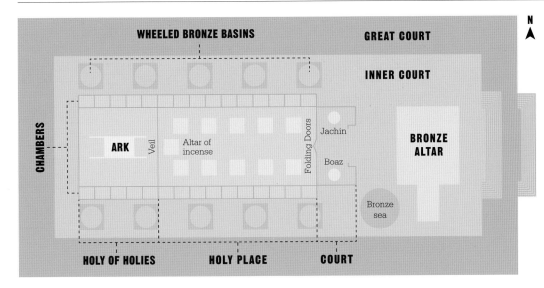

Solomon's Temple was similar to the Tabernacle but incorporated Phoenician elements such as the two columns "Jachin" and "Boaz," reflecting the input of architects and craftsmen loaned to Solomon by King Hiram of Tyre.

King of Tyre (Phoenicia), Solomon's ally and neighbor, supplies cedar for the paneling as well as labor. According to 1 Kings 6:7, the stone is finished at the quarry before being transported to the Temple, so that "no hammer, chisel or any other iron tool was heard at the Temple site while it was being built."

The priests move in

Once the Temple has been completed, the priests move God's ceremonial equipment from the tabernacle to the Temple and a feast is held for 14 days. From then on, a daily sacrifice of lamb is made in the morning, with a second lamb and cereal sacrificed by the high priest Zadok on the Sabbath. Singing and prayers are part of worship. Only the high priest is permitted to enter the Holy of Holies, and then only on the Day of Atonement (see pp. 86–87). Jerusalem is now established as a holy city. Zadok and his descendants control the Temple until the Babylonian Exile in 597 BCE.

It is difficult to pinpoint when Solomon's Temple was completed. The Bible says construction started in the fourth year of Solomon's reign and that it took seven years, which puts completion at around 964 BCE. Rabbinic sources say the Temple stood for 410 years, yet records show that it was destroyed by the Babylonians in around 587 BCE, 30 years earlier than those dates indicate. The most likely site is Temple Mount, now occupied by the Dome of the Rock, an Islamic shrine, where the Prophet Muhammad is said to have ascended to heaven. ■

When the Queen of Sheba heard about the fame of Solomon and his relationship to the Lord, she came to test Solomon with hard questions.
1 Kings 10:1

Raising funds for the First Temple

According to 1 Chronicles 22:14, King David sets aside funds and materials for the Temple before he dies. They included "a hundred thousand talents of gold, a million talents of silver, quantities of bronze and iron too great to be weighed, and wood and stone." In modern terms, this equates to 3,750 tons of gold and 37,000 tons of silver.

King David also appeals for donations. Gold, silver, iron, bronze, and precious stones are given by families, leaders of the 12 tribes, commanders, and those in charge of the works. Huge quantities of wood, especially cedar, are imported from Tyre. David promises King Hiram of Tyre to pay his craftsmen whatever wages Hiram requires; by the end of the project Solomon is greatly in debt and is forced to give 20 towns in Galilee to Hiram as payment (1 Kings 9:11).

I HAVE DIRECTED THE RAVENS TO FEED YOU THERE

1 KINGS 17:4, A PROPHET IN HIDING

IN BRIEF

PASSAGE
1 Kings 16:29–17:24

THEME
God protects His prophet

SETTING
During King Ahab's reign (873–852 BCE) Samaria and the brook Cherith, flowing east of the Jordan River.

KEY FIGURES
Elijah A prophet of God who challenges King Ahab and then must go into hiding.

King Ahab The sinful king of Israel who rejects God and worships the Canaanite god Baal.

Queen Jezebel King Ahab's wife, who encourages him to worship Baal.

The ravens Intelligent and mystical birds that feed Elijah during the drought.

The prophet Elijah makes his first biblical appearance during the reign of King Ahab. The king marries the Tyrian princess Jezebel, who persuades him to set aside God in favor of the god Baal and the goddess Asherah. Although the Bible does not explicitly say so, scholars also suggest other acts of depravity are being committed at court, including ritual sex and child sacrifice.

It is at this point that Elijah arrives, warning the errant Ahab of a drought: "There will be neither dew nor rain in the next few years except at my word" (1 Kings 17:1). However, speaking out puts Elijah's life at risk and God tells him to go to the brook Cherith (east of the Jordan River).

Elijah survives by drinking the water and eating meat brought twice a day by ravens, as God has promised, until the brook runs dry. God then leads Elijah to Phoenicia and safety within the house of a widow, where, with God's help, Elijah performs a miracle by bringing her son back to life.

God's protection of Elijah in unexpected ways—ravens, which are unclean in Israelite law, and through the poor widow—shows His care for the faithful. Ravens also reference God's protecting love in Job 38. Their ubiquity in ancient Israel was seen as a sign that God's love is everywhere. ∎

Elijah hides in the wilderness in this anonymous work from the collection of Petit Palais, Musée des Beaux-Arts de la Ville de Paris. God sends ravens to bring him food.

See also: Ruth and Naomi 108–09 ▪ Elijah and the Prophets of Baal 125 ▪ The Suffering of Job 146–47 ▪ The Good Samaritan 216–17

GO AND PRESENT YOURSELF TO AHAB, AND I WILL SEND RAIN ON THE LAND

1 KINGS 18:1, ELIJAH AND THE PROPHETS OF BAAL

IN BRIEF

PASSAGE
1 Kings 18

THEME
Authority over pagan gods

SETTING
During King Ahab's reign (873–852 BCE) Mount Carmel and the city of Jezreel.

KEY FIGURES
Elijah God's prophet, who challenges King Ahab to a religious duel in order to demonstrate the power of God.

King Ahab The king of Israel, who fails to recognize that the drought is God's wrath for his sins.

Obadiah The King's servant, who is secretly a loyal follower of God.

Queen Jezebel Ahab's wife, who seeks to kill prophets who worship God.

The story of the religious duel on Mount Carmel is a highly dramatic tale that serves to demonstrate God's power. The drought God had ordained has raged for three years when He tells the prophet Elijah to return from hiding in the wilderness and seek out Ahab. He promises rain will once again fall.

On the way, Elijah meets Ahab's administrator, Obadiah, a secret follower of God who reveals that he is hiding 100 believers from Queen Jezebel. Obadiah is afraid for his life, as he must reveal Elijah's return to Ahab. However, Elijah immediately challenges the royal couple. He blames them for the drought, as they have disobeyed God and instead worshipped Baal.

Test of two gods

To decide which god is the most powerful, Elijah proposes a public competition at Mount Carmel. The test for God and Baal is to incinerate a sacrificial bull. The 450 prophets of Baal pray, dance, and mutilate themselves, but are unable to summon lightning. Finally, Elijah takes 12 stones—one for each tribe of Israel—and builds an altar. He pours water over the wood, then prays. To everyone's amazement, a bolt of fire consumes the altar, even the water. Reminded of God's power, the people proclaim Him as the only true God. The miracle also shows how God answers the prayers of the righteous, as he sends the rain Elijah asks for and protects the faithful Obadiah. ∎

When all the people saw this, they fell prostrate and cried, 'The LORD—he is God. The LORD—he is God!'
1 Kings 18:39

See also: The Fall 30–35 ∎ Tower of Babel 42–43 ∎ The Golden Calf 84–85

LET ME INHERIT A DOUBLE PORTION OF YOUR SPIRIT
2 KINGS 2:9, THE CHARIOT OF FIRE

IN BRIEF

PASSAGE
2 Kings 2

THEME
The ascension of a prophet

SETTING
Around 850 BCE
Banks of the Jordan River.

KEY FIGURES
Elijah A prophet who urges the people of Israel to abandon their worship of Baal and return to the worship of the true God.

Elisha A faithful servant of Elijah and the prophet chosen by God to be Elijah's successor. Over the course of 60 years, he builds on Elijah's work by teaching the Israelites the ways of God.

Elijah's impressive exit from this world stands as testament to his importance as a prophet and faithful servant of God. Both he and his disciple Elisha know in advance that God will take him to heaven and are able to prepare.

Devoted to Elijah to the end, Elisha refuses three times to leave his master in his last moments. Elijah uses his cloak to part the waters of the Jordan River before asking whether there is any last request he can grant his disciple. The only thing Elisha asks of his master is "a double portion of your spirit" (2 Kings 2:9), a phrasing that references Israel's inheritance laws. Although land was shared out between a man's sons when he died, the eldest would receive a larger share—two portions of land. By asking for this, Elisha wishes to confirm himself as Elijah's spiritual heir and successor.

The prophet ascends
Elijah's ascension to heaven occurs quite suddenly as the two men walk together. He is swept away dramatically in a whirlwind, as a

Elijah

Little is known about Elijah's life before his sudden appearance as a prophet about halfway through the reign of Ahab, the son of Omri. This would put Elijah's emergence as a prophet at around 864 BCE. Mostly, Elijah's activities are confined to the northern kingdom, although he is forced to take refuge elsewhere when fleeing from Ahab's wrath. Throughout his relatively brief career, Elijah has one main purpose: This is to turn the Israelites back to the worship of the one true God and away from the worship of Baal and other pagan deities.

In the conflict with Baal's priests, Elijah aims to show the supremacy of monotheism over pagan polytheism. A man of firm and unflinching faith, Elijah constantly teaches that there is no god except the God of Israel, a statement backed up by the translation of His name, which means "My God is Jehovah."

See also: A Prophet in Hiding 124 ▪ Elijah and the Prophets of Baal 125

burning chariot divides him from Elisha. Indeed, it is more of a disappearance than a death, and he later returns to Earth, along with the prophet Moses (see pp. 234–35). The chariot of fire Elisha sees has connotations with God's heavenly host of angels, which further suggests that Elijah does not simply die, but joins the ranks of God's faithful in heaven.

When Elijah disappears, Elisha cries out and rips his garments in two, an action that is often a response to calamity in the Bible. He picks up Elijah's cloak and strikes the Jordan River with it. The waters part, just as they did for Elijah, and Elisha crosses the river on dry land. Prophets from Jericho witness the miracle and proclaim that "the spirit of Elijah is resting on Elisha" (2:15). They hail Elisha as Elijah's chosen successor.

Two contrasting leaders

Elijah and Elisha are both chosen by God, who empowers them to carry out miraculous deeds. Yet, their backgrounds could not

be more different. Elijah was born and raised in rural Gilead beyond the Jordan River, probably in a poor family, whereas Elisha is the son of a wealthy Israelite landowner.

While there is no doubting that Elijah has the harder task of the two in rekindling the Israelites' faith in God and turning them away from the god Baal, Elisha

competently carries on his legacy, counseling the rulers of the time and continuing to produce many more miracles in service to God. ▪

A fiery chariot carries Elijah to heaven in this 16th-century Russian icon. Although the Bible mentions horses of fire, the presence of angels, seen here, is not explicitly stated.

> Suddenly a chariot of fire and horses of fire appeared and separated the two of them, and Elijah went up to heaven in a whirlwind.
> **2 Kings 2:11**

SO JUDAH WENT INTO CAPTIVITY, AWAY FROM HER LAND

2 KINGS 25:21, THE FALL OF JERUSALEM

IN BRIEF

PASSAGE
2 Kings 24–25

THEME
Exile

SETTING
6th century BCE Jerusalem, central Judah.

KEY FIGURES
Nebuchadnezzar II The conquering King of Babylon, who invades Jerusalem.

Jehoiakim Puppet-king of Judah installed by the Egyptians from 609–597 BCE. Father and predecessor of Jehoiachin.

Jehoiachin King of Judah for three months in 598–597 BCE.

Zedekiah King of Judah from 597 BC up until the time of the Babylonian siege in 586 BCE. Uncle of Jehoiachin.

In 586 BCE, after a long siege, the Babylonians under King Nebuchadnezzar II, capture Jerusalem, holy city of the Israelites and capital of the kingdom of Judah. The utter destruction of both the city and the Temple of Solomon mark the start of a dark period for the Israelites: a punishment from God for their misdeeds. It is nearly 50 years before they are able to return and rebuild their city.

These dramatic events are related at the end of 2 Kings, a tumultuous book, which recounts a litany of bad rulers, catastrophe, and the ultimate loss of the two Jewish nations (the Assyrians had conquered the northern kingdom, Israel, in 722 BCE). Jerusalem's

See also: Entering the Promised Land 92–93 ▪ The Fall of Jericho 98–99 ▪ The Wisdom of Solomon 120–23 ▪ Rebuilding Jerusalem 133

The Two Nations

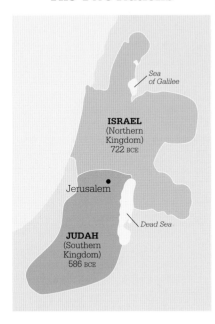

Sea of Galilee

ISRAEL
(Northern Kingdom)
722 BCE

Jerusalem

JUDAH
(Southern Kingdom)
586 BCE

Dead Sea

fortunes have ebbed and flowed over the centuries, but the death of the virtuous King Josiah while battling the Egyptians in 609 BCE prompts a dramatic downturn. Josiah is a great reformer and a devoutly religious man, who serves the Lord "with all his heart and with all his soul and with all his strength" (2 Kings 23:25). His successors fall short of this standard and their weak and impious actions have devastating consequences for Judah.

Power struggle

After Josiah's death, the kingdom of Judah becomes a pawn in the struggle between the warring nations of Egypt and Babylon. Jehoahaz, Josiah's son and heir, is deposed and imprisoned by the Egyptian pharaoh, who then installs Jehoiakim, a younger son of Josiah, on the throne of Judah

as his puppet. Egypt's power soon begins to wane, however, largely as a result of the threat posed by the Babylonians led by the conqueror Nebuchadnezzar II. He and his rampaging armies present a far greater danger to Jerusalem. As the Babylonian army approaches the walls of the holy city, Jehoiakim switches allegiances and pledges his support to Nebuchadnezzar in an attempt to appease him and persuade him to spare Jerusalem.

The arrangement works and for three years Jerusalem is unmolested. However, when a planned Babylonian invasion of Egypt fails, Jehoiakim rebels and incurs Nebuchadnezzar's wrath. In 598 BCE, the Babylonian armies attack Jerusalem and Jehoiakim then dies, possibly during the ensuing conflict.

The last days of Judah

Jehoiachin, the son of Jehoiakim, becomes the new king of Judah at only 18 years of age. He rules for just three months before Nebuchadnezzar and his armies besiege Jerusalem once more, forcing the young king to surrender. Although on this occasion he spares Jerusalem from destruction, Nebuchadnezzar carries off the king, all his family and officials, and a further 10,000 Israelites, marking the start of what is known as the Babylonian Exile or Babylonian Captivity. He also seizes treasures from the royal palace and the Temple of Solomon.

Nebuchadnezzar installs Jehoiachin's uncle, Zedekiah, on the throne of Judah, where "Only the poorest people of the land were left" (2 Kings 24:14). The Bible makes it explicitly clear that God is »

Assyria and the divided kingdom

Dating back as early as the 25th century BCE, Assyria was a huge empire and an amalgamation of numerous Middle Eastern states that continually changed in size and influence until its eventual collapse between 612 and 599 BCE. At its peak, Assyria stretched from the eastern Mediterranean to Iran, as well as into Egypt, Libya, and the Arabian Peninsula.

Assyria played a key part in Israelite history between 734 and 724 BCE, when the 10-tribe kingdom of northern Israel (called Israel) was conquered by several Assyrian monarchs and many of the inhabitants were taken captive. During this 10-year period – known as the Assyrian Exile – the groups exiled by Assyria became known as the Ten Lost Tribes of Israel as, unlike those in the Kingdom of Judah, the northern Israelite tribes were never allowed to return to their homeland.

Nebuchadnezzar II was an Assyrian King of Babylon who ruled from c.605–562 BCE. During this time, Assyria was incorporated into the Neo-Babylonian empire.

unhappy with his appointment, Zedekiah "did evil in the eyes of the Lord, just as Jehoiakim had done" (2 Kings 24:19). Zedekiah is just as bad as his predecessors and leads the holy city further away from God, into the hands of its oppressors.

After nine years of presiding over a ravaged Jerusalem, afflicted by chronic famine and shortages, Zedekiah rebels against Assyria with the help of the Egyptians. His actions are quickly countered by those of Nebuchadnezzar, who marches on Jerusalem and lays siege to the city for 18 months. Jerusalem falls into utter chaos, with the famine in the city so grave that parents eat their own children in order to survive. Finally, in July of 586 BCE, Jerusalem's walls are breached by the Babylonians. Zedekiah attempts to escape, but is captured and forced to watch the

murder of his children. The king's own eyes are then gouged out by the Babylonians, so that the last thing he ever sees is the death of his sons. Blind and defeated, he is taken to Babylon in chains.

Jerusalem destroyed

Over the following two months, Nebuchadnezzar orders a further deportation of the population of Judah and lays waste to Jerusalem. The city is completely destroyed, including the fortifications and the Temple of Solomon. The destruction of the Temple is especially significant. For nearly 400 years, the Temple had stood in the heart of Jerusalem as the ultimate symbol of the Israelite religion. Its destruction illustrates just how far the Israelites had strayed from God, and their failure to keep their covenant with Him. Having not heeded God's warnings,

The ancient city of Jerusalem lies burning after the Babylonian conquest in this engraving by 17th-century artist Jan Luyken. The people are led into exile as the city is destroyed.

they now faced exile from their devastated city and were subject to the rule of the Babylonians.

A vengeful God

Although Jerusalem lies in ruins and the vast majority of its population is deported to Babylon, there is evidence to confirm that other parts of Judah continued to be inhabited after the exile. With the loss of their holy city and Temple, those who remained must have wondered how all this could come to pass. Why would God allow a nation of idol-worshippers—the Babylonians—to overthrow His own people, who worshipped only the one true Lord? The only explanation was that Judah, and Israel before it, had neglected their worship of God. The Lord had repeatedly warned both nations that their ways were unjust and immoral, and they must repent of their own idol worship. He had made it clear that the penalty for failure to return to worship of Him alone would be exile.

The people of Judah had not changed their ways and now, as God warned in 2 Kings 21:12, a fearful judgment had come fulfilling the prophecies of Jeremiah (see pp.156–159). God's response to the Israelites' neglect follows a similar pattern to His treatment of Pharaoh in Exodus. In both cases, God delivers repeated warnings that are ignored. The judgment that follows is final.

As 2 Kings draws to a close, the situation is dire. The holy city is destroyed, the Temple has been obliterated, and all the most prominent members of Judah's society are in exile in Babylon. However, as if to offer a shred of hope after these harrowing events, 2 Kings ends with the

… Jerusalem will become a heap of rubble, the Temple hill a mound overgrown with thickets.
Micah 3:12

release of Jehoiachin from prison, when Amel-Marduk succeeds Nebuchadnezzar as king. Although still held in Babylon, Jehoiachin dines at the king's table and is even given a regular stipend.

Historical evidence
The biblical account of the fall of Jerusalem and the exile of the Judean people to Babylon largely corresponds with historical evidence. The narrative is corroborated by a wealth of archaeological findings and early accounts. These include a passage from the Babylonian Chronicles, a set of ancient tablets discovered in the 19th century that describes the sack of Jerusalem in 597 BCE, and also Jehoiachin's "rations tablets," which were unearthed from Nebuchadnezzar's royal archives during excavations in Babylon in the early 20th century. Evidence of the Babylonian rampage through central Judah in 588–586 BCE also includes pottery fragments, known as clay ostraca, and the world-renowned Lachish letters, a series of ancient Hebrew missives written in carbon ink on clay tablets, which were discovered during excavations at Tel Lachish in 1935.

The seismic events of the early 6th century BCE undoubtedly occurred as poor leadership and a difficult geographical position left the people of Judah vulnerable to their larger, more powerful neighbors. The Bible's message is clear about its cause, however. God's people strayed from His way and, as a result, were punished. ■

The failure of Sennacherib

The destruction of Jerusalem by Babylon's King Nebuchadnezzar II was not the first attempt to conquer Judah's holy city. Earlier in 2 Kings (18:17–35), the Assyrian King Sennacherib attempts to strike a deal with the people of Jerusalem that would allow him to take control of the city and become their ruler.

A hugely successful conqueror, Sennacherib has already colonized large areas of the Middle East and significantly expanded the Assyrian Empire. His reputation has made him arrogant, and he believes that taking Jerusalem will be a relatively simple undertaking. When making his proposal to the people of Judah, he blasphemes against God, saying that no god of any nation has ever been able to stand up to his might. Hezekiah, the king of Judah at that time, tells God of Sennacherib's heresy and his bold claims that he will take Jerusalem. He calls on God to deliver His people from Sennacherib and preserve the holy city. The angel of the Lord then goes into the Assyrian camp at night and strikes 185,000 Assyrian soldiers dead (2 Kings 19:35). Sennacherib is later murdered in suspicious circumstances by his own sons, and God is once more avenged.

I WILL GO TO THE KING ... IF I PERISH, I PERISH

ESTHER 4:16, QUEEN ESTHER

IN BRIEF

PASSAGE
Esther 1–10

THEME
Salvation from unlikely sources

SETTING
486–465 BCE During the reign of King Ahasuerus. The Persian capital city of Susa in modern-day Iran.

KEY FIGURES
Esther An orphaned Jew who becomes Queen of Persia.

Mordecai Esther's cousin and her only family.

King Ahasuerus King of Persia and husband of Esther. Probably the historical figure Xerxes I, known as Xerxes the Great

Haman The king's chief minister and Mordecai's sworn enemy.

The story of Esther is one of only two books in the Bible that makes no reference to God (the other is Song of Songs). The tale of a Jewish queen who speaks up to save her people, it was likely included to show how even a silent God causes good to triumph.

Esther becomes the wife of King Ahasuerus after he sets aside his previous wife, Queen Vashti, for refusing to appear before guests. A beautiful girl, Esther has been raised by a relative, Mordecai, but does not reveal her Jewish heritage to the king. The king is delighted with his wife and with Mordecai, who uncovers an assassination plot against him. Unfortunately, Mordecai offends the chief minister Haman, who vows to destroy all Jews and obtains a royal decree to murder and plunder, without telling the king whom he is targeting.

Mordecai asks the queen to intervene. She is reluctant, as it is punishable by death to approach the king, but the devout Mordecai believes God has placed Esther in her exalted position to do His work.

At a banquet, Esther reveals her heritage and pleads for her people, thus fulfilling her divine purpose. To her relief, the king turns his fury on Haman, who is executed.

Although the royal decree cannot be withdrawn, the king allows the Jews to defend themselves and no one can stand against them. This event is still commemorated as Purim, named after the Hebrew word for the lots (dice) used by Haman to decide when to kill the Jews. ∎

Who knows but that you have come to your royal position for such a time as this?
Esther 4:16

See also: Ruth and Naomi 108–09

HEAR US, OUR GOD, FOR WE ARE DESPISED

NEHEMIAH 4:4, REBUILDING JERUSALEM

Most scholars agree that Nehemiah's existence is rooted in historical fact. This great organizer and devout follower of God is credited with rebuilding the walls of Jerusalem, as well as continuing to revive the city and its people's worship of God.

While serving as the cup bearer to King Artaxerxes I, Nehemiah receives his sovereign's permission to return to his ancestral homeland of Jerusalem and rebuild the city's walls. On his arrival, he organizes the wall's restoration, but struggles to motivate the demoralized and divided Jewish people.

Faith restored

Nehemiah and the Jews are also opposed by many disparate groups: Arabs, Philistines, Ammonites, and Samaritans led by Sanballat the Horonite. Agreeing on nothing else but their opposition to the Jews, they hinder their work on the walls through insults, scorn, and terror.

Nehemiah turns to God, praying for Him to acknowledge everything His people have had to endure, and

The Jews hold weapons along with their tools as they rebuild the wall. This etching (1852–1860) by Julius Schnorr von Carolsfeld shows the threat of violence the Jews faced while working.

his faith is rewarded. The wall is rebuilt in just 52 days. Nehemiah then gathers everyone together to dedicate the newly defended city to God and hear Ezra read the Law of Moses. The people revive the feast of Sukkot, commemorating the Israelites' years in the wilderness. Jerusalem is now reborn, with Nehemiah having corrected the disobedience to God that caused the city to fall. ∎

See also: Entering the Promised Land 96–97 ▪ The Fall of Jerusalem 128–31

WISDOM
PROPHE

AND
TS

God gives Satan permission to **test Job's faithfulness** with a series of misfortunes.

↑

Collections of **wise sayings** provide advice for young persons setting out in the world.

↑

Israel, in the form of the "**Suffering Servant**," seeks comfort and hope in God.

↑

JOB
1–2:7

THE
PROVERBS

ISAIAH
52:13–53:12

THE
PSALMS

↓

Five books of 150 psalms express **praise and trust** in God.

SONG OF
SONGS

↓

The "beloved" and her companion ("He") **convey their love** for one another in sensual imagery.

JEREMIAH
1:4–9

↓

God chooses **Jeremiah** before he is even born to be a **prophet to the nations**.

Two of the most crucial, defining moments in Israelite history are the "exile," when the Israelites were forced to leave their homes in Canaan and live in foreign lands, and the "return." The exile refers to several war-induced migrations, especially the ones resulting from the Assyrian conquest of Northern Israel in 722 BCE and the Babylonian invasion of Judah in 597 BCE.

In 538 BCE, Persia's King Darius I allowed the Israelites to return home. As they rebuilt the Temple, they reflected upon their identity as God's people. Questions arose about why God would allow them to endure such suffering, then reprieve them, and what this signified about their relationship with the divine. To process these conundrums, they wrote down, edited, and collected much of the Hebrew Bible, including the poetical and wisdom literature and the books of the prophets.

An eternal quest

The poetical and wisdom literature addresses the question of how one should interact with God and the world. These writings are particularly captivating because they leave the reader without a singular conclusion; instead, they contain a chorus of responses about who God is and how one should live. Psalms focuses on the nature of the divine—as creator, provider, and rescuer—and the human response: worship. The book includes hundreds of poems, many of which are praises to God or songs of thanksgiving for divine creation and provision. Other poems are dark and sorrowful, crying out to God for help in times of trouble. Psalms provides an array of expression, validating the range of human emotions experienced by the Israelites in times of exile and return.

The mystery of why bad things happen to good people is set out in the Book of Job, the account of a blameless man who loses everything. The story creates a murky picture of how God interacts with a being called the adversary, or Satan, who may share responsibility with God for undeserved suffering.

In contrast, Proverbs and Song of Songs focus on the practicalities and pleasures of earthly life. Proverbs provides commonsensical advice on how to behave, learn, and prosper, with wisdom exalted as a treasure to be sought above all

The **fall of Jerusalem** to the Babylonians is mourned in five poems, expressing anger toward God.

LAMENTATIONS 1–5

God **shuts the mouths of the lions** when the **Prophet Daniel** is thrown into a lions' den.

DANIEL 6:22

The **Prophet Micah** fulminates against the **sinful behavior** of the citizens of Judah.

MICAH 3:1–12

EZEKIEL 37:10

The **Prophet Ezekiel** has a **vision** in which a **vast army arises** from the Valley of Dried Bones.

JONAH 1:17–2:9

God sends a fish to swallow the **Prophet Jonah**, who has **disobeyed His command** to preach to the Ninevites.

ZEPHANIAH 1–3:5

The **Prophet Zephaniah** calls on the Israelites to **repent** and warns of the coming **"Day of the Lord."**

---

else, while Song of Songs is joyful love poetry, replete with erotic imagery and descriptions of physical intimacy. Ecclesiastes, on the other hand, asks philosophical questions about the meaning of life. The author wonders at the purpose of labor and education when, ultimately, everyone dies. Nevertheless, it ends with a thread that gathers the poetical and wisdom literature together: regardless of existential realities, one must always obey God.

Major and Minor Prophets

In the Prophetic Books, the Bible returns to the theme of suffering, which is viewed as retributive punishment for Israel and Judah's sins. The prophets warn the people that if they do not follow God's laws, enemies will destroy them,

all of which happened when Assyria and Babylon came to power. Yet, during the exile, the possibility of return became real, and themes of hope and restoration begin to infiltrate the prophetic texts. The Major Prophets (Isaiah, Jeremiah, Ezekiel, and Daniel) and Lamentations contain an expectation that God will dwell among the people, love them forever, and bring them home to a new Jerusalem in the future. Daniel exemplifies what it means to act faithfully as a Jew despite constant foreign opposition.

The same themes of doom and hope are explored in the Minor Prophets, while also emphasizing commitment to God. Jonah relays the message that God accepts all those who repent and do justice, even if they are not Israelites. Yet

not all Gentiles are portrayed positively. God's threat to evil foreign powers is prominent in apocalyptic literature, and its emphasis on "the Day of the Lord," a terrifying end of the world when God will judge the wicked and reward the righteous, appears in books such as Joel, Micah, Zephaniah, and Malachi.

The idea of the Day of the Lord was later paired with a Messianic expectation that the earth will one day be ruled by God, and Israel will once again be a united kingdom in harmony with its neighbors and the divine. Many scholars believe Christians reordered the canon so that the prophets would be placed immediately before the New Testament Gospels, which used prophetic texts to support the claim that Jesus was the Messiah. ■

THE LORD IS MY SHEPHERD, I LACK NOTHING

PSALM 23:1, THE PSALMS

IN BRIEF

PASSAGE
The Psalms

THEME
The prayers of the faithful

SETTING
From 10th century BCE In the First and Second Temples of Jerusalem.

KEY FIGURES
David The second king of Israel and Judah in the 10th and 9th century BCE. An enthusiastic sponsor of singers and musicians, he was known as the "hero of Israel's songs" (2 Samuel 23:1).

Asaph A Levite, appointed by David as one of the chief musicians before the Ark of the Covenant in Jerusalem. Thought to have founded a school or guild of temple singers and musicians, known as the "sons of Asaph."

The Book of Psalms as we know it probably dates from the 6th century BCE, after the Jews returned from the Babylonian exile. It was effectively a hymn book for Israel, used in the liturgy of the Second Temple, where Psalms would have been sung to an accompaniment of lyres, harps, and cymbals.

The Psalms can be seen as the human side of a dialogue between Israel and its God. Often they are brimming with positivity, as in the ending of Psalm 23: "Surely your goodness and love will follow me all the days of my life, and I will dwell in the house of the Lord forever." At other times, feelings are bleaker and more raw: "You have put me in the lowest pit, in the darkest depths," complains the writer of Psalm 88. This broad emotional variance allows the book to cover a range of experiences relating to religious life.

Origins and usage

Like all hymn books, the Book of Psalms draws on earlier collections, many of them already hundreds of years old. Some Psalms bear

An illustration of King David marks the initial at the beginning of Psalm 1. This beautifully detailed illuminated manuscript was made in around 1450 by Leonardo Bellini.

marked resemblance to hymns used by other Near Eastern peoples—for example, Psalm 104, which has parallels with the Great Hymn to the Egyptian sun god Aten. This is more likely to be because certain types of hymns were common across the various Near Eastern religions than because one culture consciously

See also: David and Goliath 116–17 ▪ The Nature of God 144–45 ▪ Proverbs 148–51 ▪ Song of Songs 152–53 ▪ Parables of Jesus 214–15

Why are you downcast,
O my soul?
Why so disturbed within me?
Put your hope in God,
for I will yet praise him,
my Savior and my God.
Psalm 42:5

plagiarized hymns from another. Many of the common Psalm forms were also used in Babylonian and Egyptian liturgies.

Clues to the earlier collections from which the Jewish Book of Psalms was drawn can be found in the superscriptions at the top of some of the Psalms. There are the Psalms of Asaph, for example, which possibly emerged from a tradition associated with Asaph, son of Berechiah, appointed as a temple singer under King David. Another group are the Songs of Ascent, which may have been used by pilgrims to Jerusalem as they climbed the Temple Mount. Although King David is known to have composed songs, the collection labeled Psalms of David was almost certainly inspired by him and events in his life rather than actually written by him.

It is hard to confirm any exact dates for the Psalms, but scholars emphasize their link with early Temple worship before and after the exile, and traditional Jewish festivals—especially those in the fall before the harvest. It is likely that at least some of these songs and hymns were composed specifically for festival use and would have played a crucial part in the ritual life of early Jews.

Thematic groupings

The 150 Psalms are divided into five books—possibly to reflect the structure of the Pentateuch—and each book concludes with a doxology, a short formula of praise, usually starting: "Praise be to the Lord …" They contain a variety of styles and themes. Many are about royal events related to the reign of King David—73 in total bear his name—while others are more prophetic in nature, or impart an obvious moral lesson. Side by side with grand hymns of glory and devotion sit the more somber Psalms, often of individual or communal lamentation. In fact, laments constitute a major portion of the Psalms—around 40 of the total 150. They almost always conclude in trust and praise, but in their initial forthrightness

I love you, O Lord,
my strength. The Lord
is my rock, my fortress
and my deliverer;
my God is my rock,
in whom I take refuge.
Psalm 18:1–2

they say much about the heartfelt directness and honesty of Israel's liturgical life.

Crying out to God

The causes of lament vary from betrayal to imprisonment and sickness. They are often on behalf of a specific figure, who typically plunges straight into his complaint. "How long, Lord?" is Psalm 13's exasperated opening. "Will you »

Hebrew poetry

Almost a third of the Hebrew Bible is poetry. The narrative books are interspersed with poetic passages; large parts of the prophetic books are in verse; and most or all of Proverbs, Lamentations, Job, and the Psalms are poetry. Meter, as it is known in the Western tradition, does not exist in Hebrew poetry, nor does rhyme. Instead, its key building blocks are short lines in pairs, as, for example, in the opening of Psalm 24: "The earth is the Lord's, and everything in it, the world, and all who live in it." The second line often repeats the meaning of the first, to create a sense of balance or symmetry. The effect is also cumulative, with the second line amplifying the scope and resonance of the first. Another device in Hebrew poetry—one that inevitably gets lost in the translation—is the acrostic, in which each line or group of lines begins with a successive letter of the Hebrew alphabet. Nine psalms are organized in this way, notably Psalm 119.

forget me for ever? How long will you hide your face from me?" In this case the psalmist's troubles stem from the activities of an enemy. Having stated the complaint, the psalmist then makes a petition: "Look on me and answer, Lord my God. Give light to my eyes"—the light of restored vitality and joy. To add persuasive power to the petition, he gives reasons for God to act: if God fails to help him, his enemies will say they have overcome the psalmist, which may reflect badly on his God. Having now unburdened himself, the writer of Psalm 13, as in many of the other lament Psalms, switches somewhat abruptly to praise, remarking, "But I trust in your unfailing love; my heart rejoices in your salvation."

One possible reason for this sudden change of tone may lie in the context of temple worship. The psalmist's complaint and petition may have been part of a dialogue with a priest or temple official who, speaking in God's name, then pronounced an oracle telling him to go in peace, assured that God had heard his prayer. Whatever the reason, the writer concludes that God "has been good to me."

Historical laments

Other Psalms are of communal lament, many arising out of the humiliation of defeat. For the final editors of the Psalms, no defeat was more recent or searing than the destruction of Jerusalem and its temple by the Babylonians in 587 BCE. Psalm 79, one of a small number of Psalms emerging from that experience, opens with a description of the disaster: "O God, the nations have invaded your inheritance; they have defiled your holy Temple, they have reduced Jerusalem to rubble. They have left the dead bodies of your servants

> By the rivers of Babylon we sat and wept when we remembered Zion. There on the poplars we hung our harps, for there our captors asked us for songs.
> **Psalm 137:1–3**

as food for the birds of the sky, the flesh of your own people for the animals of the wild."

It continues with a mingling of praise, repentance, and anguished petitions for salvation, justice, even vengeance: "Pay back into the laps of our neighbors seven times the contempt they have hurled at you, Lord." Elsewhere, the desire for revenge burns most appallingly in another psalm of the exile, Psalm 137. Its conclusion is a howl of bloodthirsty rage: "Daughter Babylon, doomed to destruction, happy is the one who repays you for what you have done to us. Happy is the one who seizes your infants and dashes them against the rocks."

Joyous Psalms

Psalms written in the light of an answered prayer are usually more jubilant. Typically, they tell or suggest the whole story:

Hymns are sung at the Sunday celebration at the Celestial Church of Christ, Missessinto, in Benin, Africa. Psalms have been used in devotional worship since the early Church.

Psalms and their authors	
Psalms 1, 2, 10, 33, 43, 66, 67, 71, 91–100, 102, 104–07, 111–18, 119, 120, 121, 123, 125, 126, 128–30, 132, 134–37, 146–50	**Unknown**
Psalms 3–9, 11–32, 34–41, 51–65, 68–70, 86, 101, 103, 108–10, 122, 124, 131, 133, 138–45	**David**
Psalms 42, 44–49, 84–85, 87	**Sons of Korah**
Psalms 50, 73–83	**Asaph**
Psalms 72, 127	**Solomon**
Psalm 88	**Sons of Korah and Heman**
Psalm 89	**Ethan the Ezrahite**
Psalm 90	**Moses**

A shepherd and his flock

The image of a leader as a shepherd goes back to the 3rd millennium BCE when the kings of Sumer in Mesopotamia described themselves as shepherds of their people. In societies where herders were part of everyday life, it was an obvious comparison to make, and other nations followed this example.

For the Israelites, David was the archetypal shepherd-king, who literally started life as a shepherd. But above him was the one who fulfilled that role supremely: God (as stated in Psalm 23). In the 6th century BCE, during the Babylonian Exile, the prophet Ezekiel used the imagery of a shepherd in a furious tirade against Israel's leadership: "Woe to the shepherds of Israel who only take care of themselves! … you do not take care of the flock." Jesus continued the tradition, describing the crowds who followed Him as "like sheep without a shepherd," and later referring to himself as a "good shepherd [who] lays down His life for the sheep." The image lives on to this day in the word "pastor," Latin for "shepherd."

the trouble the psalmist was suffering, how he made a lament to God, and how God wonderfully intervened. "I will exalt you, Lord," begins Psalm 30, "for you lifted me out the depths and did not let my enemies gloat over me." Despite the reference to his enemies, the psalmist's distress seems to have been a sickness that brought him close to death. He cried to God for help, and God healed him, sparing him "from going down into the pit." The conclusion here is a shout of praise and thanksgiving: "You turned my wailing into dancing; you removed my sackcloth and clothed me with joy, that my heart may sing your praises and not be silent."

Songs of praise

Hymns of collective praise are among the most majestic of the Psalms. They tend to have the simplest structures: a summons to praise God, followed by reasons for that praise. "Praise the Lord, all you nations; extol him, all you peoples," the shortest psalm of all, Psalm 117, commands: "For great is His love toward us, and the faithfulness of the Lord endures forever." In other cases, the opening summons leads to a list of God's interventions on Israel's behalf.

Perhaps the most beautiful Psalms are the songs of creation, such as Psalm 104, which elicit praise by extolling the creator-God. He is the God who "makes the clouds His chariot and rides on the wings of the wind." Not only does creation reflect His splendor, but also His provision for humankind: "He makes grass grow for the cattle, and plants for people to cultivate— bringing forth food from the earth."

What is remarkable about the Psalms is the energy and feeling behind the words. Whether they are praising or petitioning God, they each show a very human side of the Bible, where people are unafraid to confess their multifaceted emotions to a benevolent Lord. ■

FROM EVERLASTING TO EVERLASTING YOU ARE GOD
PSALM 90:2, THE NATURE OF GOD

IN BRIEF

PASSAGE
Psalm 90

THEME
God's nature

SETTING
The universe All of which is created by God.

KEY FIGURES
Moses God's servant, to whom Psalm 90 is attributed.

Unlike any other ancient Near Eastern religion, the Israelite one had no family tree of the divine or account of how God came into being. The first verse of the Bible simply assumes God as creator of the world, a source of being beyond whom there is no other: "In the beginning God created the heavens and the earth."

Psalm 90—which the Bible attributes to "Moses the man of God"—picks up this concept: "Before the mountains were born or you brought forth the earth and the world, from everlasting to everlasting you are God." The sentiment behind the phrase "everlasting to everlasting" is repeated in many of the names given to God by his followers. He is "Alpha and Omega," the first and last letters of the Greek alphabet. He is *kadosh*, or holy, in Hebrew, meaning transcendent, beyond and above all normal experience.

Yet He is not cut off from humanity in some other realm. His *kavod,* glory, dwells within his creation, pervading and sustaining it—which is perhaps why, in Psalm 90, the author tells God: "Lord, you have been our dwelling place" (Psalm 90:1). The prophet Isaiah combines these two concepts in an exclamation of wonder: "Holy, holy, holy is the Lord Almighty; the whole earth is full of his glory" (Isaiah 6:3).

Wrathful God
Psalm 90 also teaches us more about the wrathful nature of God, as experienced by the ancient

God's glory dwells in the physical realm, according to Isaiah. As the creator of the vast and beautiful world that His people inhabit, Earth itself becomes a symbol of His might.

See also: Only One God 90–91 ▪ The Psalms 138–43 ▪ The Lord's Prayer 212–13

The names and nature of God

Judaism	✡	The Jewish tradition has many names for God, which recognize different attributes: from *shaddai* (judge) to *kano* (jealous) to *tzevaot* (one who battles the wicked).
Christianity	✝	The New Testament places a greater emphasis on calling God "Father," and Christians see God as having this intimate, paternal role in their lives.
Islam	☪	Muslims use the name *Allah*, which simply means "the one God." The belief that there is no other God but God ("*la ilaha ilallah*") is the central tenet of the Islamic faith.

Israelites. The prayer emphasizes the greatness of His anger: "If only we knew the power of your anger! Your wrath is as great as the fear that is your due" (Psalm 90:11). The author describes the people as fearing God's wrath above all else: "We are consumed by your anger and terrified by your indignation" (Psalm 90:7).

Collaborative nature

Relationships are at the heart of God's being. Even in the divine realm, He appears to enjoy some kind of companionship. There is a plural, for example, in the first creation account: "Let *us* make man in *our* image" (Genesis 2:26–28). From humans, God appears to seek collaboration, dialogue, and even friendship. His actions are responses to people's behavior or appeals. "I have heard them crying out," he tells Moses at the burning bush, "so I have come down to rescue them." God chooses a human, Moses, to carry out the rescue of his people, allowing God to work with and through him.

Unavoidably, the relationship brings conflict. God does not hesitate to punish His chosen people when they stray from obedience. Still, as Psalm 90 attests, God is capable of compassion: "Satisfy us … with your unfailing love, that we may sing for joy" (90:14). Although the relationship between God and His people sometimes breaks down, God loves His people, and is always working to repair it. ▪

The Lord is near to all who call on Him, to all who call on Him in truth. He fulfills the desires of those who fear Him; He hears their cry and saves them.
Psalm 145:18–19

An emotional God

The biblical writers are not afraid to give God certain human attributes, including emotions. The first chapter of Genesis shows God feeling satisfaction: "God saw all that He had made, and it was very good." A few chapters later, this joy turned to regret and grief. Faced with human corruption before the Flood, the "Lord was grieved that He had made man … His heart was filled with pain."

Expressions of God's love are as frequent in the Bible as his anger: the prophet Amos describes a fiery display of God's revulsion at rituals performed without holiness of heart. "I despise your religious feasts; I cannot stand your assemblies." However, He is shown to be open to changing His mind when His heart is appealed to: "My heart is changed within me," God tells the prophet Hosea; "all my compassion is aroused. I will not carry out my fierce anger."

In Psalm 90, Moses, depicted here in a sculpture by Michelangelo in Rome's San Pietro in Vicoli basilica, describes God's compassion and anger, as well as his omnipotence.

HAVE YOU CONSIDERED MY SERVANT JOB? THERE IS NO ONE ON EARTH LIKE HIM
JOB 2:3, THE SUFFERING OF JOB

IN BRIEF

PASSAGE
Job 1–42

THEME
The nature of suffering

SETTING
c.2000–1000 BCE Southern Edom or northern Arabia.

KEY FIGURES
Job A devoted servant of God, who is prosperous, fortunate, and righteous, yet faces terrible suffering at the hands of both Satan and God.

Bildad, Eliphaz, and Zophar Three of Job's friends, who come to comfort and debate with him.

Satan An adversary of God and His angels. He questions Job's constancy and offers God a bet on his faithfulness.

The Book of Job is one of the most engaging books of the Bible, as it deals in an accessible and dramatic way, using poetry and prose, with one of the great philosophical challenges of the Bible—if God is ethical, why do bad things happen to good people? Attempts to answer this question are called "theodicy."

Job is a shining example of God's perfect servant. He is "blameless and upright; he feared God and shunned evil" (Job 1:1).

Satan torments Job in this Gothic stained-glass window from the former Dominican Church of Strasbourg. Job's skin is shown covered in the painful sores he endures as part of his trials.

He is also blessed with numerous children, livestock, and servants. However, his entire life soon falls apart. One day, when God is holding court in heaven, he is attended by Satan, "the adversary." They discuss Job, whom God describes as uniquely faithful. Satan disagrees, contending that Job is only loyal because God protects him and gives him everything he wants. He makes a bet with God that if he is permitted to take away all of Job's possessions, Job will lose faith and curse God. This bet serves to illustrate the wider theme of the Book of Job: that goodness is hollow and worthless if it is only in search of reward.

Tests of faith

A series of disasters then befall Job. He first discovers that his oxen and donkeys have all been taken. Next, all his sheep perish in a fire. Third, his camels are stolen during an army raid. By this time, all his servants but one have perished. Finally, Job learns that a house has collapsed on all ten of his children and they have also died. Job is distraught, but refuses to curse God. In fact, such is the extent of his faith that he still

See also: The Temptations of Christ 198–99 ▪ The Way of Love 296–97

Characteristics of Satan in the Old Testament

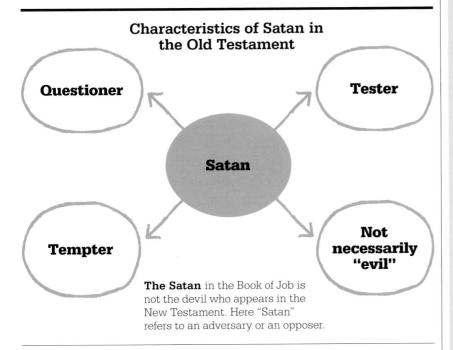

Questioner

Tester

Satan

Tempter

Not necessarily "evil"

The Satan in the Book of Job is not the devil who appears in the New Testament. Here "Satan" refers to an adversary or an opposer.

The Book of Job

There are very few clues to the author of the Book of Job, or to the time of its composition, but scholars place Job as living sometime between 2000 and 1000 BCE. It is likely that the book was written by an Israelite, due to the use of the term "Yahweh" for God. Jewish tradition attributes the book to Moses.

Whoever the author might be, it seems that the purpose of Job's book is not to give a true historical account of the man's life. Instead of writing from a purely theological perspective, the author takes a closer, sympathetic approach to Job's story, and therefore deals with the question of why humans suffer on a personal level.

When judged against the conventional criteria of what it means to be faithful, Job is one of the finest human beings depicted in the Bible— perhaps purposefully and hyperbolically good as he continues to prevail in his faith. The almost superhuman nature of his resolve, with his exemplary righteousness and strong convictions, has even given rise to the modern idiom of "having the patience of Job."

acknowledges God in his misery. The adversary does not easily give up on his bet. This time, he challenges God to harm Job in person. God duly afflicts Job with sores from head to toe. The pain is great, and Job scrapes his skin with broken pottery and sits in a pile of ashes, possibly in grief or to signal his repentance. Appalled by his suffering, Job's wife urges him to curse God and die. However, still Job will not speak ill of the Lord.

Three of Job's friends, Eliphaz, Zophar, and Bildad, arrive to comfort Job. The four companions discuss the situation, and conclude that Job must have sinned greatly to have incurred God's wrath to such a degree. The narrative then becomes more philosophical, challenging the long-standing wisdom of the time that prosperity was an indication of piety and suffering a punishment for sin. Job insists that he has not sinned and

challenges God to a fair trial. God appears to him and asks a series of questions, but Job realizes that his human brain is no match for God's wisdom and repents. In light of Job's unbreakable faith, God restores everything that Job had possessed, and more, blessing "the latter part of Job's life more than the former part" (42:12).

The mysteries of life

While the Bible often offers clear-cut solutions to vexing questions, Job presents a challenging debate on the purpose of suffering. The book serves to illustrate that suffering is a natural component of human life, and that it is how the righteous respond to that suffering that defines the strength of their faith. Ultimately, Job accepts that the mysteries of the divine, and by extension the reasoning behind suffering, are beyond human comprehension. ▪

BLESSED IS THE ONE WHO TRUSTS IN THE LORD

PROVERBS 16:20, PROVERBS

The book of Proverbs is a book of advice, or wisdom literature, which seeks to instill "knowledge and discretion" (1:4) in young men about to forge their ways in the world. The aim is that such men will not only live a fulfilling and prosperous life, but also a moral one. While the book of Proverbs makes it clear from the outset that the "fear of the Lord is the beginning of knowledge" (1:7), much of the book's focus is not directly on God, but on the choices and dilemmas faced in daily living.

The pragmatic advice comes in the form of short admonishments and pithy encouragements. A warning against laziness, for

See also: The Ten Commandments 78–83 ▪ The Wisdom of Solomon 120–23 ▪ Sermon on the Mount 204–09 ▪ The Golden Rule 210–11 ▪ Parables of Jesus 214–15

example, says: "Go to the ant, you sluggard; consider its ways and be wise!" (Proverbs 6:6). Many of the book's maxims date back millennia, and a number come from outside the Israelite tradition—some, for example, are borrowed from Egyptian wisdom literature.

Historical collection

Authorship of much of the book of Proverbs is attributed to King Solomon, although this is unlikely. It is more probable that the Proverbs were gathered into collections at various times in Israelite history and then copied at the Judean court of King Hezekiah in the late 8th century BCE. In view of the customs mentioned and the pure monotheism espoused by the text, the book as it appears today almost certainly dates from the late 6th century or 5th century BCE, after the Judeans had returned from exile in Babylon.

The scribes organized Proverbs into five sections with four short appendices at the end. The first section or prologue (chapters 1–9) most obviously bears the imprint of

Idleness is one of many vices that the proverbs warn against. In Proverb 6, sluggards are advised to follow the productive ways of the ant.

the post-Exile period, although it is labeled "The Proverbs of Solomon." Next comes a long section (10:1–22:16) of short, mostly two-line proverbs, attributed to Solomon, and then the section entitled "the sayings of the wise" (22:17–24:22), which shows Egyptian influence.

This is followed by another short section on the same theme (24:23–34), and then another longer section (chapters 25–29) attributed to Solomon. The appendices make up the last two chapters and conclude with a famous poem extolling the virtues of "The Wife of Noble Character" (see p. 151).

Twin strands

Wisdom in Proverbs is delivered through two voices. One is that of an elder—a parent, teacher, or sage—giving instruction to a younger person. The book's very first exhortation is in this style: "Listen, my son, to your father's instruction and do not forsake your mother's teaching" (1:8). The »

Wisdom literature

Proverbs, along with the Books of Job and Ecclesiastes, belongs to a well-established genre of the ancient Near East: wisdom writing. Consisting of maxims and tales that reflect upon life wisely lived, this body of literature has deep roots. One of the oldest known works is the Maxims of Ptahhotep, from the end of the 3rd millennium BCE, which details the instructions of a vizier to his son. The Instruction of Amenemopet—

written down around 1000 BCE but probably older than that—also follows a similar format. The section in Proverbs entitled "sayings of the wise" is clearly modeled on Amenemopet's maxims and includes some that are almost identical. Similarities also exist with a Mesopotamian work: the Story of Ahikar. The tale of a chief counselor at the Assyrian court, it is peppered with wise sayings. The sayings include an earlier version of the Bible's famous "spare the rod, spoil the child" proverb.

figure who conveys teaching is Wisdom, personified as a woman. "Out in the open Wisdom calls aloud, in the street, she raises her voice in the public square" (1:20), the first proverb in the book relates.

There is a contrast in tone between the two strands. While the maxims of the elder, the bulk of the book, tend to appeal to reason

St. Sophia the divine wisdom is depicted in this 16th-century Russian icon. In some forms of Christianity, her figure of personified wisdom is seen as the second part of the Holy Trinity.

and good sense, the teachings of personified Wisdom are more emotive, approaching at times the admonishing tones of the biblical prophet: "How long will you who are simple love your simple ways?" Wisdom cries out. "How long will mockers delight in mockery and fools hate knowledge?" (1:22).

Teaching in the proverbs is mostly presented in one of two forms: the instruction and the saying. Used in the first nine chapters, the former develops an idea—the perils of idleness, for example—in a poetic paragraph

a few lines long. The saying, the form that dominates most later chapters, is more succinct. It is a statement, usually of two lines, that presents a truth in a way intended to stay in the mind, often by virtue of a paradox. Possibly the most famous proverb of all works like this: "Whoever spares the rod hates their children, but the one who loves their children is careful to discipline them" (13:24).

A variation on the paradox is the numerical proverb, which lists items that have something in common and then ends with an ironic twist. One example is this reflection: "There are three things that are too amazing for me, four that I do not understand: the way of an eagle in the sky, the way of a snake on a rock, the way of a ship on the high seas, and the way of a man with a young woman" (30:19).

Domestic focus

Perhaps because of its place within the wider wisdom tradition of the Near East, the Book of Proverbs differs from much of the rest of the Hebrew Bible in that it never mentions Israel's history. Its approach is for the most part

Blessed are those who find wisdom, those who gain understanding, for she is more profitable than silver and yields better returns than gold.
Proverbs 3:13–14

Familiar Proverbs

"Open your mouth
for the mute, for the rights
of all who are destitute."
Proverbs 31:8
*Help those who cannot
help themselves.*

"Pride goes before
destruction, a haughty
spirit before a fall."
Proverbs 16.18
*Be humble before
the Lord.*

"Ponder the path of
your feet; then all your
ways will be sure."
Proverbs 4:26
*Know the road you
are taking.*

"Better a patient
person than a warrior,
one with self-control than
one who takes a city."
Proverbs 16:32
*Seek inner peace before
the peace of others.*

observational. Proverbs is clear that God lies at the heart of reality and about the need to be humble as a result. "Trust in the Lord with all your heart and lean not on your own understanding" (3:5) is one of its admonitions. Wisdom, it suggests, is learned through God. The maxims it offers on human affairs focus on areas such as family, anger, poverty, and righteousness, but cannot be truly heeded without fear of the Lord.

Wisdom incarnate
Proverbs makes intriguing claims about God and heaven in the voice of personified Wisdom. She speaks of how she is "the first of His works" (8:22), continuing: "I was there when He set the heavens in place" (8:27). She even claims to have been a craftsperson at God's side during creation.

This idea would be later picked up and developed by New Testament writers, notably the author of John's Gospel. He sets out the idea of the Logos, or Word, who "was with God in the beginning," through whom "all things were made" and who became incarnate as Jesus. Proverbs' personified Wisdom contributed to the idea of God's wisdom incarnate being a part of the Holy Trinity, leading to the establishment of the later doctrine of Jesus's incarnation (see pp. 298–99). ■

Eshet Hayil

Proverbs' final half chapter is an acrostic poem—one in which each stanza begins with a succeeding letter of the Hebrew alphabet—extolling the virtues of a woman of "valor" or "noble character." *Eshet Hayil* in Hebrew, this woman is the perfect wife and mother, whose "worth is far more than rubies" (31:10). By no means confined to the home, she works hard, has a good business head, and is generous to the poor. Presiding over her household with dignity, she brings honor to her husband, who finds himself "respected at the city gate, where he takes his seat among the elders of the land" (31:23).

The portrait the Eshet Hayil creates has resonated over the centuries, and in devout Jewish households it is often sung or recited at the start of the Kiddush, the Friday evening ceremony that ushers in the Sabbath. According to the mystical kabbalistic tradition of Judaism, it refers to God's Shekhinah, or divine presence, associated with a maternal, nurturing role. In other interpretations, it can be seen more simply as the family paying tribute to the mother. The passage that proceeds the acrostic narrates the lessons King Lemuel has received from his mother, so the poem may also be his own glorifying eulogy for her in return. In some households the Eshet Hayil is balanced with a recital of Psalm 112: "Blessed are those who fear the Lord, who find great delight in his commands."

I AM MY BELOVED'S ... MY BELOVED IS MINE.

6:3, SONG OF SONGS

IN BRIEF

PASSAGE
Song of Songs 6:3

THEME
God's love for His people

SETTING
c.970–930 BCE, Solomon's kingdom

KEY FIGURES
He An unspecified king. It could be Solomon himself, but it is not clear whether he wrote the poem or if it is about him.

She A dark-skinned woman and the king's new bride, sometimes referred to as "Shulammite" – either the female form of "Solomon" or possibly a reference to her place of origin.

Friends An unnamed chorus of commentators.

Song of Songs is one of the Bible's sweetest sections: a paean to marital ardor. The book opens with the line "Solomon's Song of Songs" and goes on to mention the ancient Israelite king six more times (Song of Songs 1:5; 3:7; 3:9; 3:11; 8:11–12), leading some scholars to believe that the book was penned by Solomon himself. This theory is supported by 1 Kings 4:32, which says that Solomon composed 1,005 songs. Others believe the link with Solomon is an editorial intervention to enhance the status of the poems.

Whoever the author was, Song of Songs is considered to be a masterpiece of erotic literature that captures the yearning of love. It is a conversation between "He" (the "king") and "She" (a woman sometimes referred to as Shulammite). The couple are occasionally interrupted by interjections from "friends," who perform the role of an audience.

Celebration of sexuality

Early in the piece, the woman entreats the king to take her to his bedchambers. Explicit

Sensuality in Song of Songs

"Let him kiss me with the kisses of his mouth" (1:1). From the opening verse of Song of Songs, sex, love, and the senses are at its heart. Throughout the book the narrators—the Beloved and her companion, the Lover—convey their love for one another with sensual imagery: perfumes incomparable to her smell, his kisses more delightful than wine, her breasts like clusters of fruit, his fruit sweet to her taste. This tantalizing imagery brings into vivid clarity the tension and

longing that exists between the two narrators, while the multiple references to vineyards and wine help build the impression of lovers who are intoxicated with one another. The image of the vineyard in bloom is just one of many metaphors drawn from nature. Twenty-five different plants, many fruit or perfume-bearing, are mentioned in the Songs, underlining the relationship between nature and fertility and sexual desire.

See also: The Psalms 138–43 ▪ Proverbs 148–51 ▪ The Way of Love 296–97

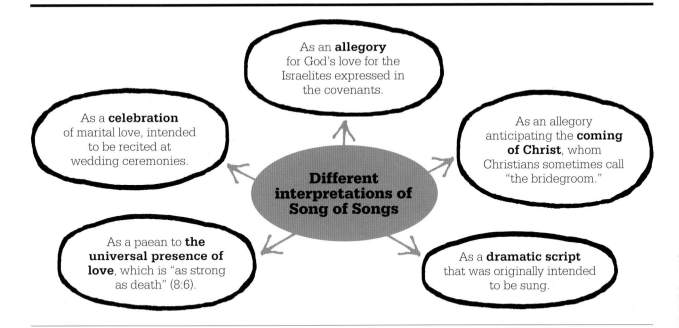

As an **allegory** for God's love for the Israelites expressed in the covenants.

As a **celebration** of marital love, intended to be recited at wedding ceremonies.

Different interpretations of Song of Songs

As an allegory anticipating the **coming of Christ**, whom Christians sometimes call "the bridegroom."

As a paean to **the universal presence of love**, which is "as strong as death" (8:6).

As a **dramatic script** that was originally intended to be sung.

sexual references follow, with the woman's body compared to a palm tree, her neck a rounded goblet, her breasts like twin fawns of a gazelle. Subsequent analogies and a series of similarly explicit metaphors make it clear that sexual love is the principal subject of discussion. Some of these comparisons may be amusing to a modern audience: 6:6, for example, says: "Your teeth are like a flock of sheep, coming up from the washing. Each has its twin, not one of them is missing."

In the course of the book, the woman describes herself to the "daughters of Jerusalem," likening her dark skin to the "tents of Kadar" and the "curtains of Solomon," while the king describes his lover's great beauty and her visits to him. The book is further embellished by the sighting of a royal wedding procession and third-party accounts of the woman's beauty.

Interpreting the Song

The meaning and purpose of Song of Songs is a matter of debate. Rabbi Saadia Gaon al-Fayyumi, a medieval Jewish commentator, described the book as resembling "locks to which the keys have been lost." God is not mentioned once in the poem. However, some commentators believe that the "king" in the poem symbolizes God, and the woman the Israelites, and what appears to be an erotic ode is an allegorical piece describing God's love for Israel. At the same time, Christians have viewed the song as a celebration of the love of Jesus for the Church. ▪

A bride and groom exchange vows during an Armenian wedding. Viewed by many as an ode to physical love within marriage, the Song of Songs is often chosen as a reading at weddings.

Many waters cannot quench love; rivers cannot sweep it away.
Song of Songs 8:7

SURELY HE TOOK UP OUR INFIRMITIES AND CARRIED OUR SORROWS

ISAIAH 53:4, THE SUFFERING SERVANT

IN BRIEF

PASSAGE
Isaiah 40–55

THEME
Suffering

SETTING
6th century BCE
The Babylonian empire, which is under threat from the Persians led by King Cyrus.

KEY FIGURES
The Suffering Servant
A metaphorical character who symbolizes the Israelites' suffering.

"Second Isaiah" Unnamed prophet who is thought to have authored chapters 40–55 of the book of Isaiah in the 6th century BCE.

Cyrus King of Persia from 558 to 530 BCE. Seen by Second Isaiah and his disciples as a savior and Yahweh's "shepherd."

Biblical scholars divide the book of Isaiah into three sections. The first, believed to be the work of Isaiah himself, was written when Assyria was expanding westward, threatening Judah. The book fulminates against the sinful leaders of Jerusalem and urges reform to avert calamity. The second section (chapters 40–55), by an anonymous source known as the Second Isaiah, or Deutero-Isaiah, is believed to have been written from exile in Babylon in the 6th century BCE, after Jerusalem has fallen; a third section (56–66), Third Isaiah, is believed to date from after the Exile.

God's chosen one

Central to the Second Isaiah are the Servant Songs: four poems that present a mysterious servant of God, His "chosen one." The poems have the same themes as First Isaiah, but preach a message of greater hope and comfort.

The Servant Songs revolve around the wretched character of the "Suffering Servant." There is nothing majestic or beautiful about him. Far from treating him with respect, people despise and reject him, beating him and plucking out his beard. He utters no words of protest. Instead, he sets his face "like flint" (50:7) and endures. He does this for the sake of God and of others, even his very tormentors. He is: a "man of sorrows" who takes up and carries the failings of others.

ESAIAS

Isaiah is one of seven Old Testament prophets painted by Michelangelo in the Vatican's Sistine Chapel (1508–1512). Isaiah (Greek "Esaias") holds the Book of Isaiah under his arm.

See also: The Suffering of Job 146–47 ▪ The Coming of Salvation 189

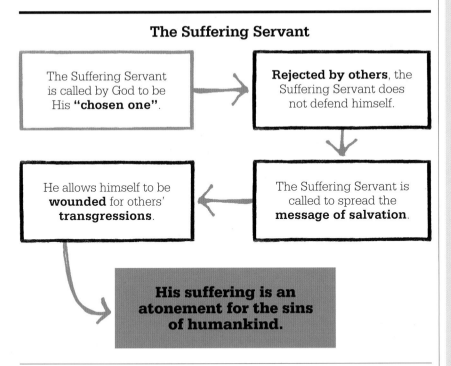

The Suffering Servant

The Suffering Servant is called by God to be His **"chosen one"**.

Rejected by others, the Suffering Servant does not defend himself.

He allows himself to be **wounded** for others' **transgressions**.

The Suffering Servant is called to spread the **message of salvation**.

His suffering is an atonement for the sins of humankind.

Anointed with God's spirit, the man is gentle and unassuming—a "bruised reed he will not break, and a smoldering wick he will not snuff out" (42:3). He is the one God calls not only to restore the exiled and dispersed people of Israel, but also to carry out an even wider task: to be "a light for the Gentiles," spreading God's salvation to the world. The life of the Suffering Servant is an atonement for sin. In exchange for him bearing "the sins of many," God will raise him up. He will "give him a portion among the great"; kings and princes will one day bow down before him.

A mysterious figure

The identity of the Suffering Servant has long been debated. One theory is that he could be Cyrus, the Persian king, who would overthrow the Israelites' hated Babylonian oppressors. Cyrus would be a friend and savior to the Jews, allowing them to return home and rebuild Jerusalem and their temple. Many Christians, however, view the Suffering Servant as a prophecy of Christ, in line with other messianic references in Isaiah. Most rabbinic scholars believe he is a metaphor for Israel itself, or rather those Israelites who have stayed true to God through humiliation and suffering. They are the "faithful remnant" (Malachi 3:15–16) of prophetic tradition, who have endured persecution not just from foreign oppressors but from the Israelites who rejected the message of repentance. Suffering has become part of their identity, but in the Servant Songs this is not a negative thing: it is redemptive and transforming. Through their suffering for the failings of others, humankind will be healed. ▪

Jesus Christ: the servant savior

The image of the Suffering Servant sank deep into the Jewish imagination, enduring into the early Christian one. In Luke's Gospel, Jesus announces His public ministry with a passage from Isaiah closely associated with the Servant passages. "Today this scripture is fulfilled in your hearing," Jesus tells the synagogue in His hometown of Nazareth. The people promptly reject Him, as was the case for the Suffering Servant. The servant theme comes up time and again in Jesus's teaching. He tells His disciples that "the Son of Man did not come to be served, but to serve, and to give His life as a ransom for many."

Echoes of the Servant Songs are unmistakable. Peter writes about Jesus's silence in the face of His accusers. "When they hurled their insults at Him … He did not retaliate."

The face of Christ on a statue in Paris. The Book of Isaiah contains so many messianic references that it is sometimes called the fifth Gospel.

BEFORE I FORMED YOU IN THE WOMB I KNEW YOU

JEREMIAH 1:5, THE PROPHET JEREMIAH

IN BRIEF

PASSAGE
Jeremiah 1–52

THEME
Predestination

SETTING
Around 626–570 BCE
Jerusalem.

KEY FIGURES
Jeremiah Selected by God to
be a prophet "to the nations."
Born in Anathoth, a few miles
north of Jerusalem, where his
father Hilkiah was a priest.

Hananiah A false prophet
preaching against Jeremiah.

When God declares Jeremiah a prophet He assigns him an unenviable mission: Jeremiah must make the people of Judah repent for years of bad behavior. Though faced with hatred and adversity, the reluctant prophet continues to discharge his task and spread the word of God right up until the end of his life.

Jeremiah is regarded, after Isaiah, as the second major prophet of the latter "writing" prophets in Judaism (earlier figures, such as Elijah, were "oral" prophets, who did not record their words). He is also known as the "Weeping Prophet," as his eponymous book, written around 585 BCE, with the help of the scribe Baruch, is deeply melancholic. The epithet is apt, given the nature of the prophet's lifelong travails. Such is the notoriety of Jeremiah's thankless struggles that to this day an angry or miserable person is often referred to as a "Jeremiah."

The desolation of Jeremiah is captured with dramatic intensity in *Cry of prophet Jeremiah on the Ruins of Jerusalem*, painted in 1870 by the Russian artist Ilya Yefimovich Repin.

God selected Jeremiah before he was even born to exhort the people of Judah to mend their idolatrous and disrespectful ways. He later tells Jeremiah He made him a prophet "in the womb" (Jeremiah 1:5). Despite an initial reluctance to accept his role, Jeremiah ultimately accepts that his life's work is predestined, and faithfully follows God's carefully mapped plan throughout his life.

Called to God's work

Jeremiah was born in Anathoth, a small village 4 miles (6km) north of Jerusalem, the son of Hilkiah, a priest. His lineage can be traced back to Moses, and there are several parallels in the two men's lives. Just as Moses demurs when God instructs him to lead the Israelites out of Egypt, the young Jeremiah makes excuses as to why he is not fit to extract the repentance of the people of Judah and fulfill the mission that God has assigned to him. He protests to God that he is too young to take on such a role and, like Moses, is not a sufficiently good speaker to cope with such a weighty task. In response, God reassures Jeremiah, as He did Moses, telling the prophet not to fear, as He will support and rescue him. The Lord then touches Jeremiah's mouth and says to him, "I have put my words in your mouth. See, today I appoint you over nations and kingdoms to uproot and tear down, to destroy and overthrow, to build and to plant" (1:9–10).

A dangerous mission

Won over by God's words, Jeremiah prepares to try and reconvert the errant sons and daughters of Judah. He begins his ministry around 626 BCE, in what was a tumultuous period for the people of Israel. The message was dire. God was

> Call to Me and I will answer you and tell you great and unsearchable things you do not know.
> **Jeremiah 33:3**

calling on him to prophesy a severe, cataclysmic event to the people—the destruction of their holy city Jerusalem by the Babylonians. Jeremiah's task was to remind the people of their covenant with God and to dissuade them from breaking the laws associated with it, despite any opposition he faced. Of their many crimes, the idolatrous worship of the false god Baal represented a particularly disturbing offense. »

Predestination

The theological concept of "predestination" holds that all events are willed and predetermined by God. The theory is aired in the Bible in Jeremiah 1:5, Romans 8:29, and Ephesians 1:5–14. The "paradox of free will," long a subject of theological debate, is the apparent incompatibility between God's omniscience and the free will of a human being. In the ways shown in the Bible, predestination usually amounts to a form of religious determinism or predeterminism. The dilemma that Christians face is whether they are able to freely make choices of their own volition, as opposed to choices that are predetermined by God. Scholars have labored over the question for centuries. The general consensus is that not all people live predestined lives and therefore enjoy free will. However, in Jeremiah's case, he had little choice in the path that his life would take; the events shaping his existence were preordained by God when he was in his mother's womb.

coming enslavement of the Israelite people to the Babylonians. The prophet then goes to Zedekiah, wearing the yoke, and says, "Bow your neck under the yoke of the king of Babylon" (27:12–13), so that he and the nation might not die by "the sword, famine, and plague." Jeremiah denounces the false prophets who favor opposition to Babylon, as God has told him that can only lead to Judah's downfall. He goes on to tell the priest and people, "Serve the king of Babylon and you will live. Why should this city become a ruin?" (27:17).

The people, angry and afraid, react badly to Jeremiah's words. Later, the false prophet Hananiah seizes his chance and tears the yoke from Jeremiah's neck and breaks it on the ground, declaring that the Lord will break the yoke of Nebuchadnezzar II within two years.

As in many other parts of his story, Jeremiah continues his mission despite his humiliation. The Lord tells him to go to Hananiah and say that in place of a wooden yoke, he will get a yoke of iron. Jeremiah also prophesies that Hananiah will be dead within a year, for inciting rebellion against the Lord—a statement that proves accurate.

Destruction foretold
Jeremiah's terrible prophecies do eventually come true; the people witness their city being completely destroyed by the Babylonians and most of their people are taken into captivity. The survivors go to Jeremiah and ask for forgiveness. They acknowledge that they should

They had constructed high altars to Baal, in which they burned their own children as sacrificial offerings.

Jeremiah's prophecies of doom and destruction are unpopular and he becomes the target of much mockery, and several attempts are made to kill him. When Jeremiah complains to God that he has become a laughing stock for spreading the word of the Lord, he is told that he is destined to endure more painful attacks over the course of his mission. He cries and laments (the following biblical book, Lamentations, is a further highly poetic expression of grief). Still God insists that the prophet must continue to disseminate His dire warnings to the people of Judah. Further misfortunes befall Jeremiah; he is beaten and held in

the stocks for a day (20:2), and at one point is thrown into a dark and muddy well (38:6).

Battles with false prophets
While Jeremiah is busy spreading his apocalyptic messages, other prophets are at work, sending out a more positive message of peace and prosperity (Jeremiah 27–28). The most famous of these is Hananiah, with whom Jeremiah clashes throughout much of the central part of his narrative.

Things come to a head early in the reign of King Zedekiah in Jerusalem. Jeremiah is determined to ensure Jerusalem's surrender in the face of the rapidly advancing Babylonian forces. He puts on a yoke, or oxen harness, to symbolize what God has told him about the have listened to him and repented of their wrongdoing. They also ask his advice for where to go next. However, when he tells them "Do not go to Egypt" (42:19), Jeremiah is once more maligned by the people he is trying to save: he is branded a liar and taken to Egypt with the Israelites, where he dies soon afterward. Some extra-biblical sources suggest that he was stoned to death by his angry countrymen.

A new covenant

Not all of the Book of Jeremiah prophesies misery and despair. Chapters 29–31 strike a fresh tone of positivity. In a letter to those exiled in Babylon, God speaks through Jeremiah, telling him he will bring them back after 70 years and promising them a new covenant. This covenant will succeed because God will put it in their mind, "write it on their hearts" and "forgive their wickedness and will remember their sins no more" (Jeremiah 31:33–34).

This prophecy at the heart of the Book of Jeremiah gave the Jewish people great hope after the fall of Jerusalem in 586 BCE. Early Christians often applied the prophecy to Jesus. His death on the cross was seen to herald the promised new covenant, as it showed God's forgiveness of their sins (Luke 22:20). ∎

Jeremiah

The Prophet Jeremiah was the last prophet that God sent to preach to the southern kingdom, home to the tribes of Benjamin and Judah. God had repeatedly warned the Israelites to cease their idolatrous worship and evil deeds, but his preaching had been continually ignored. With the 12 tribes split, and the 10 northern tribes lost among the Assyrians, God's decision to appoint Jeremiah as His prophet constituted His final attempt to bring the errant southern tribes back into His fold. Jeremiah was around 17 years old when God called upon him. Privy to God's most terrible plans for his compatriots, he cried tears of sadness, because not only did he know what was going to happen to the Israelites, he was unable to convince them of his knowledge. Although he preached for 40 years, often entirely unaided, he was unable to change or soften the stubborn hearts and minds of the Israelite people. In the face of great hardships, Jeremiah's legacy lies in the courage he showed by teaching the word of God despite the significant aversion to His message.

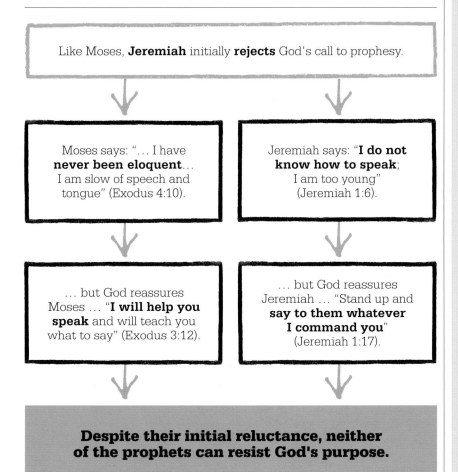

Like Moses, **Jeremiah** initially **rejects** God's call to prophesy.

Moses says: "… I have **never been eloquent**… I am slow of speech and tongue" (Exodus 4:10).

Jeremiah says: "**I do not know how to speak**; I am too young" (Jeremiah 1:6).

… but God reassures Moses … "**I will help you speak** and will teach you what to say" (Exodus 3:12).

… but God reassures Jeremiah … "Stand up and **say to them whatever I command you**" (Jeremiah 1:17).

Despite their initial reluctance, neither of the prophets can resist God's purpose.

MY HEART IS POURED OUT ON THE GROUND

LAMENTATIONS 2:11, LAMENT FOR THE EXILES

IN BRIEF

PASSAGE
Lamentations 1–5

THEME
God suffers when His people suffer

SETTING
586 BCE, Jerusalem

KEY FIGURES
Narrator Widely believed to be Jeremiah, the "Weeping Prophet," to whom the Book of Lamentations is attributed.

The people of Jerusalem Survivors of the Babylonian invasion, desperately trying to remain alive.

Nebuchadnezzar II King of Babylon, who leads his army in destroying the holy city of Jerusalem and is supported by God as punishment for the Judeans' unfaithful behavior.

The aptly named Book of Lamentations concerns the destruction of Jerusalem at God's behest. The book is traditionally attributed to Jeremiah, known as the "Weeping Prophet," and it serves as a postscript to the Book of Jeremiah. However, most scholars believe that it is by an anonymous source.

The book comprises five poems, each arranged in a series of short, rhymeless stanzas, describing the state of Jerusalem after its annihilation by the Babylonians under Nebuchadnezzar II. The prophet Jeremiah lived in Judah during the Babylonian invasion, which culminated in the siege of the holy city in 586 BCE.

Lamentations opens with the foreboding words "How deserted lies the city, once so full of people!" From this gloomy start, the narrative becomes progressively darker, describing the Babylonian army breaching the city walls of Jerusalem, killing or enslaving

By the Waters of Babylon (1882–1883), an oil painting by Evelyn De Morgan, depicts an exiled patriarch (under the tree) with other exiles weeping over the loss of their Promised Land.

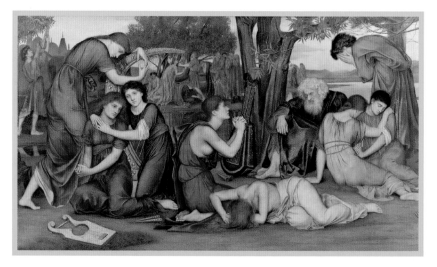

See also: Entering the Promised Land 96–97 ▪ The Fall of Jerusalem 128–31 ▪ The Prophet Jeremiah 156–59 ▪ Daniel in Babylon 164–65

all the people, and burning the city to the ground. The survivors are described in detail, with harrowing accounts of how mothers ate their own children in order to survive, children beg for bread but no one gives them any, and young and old lie in the dust of the streets (Lamentations 2:20–21 and 4:4).

Terrible punishments

After the fall of Jerusalem, worldly possessions and wealth now mean nothing: Chapter 4:1 describes how gold has lost its luster and precious stones are scattered on every street corner. It appears that all hope is lost, such is the misery and despair that is recounted. Nevertheless, despite inflicting such a terrible punishment on His people, Jeremiah suggests that there is still reason to hope: "For no one is cast off by the Lord for ever. Though He brings grief, He will show compassion, so great is His unfailing love. For He does not willingly bring affliction or grief to anyone" (3:32–33).

Lamentations is full of references to tears and crying, including the agonizing and despair of Jeremiah himself. Lamentations 4:6 states that the punishment of the people of Jerusalem is greater even than that of the people of Sodom. The extent of God's wrath is made abundantly clear as the narrative unfolds. However, the underlying tone throughout the book is that, though His anger knows no limits, God suffers Himself at having to wreak such terrible carnage in the first place.

At the heart of Lamentations is an important message of peace and reconciliation, which points to the inexhaustible possibilities for redemption and forgiveness if the exiles maintain their faith in God. He is angry—but He also grieves that the longstanding heinous behavior by the Israelite people has forced Him to punish them so harshly. The message of Lamentations is clear: when God's people suffer, God suffers, too. ▪

City of Babylon

Babylon, where the Israelites were taken as slaves and exiles, was the capital city of Babylonia in southwest Asia, now southern Iraq. The city sat on the Euphrates River, north of the modern town of Hillah.

The fall of the city, and the end of the neo-Babylonian empire with it, is predicted by the prophets in Isaiah 14:4 and 21:9, as well as Jeremiah 50–51. The city was under Babylonian control until 539 BCE, when Cyrus the Great of Persia invaded and killed king Belshazzar. However, Babylon was fairly unscathed by the invasion and continued to flourish under Persian rule.

Genesis 6:6: God **grieves** over the wickedness of humankind.

Hosea 11:8 God **cannot bear** to punish His people for rejecting Him.

Luke 19:41 Jesus weeps for the **lost souls** of Jerusalem.

Jeremiah 14:17 God's eyes overflow with **tears** for the Israelites' suffering.

God suffers with His people.

John 11:35 Jesus **weeps** when He sees Mary grieving over Lazarus.

I WILL REMOVE ... YOUR HEART OF STONE AND GIVE YOU A HEART OF FLESH
EZEKIEL 36:26, THE PROPHET EZEKIEL

IN BRIEF

PASSAGE
Ezekiel 1–48

THEME
God's people will be restored

SETTING
c.590s–570s BCE Babylon, Mesopotamia.

KEY FIGURES
Ezekiel A priest from the Temple in Jerusalem, now exiled in Babylon. He is a prophet of the Lord, appointed to help instruct the exiles.

The Israelites God's chosen people, now living in exile in Babylon, Mesopotamia.

The Book of Ezekiel charts the lives and experiences of the Israelites during Babylonian captivity. For most of the book, the picture is bleak but the last section (Ezekiel 33–38) offers hope and the prospect of revival and redemption in the wake of the destruction of Jerusalem.

Ezekiel was a contemporary of the prophet Jeremiah and a priest at the Temple of Jerusalem, prior to the destruction of the city. He therefore occupied a prominent role in Israelite society. Owing to his elevated status, Ezekiel was among the first wave of exiles that went to Babylon with King Jehoiachin and his court in around 597 BCE, nine years prior to Jerusalem's final destruction in 586 BCE. This meant that, while Jeremiah stayed in Jerusalem, trying to persuade the Israelites to reform their ways, Ezekiel was prophet to the exiles, 1,000 miles (1,600km) away in Babylon.

Amazing illusions
Ezekiel's strange, intensely mystical career as a prophet begins when he experiences an incredible vision beside the River Chebar. God appears before him in the form

In Raphael's *Ezekiel's Vision* (c.1518), the prophet sees God in all His majesty raised by cherubim—fantastical winged creatures that perform a protective role in the Bible.

of a man, yet from the "waist up He looked like glowing metal, as if full of fire ... and brilliant light surrounded Him" (1:27). God is standing astride a throne-like chariot made of lapis lazuli with wheels that resemble topaz. The chariot flies through the air at great speed and is surrounded by a ring of fire. It is borne by cherubim with lions' bodies and eagles'

See also: Entering the Promised Land 96–97 ▪ The Fall of Jerusalem 128–31 ▪ Lament for the Exiles 160–61 ▪ The New Jerusalem 322–29

wings, each of which have four aspects to their faces—one of a human, one of a lion, one of an ox, and one of an eagle.

God hands Ezekiel a scroll with the words, "Son of man, eat what is before you, eat this scroll; then go and speak to the people of Israel" (3:1). He tells Ezekiel to eat the scroll, so that his words will literally be those of God. Ezekiel does as he is bidden and then climbs aboard God's incredible flaming chariot. He is then transported to Babylon, where Ezekiel joins the exiles and begins his life's work preaching about the restoration of the Jewish people and nation.

Coming redemption

Ezekiel's strange vision is designed to emphasize two key points at this important stage in the plight of the Jewish people. First, it is made clear that although God's chosen people are in exile in Babylon, He will still be with them. This is why He flies in His flaming chariot from Jerusalem to Babylon. Second, God's appointment of Ezekiel as His spokesman—which is forcefully underlined by His command to eat the scroll—shows that the Lord is leaving an important prophet, whose word is true, with the exiles. Thus, the Israelites are assured that if they follow Ezekiel's prophecies and return to God, their nation will ultimately be restored.

This message is reinforced by three more significant visions. In the first, Ezekiel is taken to the Temple of Jerusalem, and finds it covered in crawling things and unclean animals. As he stands there, the "glory of God" rises from the sanctuary and leaves the temple and Jerusalem. In the second, however, he is shown a valley of dried human skeletons, called "the people of Israel," whom God restores to full life before his eyes (37:11). The third is a profoundly positive vision of the future. Ezekiel sees Jerusalem's Temple—huge and magnificent— and imagines a "New Jerusalem," a fully restored Israelite kingdom that henceforth will be ruled only by God (40–48). ▪

Visions of Ezekiel

The wheels of God's chariot are able to move "in any one of four directions." This is a metaphor for His omnipresence.

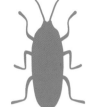

Crawling things and unclean animals (Ezekiel 8:10) are symbolic of the false idolatry that led to the downfall of the Israelites.

The dry bones of "the people of Israel" are given life in Ezekiel's visions, which represent their ultimate return to their own land.

Jerusalem's future temple will be measured according to God's law. Once restored, it will be honest, pure, and true.

A tetragrammaton as depicted in the window of the Karlskirche, Vienna. Often translated as Yahweh, this symbol asserts God's omnipotence.

Glory of God

In the Christian religion, "glory"— derived from the Latin *gloria*, meaning "renown"—is used to describe the manifestation of God's presence when it is actively perceived by human beings. In Ezekiel, and elsewhere in the Bible, God appears in many different guises and various fantastical forms—or is merely heard or sensed by His subjects. Divine glory is an extremely important motif in theology, in which God is the most glorious being in existence.

However, due to the fact that human beings are created in His image, they can share (albeit imperfectly) in disseminating divine glory as "image bearers." They cannot match the glory of God Himself, but can spread it among others. This concept is best explained in Matthew 5:16, which states: "let your light shine before others, that they may see your good deeds and glorify your Father in heaven."

In religious media today, glory is often conveyed by the use of a halo, or white robes, crowns, jewels, gold, or stars.

MY GOD SENT HIS ANGEL, AND HE SHUT THE MOUTHS OF THE LIONS

DANIEL 6:22, DANIEL IN BABYLON

IN BRIEF

PASSAGE
Daniel 1–12

THEME
God's protection

SETTING
c.605–538 BCE Babylon.

KEY FIGURES
Daniel Wise man and prophet in exile from Judea and interpreter of dreams.

Nebuchadnezzar II King of Babylon, patron of Daniel, and destroyer of Jerusalem.

Belshazzar Son of King Nabonidus and the final documented ruler of Babylon.

Darius the Mede Successor to Belshazzar as King of Babylon, according to the Book of Daniel. His historical existence is doubted by most researchers.

The eventful Book of Daniel celebrates people of vision and courage—those who dare to stand steadfast in their faith in the Lord, whoever the adversary and no matter how bad the situation.

In 586 BCE, Nebuchadnezzar II of Babylon destroys Jerusalem and deports many of its citizens to Babylon. Several of the exiled aristocrats are given official positions, including the Judean Daniel. Despite being offered choice food and wine from the royal table, Daniel remains true to his religion,

resolving to "not defile himself" (Daniel 1:8) by eating food the Israelites considered unclean.

Although he is a Judean exile, Daniel is made "ruler of the entire province of Babylon" (2:48) after he interprets a mystifying dream of Nebuchadnezzar's. Daniel's elevated status lasts into the reign of the king's successor, Belshazzar.

Writing on the wall

In Daniel 5, a hand appears from thin air to write on the wall as King Belshazzar holds a banquet. Daniel is brought in to translate and interpret the four Hebrew words for the astonished king: "God has numbered the days of your reign … You have been weighed on the scales and found wanting … Your kingdom is divided" (5:26–28). Daniel is again rewarded for his efforts and becomes the third highest ruler in the kingdom. King Belshazzar is slain "that very night" (5:30). Darius the Mede becomes the new

Blessed with the protection of an angel of the Lord, Daniel is saved from the lions' mouths in the den. He is replaced by King Darius's jealous advisers, who are all eaten alive.

See also: ▪ Joseph the Dreamer 58–61 ▪ The Fall of Jerusalem 128–31 ▪ The Prophet Jeremiah 156–59 ▪ Lament for the Exiles 160–61

Nebuchadnezzar's dream

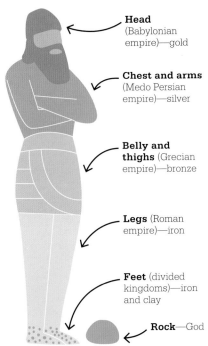

Head (Babylonian empire)—gold

Chest and arms (Medo Persian empire)—silver

Belly and thighs (Grecian empire)—bronze

Legs (Roman empire)—iron

Feet (divided kingdoms)—iron and clay

Rock—God

Nebuchadnezzar dreamed of a statue made of various materials that crumbled as a rock struck its base. Daniel interpreted the dream as the impending destruction of all kingdoms.

king. Advisers jealous of Daniel's growing power dupe King Darius into decreeing that all should pray only to him, knowing that Daniel would refuse. When Daniel violates the decree by continuing to pray to God, Darius reluctantly has him thrown into the lion's den overnight as punishment. The king returns to his palace and frets over Daniel's fate.

When Darius returns the next morning, he finds Daniel unharmed. Daniel tells him, "My God sent His angel, and He shut the mouths of the lions. They have not hurt me, because I was found innocent in His sight" (6:22). Darius issues a decree that praises both God and Daniel.

The episode of Daniel in the lions' den is thus seen as proof that God protects those who honor Him.

Purpose and meaning

After Daniel 6, the book shifts and becomes apocalyptic in tone. Daniel interprets his visions and describes events in which empires will fall and the kingdom of heaven will be established forever. For many readers, this signifies the literal end of the world.

Notably, in the Hebrew canon Daniel is not regarded as a prophet. However, in the Christian Bible the book of Daniel is included among the Major Prophets. As the Book of Daniel was largely written in Aramaic, and explicitly describes the coming of Alexander (10–12) and the wars that followed, scholars date it to the period after the region was conquered by Alexander the Great. For this reason, some believe the Book of Daniel essentially functions as propaganda, describing the fall of an oppressive empire and the rise of an Israelite kingdom. ▪

No wise man, enchanter, magician, or diviner can explain to the king the mystery he has asked about, but there is a God in heaven who reveals mysteries.
Daniel 2:27–28

Daniel

The name Daniel means "God is my Judge." He is said to have been selected to be an official for Nebuchadnezzar because he was handsome, without blemish, and "quick to understand" (Daniel 1:4). However, Daniel believes he derives all of his abilities from the Lord. As an interpreter of dreams for a foreign king, Daniel's experience echoes that of Joseph in Genesis (37–50), who interprets dreams for Pharaoh in Egypt.

Daniel is considered a prophet by Christians and his apocalyptic visions are mentioned in the Apocryphal book 2 Esdras and in Matthew 24. In Judaism, Daniel is often represented as a wise man, but his book is not included in those of the prophets in the Jewish canon. In pre-Israelite Canaanite literature, there was a figure named Daniel, who was a wise man and adjudicator of justice. Scholars liken the biblical Daniel to this figure.

Regardless of the slightly differing views of his status, Daniel is consistently described as being devout, morally astute, and unwavering in his devotion to God.

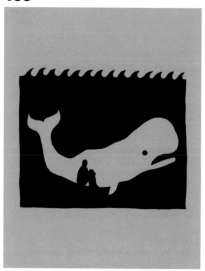

JONAH WAS IN THE BELLY OF THE FISH THREE DAYS AND THREE NIGHTS
JONAH 1:17, THE DISOBEDIENT PROPHET

IN BRIEF

PASSAGE
Jonah 1–4

THEME
God's omnipresence

SETTING
786–746 BCE The reign of
Jeroboam. The Mediterranean
Sea; Nineveh, the capital
of Assyria.

KEY FIGURES
Jonah Reluctant prophet,
son of Amittai.

Sailors The polytheistic crew
of a ship that Jonah boards
to escape God's command to
preach in Nineveh.

Fish or whale An instrument
of God.

The Ninevites Enemies of
Israel whose wickedness has
drawn the attention of God.

The story of Jonah, which also occurs in the Qur'an, is found among the short prophet books, often called the Minor Prophets or the Twelve Prophets. Most biblical scholars extrapolate two major themes from the story of Jonah: first, the omnipresence of God, and second, His willingness to forgive those who repent. Although Jonah hears God, he does not want to listen.

Punished prophet
The story opens with God telling Jonah to go to Nineveh, the capital of Assyria, to preach against sin. Instead, Jonah runs away to Joppa (Jaffa) and boards a ship sailing to Tarshish, whose location is unknown today. However, he cannot run from an omnipresent God. While Jonah is on the boat, the Lord sends a violent storm.

When the sailors discover that Jonah is a Hebrew, and that the Lord is angry with him, they ask Jonah what to do to calm the sea. Jonah tells them to throw him into the water. At first, they ignore Jonah's advice, as they do not want to kill an innocent man, but when their attempts to row back to land fail, they throw him overboard. The

Jonah is devoured by a "huge fish" with gills in this 15th-century French miniature from the Bible of St. John XXII. Contrary to popular myth, the Bible does not specify a whale.

sea calms and the sailors offer a sacrifice to the Lord. God then sends a fish to swallow Jonah, who stays in the belly of the fish for three days and nights.

Jonah's prayer
While in the fish, Jonah says a prayer in poetic form similar to that of many of the Psalms of lament. He

See also: The Tower of Babel 42–43 ▪ Sodom and Gomorrah 48–49 ▪ The Ten Commandments 78–83 ▪
The Psalms 138–43 ▪ The Empty Tomb 268–71

describes how he has been brought low, but the power of the Lord will save him, suggesting he is willing to do what is commanded of him. Jonah appears to allude to the Psalms in the prayer. He includes the word *sheol* in Hebrew, which is typically translated in the Psalms, and elsewhere, as the grave, or abode of the dead. Little is known about the ancient concept of *sheol*, but scholars believe it is a place where the presence of the Lord cannot be felt.

Jonah ends the prayer by vowing to reform. Echoing Psalm 3:8, he says: "Salvation comes from the Lord" (Jonah 2:9). After this, the fish spits Jonah out.

God's compassion

Chastised by his experience, Jonah travels to Nineveh, where he fulfills God's command. He tells the sinful Ninevites to repent and prophesies their destruction. However, when they do repent, and the Lord forgives them, Jonah is angry that God should show mercy to enemies of Israel and deny his prophecy. He obstinately sits outside the city, waiting for its destruction.

The disobedience of Jonah

Jonah shirks God's command to **preach in Nineveh** and flees.

⬇

He is angry that **God is compassionate** toward Nineveh.

⬇

He then asserts his own **prophecy and judgment**.

⬇

Jonah is rebuked by God for wanting to influence what only He controls.

To teach Jonah a lesson—prophets are the messengers of the Lord; they are not supposed to punish or act independently—God grows a vine (generally thought to be a gourd) over Jonah to provide shade while he waits near Nineveh, but then commands a worm to eat the vine, and sends a scorching east wind so that Jonah grows faint.

Through this act, God both forgives and punishes Jonah. But Jonah remains angry. God then says to Jonah, "Should I not have concern for the great city of Nineveh, in which there are more than a hundred and twenty thousand?" (4:10). While Jonah believes salvation should be for the Israelites alone, God's mercy extends to all. ▪

Interpretations of the story of Jonah

For many, it is puzzling to see a prophet of the Lord being disobedient and the enemies of Israel receiving forgiveness. However, God mentions that all nations are under the Lord's dominion and Ezekiel 21 states that even Babylon is the tool of the Lord. In Matthew 12:39–41, Jesus equates Himself to Jonah: He applauds that the people of Nineveh repented, but says that His work will be greater. Jesus also mentions that, just as Jonah was in the fish for three days, He will be three days and nights "in the heart of the earth."

Many readers focus on the fish, or whale, but what all the interpretations show is the centrality of repentance and forgiveness. In Judaism, Jonah is read during Yom Kippur (Day of Atonement) in remembrance of God's forgiveness, even to the enemies of Israel.

A 4th-century mosaic in the Basilica di Santa Maria Assunta, Aquileia, Italy, shows Jonah resting under the gourd vine sent by God.

AND WHAT DOES THE LORD REQUIRE OF YOU?

MICAH 6:8, THE PROPHET MICAH

For hundreds of years, the ancient Assyrian Empire, based in the northeast of what is now Iraq, posed a constant threat to smaller, neighboring nations, including the two Israelite kingdoms of Israel and Judah. In 722 BCE, during the prophet Micah's lifetime, the Assyrians destroyed Samaria, the capital of the Northern Kingdom of Israel, and deported the

See also: The Fall of Jerusalem 128–31 ▪ The Suffering Servant 154–55 ▪ Lament for the Exiles 160–61 ▪
The Birth of Jesus 180–85

bulk of its population. In 701 BCE, they came close to doing the same to the Judean kingdom and its capital, Jerusalem, in the south.

Micah was from Judah. Unlike the urban aristocrat Isaiah, Micah was a country dweller from the

An 1865 engraving of Micah by Gustave Doré. The prophet reproaches the Israelites for idolatry in the days of Jotham and Hezekiah, kings of Judah, and exhorts the people to repent.

village of Moresheth, southwest of Jerusalem. Micah was aware of the Assyrian threat to Judah, but his main concern was the suffering he saw in the farmsteads, villages, and small towns of Judah, caused not by foreign oppressors, but by his people's own rulers and leaders.

Inspired by God
The book that bears Micah's name alternates between threats of doom and promises of God's mercy. As a prophet, Micah speaks not in his own name, nor even in the name of a

cause or of an abstract concept of justice. Instead, he speaks to the people on behalf of God. He has holy visions, and is "filled" with God's power and spirit (Micah 3:8).

Micah paints a disturbing picture of Judah. He describes how, in the early hours of the morning, people who are already rich and powerful lie in bed plotting ways in which to further increase their wealth. The moment dawn breaks, they start executing their plans, seizing the fields and houses of the poor and weak. Micah describes how the women of Judah are driven onto the streets, their children deprived of a secure home; social dysfunction and injustice are rampant as the rich get away with murder; and the poor and »

The Book of the Twelve

The Hebrew Bible's 12 short writings known as the "Minor Prophets" were kept on a single scroll and regarded as one book, the Book of the Twelve. These writings clearly reflect the historical context in which each prophet was active. Hosea, Amos, and Micah, for example, are contemporaries of Isaiah, and date from the 8th century BCE—a time dominated by the threat of the Assyrian Empire, which destroyed Israel's capital of Samaria in 722 BCE. Habakkuk, Zephaniah, and Nahum prophesied just prior to the fall of Nineveh in 612 BCE. By this time, Assyria was in decline and a renewed Babylon now threatened the southern Kingdom of Judah.

Hosea	Prophesies to the Northern Kingdom, Israel.
Joel	Prophesies after the rebuilding of the Jerusalem temple.
Amos	Prophesies to Israel, though he was from Judah.
Obadiah	Prophesies against the Edomites.
Jonah	Disobeys God's command to prophesy to the city of Nineveh.
Micah	Prophesies to the Southern Kingdom, Judah.
Nahum	Prophesies against the city of Nineveh.
Habakkuk	Dialogues with God about injustice in the world.
Zephaniah	Prophesies to Judah.
Haggai	Exhorts returned exiles to finish rebuilding Jerusalem's temple.
Zechariah	Foretells the coming of a savior or Messiah.
Malachi	Prophesies a cataclysmic future Day of Judgment.

in Judah try to silence Micah, convinced that his message of doom is exaggerated. They ask, "Is not the Lord among us?" (3:11) and give bland, empty assurances that no disaster would befall the nation. Micah, however, is adamant. Through its sins, the nation is treating God as an enemy. Judah could not expect Him to continue to give His protection.

Repentance and mercy

By Micah's final chapter, Judah is depicted as a dystopia: a society in which "the powerful dictate what they desire" (7:3). People cannot trust their neighbors or friends, even spouses have to be careful what they say to each other, and family members turn on each other and become enemies.

Yet judgment alternates with mercy, or the possibility of it, arrived at through repentance. God asks His people to explain themselves: "What have I done

> I am filled with power, with the Spirit of the Lord, and with justice and might, to declare to Jacob his transgression, to Israel his sin.
> **Micah 3:8**

vulnerable have no redress. Crying out in God's name, the prophet compares his nation's rulers to cannibals "who eat my people's flesh, strip off their skin, and break their bones in pieces" (3:3).

Nation of sin

God's feelings toward the sinful people of Judah are expressed in an alarming vision at the start of the Book of Micah, in which, enraged, He comes "from his dwelling-place" treading the "heights of the earth"; this causes mountains to melt and valleys to split asunder (1:3).

Micah warns that the Israelites' sins have mounted to the point where God can no longer ignore them. Divine judgment has become necessary, and God

delivers this judgment through the foreign, Assyrian oppressor. In Micah's prophecy, God promises to turn Samaria into rubble: "I will pour her stones into the valley and lay bare her foundations" (1:6). This reference to the brutal destruction of the Northern Kingdom shows what could also happen to Judah: society itself is broken, so judgment will come from an outside source.

The sins of Judah are myriad: they include idolatry; the rich dispossessing the poor of land and houses; cheating by merchants and traders; judges who take bribes; and thuggery. Religious leaders are as venal as the rest, with priests teaching "for a price" and so-called prophets telling fortunes for money. Other prophets

> Your rich people are violent; your inhabitants are liars and their tongues speak deceitfully. Therefore, I have begun to destroy you, to ruin you because of your sins.
> **Micah 6:12–13**

to you? How have I burdened you?" (6:3). He reminds them how He brought them out of Egypt and into the Promised Land.

The people do not know how to respond. Should they come before the Lord with extravagant ritual sacrifices: burnt offerings, calves a year old, thousands of rams, whole rivers of olive oil? They even go as far as to suggest child sacrifice as a means of regaining God's favor. Nothing could be farther from God's mind, however. "He has showed you, O man, what is good," Micah announces. The answer is simple: to "act justly and to love mercy and to walk humbly with your God" (Micah 6:8). Sincere internal repentance reaches God, not empty external displays.

Scholarly interpretation

The Book of Micah is not confined to the words of the prophet alone. For the ancient Israelites, prophecy was for all time. The words of a prophet would be reflected upon, edited, reinterpreted, and added to over generations in the light of time and unfolding circumstances. Key later events that affected the text of Micah were the fall of Jerusalem to the Babylonians in 587–586 BCE, the Jews' subsequent exile in Babylon, and their return from exile 50 years after the fall of the capital. It is thus impossible to fully disentangle Micah's original prophecies from later editing and additions.

Generally, however, it seems that the messages of doom are Micah's. Many, but not all, of the messages of hope were added later. The experience of divine mercy in the return from exile did not detract from the prophet's original stern message, but provided it with a setting. Judgment leading to a change of heart and repentance came to be seen as evidence of God's love for His people. The final verses of Micah, almost certainly a later addition, show this: "You will again have compassion on us; you will tread our sins underfoot and hurl all our iniquities into the … sea. You will be faithful to Jacob, and show love to Abraham, as you pledged on oath to our ancestors in days long ago" (7:19–20). ∎

> Who is a God like you, who pardons sin and forgives the transgression of the remnant of his inheritance? You do not stay angry for ever but delight to show mercy.
> **Micah 7:18**

The Bethlehem prophecy

Micah prophesies that the Messiah will be born in Bethlehem. But after Jesus's birth, wise men, or magi, arrive in Jerusalem from the east asking for "the one who has been born king of the Jews." They have seen his star and come to worship him. Puzzled, Jewish priests and scholars inform them that, according to prophecy, Israel's expected savior will be born in Bethlehem.

The magi head to Bethlehem, where they find the baby Jesus and his parents. While it may have been elaborated after Micah's time (during the Babylonian exile or later), the prophecy was part of a growing expectation among the Jews that a new ruler would emerge to restore the nation's greatness. In the Micah prophecy, he would be a true shepherd under whom Israel would live peacefully.

Bethlehem was significant. It was King David's birthplace, suggesting a new ruler from the same royal line, and it was small and rural. For Micah and the tradition he represented, that was important. Like David, the new ruler would be from the fringes, not the center of society.

THE REMNANT OF ISRAEL WILL TRUST IN THE NAME OF THE LORD
ZEPHANIAH 3:17, CALL FOR REPENTANCE

IN BRIEF

PASSAGE
Zephaniah 1–3

THEME
God's righteous remnant

SETTING
640–609 BCE Jerusalem.

KEY FIGURE
Zephaniah Prophet of Judah.

The Book of Zephaniah is the ninth book within the short prophetic texts called the Minor Prophets, or the Twelve Prophets. The book was written during the reign of King Josiah (640–609 BCE) by, it says, the son of Cushi and a descendant of King Hezekiah. This has led some scholars to believe that the author may have been from Cush in Ethiopia or a descendant of King Hezekiah, a former ruler of Judah.

The book probably formed part of the religious reforms of Josiah, who outlawed the non-Yahwistic cults that had sprung up during Assyrian domination of Judah. It calls Judah "you shameful nation" (2:1) and berates Jerusalem whose priests "profane the sanctuary and do violence to the Law" (3:4).

The text, modeled on many other prophecies and structured in a similar way to other biblical narratives, is about destruction and restoration. The people of Judah and its neighbors Philistia, Moab, Ammon, Cush, and Assyria have angered the Lord. Their prophesied destruction on the Day of Judgment, the "great day of the Lord," is described in words that centuries later will be turned into the somber Latin hymn *Dies israe* (Day of Wrath) used in the mass for the dead.

Rising from the ashes
The restoration portion of the book begins at Zephaniah 3:9. Some scholars believe this section was written after the fall of Jerusalem and the Babylonian exile because it mentions the "remnant" of Israel and gathering those who have been scattered. It describes how the Lord will punish Israel's enemies and save the righteous, who are now purged from sin. Chapter 3:14–20, beginning "Sing daughter Zion; shout aloud Israel" tells how the Lord will remove sorrow and punishment from the Israelites. ∎

'I will sweep away the birds of the air and the fish of the sea. The wicked will have only heaps of rubble when I cut off man from the face of the earth,' declares the Lord.
Zephaniah 1:3

See also: The Fall 30–35 ∎ The Flood 40–41 ∎ Sodom and Gomorrah 48–49 ∎ The Fall of Jerusalem 128–31 ∎ The Final Judgment 316–21

SURELY THE DAY IS COMING; IT WILL BURN LIKE A FURNACE

MALACHI 4, THE DAY OF JUDGEMENT

IN BRIEF

PASSAGE
Malachi 1–4

THEME
Wrath and judgment

SETTING
500–600 BCE Judah.

KEY FIGURE
Malachi Prophet of Judah.

Malachi is the last book of the Minor Prophets, or the Twelve Prophets, and for Christians, it is the last book of the Old Testament. It is hard to know when it was written, but use of the word *pechah* (governor) in 1:8 fits the period after the Persian conquest of Judah (539 BCE) and the building of the Second Temple.

Malachi means "my messenger," or "angel," and Malachi says that "God will send a messenger who will prepare the way before me." Some believe this "messenger" is Malachi, although the phrase is also used by Jesus to describe John the Baptist (Luke 7:27), leading Christian commentators to see the promised messenger as Christ.

Catalogue of rebukes

The text begins by invoking the Genesis story of Jacob and his brother Esau (see pp. 54–55), in which Jacob is loved by God, and receives His blessing, while Esau is rejected. This sets the stage for the remainder of the text, in which God reminds the Israelites of His covenants with the ancestors and asks "Where is the respect due me?" (1:6). He rebukes the priests for not keeping the Law and the people for disobedience; taking wives who worship foreign gods; and sacrificing blind, lame, or diseased animals as offerings.

The book ends with a proclamation that the Day of the Lord will come, when "every evil-doer will be stubble" (4:1) to be set on fire. However, God renews His covenant with the faithful and states that He will send the prophet Elijah—a precursor to the Messiah in Judaism and to Jesus Christ in Christianity—before striking the land with "total destruction" (4:6). ∎

Christ sits above a rainbow in Crispin van den Broeck's *The Last Judgment* (1560), recalling the rainbow that God created as a symbol of his covenant with Noah after the Flood.

See also: The Flood 40–41 ▪ Covenants 44–47 ▪ Esau and Jacob 54–55 ▪ The Ten Commandments 78–83 ▪ The Coming of Salvation 189 ▪ The Final Judgment 316–21

THE GOS

PELS

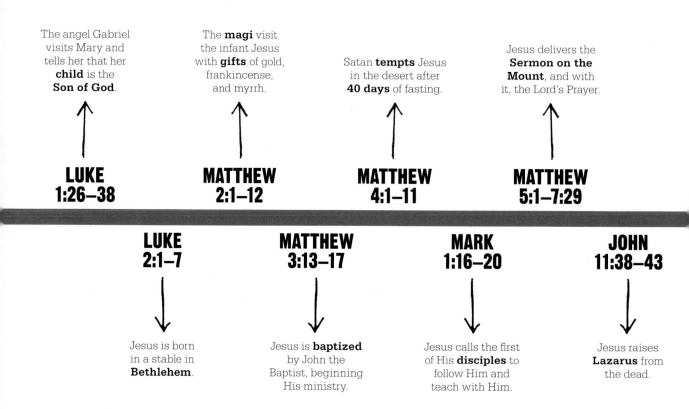

The angel Gabriel visits Mary and tells her that her **child** is the **Son of God**.

LUKE 1:26–38

The **magi** visit the infant Jesus with **gifts** of gold, frankincense, and myrrh.

MATTHEW 2:1–12

Satan **tempts** Jesus in the desert after **40 days** of fasting.

MATTHEW 4:1–11

Jesus delivers the **Sermon on the Mount**, and with it, the Lord's Prayer.

MATTHEW 5:1–7:29

LUKE 2:1–7

Jesus is born in a stable in **Bethlehem**.

MATTHEW 3:13–17

Jesus is **baptized** by John the Baptist, beginning His ministry.

MARK 1:16–20

Jesus calls the first of His **disciples** to follow Him and teach with Him.

JOHN 11:38–43

Jesus raises **Lazarus** from the dead.

Christians first used the Greek word *euangelion* ("gospel" or "good news") to refer to the message of salvation from sin and judgment through faith in Jesus Christ. By the middle of the 2nd century CE, however, it was also used to refer to the four canonical books of the New Testament written in the second half of the 1st century CE. While none of the four Gospels names its author directly, two are traditionally attributed to the Apostles Matthew and John, and two are associated with the Apostles Peter (Mark) and Paul (Luke).

The central figure in the Gospels is Jesus, an itinerant preacher born in Bethlehem and raised in Nazareth, a small town in Galilee. His life and ministry are set against the background of the Roman occupation of Israel and prophecies of a divinely anointed leader, a Messiah. Although the details of this expectation varied widely, popular belief looked for a military-political leader such as Moses or David, who would liberate Israel from Roman control and reestablish the Davidic monarchy. Jesus's claim to be the Messiah combined many of these ideas, but rejected the establishment of an earthly kingdom as His immediate goal. Instead, it seems Jesus saw sin and alienation from God as the primary enemy to be defeated.

All four Gospels relate the miracles that Jesus performed—feeding the hungry, healing the sick, casting out demons, calming storms, and even raising the dead. They also report His teaching, public preaching, and His private conversations with His disciples. Through sermons and parables, Jesus repeatedly called for His followers to repent and submit to the coming Kingdom of God.

Disputes between Jesus and Jerusalem's religious leaders punctuate the Gospels. In private and public settings, these leaders show a growing concern over His fellowship with "sinners" (Jews who did not obey God's commandments) and His seeming blasphemy by claiming a status equal to God and the authority to forgive sins. Jesus, in turn, rebuked the religious leaders by cleansing the Temple, warning against their teaching and the example they set, and declaring God's judgment on them. This conflict, along with alarm at His popularity, led the religious leaders

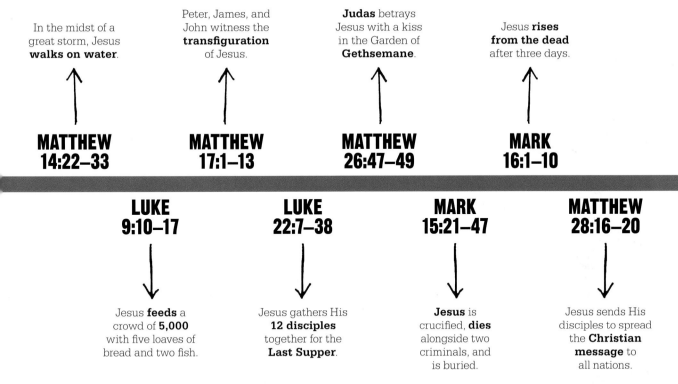

In the midst of a great storm, Jesus **walks on water**.

MATTHEW 14:22–33

Peter, James, and John witness the **transfiguration** of Jesus.

MATTHEW 17:1–13

Judas betrays Jesus with a kiss in the Garden of **Gethsemane**.

MATTHEW 26:47–49

Jesus **rises from the dead** after three days.

MARK 16:1–10

LUKE 9:10–17

Jesus **feeds** a crowd of **5,000** with five loaves of bread and two fish.

LUKE 22:7–38

Jesus gathers His **12 disciples** together for the **Last Supper**.

MARK 15:21–47

Jesus is crucified, **dies** alongside two criminals, and is buried.

MATTHEW 28:16–20

Jesus sends His disciples to spread the **Christian message** to all nations.

to try Jesus for blasphemy, and then pressure the Roman governor Pilate to crucify Him.

The Gospels all indicate that Jesus expected His betrayal and crucifixion. This confused His disciples, who could not grasp how Jesus's execution could be the culmination of God's plan for the one they regarded as the Messiah.

The climax of the Gospels is Jesus's resurrection. Luke and John report the incredulity of the disciples, and how Jesus overcame their doubts and prepared them for their own mission to preach the "good news" to all nations.

Similarities and differences

The first three Gospels—Matthew, Mark, and Luke—are called the Synoptic Gospels (literally, "looking together") because they relate many of the same events in much the same order, often using similar or even identical language. Such similarities have led many scholars to the view that one Gospel, and possibly other documents, was the primary source for the others. Debate about which Gospel was written first, the exact nature of their relationship to one another, and related issues, are known as the "Synoptic problem."

Differences between the Gospels have also been intensely analyzed. Ancient scholars tended to see these as harmonious rather than contradictory, collectively painting a richer picture of Jesus's life and teaching than any single account. Some modern scholars see the differences as conflicting and evidence of myth-making. Others see them as an attempt to address different audiences or theological themes present in Jesus's life and teaching. While Matthew stresses Jesus's fulfillment of Old Testament prophecy, Mark depicts Him as the "Suffering Servant." Luke's account primarily appeals to Gentile audiences, while John, whose account is markedly different from the Synoptic Gospels, often elaborates on Christ's divinity.

Scholars have also debated the literary genre of the four books. The traditional view of the Gospels as biographies lost favor among 20th-century scholars, who pointed out that as a genre, biographies tend to explore the personality, psychology, and forming influences of their subject. In the Bible, these aspects are secondary to the depiction of Jesus as divine and the espousal of His teachings. ■

AND BEHOLD, YOU WILL CONCEIVE IN YOUR WOMB AND BEAR A SON

LUKE 1:31, THE ANNUNCIATION

IN BRIEF

PASSAGE
Luke 1:31

THEME
The Annunciation

SETTING
c.7 BCE Nazareth, a town of Galilee.

KEY FIGURES
Mary A young Galilean Jewish woman. Luke's Gospel traces her lineage from King David.

Joseph Betrothed to Mary and, according to Matthew's Gospel, a descendant of King David.

The angel Gabriel God's heavenly messenger and the bearer of the Annunciation.

The Gospel of Luke is the only place in the Bible in which the announcement to Mary of Jesus's birth is recorded. In an event now known as the Annunciation, the angel Gabriel visits a young woman named Mary in Nazareth and declares that she will soon bear a son. She is surprised to hear that she is going to give birth, as she is a virgin, not yet married to her betrothed, Joseph. In reassurance, the angel Gabriel tells her: "The Holy Spirit will come on you, and the power of the Most High will overshadow you. So the holy one to be born will be called the Son of God" (Luke 1:35).

Elsewhere in the Gospels—in Matthew 1:20—Joseph is informed by another angel that his wife-to-be is expecting a child of the Lord. The angel tells Joseph, who has been considering breaking his engagement to Mary because she has become pregnant, that the pregnancy has been divinely orchestrated and that he should marry her without delay and name their child Jesus, which means "the Lord saves." The significance of this name is confirmed by the angel, who states that "he will save his people from their sins."

Davidic inheritance

One of the most important aspects of Jesus's birth is His ancestry—the lineage of both His parents. Although Joseph and Mary are of humble means, they are of noble birth, as descendants of the Israelite King David. This connection is of great significance in Judaic culture and religion, because many Jews at the time expected not only a Messiah but

Gabriel appears to Mary in the central panel of this oil on oak triptych. This depiction of the Annunciation was painted by Carlo Crivelli c.1440.

See also: The Birth of Jesus 180–85 ▪ The Magi 186 ▪ Herod's Infanticide 187 ▪
The Divinity of Jesus 190–93

Angels announce Mary's conception

Luke's Gospel focuses on **Mary.**	Matthew's Gospel focuses on **Joseph**.
↓	↓
Mary, a **virgin**, is **pledged** to marry Joseph.	Mary is pledged to Joseph but becomes **pregnant**.
↓	↓
Gabriel tells Mary she has found favor with God.	Joseph, **"son of David,"** decides to leave her quietly.
↓	↓
Gabriel says she will conceive a child by the **Holy Spirit**.	An **angel** explains that Mary conceived by the Holy Spirit.
↓	↓
Mary **accepts** Gabriel's word and promises to serve God.	Joseph **marries** Mary but the union is not consummated.

Jesus is born in Bethlehem.

a Davidic Messiah, or king, who would deliver them from their enemies—at that time, the Romans. As Isaiah had prophesied: "He will reign on David's throne and over his kingdom, establishing and upholding it with justice and righteousness" (Isaiah 9:7).

A common name given to Jesus refers back to this idea of Him as the prophesied savior. *Messiah* means "anointed one" in Hebrew—that is, Jesus has been blessed by God to lead His chosen people—and translates as *Christos* in Greek, hence the English name "Jesus Christ."

Son of Man
While the Bible is full of miraculous signs, it is noteworthy that the means of Jesus coming to earth is genuinely human: through Mary's pregnancy and childbirth. Although Jesus proves Himself to be the Son of God, His conception in Mary by the Holy Spirit makes Him both human and divine. ∎

Mary

An obscure young woman living in Nazareth and betrothed to Joseph, Mary rises to everlasting adoration by the Annunciation of the angel Gabriel. Mary humbly accepts her extraordinary situation without challenge and immediately prepares herself to deliver the son of the Lord. She gives birth to Jesus in a stable in Bethlehem.

Mary encourages Jesus to perform His first miracle at Cana. After Jesus leaves home to begin His ministry, Mary rarely appears in the Bible, but she is present at the foot of the cross during the crucifixion and continues to meet with the disciples after this and the resurrection. Mary's devotion to God is attested to by her psalm of thanksgiving (canticle) in Luke 1:46–55. This "Song of Mary" is also called the Magnificat, and is incorporated into the liturgical services of the Catholic Church. It is one of the most ancient of all Christian hymns.

The Virgin of Guadalupe, in a clay wall hanging in Metepec, Mexico. The name dates back to 1851, when a peasant saw a vision of Mary near Villa de Guadalupe.

A SAVIOR HAS BEEN BORN TO YOU; HE IS THE MESSIAH

THE BIRTH OF JESUS, LUKE 2:11

IN BRIEF

PASSAGE
Luke 2:1–40

THEME
Christ's humble origins

SETTING
c.6–4 BCE A cave or barn on the outskirts of Bethlehem.

KEY FIGURES
Mary A young woman from Nazareth, Galilee.

Joseph Husband of Mary, a carpenter, possibly descended from the royal House of David.

Jesus Mary's newborn baby, who is the Messiah and Son of God.

Three shepherds Herdsmen watching their sheep through the night near Bethlehem.

Simeon An old and devout man in Jerusalem.

Anna An 84-year-old widow in Jerusalem.

The Nativity scene in Joan Mates's *Altarpiece of St. James* (c.1400) from Vallespinosa, Spain, depicts a troubled Joseph struggling to come to terms with the divine birth.

T he story of the birth of Jesus, widely known as the Nativity, is presented as a simple tale in the Gospel of Luke. Probably writing in the early 80s CE, the author draws on earlier written accounts of Jesus's life alongside oral traditions handed down in various 1st-century Christian communities. It is believed that the author was also highlighting parallels with birth narratives in the Hebrew Bible—notably, the story of the birth and infancy of the prophet Samuel. Matthew's account stresses the fulfillment of Old Testament prophecies and begins with a genealogy tracing Jesus's ancestry to Abraham through King David.

The birth of Jesus

When the Roman emperor orders a census requiring the heads of all households to register in their ancestral communities, Joseph needs to return to the town of Bethlehem. He travels there with his heavily pregnant wife Mary, finally arriving at an inn.

Mary and Joseph arrive too late in the evening to find suitable accommodations—the Greek phrase in Luke 2:7 translates as "there was no room at the inn"—and they must find makeshift shelter elsewhere: a stable, or possibly a cave, on the town's outskirts. In these unlikely surroundings, Mary gives birth to a son. Like all mothers of the time, she wraps her newborn baby with swaddling cloths. She then places her child in the only crib available: a feeding trough for animals. The modest birth story of God's son serves to indicate how Jesus was born as an ordinary member of mankind—a status that would enable Him to establish His close relationship with the people of God.

Like the author of Matthew's Gospel, the writer of Luke also places the birth in Bethlehem, about 6 miles (10km) south of Jerusalem. This has symbolic significance, as it links Jesus with

See also: The Prophet Samuel 110–15 ▪ The Suffering Servant 154–55 ▪ The Prophet Micah 168–71 ▪ The Annunciation 178–79 ▪ The Magi 186 ▪ Herod's Infanticide 187 ▪ The Coming of Salvation 189 ▪ The Divinity of Jesus 190–93

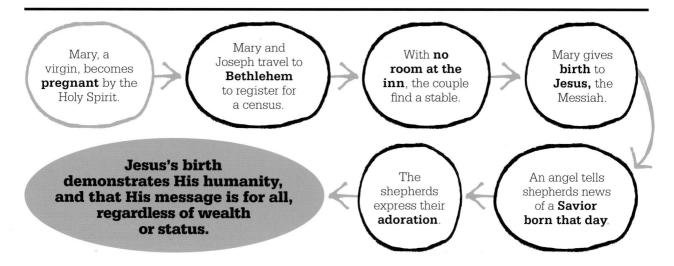

Mary, a virgin, becomes **pregnant** by the Holy Spirit.

Mary and Joseph travel to **Bethlehem** to register for a census.

With **no room at the inn**, the couple find a stable.

Mary gives **birth** to **Jesus,** the Messiah.

An angel tells shepherds news of a **Savior born that day**.

The shepherds express their **adoration**.

Jesus's birth demonstrates His humanity, and that His message is for all, regardless of wealth or status.

King David, who was also born in Bethlehem, and with the prophet Micah's foretelling that a savior, or Messiah, of David's line would be born there. Ascribing Jesus's birthplace to Bethlehem is not purely symbolic, however, as traditions in the early Church also say that Jesus was born there.

Luke's dating of the birth is more uncertain. He identifies the census that obliges Mary and Joseph to travel to Bethlehem as the one that was ordered by Quirinius, the Roman governor of Syria, in 6–7 CE. This census provoked a revolt among the Jews. However, this does not fit with later references in the Gospels. Both Luke and Matthew make clear that Jesus was born during the reign of King Herod the Great of Judea, who died in 4 BCE. Luke may have confused the census that took place under Quirinius with an earlier one carried out by Herod within his own realms. Although still contested, scholars generally place the birth of Jesus between 6–4 BCE.

The news spreads

Rejoicing at the birth of Jesus extends beyond Mary and Joseph. Just as the birth is preceded in Luke's account by the annunciation of the angel Gabriel, who appears to Mary in her home village of Nazareth, so it is followed by an another annunciation. An angel »

Joseph, husband of Mary

Joseph is mentioned only in the Gospels of Matthew and Luke, where he is said to be descended from King David. This is not impossible: although a humble carpenter, he might come from a minor, impoverished branch of the former royal house.

Matthew's Gospel—in which an annunciation happens to Joseph rather than Mary—shows a very human figure caught in a struggle between his sense of justice and his compassion for Mary. According to Law, Mary, if guilty of adultery, should be stoned to death. Unlike Mary,

Joseph does not feature in the ministry of Jesus, perhaps because he had died by then. He must have died by the time of the crucifixion, as John 19:26 states that Mary went to live with the "disciple whom He loved." From the 2nd century CE, tradition portrayed Joseph as a widower when he married Mary, with children from a previous marriage. This preserved the doctrine of Mary's perpetual virginity while also helping to explain the brothers and sisters of Jesus mentioned in Mark 6:3 and Matthew 13:55–56.

appears to shepherds in the fields nearby, as they watch over their sheep during the night. The angel announces the birth of a "Savior," a word with double significance. In Jewish minds, it would recall Moses, who saved the Israelites by leading them out of slavery in Egypt. On another level, it would also evoke the Roman Emperor Augustus, a self-proclaimed "savior" who had brought much-needed peace to the empire. This child, the angel is saying, born in such lowly circumstances and announced to such humble people, will come to be a savior to all of humankind.

In the eyes of many at the time, shepherds would be regarded as unworthy of receiving a divine revelation. Although King David started life as a shepherd, and kings in the ancient Near East generally liked to describe themselves as shepherds of their people, in everyday life shepherds were despised and shunned. Spending so much time in the fields with animals, they were dirty and foul-smelling, and they also had to deal regularly with animal carcasses, making them ritually unclean in Jewish eyes.

Like other marginalized figures in Luke, the shepherds, although initially afraid, are open and trusting, and their response to the angel is immediate. They hurry off to find the baby, and then share all that they have heard and experienced with Mary and Joseph. Mary is described as "treasuring up" the things they tell her and "pondering" them in her heart (Luke 2:19).

A humble sacrifice

On the eighth day after the birth, the baby is circumcised, as is customary, and named Jesus, meaning "the Lord saves." Later, He is taken to the Temple in Jerusalem, in an episode which recalls the earlier story in the Hebrew Bible of the young Samuel's presentation by his mother Hannah at the "house of the Lord" in Shiloh (1 Samuel 1:24). Here, Luke seems to have conflated two different rituals. The first concerns the redemption of the firstborn,

A Savior has been born to you; He is the Messiah, the Lord. This will be a sign to you: You will find a baby wrapped in cloths and lying in a manger.
Luke 2:11–12

whereby all firstborn males were redeemed—effectively, bought back from God—through the payment of money to the religious authorities. This did not necessarily involve going to Jerusalem. The second required a mother to go to the Temple for her ritual purification just over a month after childbirth. There, the mother would make a sacrificial offering. For those unable to afford anything more elaborate, this consisted of "a pair of doves or two young pigeons" (Luke 2:24). This is the approach Mary takes, again emphasizing the family's humble background.

Blessing the child

While they are in the Temple, Mary and Joseph encounter two people, a man named Simeon and a woman called Anna. Luke often pairs men and women in this way, perhaps to indicate that they are equal and complementary before God. Both

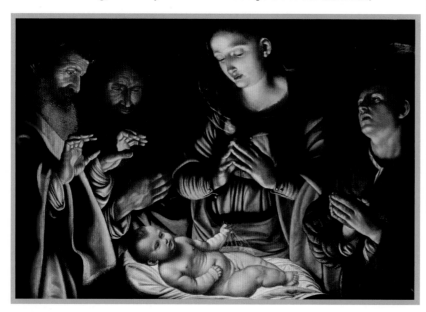

Giovanni Girolamo Savoldo's *Adoration of the Shepherds* (c.1530s) depicts the shepherds and the Virgin Mary bathed in the luminous and symbolic light of the Christ child.

Celebrating Christmas

The Bible gives no indication as to the year of Jesus's birth, and many leaders of the early Church disapproved of marking the event, preferring to honor martyrs on the anniversary of their martyrdom. In spite of this, efforts were made to assign a date to the Nativity, using the seasons as a guide.

The spring equinox in March was associated with creation, the emergence of new life. This seemed right for the date of Jesus's conception. Nine months later came the winter solstice—December 25, in the Julian calendar of the time. In Rome this was also the feast of the invincible sun, *Sol Invictus*, the turning point at which light starts to drive back darkness. Jesus had long been identified as the "Sun of righteousness"; the symbolism was compelling and the date gradually gained acceptance. There is evidence that, by 336 CE, the feast of the Nativity—Christmas—was already being celebrated liturgically in Rome on December 25. Within a century, the holy festival had become widespread.

are old, righteous, and devout, belonging to a recognizable group known in the Bible as the "faithful remnant," described by Zephaniah, Malachi, and other prophets. They care passionately about the redemption of Jerusalem and Israel.

Simeon arrives first, divine inspiration leading him to the couple from provincial Galilee. He takes the child Jesus in his arms and utters the song, or canticle, known by its first two words in

This child is destined to cause the falling and rising of many in Israel, and to be a sign that will be spoken against, so that the thoughts of many hearts will be revealed.
Luke 2:34–35

The traditional place of Christ's birth, Bethlehem's Church of the Nativity, is an important pilgrimage site for Christians. A silver star marks the supposed birthplace.

the Latin Bible, *Nunc Dimittis*. Years earlier, God had revealed to Simeon that he would not die until he had seen the promised Messiah. Now the old man declares that promise has been fulfilled. He can die peacefully, for in the child he holds in his arms he sees God's salvation. This, he proclaims, is for the whole world, not just Israel, saying the child will be "a light for revelation to the Gentiles" (Luke 2:32). This universalism is another characteristic of the Gospel of Luke, which was written chiefly for a Christian audience from a Gentile, rather than a Jewish, background.

Simeon then adds two warnings: people's responses to Jesus will be mixed. Not all shall welcome Him; many will reject Him. In an aside to Mary, he tells her that a sword will one day pierce her soul. This may be a foretelling of Mary's later sufferings at the crucifixion, or it may refer to her need, when the

adult Jesus embarks upon His public ministry, to let go of her son for the greater good.

Anna, an 84-year-old widow, joins the group, also recognizing that the child is the one promised by God. She gives loud thanks for what she is seeing. Having fulfilled all that is required of them and their baby by "the Law of the Lord", and marveling at what they have seen and heard, Mary and Joseph set off home to Nazareth. The child Jesus grows and becomes strong, "filled with wisdom, and the grace of God was upon Him" (Luke 2:40). ∎

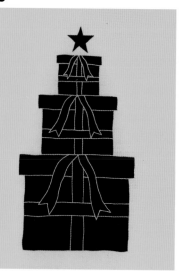

THEY ... PRESENTED HIM WITH GIFTS OF GOLD, FRANKINCENSE, AND MYRRH

MATTHEW 2:11, THE MAGI

Although divination was forbidden in the Jewish scriptures, it was common in other Greco-Roman and ancient Near Eastern societies. Magi were respected professionals, who studied the constellations and then interpreted the movements of the stars as divine portents.

A new king

The journey of the magi is recorded only in Matthew's Gospel. In his account, the magi travel from the east to Judea searching for the newly born "king of the Jews." On hearing of the magis' quest, King Herod is alarmed by the potential threat to his rule. When his chief priests tell him that the Christ is to be born in Bethlehem, he tells the magi to go to that city and return with the exact location of the baby, on the pretense that he wishes to pay his respects.

The magi follow a unique star to Bethlehem and find Jesus with His mother, Mary. Overjoyed, the magi kneel down before the child and offer gifts of gold, frankincense,

The Adoration of the Magi by Quentin Matsys shows the magi with a huge retinue. None of the Gospels suggest this was the case.

and myrrh. Finally, on account of a dream warning them against returning to Jerusalem, they journey back home to the east.

The story of the magi shows that Jesus is not only fulfilling Jewish prophecies but also Gentile predictions. As such, Jesus is depicted as a divinely chosen ruler whom all peoples and nations should glorify. ∎

See also: The Birth of Jesus 180–85 ∎ Herod's Infanticide 187 ∎ The Council of Jerusalem 292–93

HE GAVE ORDERS TO KILL ALL THE BOYS IN BETHLEHEM
MATTHEW 2:16, HEROD'S INFANTICIDE

IN BRIEF

PASSAGE
Matthew 2:13–18

THEME
Persecution

SETTING
6–4 BCE During the reign of King Herod. Judea and Egypt.

KEY FIGURES
Herod King of Judea, appointed by the Romans, who also called him "King of the Jews."

Joseph The adoptive father of Jesus and husband of Mary.

The angel A divine messenger who warns Joseph of King Herod's plot to kill the infant Jesus.

The first two chapters in the Gospel of Matthew recount the early years of Jesus's life. In each scene, the author calls on the words of the prophets, including Jeremiah and Hosea, to demonstrate how Jesus is the anticipated Messiah.

Exodus reinterpreted

Worried about a prediction that his royal replacement, the Christ, has been born in Bethlehem, Herod orders the killing of all babies under the age of 2 in the city. In a moment of divine intervention, an angel appears to Joseph and urges him to flee with Mary and Jesus. Following the angelic command, Joseph resettles his family in Egypt. They do not return to Judea until after the death of King Herod several years later.

The king's actions mirror those of Pharaoh in the Exodus story, who also ordered mass infanticide. Like Moses, Jesus flees from the land of His birth after a king threatens His life, but later returns to become an influential religious teacher.

The author builds on these connections between Jesus and the Exodus story by proclaiming that Jesus's stay in Egypt fulfills a text in Hosea in which God calls His son out of Egypt: "When Israel was a child, I loved him, and out of Egypt I called my son" (Hosea 11:1). The original passage referred to God rescuing the people of Israel from slavery in Egypt. The author of Matthew's Gospel reinterprets the divine claim, making Jesus the Son of God. ∎

Escape to Egypt. Stay there until I tell you, for Herod is going to search for the child to kill him.
Matthew 2:13

See also: Moses and the Burning Bush 66–69 ▪ The Ten Plagues 70–71 ▪ The Exodus 74–77 ▪ The Prophet Micah 168–71 ▪ The Birth of Jesus 180–85

188

DIDN'T YOU KNOW I HAD TO BE IN MY FATHER'S HOUSE?

LUKE 2:49, A CHILD IN THE TEMPLE

Every year, Jesus and His parents travel to Jerusalem for the feast of Passover. One year, when Jesus is 12 years old, He stays in Jerusalem after His parents have set out for home. Thinking their son is among their fellow travelers, Mary and Joseph do not realize He is missing until a whole day has passed, at which point they return to Jerusalem to look for Him. After three days of searching, they find Him debating with the rabbis in the Temple.

Everyone who listens to Jesus is amazed by Him, but Mary rebukes her son. In an instant, Jesus turns from His debate with the rabbis to address His mother: "Why were you searching for me? Didn't you know I had to be in my Father's house?" (Luke 2:49). Jesus's reply confuses His parents, who do not understand that He is revealing His knowledge of His divine lineage.

The author's use of dramatic irony was probably intended to amuse early Christian readers of Luke. Other literary devices include foreshadowing and allusion: Jesus's three-day absence from His family anticipates His three days in the grave after His death, and the combination of the Passover setting and Jesus's claim to be the Son of God allude to the Exodus, in which Israel is also called God's son (Exodus 4:22). Such devices, and the fact that this is the only depiction of Jesus's adolescence in the Gospels, lead some scholars to view the episode as theological fiction rather than historical fact, the main purpose of which is to highlight Jesus's divinity. ∎

In William Holman Hunt's highly symbolic *The Finding of the Savior in the Temple* (1860), a blind rabbi (bottom left) clutches the Torah as though he and his religion are under threat.

See also: The Exodus 74–77 ▪ The Annunciation 178–79 ▪ The Birth of Jesus 180–85 ▪ The Magi 186 ▪ The Coming of Salvation 189

PREPARE THE WAY FOR THE LORD
LUKE 3:4, THE COMING OF SALVATION

IN BRIEF

PASSAGE
Luke 3:1–18

THEME
The prophecy fulfilled

SETTING
c.26 CE The country around the River Jordan.

KEY FIGURES
John the Baptist Son of Elizabeth and Zechariah. A prophet who baptizes Jesus and is later beheaded by King Herod.

Isaiah An ancient Israelite prophet, to whom the Book of Isaiah is ascribed.

Jesus The Messiah and Son of God in the period before He begins His ministry.

John the Baptist was a Jewish prophet who heralded Jesus in the Gospel of Luke. In Luke 3, John goes out into the country and calls the people to repent and be forgiven. He baptizes those who accept his message in the River Jordan.

The author of Luke presents John's actions as the fulfillment of a prophecy in the Book of Isaiah. John quotes Isaiah 40:3, in which a voice in the wilderness exhorts listeners to prepare the way for the Lord. They are to make the path straight, level, and smooth, and then all will see the coming of God's salvation. Although Isaiah's prophecy spoke first about God's rescue of the Israelites from exile in Babylon, the Gospel of Luke reports that John the Baptist interpreted it to have a further fulfillment in his own ministry.

Baptism by fire
In the next scene, the followers of John begin to wonder if he is the Christ. John affirms his role as messianic precursor, declaring that

The ax is … at the root of the trees, and every tree that does not produce good fruit will be cut down.
Luke 3:9

he is not worthy to untie the sandal of the one who is to come. He says that while he baptizes with water, the one more powerful than him will baptize with the Holy Spirit and fire. John concludes his message with an image of Christ as a winnower, separating the wheat from chaff and burning the chaff with unquenchable fire (3:17), symbolizing the Final Judgment. John hopes that all will hear the news of the coming Christ, repent, and be saved. ■

See also: The Suffering Servant 190–93 ▪ The Divinity of Jesus 190–93 ▪ The Baptism of Jesus 194–97 ▪ The Empty Tomb 268–71

THE WORD BECAME FLESH AND MADE HIS DWELLING AMONG US

JOHN 1:14, THE DIVINITY OF JESUS

For Christians, Jesus of Nazareth is the central figure in the Bible. Although prophets, priests, and kings have come before Him, none taught as He did, nor provoked such loyalty and hostility. Jesus's life, teaching, death, and resurrection are the substance of Christian teaching.

Word of God

The Gospel of John is the last of the four Gospels to be written. One of the main concerns in the Apostle John's New Testament writings, which include the epistles of 1–3 John, is to encourage those who believe in Jesus that He is the Son of God. It begins like Genesis 1 with the creation of the world. Just as Genesis 1 assumes the existence of God, "In the beginning God …" and goes on to assert that this God is the creator, "and God said, 'Let there be light,'" John opens with, "In the beginning was the Word, and the Word was with God, and the Word was God …

See also: The Exodus 74–77 ■ The Suffering Servant 154–55 ■ The Crucifixion 258–65 ■ The Empty Tomb 268–71 ■ The Coming of Salvation 301

Fra Angelico's fresco *Christ the Judge Amongst the Angels*, from the Chapel of San Brizio, Orvieto, Italy, shows Christ presiding in judgment on a heavenly throne.

All things came into being through Him." The foundation of all things, according to John, was the Word, who was in some sense God, and yet somehow distinct from God.

In John 1:14–18, the Apostle returns to the connection he made between the divine Word and creation. John declares that "the Word became flesh, and dwelt among us ..." and God exhibited His glory as His "one and only" Son.

John the Apostle's claim that Jesus was also the creator did not arise with his Gospel nor was the realization that Jesus was, and claimed to be, something more than a Galilean carpenter or a preacher a late invention. Jesus's behavior itself implies divinity. The first three Gospels portray Him acting in ways that parallel God's interventions in the Old Testament, such as feeding the 5,000 with loaves and fish (God feeds the Israelites in the wilderness) and »

Awaiting the Messiah

The prophet Isaiah had predicted that the Messiah would be born to a virgin and be called "Immanuel" (Isaiah 7:14), meaning "God with us." In the New Testament, the author of the Gospel of John reports how John the Baptist, proclaiming Jesus's higher rank, says, "He was before me" (John 1:15). The implication is that Jesus, who was younger than John the Baptist, existed eternally.

The other Gospels report that even during Jesus's lifetime, people see and hear things about Him that are extraordinary. When Herod hears that magi from the east are visiting the infant Jesus, he sees the child as a threat and asks his chief priests "where the Messiah was to be born" (Matthew 2:4).

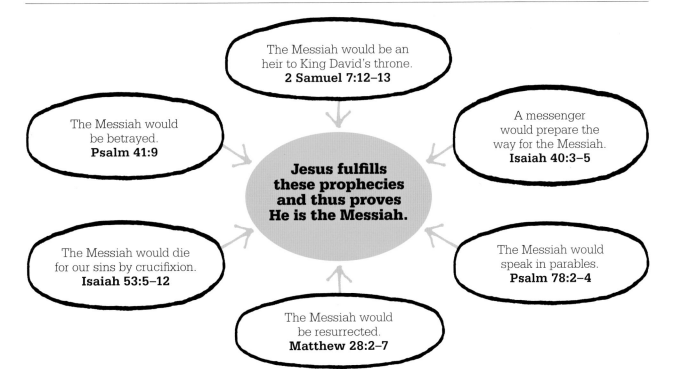

St. Simeon

Eight days after His birth, Mary and Joseph present Jesus for circumcision at the Temple in Jerusalem. Luke's Gospel tells how an elderly priest, Simeon, who was longing for the coming of Israel's Messiah, is in the Temple courts that day (Luke 2:25–35). God had promised Simeon that he would not die until he had seen the Messiah. Led by the Holy Spirit, Simeon takes the infant Jesus in his arms and blesses Him. In Simeon's Song, he praises God for keeping His promise, both to him and to Israel. He identifies Jesus as the salvation for both Israel and for the world.

Simeon's expectation echoed the universal scope expressed by Isaiah, who talks of the Israelites being a "light for the Gentiles" (Isaiah 49:6). Salvation would come first to the Jews, but would not be for them alone. God's plan was to save people from all nations. The praise in Simeon's Song anticipates an important theme in Luke's Gospel and in Acts—the salvation of the wider world.

stilling storms (as God does in Jonah when the prophet runs away to sea).

Matthew, Mark, and Luke's Gospels also report incidents in which several religious leaders understand Jesus to be claiming divine status. Most famously, the night before His crucifixion, Jesus faces a trial before a large group of religious leaders. They demand to know if He is the Christ, the Son of God. Jesus affirms that He is, saying they will see Him "sitting at the right hand of the Mighty One, and coming on the clouds of heaven" (Matthew 26:64).

The Apostle Paul, preaching across the Roman Empire after Jesus's death, writes that Jesus is divine. He refers to Jesus as God twice in his letters and calls Jesus "Lord," a Hebrew term for God. Paul anticipates John's teaching that all things are created through Jesus (1 Corinthians 8:6) and insists that Jesus possesses every attribute of divinity (Colossians 1:19, 2:9), such as omnipotence, eternality, and omnipresence.

John's evidence
The Gospel of John provides the most explicit case for Jesus's divinity. After healing a man on the Sabbath day, Jesus answers the

> Christ was not … a being half human and half not, like a centaur, but both things at once and both things thoroughly, very man and very God.
> **G.K. Chesterton**

rabbis' criticism by equating God's work with His own, calling God His Father, and making Himself equal with God. In another dispute, Jesus states that "before Abraham was, I AM," thus making a claim to preexist Abraham (John 8:58). The rabbis understand these words, but deny their truth, and pick up stones to kill Jesus for blasphemy. Later, when pressed to declare if He is the Messiah, Jesus says, "I and the Father are One" (John 10:30), echoing Deuteronomy 6:4—"Hear O Israel, the Lord our God, the Lord is One"—but replacing the second "Lord" with "I and the Father."

Fully man, fully God

Humanity   Deity

The Chalcedonian Creed asserts that Jesus Christ has two natures— human and divine. Each is complete and distinct, yet "not parted or divided" into two persons.

Spatial, temporal existence, subject to birth, life, and death

Omnipresent, eternal, infinite existence, with power over life and death

The supreme act in support of Jesus's claim to be divine is His resurrection. After His execution by the Romans for being a rebel, Jesus's resurrection would have stood as God's vindication of Jesus's words and deeds. When Thomas finally sees the resurrected Jesus, he addresses Him as "My Lord and my God" (John 20:28).

The incarnation

Jesus of Nazareth is a man who eats and sleeps, yet He also claims to be God. Affirming these two ideas together is the doctrine of the incarnation: the Word becoming flesh. Some early teachers tried to resolve this paradox by saying Christ was fundamentally human, but had been "adopted" as God's Son. Others, affirming the genuine deity of Jesus, taught that He only "seemed" to be human. Yet others insisted that Jesus could really be God because He was the Father in disguise. Later teachers affirmed the humanity and deity of Jesus, but struggled to find a consistent explanation for how He could be both. In the 5th century some teachers affirmed that Jesus had a human body and soul, but that the divine Word took the place of His human spirit. Others taught that the human and divine had merged in Jesus, and that He was neither purely divine nor human.

In 451 CE, Church leaders at the Council of Chalcedon in Turkey affirmed that Jesus possessed two natures, one divine and the other human, in His one person. Each of these natures was complete, not lacking any attribute proper to being either divine or human. The Chalcedonian Creed became the affirmation of the incarnation.

The Christ the Redeemer statue on the Corcovado mountain in Rio de Janeiro was built in the 1920s, reputedly in response to a rising tide of godlessness in the city.

The doctrine of the incarnation arose as a recognition of the validity of Jesus's claim to be God; an assertion vindicated by His resurrection. Yet it also protected Christianity from the possibility of a fatal internal contradiction. Jesus accepted worship as God from His followers and commanded them to trust in Him for their salvation. If Jesus were not God, then His followers were guilty of idolatry, an offense for which there was no atoning sacrifice under the Law of Moses. But worship of and trust in Jesus would not be idolatry if Jesus were God, and salvation in His name would not be blasphemy. ∎

THIS IS MY SON, WHOM I LOVE; WITH HIM I AM WELL PLEASED

MATTHEW 3:17, THE BAPTISM OF JESUS

N ear the beginning of the Gospel according to Matthew, at the start of the New Testament, Jesus undergoes a baptism (ritual washing by immersion in water) at the hands of a man named John the Baptist. Such is the significance of this event—because it marks the beginning of Jesus's ministry—that it is mentioned in all four Gospels of the New Testament. In addition to Matthew 3, referenced here, Mark 1 and Luke 3 both give full details of the baptism, while in John 1, it is discussed in passing.

Baptisms in the New Testament

Baptism by John	(Matthew 3:6)
Baptism of Jesus	(Mathew 3:13–17)
Baptism by the Holy Spirit	(1 Corinthians 12:12–13; Galatians 3:27)
Baptism with fire	(Luke 3:16)
Baptizing believers	(Acts 2:41; 8:36)
Baptism of the Israelites	(1 Corinthians 10:1–2)
Baptism for the dead	(1 Corinthians 15:29)

This detail from *The Baptism of Christ*, by A.H. Philippe Sauvan-Magnet, c.1500, shows John pouring water over Jesus's head. Matthew's account suggests He was submerged.

According to Luke (3:23), Jesus is about 30 years old at the time of the baptism. He travels to the River Jordan from Galilee to meet with John. The latter has gained a reputation for the act—exhorting local people to confess and repent of their sins, and then washing them clean in the water of the river.

When the two men first meet, John is surprised by Jesus's request to be baptized, because he knows that Jesus is the Messiah. John exclaims: "I need to be baptized by You, and do You come to me?" (Matthew 3:14). Reassured by Jesus that there is no mistake, John then lowers Jesus into the waters and baptizes Him.

Purpose of the act
Biblical scholars have long debated the precise significance of this event, since the stated purpose of John's baptism is a "baptism of repentance for the forgiveness of sins" (Mark 1:4). However, as the New Testament confirms, Jesus was completely without sin—Paul writes in 2 Corinthians 5:21 that "God made Him who had no sin to be sin for us." Jesus therefore has nothing to repent for, yet still asks for baptism. The general consensus is that, in this case, the act of cleansing is merely symbolic. »

John the Baptist

Like Jesus, John the Baptist is born in miraculous circumstances. In Luke (1:5–23), an angel of the Lord visits Zechariah, an aged priest, and his barren wife Elizabeth. He announces that they will have a son and that he will become a great man of God. Such is Zechariah's disbelief at this revelation—owing to their age—that God strikes him dumb.

Zechariah recovers his speech when Elizabeth gives birth to their son, John. Luke confirms that the birth occurs just months prior to that of Jesus (1:36). John becomes a preacher, living an austere and hermitic life in the desert. He preaches a message advocating both confession and repentance, and offers baptism in the River Jordan to all who heed him. John speaks, above all, of a "greater one" who will come after him—the Messiah prophesied in the scriptures.

John's preaching ultimately leads to his downfall, when he warns King Herod against marrying his brother's wife. The king marries her anyway, but she never forgives John, and John is eventually beheaded on the whim of her daughter, Salome.

Some scholars debate whether or not John knew before he baptized Him that Jesus was the Messiah. According to Luke's account, as Jesus comes up out of the river, the heavens above Him open and "the Holy Spirit descended on Him in bodily form like a dove" (Luke 3:22). A voice from heaven simultaneously booms out: "This is my Son, whom I love; with Him I am well pleased" (Matthew 3:17). John's Gospel suggests John did not know who was in front of him until he saw the dove: "And I myself did not know Him, but the one who sent me to baptize with water told me, 'The man on whom you see the Spirit come down and remain is the one who will baptize with the Holy Spirit'" (John 1:33). John claims to have decided to baptize Jesus simply because then the man "might be revealed to Israel" (1:31).

The affirmations of God and John the Baptist, made in front of the witnessing crowd, both confirm that Jesus is the Son of God and the Messiah. He is symbolically cleansed in order to commence His ministry and is now ready to encounter the forces of darkness. Immediately after the baptism, Jesus goes into the desert, where He fasts for 40 days. Here, He is tempted by Satan (Matthew 4),

> He will baptize you with the Holy Spirit and fire.
> **Matthew 3:11**

in a series of tests that resonate with universal human desires and concerns. Jesus maintains His resolve—His baptism has been successful—and He returns to society to begin preaching to the people and working miracles.

Historical ramifications

The baptism of Jesus is one of five key events in the Gospel narrative of the life of the Messiah. The other four are: the Transfiguration; the Crucifixion; the Resurrection; and Jesus's Ascension into heaven. Nearly all denominations of Christianity celebrate the event, and the baptism of Jesus shaped the Christian rite of baptism that is practiced worldwide to this day.

The majority of theologians assign a high degree of certainty to the actuality of Jesus's baptism, using it as a starting point from which to assert Jesus's historicity. It is also highly likely, based on

The dove of the Holy Spirit in this 14th-century fresco by Giusto de' Menabuoi, in the Baptistery in Padua, is a symbol of renewal, like the dove sent out by Noah after the Flood.

historical records, that John the Baptist lived at the same time as Jesus. The 1st-century historian Flavius Josephus attested to the existence of John the Baptist at the same time as Jesus in his work *Antiquities of the Jews*. He stated that John's ministry began around 28–29 CE, shortly before that of the Messiah, and most modern theologians accept this view.

Once he has baptized Jesus, John the Baptist's popularity as a preacher begins to wane. This is largely due to people beginning to follow Jesus instead of him. John's response to this change in his circumstances is typical of his renowned humility, as well as affirming his role as a precursor

Methods of baptism				
Denomination	**Sprinkling**	**Pouring**	**Immersion**	**Do Not Baptize**
Adventist			✓	
Anglican	✓	✓	✓	
Baptist		✓	✓	
Roman Catholic		✓	✓	
Eastern Orthodox			✓	
Episcopalian	✓	✓	✓	
Methodist	✓	✓	✓	
Presbyterian	✓	✓	✓	
Quaker				✓
United Church of Christ	✓	✓	✓	

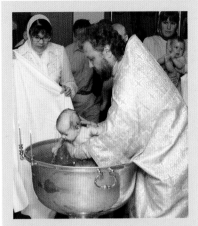

Baptism

The Christian rite of baptism—which consists of sprinkling or pouring water on a person's forehead or immersing them in water—symbolizes spiritual and physical purification. The rite of baptism confers an individual's admission to the Christian Church. Before His Ascension, Jesus bids his disciples to "make disciples of all nations, baptizing them" (Matthew 28:19).

In many denominations, baptism is performed on very young children, accompanied by name giving. The doctrine of original sin, propounded by St. Paul and developed by the early Church, made the baptism of infants, who might die suddenly or unexpectedly, of vital importance. The early church frowned upon the practice of "baptism of the dead," in which a living person was baptized on behalf of the deceased.

Today, some Christian denominations, including Baptists, do not baptize children, on the grounds that the basis for baptism is a credible profession of faith. Other groups, including Quakers, view baptism as an unnecessary ritual.

to Christ. In John 3:30, John states: "He [Jesus] must become greater; I must become less."

Holy waters

Most scholars agree that the baptism took place near the Jordan River, in the countryside of Roman Judea. Some accounts suggest that the immersion was conducted in one of the many desert springs or waterholes in the area, rather than in the river itself. Specific references in the book of John point to the town of Bethany on the eastern bank of the Jordan River, near Jericho (1:28), or to the settlement of Aenon near Salim "because there was plenty of water, and people were coming and being baptized." (3:23).

Given the meaning of the word baptize—"to dip"—many Christian denominations insist upon baptism by total immersion, often three times, to symbolize Jesus's death and resurrection; others favour sprinkling or pouring to represent the Holy Spirit descending from above. Some Christians believe that baptism is a sacrament that is necessary for salvation; other groups, such as Lutheran Protestants, associate baptism with spiritual regeneration. ■

Heaven was opened and he saw the Spirit of God descending like a dove.
Matthew 3:16

JESUS SAID TO HIM, "AWAY FROM ME, SATAN!"

MATTHEW 4:10, THE TEMPTATIONS OF CHRIST

IN BRIEF

PASSAGE
Matthew 4:1–11; Mark 1:12–13; Luke 4:1–13

THEME
Resisting temptation

SETTING
c.26–27 CE The Judean Desert, near the Dead Sea.

KEY FIGURES
Jesus The Messiah and Son of God at the start of His ministry, recently baptized by John the Baptist.

Satan The accuser and tempter, whom early Christians later identify as the serpent in the Garden of Eden and the great dragon of Revelation.

The temptations of Jesus in the wilderness are a theological battle between Jesus and Satan. Both figures quote the Old Testament—Satan to taunt Jesus into proving that He is the promised Messiah, beginning each of his challenges with the words "If you are the son of God" (Psalm 91:11, 12), and Jesus to assert His divinity: "Do not put the Lord your God to the test" (Deuteronomy 6:16). The encounter is described in Matthew, Mark, and Luke, although Mark mentions it in only two verses (Mark 1:12–13). Applying the scholarly assumption that Mark is the oldest Gospel, it is likely that Matthew and Luke expanded on the stories using a source known as Q—named for the German *Quelle*, meaning source.

Satan speaks

In all three Gospels, Jesus is sent or led to the desert by the "Spirit." There, after 40 days and 40 nights of fasting, Jesus is suddenly confronted by Satan, who poses three questions to Him.

He first asks Jesus to sate His hunger by turning stone to bread. In reply, Jesus tells him that man shall not live on bread alone. Then Satan asks Jesus to demonstrate the extent of His power by throwing Himself from a mountain so that angels can save Him. Jesus refuses, telling him not to put the Lord your God to the test. Finally, Satan tells Jesus he will give Him the world if He worships him. Again, Jesus refuses, saying that only God should be worshipped. In Matthew, Jesus then cries: "Away from me, Satan!"

Even though Jesus never tells Satan that He is the Son of God, it is implied that He is not only God's Son, but also the embodiment of God on earth. The Gospels suggest that while humans would succumb to the temptation of

Christ in the Wilderness (1872), by Russian artist Ivan Kramskoi, emphasizes the human in the divine, depicting a figure pondering the heavy responsibilities that await Him.

See also: The Fall 30–35 ▪ The Flood 40–41 ▪ The Exodus 74–77 ▪ The Suffering of Job 146–47 ▪ The Lord's Prayer 212–13 ▪ Demons and the Herd of Pigs 224–25

Satan, Jesus passes each test. His divinity is confirmed in Mark and Matthew's description of angels attending Jesus when Satan leaves.

Fulfilling the prophecy

In all three Gospels, the temptation of Christ occurs after He has been baptized by John, creating a sequence of birth, baptism, and then temptation that culminates in His ministry. As in many passages from the New Testament, the Gospel authors also allude to the fulfillment of Isaiah's Messianic prophecy through Jesus. Other echoes of the Old Testament include the Fall, when Adam and Eve are tempted to eat from the Tree of the Knowledge of Good and Evil by the serpent (whom Christians later identify as Satan), and the significance of the number 40. Like Noah's flood, which destroys the world's sins, Jesus's fast lasts 40 days and 40 nights, and there are echoes of the Israelites' 40-year wandering in the wilderness, when God sates their hunger with manna from heaven. ▪

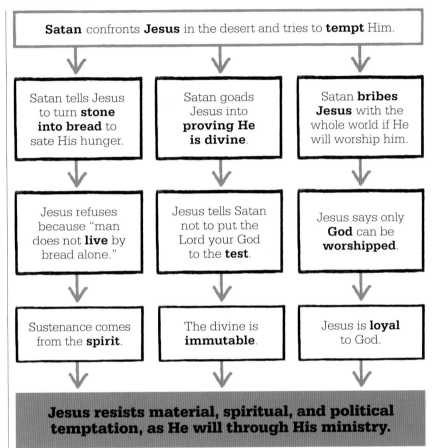

Satan confronts **Jesus** in the desert and tries to **tempt** Him.

Satan tells Jesus to turn **stone into bread** to sate His hunger.	Satan goads Jesus into **proving He is divine**.	Satan **bribes Jesus** with the whole world if He will worship him.
Jesus refuses because "man does not **live** by bread alone."	Jesus tells Satan not to put the Lord your God to the **test**.	Jesus says only **God** can be **worshipped**.
Sustenance comes from the **spirit**.	The divine is **immutable**.	Jesus is **loyal** to God.

Jesus resists material, spiritual, and political temptation, as He will through His ministry.

Satan in the New Testament

Throughout the Bible, from the writing of Job to the Gospels, the figure of the *satan* (Hebrew for "adversary") is portrayed as an antagonistic being who, despite an existence predicated on God's will, is intent on destroying His followers and discrediting Him.

The "devil" appears most often in the New Testament. In Luke 22:3, Satan enters Judas Iscariot, and in Luke 13:10–15, Jesus cures a crippled woman whom Satan "has kept bound" for 18 years. In Revelation 20:2, Satan, "who leads the whole world astray," is hurled to the earth and bound for 1,000 years.

The belief in Satan as an independent, evil figure who contrasts with God's goodness is known as "dualism." The concept became popular among medieval Christian sects such as the Paulicians and the Cathars. Its origins may lie in the spread of Greek culture after Alexander the Great's conquest of the Phoenician Empire in 331 BCE.

"FOLLOW ME," JESUS SAID, " ... I WILL SEND YOU OUT TO FISH FOR PEOPLE"

MARK 1:17, THE CALLING OF THE DISCIPLES

IN BRIEF

PASSAGE
Mark 1:17

THEME
Jesus calls His disciples for ministry

SETTING
c.26–27 CE, Roman Judean countryside, beside the Sea of Galilee.

KEY FIGURES
Jesus The Messiah and Son of God at the start of His ministry in Galilee.

The 11 "good" disciples These include (Simon) Peter, Andrew, James, John, Matthew (Levi), and Simon the Zealot.

Judas Iscariot The disciple who will betray Jesus.

E arly in His ministry, Jesus selects 12 disciples. This is a step to securing His legacy and has huge significance: the 12 men He chooses will go on to spread the word of Jesus and build a new Israel: a new Church.

In the Ancient Near East, the gathering of students, or "disciples," around a master teacher was an established practice. At the time, knowledge was largely imparted via the spoken word, and the more disciples that were amassed, the farther that word would spread. Jesus was aware of this, and the selection of as many as a dozen disciples gives an indication of the intended scale of His ministry. In Mark 1, Jesus is walking beside the Sea of Galilee one day, when He sees Simon (whom Jesus calls

See also: Jesus Embraces a Tax Collector 242–43 ▪ Peter's Denial 256–57 ▪ The Great Commission 274–77

The Miraculous Draught of Fishes, by Jean Jouvenet (1644–1717), depicts Jesus recruiting Peter and Andrew, and filling their previously empty nets with fish.

Peter) and his brother Andrew hauling in an empty net. Jesus walks up to the men and exhorts them to cast their net again. When they draw the net in, it is brimming with fish. "Follow me … to fish for people," Jesus tells them (1:17). Without hesitating, the men leave their nets to go with Him to recruit more disciples. Jesus then meets two more fishermen—James and John—in a boat with their father Zebedee and some hired men. Like Peter and Andrew, James and John join Jesus as soon as He asks them. The four fishermen become the first of Jesus's 12 disciples.

Lowly profession

Just as it is symbolic that Jesus chooses 12 disciples—to represent the totality of the nation of Israel— it is also telling that He selects four fishermen and, ultimately, possibly as many as six. Such an elevation of this relatively lowly profession indicates that knowledge of God should not be confined to the learned or priestly classes. As stated in 1 Corinthians 1:27: "God chose the foolish things of the world to shame the wise; God chose the weak things of the world to shame the strong." There may also be some significance in the fact that fishermen have to be patient in their work; Jesus knew that to change the world as He intended would take great patience.

Courting controversy

Jesus's choice of His remaining eight disciples is also significant. First, He chooses a tax collector, Levi, who also goes by the name of Matthew, and is the reputed author of the Gospel of that name. Initially, this seems like an odd choice. As the Bible repeatedly demonstrates, tax collectors were particularly unpopular at the time; Jesus's selection of Levi therefore earns Him disdain from the Pharisee teachers of the Law: "Why does He eat with tax collectors and sinners?" (Mark 2:16). Jesus responds: "It is not the healthy who need a doctor but those who are sick. I have not come to call the righteous, but sinners" (2:17).

Jesus next chooses the Zealot, Simon. Again, the appointment is symbolic. After their experiences in Egypt and in the wake of the ceaseless invasions of their nation, the Jewish people had developed an intense dislike of foreign rule. No group is still more active in »

Disciples as learners

A "disciple" is someone who adheres to the teachings of a master or instructor. In the New Testament, it is made clear on numerous occasions that Jesus is the ultimate master on earth. It is upon Jesus that all authority in heaven and on earth has been bestowed (Matthew 28:18); it is to Jesus that every knee will bow (Philippians 2:10); it is on account of Jesus that all the tribes of the earth will mourn (Revelation 1:7); and from Jesus that the absolute fury of God's wrath will be executed (Revelation 19:15). It is incumbent upon the 12 disciples that they learn to live like Jesus, and to teach others to behave in the same way. Essentially, they should learn to become "little Christs," or "Christians" (Acts 26:28; 2 Corinthians 1:21). The four Gospels demonstrate what it means to be a disciple of Jesus. In particular, John classifies the role in three ways: worshipper (or learner/follower), servant, and witness.

encouraging resistance to foreign control and religion. As their name implies, they are "zealous" in asserting the ancestral traditions of the nation of Israel and repelling the depredations of invaders and false gods. For many Zealots, the end objective was the overthrow of Rome itself. By appointing Peter, as with Levi (Matthew), Jesus appears to be courting controversy. He condemns violence, yet also paradoxically chooses a disciple who supports it. The selection of Simon the Zealot shows that ideological orientation is no barrier to admission to God's kingdom.

The professions of the other six disciples are not specified by the Gospel writers, but it seems likely that at least two more of

The things you have heard me say … entrust to reliable people who will also be qualified to teach others.
2 Timothy 2:2

them were fishermen. The names of the six are: Philip; Bartholomew, also referred to as "Nathanael" in John and probably Philip's brother; Thomas, who went on to doubt the resurrection of Jesus, giving rise to the term "Doubting Thomas"; another James (not the brother of John); Thaddaeus, also known as Judas; and Judas Iscariot, who eventually betrays Jesus.

These 12 disciples are also known as "Apostles" in the Bible and the two terms are employed interchangeably in the Gospels. Indeed, such was their importance to the spread of Christianity that the period in which they lived is known as the "Apostolic Age."

Martyrdom

Christian tradition maintains that all but one of the 12 disciples were martyred, with John alone surviving into old age and dying peacefully. However, only the death of James—fisherman and son of Zebedee—is described in the New Testament. There may be a reason for this: according to the 18th-century English historian Edward Gibbon, early Christians believed that among the original 12 disciples only James and Peter died for their faith in Jesus.

There are various reports of the death of Judas Iscariot. Matthew 27:5 records that he throws down

Each of the Apostles in this gilded and painted alabaster representation (c.1450) from England holds his emblem and a colored scroll inscribed with a sentence of the creed in Latin.

the silver he receives for the betrayal of Jesus in the Temple and then hangs himself. Acts 1:18 states that he purchases a field with his blood money, and then plunges headlong into a pit in the field and bursts open. In any event, Judas Iscariot is dead by the time of Christ's resurrection. The disciples replace Judas, by election, with Matthias.

New disciples

The Christian teachings inspired by the short life of Jesus were not just taught by 11 of the 12 original disciples and Matthias. Instead, Eastern Christian tradition maintains that there were as many as 70 Apostles during the time of Jesus's ministry. A number of other prominent figures, such as St. Paul (who was also martyred), were also known as Apostles, even though they did not follow Jesus during His earthly ministry.

The Apostles would become the foundations of the early Church. During the 1st century CE, they established churches throughout the Mediterranean, as well as across the Middle East, Africa, and India, in spite of persecution, which continued into the 4th century. The reputation of these men, and the esteem in which they were held, grew as the Church spread through the world.

Holy lineage

To this day, churches that are believed to have been founded by one of the Apostles are referred to as "apostolic sees," among which the Holy See of Rome is pre-eminent. Bishops throughout the Christian world have traditionally claimed their authority via "apostolic succession"—claiming to trace their roots back to the original 12 disciples. In practice, this means that bishops today are consecrated by older bishops, who in turn were consecrated by bishops before them, with a chain stretching directly back to the 12 Apostles.

Today, personal apostolic succession is still a requirement for a bishop's ordination in many Christian denominations—notably the Roman Catholic, Eastern Orthodox, and Anglican churches. ∎

Fishing and the Ichthys

Just as fishermen bear great symbolism in the New Testament as "fishers of men," so do fish themselves. The most famous reference to fish in the Gospels is the feeding of the 5,000 using just five loaves of bread and two fish, which is reported in all four (Matthew 14:13–21; Mark 6:30–44; Luke 9:10–17; John 6:1–15). In Matthew 13:47–52, in the Parable of the Net, Jesus compares God's Final Judgment on who goes to heaven and who to hell to fishermen sorting out their catch, keeping the good fish and throwing the bad away. After His resurrection, Jesus is offered grilled fish to eat in Luke 24:41–43.

The many mentions of fish in the New Testament may explain why the ichthys (Greek for "fish"), the elliptical shape ending in a fish tail, became a symbol of early Christianity. Deployed as a secret code by Christians during times of persecution, the ichthys is sometimes seen etched into walls or in floor mosaics in early Christian basilicas. To this day, Christians incorporate the fish symbol in jewelry and clothing.

The Apostles of Jesus

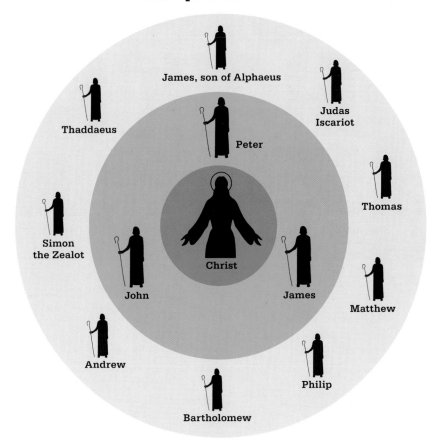

James, son of Alphaeus

Judas Iscariot

Thaddaeus

Peter

Thomas

Simon the Zealot

Christ

John

James

Matthew

Andrew

Philip

Bartholomew

The disciples closest to Jesus were Peter, James, and John. They spent the most time with Him and witnessed more of His miracles. In any list of the Apostles, Peter is always first.

LOVE YOUR ENEMIES, AND PRAY FOR THOSE WHO PERSECUTE YOU

MATTHEW 5:44, SERMON ON THE MOUNT

IN BRIEF

PASSAGE
Matthew 5:1–7:29

THEME
The wisdom of God's Kingdom

SETTING
c.27–29 CE A mountainside in Galilee.

KEY FIGURES
Jesus The Messiah and Son of God at the start of His ministry in Galilee.

Disciples Jesus's close group of 12 followers.

Crowds People from Galilee, the Decapolis, Jerusalem, and "beyond the Jordan" who have begun to follow Jesus out of curiosity and amazement.

News of Jesus and His preaching and healing ministry was beginning to spread far and wide. In addition to His band of 12 close disciples, large crowds started to follow Jesus, eager to hear Him teach about the Kingdom of God and to watch Him perform miracles.

Seeing an opportunity to address the crowds one day, Jesus climbs up a mountainside and sits down, adopting the typical position of an authoritative teacher, or rabbi. The disciples and crowds gather around and Jesus begins to teach. Often known as the "Sermon on the Mount," His speech to the people reads as His manifesto, announcing how life will be in God's kingdom.

Jesus begins by turning usual expectations upside down in a short passage known as "the beatitudes." He announces a blessing on those who are aware of the powerlessness of their own lives; it is they, rather than the strong and self-sufficient, who shall receive a place in God's kingdom. Conventional ideals of wealth and

The Roman Catholic Church of the Beatitudes stands on a hill overlooking the Sea of Galilee in Israel. It was built on the traditional site of Jesus's Sermon on the Mount.

success are rejected as Jesus declares that those who appear to have been overlooked in their present life shall receive God's reward in heaven.

In Jesus's inverted vision of the world, those who follow Him are to be "salt" and "light," bringing out God's flavor in the world and shining God's light into the darkness. The purpose of the positive attitudes and actions of such people is that others "may see your good deeds and glorify your Father in heaven" (Matthew 5:16). From just a little salt and a little light, Jesus knows that God's kingdom can reach the world.

A parallel with Moses

Those listening to Jesus are predominantly Jewish, brought up to honor and obey the Law of Moses given centuries earlier.

The Beatitudes

The concept of bestowing a blessing on those who faithfully follow God's commandments is familiar from the Old Testament. However, at the beginning of the Sermon on the Mount, Jesus delivers His idea of "blessing" in a different way, through eight statements that are collectively known as the "beatitudes," a word deriving from the Latin for "blessed" (*beatus*).

Instead of saying "you will be blessed if you do this," Jesus's beatitudes announce that certain people will be blessed without condition—specifically, the poor in spirit,

those who mourn, the meek, the merciful, those who hunger and thirst for righteousness, the pure in heart, the peacemakers, and the persecuted. Also, God's benchmark for blessing is at odds with that of the earthly world: people will not be measured in terms of their visible successes, but rather by an awareness of their own brokenness and dependence on God for all things.

Some versions of the Bible translate "blessed are" as "happy are," but Jesus's teaching remains the same: it is those who are least expecting it who will find themselves recipients of God's favor.

See also: The Ten Commandments 78–83 ▪ The Golden Rule 210–11 ▪ Parables of Jesus 214–15

There are several parallels in Jesus's Sermon on the Mount that would not have been lost on His audience, for it strongly echoes the giving of the Ten Commandments to Moses on Mount Sinai (Exodus 20): just as Moses went up the mountain and received God's word, so Jesus here ascends a mountainside and teaches with God's authority.

Moses's Law showed the Israelites how to live as God's new community following their deliverance from slavery in Egypt. Jesus is less concerned about establishing a moral code for a defined earthly kingdom; instead, He presents a picture of life in God's spiritual kingdom of heaven that is accessible to all people at all times. To some in His audience, it may have seemed that Jesus was contradicting Moses. However, in a large section of the Sermon on the Mount, Jesus addresses this question directly: "Do not think that I have come to abolish the Law or the Prophets; I have not come to abolish them but to fulfill them" (Matthew 5:17). Jesus is God's new Moses, instructing the crowds as they follow Him.

Be perfect, therefore, as your heavenly Father is perfect.
Matthew 5:48

Other religious leaders at the time—in particular, the Pharisees—encouraged people to follow the law down to its last letter. However, Jesus says that such rigid adherence to Moses's Law is not sufficient to guarantee people a place in God's kingdom: "I tell you that unless your righteousness surpasses that of the Pharisees and the teachers of the Law, you will certainly not enter the kingdom of heaven" (5:20).

Instead, in the Sermon on the Mount, Jesus intensifies the meaning of the Law by declaring that it is not enough simply to obey God's commands outwardly; rather, His Law must transform the desires and motivations of the heart of those who seek to obey Him.

In a series of teachings that take the form, "You have heard that it was said … but I say to you," Jesus takes some of the most familiar commandments from Moses's Law and broadens their application. His disciples must not simply refrain from murder, but must avoid anger or ridiculing others, and prioritize forgiveness

In the Vatican's Sistine Chapel, this fresco of the *Sermon on the Mount* (c.1461) by Cosimo Rosselli is opposite the artist's fresco of Moses receiving the Ten Commandments.

and reconciliation. Lustful looks are to be considered as perilous as adultery, and marriage relationships should not be broken except in clear cases of unfaithfulness. Disciples should not merely keep the oaths they have made to God, but rather be faithful to every word that they speak.

Exercising humility

Moses's law had sought to restrict overly harsh punishments by commending the principle of "eye for eye, tooth for tooth" (Leviticus 24:20); but Jesus rejects the notion of giving "as good as you get." Instead, He tells His disciples to exercise restraint, never fighting back, but always praying for those who would seek to bring harm to them. By loving their enemies, they would be showing that they belonged with Jesus as children » of God, since they would be imitating Jesus's love for His enemies, as He would demonstrate on the cross.

Having asked His disciples to "exceed" the righteousness of the Pharisees, Jesus then warns them not to become "self-righteous," or smug: "Be careful not to practice your acts of righteousness in front of others to be seen by them" (Matthew 6:1). They should not "trumpet" their good works to the world, but rather be discreet, confident that God sees what they do. The same humility should be evident, He says, when people pray.

Jesus teaches that God does not listen to prayers because they are loud and long, but because they are offered in humble dependence on God. "Go into your room, close the door, and pray to your Father … who sees what is done in secret" (6:6). In short, Jesus encourages His followers to look for God's favor more than the applause of the people around them. "Do not store up for yourselves treasures on Earth … but store up for yourselves treasures in heaven" (6:19–20).

One of the key themes in Jesus's Sermon on the Mount is the faith that His disciples should have in

> Can any one of you by worrying add a single hour to your life?
> **Matthew 6:27**

God. They must be confident that God's goodwill is all they need for their lives to flourish. Instead of being anxious about finding food and clothing, they should focus on the life of God's kingdom. In much the same way, His disciples should not spend their lives looking for faults in other people, but rather leave all judgment to God. At its heart, this part of Jesus's teaching is emphasizing that God is good and is to be trusted.

At the end of His sermon, Jesus reminds His listeners to practice what He preaches: "Everyone who hears these words of mine and puts them into practice is like a wise man who built his house on the rock … and not the foolish man who built his house on sand" (7:24–26).

Revolutionary message

Jesus's listeners are amazed by His teaching, because they recognize that He teaches with God's supreme authority, and not simply with human skill. When Jesus finishes teaching and comes down the mountainside, He is followed by large crowds (8:1).

The Sermon on the Mount describes a world that has been turned upside down by God's

Teachings from Jesus's sermon

If your **right eye** causes you to stumble, gouge it out and **throw it away** (5:29). →	**Believers** must give up things that stand in the way of their **faith**.
When you **give** to the needy, do not let your **left hand** know what your **right hand** is doing (6:3). →	Do not practice **good deeds** in order to receive **praise** or recognition.
Watch out for **false prophets**. They come to you in **sheep's clothing** (7:15). →	The **enemies** of God often disguise themselves as **friends**.
Enter through the **narrow gate**. For wide is the gate … that leads to **destruction** (7:13). →	It is easy to stray from Christ's **instructions** if you don't live well.

Jesus warns against judging others in *The Parable of the Mote and the Beam* (c.1619) by Domenico Fetti. The painting was one in a series of 13 works illustrating the parables.

The sermon as a far-reaching influence

From the earliest days of Christianity, Jesus's Sermon on the Mount has been considered central to His teaching, giving His followers a clear pattern for their lives. Church leaders and prominent thinkers point to the sermon when giving ethical guidance to Christians in such diverse areas as conflict resolution, personal relationships, wealth, and justice. Some groups, such as the Amish, are renowned for seeking to live simply in accordance with the Sermon on the Mount.

The influence of the sermon reaches beyond the Christian Church. Some phrases have become idioms in wider usage, not least owing to influential literary figures such as Dante, Chaucer, and Shakespeare. "Don't hide your light under a bushel," "salt of the earth," and "don't throw your pearls before pigs" all come from Jesus's teaching.

kingdom. It is a world in which the weak and powerless are considered to be God's treasured children, a place where generosity and forgiveness are valued more highly than strength. Here, trust in God matters more than any other virtue. The idea of such a world must have seemed an impossible utopia for those listening to Jesus, yet they recognized God's authority in Jesus's words. He was not simply presenting a picture of an ideal life; He was saying that they could be part of this kingdom, if only they would build their lives on the "rock" that He was.

Jesus knew that not everyone would accept this way of life. It was a "narrow gate" for people to enter, compared to the broad road of living as you please, but the narrow path would lead to God's blessing (7:13–14).

Jesus's story continued to unfold. His death and resurrection became powerful reminders to Jesus's disciples and followers to teach and live by the lessons of the Sermon on the Mount. ∎

Ask and it will be given to you; seek and you will find; knock and the door will be opened to you ... For everyone who asks receives.
Matthew 7:7–8

DO TO OTHERS AS YOU WOULD HAVE THEM DO TO YOU
LUKE 6:31, THE GOLDEN RULE

IN BRIEF

PASSAGE
**Matthew 7:9–12;
Luke 6:27–36**

THEME
Fulfilling the Jewish law

SETTING
c.27–29 CE The Sermon on
the Mount (in Matthew), a
mountainside in Galilee; the
Sermon on the Plain (in Luke),
a plain near Capernaum.

KEY FIGURES
Jesus The Messiah and
Son of God at the start of
His ministry in Galilee.

Jesus's disciples A group of
Jewish men and women who
travel with Jesus during His
ministry. The 12 closest to
Him are tasked with spreading
the word about Him and His
teachings after His death.

The saying, "Do to others what you would have them do to you," has become known as the Golden Rule, and finds expression in the ethical code of most of the world's religions. In the Bible, it is taught by Jesus as part of the Sermon on the Plain in Luke 6:31 and the Sermon on the Mount in Matthew 7:12, where Jesus says that it "sums up the Law and Prophets."

The Golden Rule emphasizes the necessity of positive ethical behavior. It is not simply enough

Jesus preaches to His followers in this stained-glass detail of one of the four scenes gifted to St. Leonard's Church in Charlecote, England, in the late 19th century.

to refrain from doing what is wrong; rather, those who would live by the Golden Rule must actively seek to do good to and for others, just as they would hope to be treated themselves. When Jesus claims that this sums up all the Law and Prophets, it is a reminder that God's commandments are not primarily

See also: Sermon on the Mount 204–09 ▪ The Lord's Prayer 212–13 ▪ The Good Samaritan 216–17

a list of dos and don'ts, but rather a blueprint for healthy relationships between people. Ethical behavior requires us to treat every person as equally valuable.

Emulating God
Jesus's teaching contains a distinctive perspective on the Golden Rule. In Luke's version, Jesus points out that if His disciples apply this rule only to those who are already good to them, then they have missed the point. Following the Golden Rule will mean that they will seek to do good even to their enemies, even though they might never treat them with respect in return. By blessing others, even when they do not respond in a like manner, Jesus's disciples show that they have truly become children of God through their imitation of God's character.

In Matthew's account, Jesus gives the Golden Rule immediately after describing the willingness of God to listen to prayer: "Ask and it will be given to you; seek and you will find; knock and the door will be opened to you." Jesus makes the point that good parents give good gifts to their children, and would never think to serve up a stone rather than bread to eat, or give a child a snake instead of a fish.

If human parents are like this, Jesus says, then "how much more will your Father in heaven give good gifts to those who ask Him!" (Matthew 7:11). Since God responds so readily to the needs of Jesus's followers, blessing them with love despite their many failings, they in turn should willingly act for the good of others, regardless of what the response might be.

Basis of morality
It is important to remember that the Golden Rule is positive in form. Too often the negative form—do not do things to other people that you would not want done to you—is used, which ensures that there is a minimum level of ethical behavior. However, Jesus's Golden Rule seeks to guide His disciples in a life of kindness, generosity, and justice that goes beyond strict moralism.

Love the Lord your God with all your heart and with all your soul and with all your strength and with all your mind.
Luke 10:26–27

The Golden Rule is sometimes called the "ethic of reciprocity" when discussed outside of a Christian context. This name has sparked some debate: while, in a philosophical context, the concept is seen as a moral contract between two parties (one treats the other well, in expectation of this kindness being reciprocated) in the Golden Rule, the *actual* or presupposed behavior of others has no bearing on how one should treat them. ▪

The Qur'an tells Muslims to do good to everyone, including wayfarers, "neighbors who are strangers," and slaves (Q:4:36).

The Golden Rule in other religions
As a fundamental ethical idea, the Golden Rule is found in many of the world's religions and moral codes. However, different religions each approach the rule with a slightly different emphasis, and many Eastern religions take the negative form. Buddhism says: "Hurt not others in ways that you yourself would find hurtful (Udana-Varga 5:18), while Hinduism says: "Do not do to others what would cause pain if done to you" (Mahabharata 5:1517). The Confucian Doctrine of the Mean says: "Do not impose on others what you yourself do not desire" (13.3).

The Abrahamic religions are united by the use of the positive form to express the Golden Rule. Islam preaches that "None of you believes until he wishes for his brother what he wishes for himself" (Hadith-Nawawi 13), while Judaism's expression of the Golden Rule can be found in Leviticus 19:18, with the simple commandment to "Love your neighbor as yourself."

THIS, THEN, IS HOW YOU SHOULD PRAY

MATTHEW 6:9, THE LORD'S PRAYER

IN BRIEF

PASSAGE
Matthew 6:9–13
Luke 11:2–4

THEME
Teaching on prayer

SETTING
c.27–29 CE The Sermon on the Mount (in Matthew), a mountainside in Galilee. Luke says only that Jesus teaches the prayer "in a certain place."

KEY FIGURES
Jesus The Messiah and Son of God during His ministry in Galilee and Judea.

Jesus's disciples A group of Jewish men and women who travel with Jesus during His ministry, and spread the word about Him and His teachings after His death.

Christianity's most famous prayer, which was taught to the disciples by Jesus Himself, starts on a striking note: "Our Father." By opening what became known as the Lord's Prayer with those two words, Jesus was encouraging His disciples to enter into an extraordinary intimacy with God—similar to the one that He Himself enjoyed.

The image of God as a loving parent was not unknown in the Hebrew scriptures. As early as Exodus 4, the Lord refers to Israel as His "firstborn son." Nowhere in the Old Testament, however, is the idea of God as the Father as central as it is in Jesus's teachings. In telling His followers to say "Our Father," He encourages them to approach God boldly, just as a child would approach a parent whose care, provision, and protection they otherwise take for granted.

Learning to pray

In Luke's Gospel, Jesus gives the prayer in response to a request from one of the disciples: "Lord, teach us to pray, just as John [the Baptist] taught his disciples." Luke's version

Translations

The oldest known English versions of the Lord's Prayer date from before 1000 CE. John Wycliffe, leader of the reformist Lollard movement, translated it into English (along with the rest of the Bible) in the 1380s, and William Tyndale followed suit in the 1520s and 1530s. After the English Reformation, Tyndale's version of the Prayer was included with a few changes in the new Church of England's Book of Common Prayer, compiled by Thomas Cranmer,

Archbishop of Canterbury, and first published in 1549. This has survived with only a few modifications as the traditional form of the prayer in English, which is still the most familiar version for many people.

The doxology (a short verse praising God) at the end of the prayer—"For thine is the kingdom …"—is not found in the Bible, but versions of it have been used for hundreds of years, particularly in the Eastern and Orthodox Church. In its present form, the doxology is mostly used by Protestants.

See also: The Origin of Prayer 38–39 ▪ The Divinity of Jesus 190–93 ▪ Sermon on the Mount 204–09 ▪ Parables of Jesus 214–15 ▪ The Nature of Faith 236–41

> The Lord's Prayer is the most perfect of prayers. … This prayer teaches us not only to ask for things, but also in what order we should desire them.
> **Thomas Aquinas**

of the prayer is more pared down than Matthew's and includes just five petitions. In Matthew's Gospel, the prayer is the focal point of the Sermon on the Mount and includes the salutation and seven petitions familiar to Christians today. Different religious traditions had their distinctive prayers, and Jesus intended the Lord's Prayer to be for His followers to say. The early Christians recited it three times a day in the same way that Jews recite the 18 Benedictions.

Seven petitions

The prayer has become central to Christian liturgies, but it is also seen as a "school of prayer." The opening salutation stresses the person's membership in a family of fellow children of God: *"Our* Father." Three so-called "you-petitions" follow—hallowed be *your* name; *your* kingdom come, *your* will be done on earth as it is in heaven— succeeded by four "we-petitions": give *us* our daily bread; forgive *us* our trespasses; lead *us* not into temptation; and deliver *us* from evil.

Our Father, which art in Heaven.

Reciting the Lord's Prayer was once a daily ritual in many Christian families, as shown in this illustration from Berlin, dating from around 1900.

While the you-petitions concern God's desire for love and justice among people, in the we-petitions the believer grapples with the challenges of living out that vision: the need for material and spiritual sustenance, forgiveness, mercy, and the ability to persevere.

In both Matthew's and Luke's Gospels, the prayer is followed shortly afterward by other famous pronouncements of Jesus: "Ask and it will be given to you; seek and you will find; knock and the door will be opened to you …" Through the Lord's Prayer, Jesus repeatedly demonstrates His belief in making petitions to God, thus encouraging people to pray. ▪

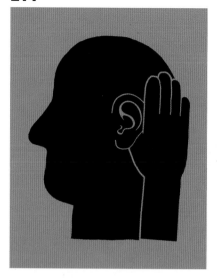

WHOEVER HAS EARS, LET THEM HEAR

MATTHEW 13:43, PARABLES OF JESUS

IN BRIEF

PASSAGE
Matthew 13:1–53,
Luke 8–20, Mark 4–13

THEME
Teaching through stories

SETTING
c.27–29 CE The Galilee region.

KEY FIGURES
Jesus The Messiah and Son of God during His ministry in Galilee and Judea.

Jesus's disciples A group of Jewish men and women who call Jesus their rabbi or teacher. They travel with Him during His ministry and preach about Him and His teachings after His death.

One of the many reasons the Bible is still so popular today is its use of story. As humans, we are captivated by the power of narrative, so skilled orators use stories to convey concepts. Jesus is no exception. He uses short, meaningful stories called "parables" to engage and teach His listeners.

The word "parable" comes from the Greek *parabole*, meaning "placing beside" or "comparison," and refers to the fact that parables use extended analogies to explain God's teachings. Parables allow readers to draw comparisons with

A farmer sows his seeds in Marten van Valckenborch's 1590 depiction of the parable of the sower. The painting also shows Jesus (in a boat) telling the story to His followers.

the situations in the stories and their own lives as servants of God. They are sometimes called earthly stories with heavenly meanings, as Jesus uses common socio-cultural contexts, such as farming, to explain the kingdom of heaven. In Matthew 13:3–8, for example, Jesus tells the story of a farmer whose seed falls variously on a path, rocky ground, thorns, and good soil.

See also: The Good Samaritan 216–17 ▪ The Prodigal Son 218–21 ▪ Workers in the Vineyard 223

Unsurprisingly, only the seeds on the good soil yield abundant crops. Jesus explains what the parable signifies: the seed stands for the truth of the kingdom, while the various soils represent the people hearing the truth (18–23). If people are not "good soil"—receptive to the word of God—they will not come to understand it. Only those who comprehend the word and let it transform their lives will bear fruit.

Speaking in parables

Jesus uses everyday images, but some fail to grasp the complex spiritual truths they communicate. For instance, after Jesus tells them several parables, the disciples ask Him to explain the story about the weeds in the field (13:36), which explains the existence of good and evil people in the world.

Once Jesus explains them, the stories make complete sense to the disciples. However, when Jesus does not clarify their meaning, they

> Jesus spoke all these things to the crowd in parables; he did not say anything to them without using a parable.
> **Matthew 13:3**

are not always so obvious. This is the very nature of parables—and one of the reasons Jesus uses them. He uses parables not just to convey the truth to those who believe, but to conceal it from those who harden their hearts to Him. They will not know the truth because "they hardly hear with their ears … they have closed their eyes" (13:15). ▪

The oral tradition

Before the Jewish and Christian traditions existed in written form, they were almost always passed down orally. The history, values, and folklore of these communities were verbally transmitted from teacher to student in familial or educational circles. Since the spoken word was the main form of education, students refined their listening skills, while teachers sought to be riveting orators. They used rhetorical devices to help structure their teachings and make them more memorable.

Jesus learned and taught in this method, which is why He often quoted the scriptures from memory and chose to teach with parables: they were short, rich with meaning, and easy to remember. The number of parables recorded in the Gospels—decades after Jesus's death—demonstrates their memorability and His skill as a rabbi and storyteller.

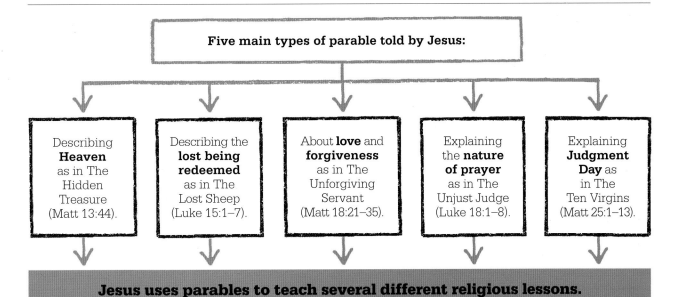

Five main types of parable told by Jesus:

Describing **Heaven** as in The Hidden Treasure (Matt 13:44).

Describing the **lost being redeemed** as in The Lost Sheep (Luke 15:1–7).

About **love** and **forgiveness** as in The Unforgiving Servant (Matt 18:21–35).

Explaining the **nature of prayer** as in The Unjust Judge (Luke 18:1–8).

Explaining **Judgment Day** as in The Ten Virgins (Matt 25:1–13).

Jesus uses parables to teach several different religious lessons.

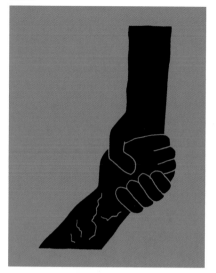

WHEN HE SAW HIM, HE TOOK PITY ON HIM

LUKE 10:33, THE GOOD SAMARITAN

IN BRIEF

PASSAGE
Luke 10:25–37

THEME
Charity to the unfortunate

SETTING
c.27–29 CE The road from Jerusalem to Jericho during the time of Christ's ministry.

KEY FIGURES
Jesus The Messiah and Son of God during His ministry in Galilee.

Expert of the Law Possibly a priest, who has studied the Torah.

The Good Samaritan A traveler who shows compassion for a stranger.

The stranger A man traveling the road to Jericho.

The Parable of the Good Samaritan is one of several stories told by Jesus, and, like many parables, only appears in the Gospel of Luke. At the heart of it is the Golden Rule—that we must treat others as we would expect to be treated ourselves.

The story begins with "an expert in the Law" asking Jesus how to inherit eternal life. When Jesus asks the expert to consider the Law, he begins by quoting Deuteronomy 6:5, which says to love the Lord with all your heart, soul, and strength. The expert then quotes Leviticus 19:18, that you

must also love your neighbor. Jesus tells the expert that he has found his answer, but when the expert is not satisfied, Jesus uses a parable as a novel means of getting him to seek the answer out himself.

The story concerns a man who is going from Jerusalem to Jericho, when he is robbed and left for dead by the side of the road. A priest passes and does nothing. Then a Levite passes and does nothing. Yet when a Samaritan comes past, he stops, takes care of the man's wounds, and gives him food, before paying for the man to stay in an inn. Jesus ends the story by asking the expert who is the better neighbor.

A story of Luke
Although Matthew (22:34–40) and Mark (12:28–34) include the Law expert's question, they do not include this parable. Because of this omission, some scholars question the authenticity of the story as a true parable of Christ. Nonetheless, the story gives the

The stranger is helped onto the back of the Samaritan's horse, while other passers-by disappear into the distance, in this 1890 depiction by Vincent Van Gogh (after Eugène Delacroix).

See also: The Golden Rule 210–11 ▪ Parables of Jesus 214–15 ▪
The Prodigal Son 218–21 ▪ Workers in the Vineyard 223

Early Christian allegorical reading of The Good Samaritan

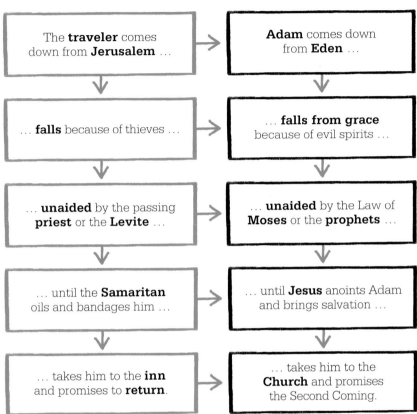

The **traveler** comes down from **Jerusalem** … → **Adam** comes down from **Eden** …

… **falls** because of thieves … → … **falls from grace** because of evil spirits …

… **unaided** by the passing **priest** or the **Levite** … → … **unaided** by the Law of **Moses** or the **prophets** …

… until the **Samaritan** oils and bandages him … → … until **Jesus** anoints Adam and brings salvation …

… takes him to the **inn** and promises to **return**. → … takes him to the **Church** and promises the Second Coming.

Samaria

Samaria is a region in modern Israel that roughly equates to the biblical Northern Kingdom of Israel. Samaria was also the name given to the city built in the 9th century BCE by King Omri, who declared it capital of the region. In 722 BCE, following the fall of the city of Samaria to the Assyrian empire, many foreign groups (2 Kings 17:24) were moved into the land by the Assyrians, eventually forming what would become known as Samaritans. These groups were largely composed of Gentiles, and for this reason, Judeans were wary of the Samaritans, who were not viewed as ethnically or religiously Jewish. Over time, Samaritans came to be seen as unclean people, who lived sinfully and worshipped at the altars of pagan gods.

In the New Testament, Jesus initially commands His disciples to avoid frequenting any Gentile or Samaritan city. Later, however, Jesus visits Samaritan areas, healing the sick, casting out demons, and showing compassion where others had not. It seems fitting, therefore, that the merciful man in this parable should be a Samaritan.

reader an insight into the theology of the author of Luke. Given that he was probably a Greek-speaking Gentile, the parable is a perfect analogy of Jesus extending His favor to non-Jews.

In particular, the positioning of a non-Jew—and Samaritan—as the protagonist of a parable would have shocked contemporary Jewish audiences, due to a longstanding rivalry between the Jews and the Samaritans since the 5th century BCE. In telling this parable, Jesus helps His audience to see the kindness in a figure they would traditionally consider an adversary, emphasizing the message of the parable: to love your neighbor, and enemy, as you love yourself.

Road from Jerusalem

Roads and pathways are "liminal" spaces—they signify a transition from one place to another. In a literal sense, roads are ungoverned, dangerous spaces. With Jerusalem being a popular destination for trade and pilgrimage, it would come as no surprise to find bandits lying in wait. In the Bible, roads are often metaphorical, suggesting a pathway to wisdom, immorality, goodness, or God. ▪

THIS BROTHER OF YOURS WAS DEAD ... HE WAS LOST AND IS FOUND

LUKE 15:32, THE PRODIGAL SON

IN BRIEF

PASSAGE
Luke 15:32

THEME
God seeks out the lost

SETTING
c.27–29 CE The road
to Jerusalem.

KEY FIGURES
Jesus The Messiah and Son
of God during His ministry
in Galilee.

The father A farmer.

The prodigal son The
farmer's younger son.

The older son The farmer's
older son.

O f all of the allegorical and moral tales that Jesus told during His ministry, the parable of the prodigal son is one of the most beloved and well-known. Widely regarded as one of the greatest short stories ever told, the tale offers profound insights on the human condition, and its essential message of repentance, forgiveness, and redemption has ensured its timeless popularity.

Presumption and pigs
The parable concerns a farmer with two sons, who will jointly inherit his land. Rather than wait until the death of his father, the younger son asks for his share of the family estate, and the father divides up his property accordingly.

The son swaps the land he has been given for cash and sets off for an unnamed distant country. It does not take long for him to spend all of his money—leading to the moniker

See also: Proverbs 148–51 ▪ The Prophet Micah 168–71 ▪ Call for Repentance 172 ▪ The Good Samaritan 216–17

of "prodigal," meaning "recklessly extravagant." At the same time, however, famine strikes the land. The prodigal son, reduced to penury, is forced to hire himself out to a local farmer, who puts him to work looking after his pigs. In his miserable state, he longs to eat the same food that the pigs are eating. The choice of pigs is deliberate. According to Mosaic Law, swine are classed as unclean. Eating and even touching them is forbidden (Leviticus 11:7–8). The fact that the prodigal son is contemplating eating pig slops is therefore a highly significant demonstration of his hunger, desperation, and moral depths to which he has fallen.

Faced with poverty, the prodigal son is finally made to confront his sinful actions. He recognizes how greedy he has been and decides to return to his father and beg for forgiveness. He even rehearses the plea of contrition that he will use in order to win his father's favor. "Father, I have sinned against heaven and you," he says. "I am no longer worthy to be called your son;

make me like one of your hired servants" (Luke 15:18–19). Having practiced his apology, he journeys home to beg forgiveness from his unwitting father and brother.

Healing the rift

When his father spots the prodigal son in the distance, he does not feel the urge to rebuke him for his misdeeds. Instead, he is filled with compassion for his long-lost child. The father runs hastily to greet his returning son, embraces him, and seals the reconciliation with a kiss.

The prodigal son only gets as far as the end of the second sentence of his prepared speech before his father interrupts him. He tells his servants to bring him the best robe they can find and clothe his son with it. Similarly, they are told to put a ring on one of his fingers and sandals on his feet. Following »

The Prodigal Son depicted as a swineherd in 1608, by the Flemish master David Vinckboons, and printed by Claes Jansz Visscher. The protagonist looks enviously at the pigs' food.

The youngest son leaves his family, an act that symbolizes a **turning away from God**.

⬇

He lives a **profligate** life of **sinful** behavior.

⬇

Famine strikes the nation, echoing his **spiritual drought**.

⬇

He **returns** home, like a sinner **returning to God**.

⬇

His story shows it is never too late to repent and be forgiven.

The Return of the Prodigal Son by Bartolomé Esteban Murillo (1618–1682), painted sometime around 1667–1670. The riches of the father contrast with the son's dirty feet and ragged clothes.

this, the celebrations begin with the slaughter of a fattened calf—a lavish expense—followed by feasting, singing, and dancing.

Undeserved welcome

Meanwhile, the prodigal son's older brother, who has spent the day laboring in his father's fields, hears the music as he approaches home. A servant tells him why his father has ordered such rejoicing.

When he learns the reason for the celebrations, the older brother becomes infuriated. He refuses to join the party, despite his father's pleadings. He tells his father that while he, the elder brother has worked tirelessly and obediently for his father for many years, he has never been rewarded. In contrast, he says, "when this son of yours who has squandered your property with prostitutes comes home, you kill the fattened calf for him!" (Luke 15:30) However, his father does not see it this way. "My son," he says, "you are always with me and everything I have is yours. But we have to

celebrate … [your brother] was dead and is alive again; he was lost and is found" (Luke 15:28–31).

When engaging with the parable of the prodigal son for the first time, it is easy or even natural to identify with the helpless rage exhibited by the elder son. His belief that he has suffered an injustice is certainly not unfounded and, having worked hard for his

father for years with little to no acknowledgment, his resentment is understandable. This sense of identification with the plight of the elder brother only heightens the power of the parable's conclusion.

While the older brother has been open and honest in his assertions, his self-righteous and self-centered attitude is condemned by Jesus. In the older brother's fury at the lack of recognition that his father has given to his good deeds, or works, he is unable to exhibit the grace of his father and welcome his brother home. What is more, the older brother cannot share in his father's gratitude that the prodigal son has owned up to his mistakes and sought out forgiveness. We never learn whether the older brother repents for his behavior.

Lost but redeemed

In the Bible, important principles are often repeated for emphasis. This is exemplified by Luke 15, which, in

Familial relationships and inheritance

In the ancient world, land was a family's most important asset. For this reason, laws evolved that governed the rights of inheritance. Though the Bible varies in what it says these laws stipulate—probably because the texts setting them out were written at different times—it is clear that a man's principal heirs were sons born to him by his wife or wives. As stated in Deuteronomy 21, the eldest son inherits a double share. So if, for example, there were four sons,

the oldest would get 40 percent of the estate and the others 20 percent each. Daughters did not inherit, but were provided with a dowry that went to their husband's family when they married. They could only inherit their father's estate if there were no sons to do so.

Contrarily, the New Testament focuses on spiritual, rather than physical, inheritance. Indeed, in Luke 12:13–21, Jesus specifically states that life "does not consist of an abundance of possessions."

addition to the prodigal son, contains two other parables linked by a common theme—the lost sheep and the lost coin. In the first of these parables, Jesus is not worried about the sheep that are safe—all 99 of them; he is concerned about the one sheep that is lost. The point is reiterated in the second parable, about a lost coin which, when rediscovered, becomes all the more treasured. Throughout these first two parables, Jesus repeatedly states the possibility of forgiveness and redemption, saying: "there is rejoicing in the presence of the angels of God over one sinner who repents" (15:10).

In the parable of the prodigal son, this message is taken further, with the lost being contrasted against the faithful. The prodigal son represents any person who has—one way or another, through greed or negligence—strayed from God. His older brother represents the loyal believers who, basking in their self-righteousness, may be blind to the sin of their own arrogance; his presence in the story reminds those who hear it that the grace of God is above petty human notions of justice and fairness.

> When he came to his senses, he said, 'How many of my father's hired servants have food to spare, and here I am starving to death!'
> **Luke 15:17**

> His father saw him and was filled with compassion for him; he ran to his son, threw his arms around him, and kissed him.
> **Luke 15:20**

The father figure represents God Himself. Despite having been wronged by his son's actions, he loves him and welcomes him home with open arms—just as God, throughout the Bible, forgives His people for their misdeeds on the basis of His grace. The message of the Prodigal Son is clear. It is the people who are lost that need to be shown God's mercy and forgiveness the most, so that they may be found again.

Context of Luke

Though Luke was not present with Jesus at the time of His ministry—in all likelihood, he did not convert until after the resurrection—it is notable that his Gospel account is the only one to include the parable of the prodigal son. While the Synoptic Gospels of Matthew, Mark, and Luke are broadly similar in content, the Gospel of Luke in particular addresses a specific challenge often put to Jesus—that in associating with sinners, He Himself is acting sinfully. It is therefore perhaps not surprising that Luke alone would focus on a tale that encourages forgiveness of the wayward sinner, regardless of any transgressions in his past. ■

Lost and found

As well as the three parables in Luke 15, the notion of things that are "lost" and "found" features elsewhere in the Bible, such as Luke 19:10 and Psalm 119. In Psalm 119 in particular, the idea is highly relevant. This acrostic poem is a prayer to God, which tells Him: "I have strayed like a lost sheep. Seek your servant, for I have not forgotten your commands" (Psalm 119:176).

Isaiah 41:10 sums up God's reaction to all such pleas from the lost who pray for guidance: "So do not fear for I am with you; do not be dismayed, for I am your God. I will strengthen you and help you; I will uphold you with my strong right hand." Solomon, the son of King David, also preaches about the need to trust in God, and to do so fully, "with all your heart and lean not on your understanding" (Proverbs 3:5). He goes on to say that if you acknowledge God "in all your ways" and "submit to him," then God will "make your paths straight" (Proverbs 3:6). According to Solomon, by following the word of God and obeying His will, His people will be guided through life and not become "lost" or sinful.

FROM WHOM DO THE KINGS OF THE EARTH COLLECT DUTY AND TAXES?

MATTHEW 17:27, THE TEMPLE TAX

IN BRIEF

PASSAGE
Matthew 17:27

THEME
God's provision

SETTING
c.27–29 CE Capernaum at the Sea of Galilee.

KEY FIGURES
Jesus The Messiah and Son of God during His ministry in Galilee.

Peter A fisherman by trade and one of Jesus's most favored disciples.

Tax collectors State officials generally disliked for their corrupt practices.

In addition to the taxes that were imposed on the people of Judea by Rome, a voluntary Temple tax was levied on Jewish males over the age of 20 to pay for sacrifices and incense in the Temple. In Matthew 17, the Apostle describes Jesus and His disciples arriving in Capernaum, where Peter is confronted by the collectors of the Temple tax. When the officials ask Peter if His master pays the tax, Peter affirms that He does.

A little later, Jesus challenges Peter, asking if taxes are paid by the children of the "kings of the earth" (Matthew 17:25). In response, Peter grants that taxes are not paid by the children of kings. Then, in a miraculous twist, Jesus tells Peter to catch a fish and open its mouth. There he will find a four-drachma coin with which he is to pay both his own tax and Jesus's.

The tax is paid

When Jesus speaks of the children of kings, He casts Himself and His disciples as sons of God who are therefore exempt from the taxation

Peter finds a coin in the mouth of a fish on the shores of Lake Capernaum, in a 17th-century Dutch engraving by Salomon Savery after a painting by Peter Paul Rubens.

that is imposed on the house of God. Yet Jesus instructs Peter to fish for the coin, explaining it must be done "so that we may not offend" the tax collectors (Matthew 17:27).

Jesus's actions suggest that it is sometimes necessary to comply with the views of others in order to keep the peace. However, they do not pay from their own pockets: the miracle of the coin in the fish's mouth shows God's generosity and His capacity to lovingly provide for both His Son and His people. ∎

See also: A Child in the Temple 188 ▪ Jesus Embraces a Tax Collector 242–43 ▪ Cleansing the Temple 244–45

SO THE LAST WILL BE FIRST, AND THE FIRST WILL BE LAST
MATTHEW 20:16, WORKERS IN THE VINEYARD

IN BRIEF

PASSAGE
Matthew 20:16

THEME
God operates through unending grace

SETTING
c.27–29 CE The region of Galilee.

KEY FIGURES
Jesus The Messiah and Son of God during His ministry in Galilee.

The landowner Owner of the vineyard and the purveyor of God's grace.

The workers The employees of the landowner gathered from the marketplace.

The parable of the workers in the vineyard is one that many readers with modern notions of fairness struggle to accept. However, it functions very well as a demonstration of how God deals with people on the basis of grace, rather than works.

In the parable, a landowner goes out early one morning to recruit workers. He agrees to pay each of the laborers a denarius for the day. Later in the day, the vineyard

These who were hired last … you have made … equal to us who have borne the burden of the work and the heat of the day.
Matthew 20:12

owner goes out again four times—at 9 am, midday, 3 pm, and 5 pm. Each time he leaves, he encounters more men doing nothing and offers them work in his vineyard too, which Jesus says represents "the kingdom of heaven" (Matthew 20:1).

When evening comes, the landowner gathers the workers. He pays all of them the same amount—one denarius each. The men who worked longer hours are outraged. The landowner, however, brushes away their objections, saying that he is generous and has the right to use his money as he sees fit.

Interpreting the tale
The story of the workers in the vineyard shows us that God's grace can supersede human logic. One interpretation of the parable is that those who turn to God late in life are just as worthy of salvation as those who have always believed. Other theologians go further, presenting the first laborers as Jews, and the latecomers as Gentiles—both equally deserving of God's love and salvation. ∎

See also: Parables of Jesus 214–15 ▪ The Good Samaritan 216–17 ▪ The Prodigal Son 218–21

MY NAME IS LEGION, FOR WE ARE MANY

MARK 5:9, DEMONS AND THE HERD OF PIGS

IN BRIEF

PASSAGE
Mark 5:1–20
Luke 8:26–39
Matthew 8:28–34

THEME
Jesus's authority over the spiritual realm

SETTING
c.27–29 CE Gerasene shores of the Sea of Galilee.

KEY FIGURES
Jesus The Messiah and Son of God at the height of His ministry in Galilee.

The demoniac An immensely strong demon-possessed man who lives in tombs near the shores of the Sea of Galilee.

Pig-keepers The unfortunate herdsmen who see their pigs drown and inform the local people of Jesus's miracle.

Often referred to as the Miracle of the Gadarene Swine, the miracle of the demons and the herd of pigs demonstrates the total authority of Jesus over the spiritual realm.

The story is recounted in three of the Gospels—Mark 5:1–20, Luke 8:26–39, and Matthew 8:28–34—but the fullest account is in Mark. Jesus crosses the Sea of Galilee with His followers and arrives in the land of the Gerasenes. As He gets out of His boat, a man possessed by a demon, a demoniac, comes down from some tombs to meet Him. The man is so strong that he cannot be bound, breaking his chains and cutting himself with stones, while crying out at the top of his voice.

Jesus heals the demoniac in this 6th-century mosaic from the Basilica of Sant'Apollinare Nuovo in Ravenna, Italy. The drowning pigs are depicted next to the possessed man.

See also: The Raising of Lazarus 226–27 ▪ Feeding the 5,000 228–31 ▪ Healing of the Beggar 284–87 ▪ The Final Judgment 316–21

Jesus approaches the man and calls for the demon to come out of Him. The demon replies: "What do you want with me, Jesus, Son of the Most High God? In God's name, don't torture me!" (Mark 5:7) Jesus asks for the name of the demon, who tells Him it is "Legion, for we are many."

Unclean and unwanted

The demons plead with Jesus not to send them away, but rather to send them into the bodies of a large herd of pigs grazing nearby. When Jesus grants the demons their wish, the pigs hurtle down the steep hillside into the lake and are drowned, demonstrating Jesus's dominion over spiritual creatures.

The pig-keepers are angry at the loss of their property and when the local people hear about the carnage, they remonstrate with Jesus and ask Him to leave. As He climbs back into His boat, however, Jesus is hailed by the cured demoniac. The man begs Jesus to let him travel with Him, but Jesus refuses, telling the man to go home to his own people and tell them how much the Lord has done for him.

A boy.
Mark 9:17–29

A man in the synagogue at Capernaum.
Luke 4:35

A Canaanite woman's daughter.
Matthew 15:21–28

Subjects of exorcism

A mute man.
Matthew 9:32–34

A blind and mute man.
Matthew 12:22–32

The traditional interpretation of this story is that, in casting out the demons and condemning the pigs, Jesus prioritized the soul of the man. Medieval scholar St. Thomas Aquinas argued that Jesus acted to save the demoniac's soul rather than his body or the property of the pig-keepers. Thus, the miracle is a judgment on the townsmen's concern for their pigs over the possessed man. The tale may also have symbolic meaning. Judaism regards pigs as unclean, and therefore the herd might be a good place to bury impure spirits. ▪

Demonic Possession

According to French Benedictine monk Antoine Augustin Calmet, writing in the 18th century, in the Bible there are two forms of demonic attack—"possession" and "obsession." The former usually involves the internal "ownership" of the individual by an evil spirit. This manifests in the form of physical agitation, a furious temper, speaking in tongues, and uttering blasphemy. "Obsession" occurs when the demon acts externally against its victim. This can involve unexplained lesions, epileptic seizures, and facial deformation.

In the Old Testament, evil spirits are mentioned in 1 Samuel, 1 Kings, and Job. There is a greater number of demonic attacks in the New Testament. However, Calmet notes that what seemed to be demons may have often represented little more than simple maladies that could not be explained by contemporary physicians.

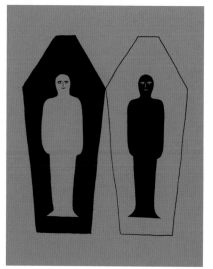

THE MAN WHO HAD DIED CAME OUT

JOHN 11:44, THE RAISING OF LAZARUS

IN BRIEF

PASSAGE
John 11:1–57

THEME
Resurrection through Christ

SETTING
c.29–33 CE Bethany, south of Jerusalem.

KEY FIGURES
Jesus The Messiah and the Son of God.

Mary and Martha Two of Jesus's followers and friends.

Lazarus The brother of Mary and Martha, and one of Jesus's closest friends.

Disciples The 12 Apostles chosen by Jesus at the beginning of His ministry.

The Book of John is full of signs and wonders that are seen as proof that Jesus was not simply a prophet but the Son of God. When compared to the Synoptic Gospels—the books of Matthew, Mark, and Luke—the Book of John contains few parables, with more emphasis placed on the miracles that Jesus performs.

A plea for help

One of the most well known of these miracles is the story of Lazarus, a name which means "God helped," and possibly foreshadows the events that occur in the story. Lazarus and his sisters Mary and Martha—close friends of Jesus— live in the town of Bethany. When Lazarus becomes deathly ill, his sisters send word to Jesus, asking for His return so that He may heal their brother. Jesus and His disciples are about one day's travel away, but when word reaches them, the disciples do not want Jesus to go to Bethany due to rising hostility toward Him in nearby Jerusalem.

However, Jesus rebukes them, saying "A man who walks by day will not stumble, for he sees by this world's light" (John 11:9). In this way, Jesus shows His disciples that

Friedrich Overbeck's 1882 painting *Raising of Lazarus* was born out of the Nazarene movement of 19th-century Rome. Art from this movement was dominated by religious subjects.

through faith in God any obstacle can be surpassed, including death itself—a theme emphasized in the story of Lazarus.

Jesus wept

By the time Jesus returns to Bethany, Lazarus has already been dead for four days. On His arrival, Jesus greets Martha, saying "your brother will rise again" (John 11:23). Jesus then calls Mary to meet Him, and when He sees her grief, Jesus weeps alongside her.

See also: Demons and the Herds of Pigs 224–25 ▪ Jesus Anointed at Bethany 246–47 ▪ The Empty Tomb 268–71

Jesus asks Mary to take Him to the tomb of Lazarus and she obliges. When He ask the crowd to roll away the stone from the front of the tomb, Martha initially objects, expressing fear that the corpse will smell, but then acquiesces. In a loud voice, Jesus shouts "Lazarus, come out!" (John 11:43). Immediately, Lazarus rises and exits the tomb.

Purpose of the miracle

In one of the many miracles that Jesus performs, He resurrects Lazarus for the purpose of proving that He is the Messiah. Jesus states this when Martha asks Him to return to Bethany: He says that it will be done "so that God's son may be glorified through it" (John 11:4).

When Jesus approaches the tomb, the doubtful crowd suggests that if He were truly the Son of God, He would have healed Lazarus before his death. Jesus then prays to God, telling Him that He is enacting the resurrection out loud for the benefit of the crowd, so that they may see the glory of God. These details suggest that the primary purpose of raising Lazarus is to inspire the watching audience

Did I not tell you that if you believed, you would see the glory of God?
John 11:40

to discuss the figure of Jesus and, ultimately, have faith in the power of Christ above and beyond death.

However, the importance of the story of Lazarus extends further. When Martha and Mary send word to Jesus that Lazarus is dying, their message reads "Lord, the one you love is sick" (John 11:3) and Jesus's compassion is clearly visible from His interactions with Mary. More than simply a display of divinity, the story of Lazarus shows an emotional depth in Jesus, which acts as a powerful reminder that, like God, Jesus feels profound love and compassion for His people. ▪

Healing the sick

The curing of illnesses and casting out of demons were often considered one and the same in ancient Near Eastern thought. In fact, many ancient people believed that demons were the root cause of any given illness. For example, in Babylon, the god Marduk was called upon to cure common ailments such as headaches or toothaches through exorcism.

With this in mind, it is no surprise that over the course of His ministry, Jesus would heal those with more serious ailments in order to show His holiness. In the Bible, demonic possession is sometimes described in similar terms to what we regard as mental illness today. One such example comes in Mark 5, when Jesus exorcizes multiple demons from a man in Gerasa.

In ancient times many of those who were sick, such as lepers, were cast out of society out of fear and hatred. Jesus focused on these individuals during His mission and, in doing so, taught His followers that nobody is beyond Christ's redemption if they have faith.

The **"seven signs"** proving that Jesus is the Christ form the structural backbone of the Book of John. These miracles become increasingly more impressive as the Gospel goes on.

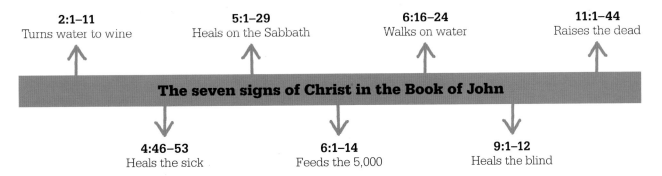

2:1–11
Turns water to wine

5:1–29
Heals on the Sabbath

6:16–24
Walks on water

11:1–44
Raises the dead

The seven signs of Christ in the Book of John

4:46–53
Heals the sick

6:1–14
Feeds the 5,000

9:1–12
Heals the blind

AND TAKING THE FIVE LOAVES, AND THE TWO FISH, HE LOOKED UP TO HEAVEN

LUKE 9:16, FEEDING THE 5,000

IN BRIEF

PASSAGE
Matthew 14:13–21
Mark 6:31–44
Luke 9:12–17
John 6:1–14

THEME
God satisfies material and spiritual hunger

SETTING
c.27–29 CE Bethsaida.

KEY FIGURES
Jesus The Messiah and Son of God during the height of His ministry in Galilee.

The 12 disciples Jesus's chosen followers, who help Him to heal the sick and feed the multitude.

The crowd Mainly Jewish residents of the settlements near the town of Bethsaida.

The feeding of the 5,000—also known as the Miracle of the Five Loaves and Two Fish—is one of the most celebrated moments in the Bible. In fact, it is the only miracle, other than the resurrection, to appear in all four of the Gospels, which underlines its significance. God's compassion and limitless ability to satisfy both physical and spiritual hunger are shown here at their greatest.

Although this miracle is most often referred to as "the feeding of the 5,000," the number of people present could have been far greater. Matthew 14:21 estimates the number of men alone at "about five thousand," and goes on to say that

See also: The Origin of Prayer 38–39 ▪ The Lord's Prayer 212–13 ▪ The Last Supper 236–41 ▪ The Empty Tomb 268–71

women and children were there, too. Some Bible scholars believe there may have been as many as 20,000 people fed in total.

Jesus seeks solitude

According to Luke's Gospel, upon hearing that John the Baptist has been killed, Jesus withdraws to a

They do not need to go away. You give them something to eat.
Matthew 14:16

remote place near the town of Bethsaida, likely located on the River Jordan just north of the Sea of Galilee. However, the crowds find out where He is, and they leave their towns and villages to follow Him there. Despite His desire for solitude, when Jesus sees the large crowd of people gathering around Him, He feels compassion for them. He speaks to them about the kingdom of God and begins to heal those who are sick.

Feeding the multitude

Late in the afternoon, all 12 of the disciples approach Him, and remind Him of their remote location. They suggest that He send the people away to the surrounding settlements so they can find food and lodging for the night. Jesus instead tells His disciples to give the hungry people something to eat where they stand.

The Feeding of the Five Thousand is depicted by Flemish Renaissance artist Joachim Patinir. The painting, from the Monasterio de El Escorial, Spain, has the Sea of Galilee in the background.

The disciples explain that this is impossible, as they only have five loaves of bread and two fish with which to feed the thousands.

Jesus instructs the disciples to make the crowd sit down in groups of about 50 people. He takes the loaves and fish, looks up to heaven, and gives thanks. He then breaks the loaves and fish into pieces and hands them to the disciples, who then feed everyone at the gathering until they are all satisfied. There are even 12 basketfuls of broken bread left over at the end of the meal.

The miracle that Jesus has just performed is symbolic of God's endless love and compassion for »

Bread as a symbol of life

Bread is mentioned throughout the Bible. While this was one of the most important foods of ancient times, it also has a symbolic status as a manifestation of human life itself. Nowhere is this idea underlined more thematically than in the Miracle of the Five Loaves and Two Fish. Shortly after performing His miracle, Jesus states, "I am the bread of life. Whoever comes to me will never go hungry" (John 6:35).

The breaking of loaves of bread to feed the multitudes also foreshadows Jesus's same action during the last meal He shares with His disciples. It is during this event that Jesus establishes that the bread and His flesh are one and the same, at least symbolically.

As well as providing the people with sustenance, bread also represents a connection to Jesus. Its multiplication and distribution in this miracle shows Jesus's desire to satisfy the people's hunger, and also to spread the word of God.

Bakers check the quality of the matza bread at a handmade matza factory in Kfar Chabad, Israel.

His people. From an impossibly small amount of food, an enormous crowd is fed. The fact that they are in such a remote setting shows the wide reach of God's love, suggesting that no matter where one is, God's love can still be felt.

Giving thanks to heaven

The sustenance that God provides can be thought of as both physical and spiritual. Although the story focuses on the necessary physical nourishment the bread provides, this is also a symbolic gesture of compassion. Many Christians interpret this miracle as proof that if they remain faithful and grateful to God, He will provide them with everything they need, both physically and spiritually. The 12 baskets of leftover bread exemplify the endless nature of God's love for His people, and serve as an illustration of why He deserves their worship.

It is also noteworthy that in three of the Gospels—Matthew, Mark, and Luke—Jesus does not hand the food out Himself; instead, He gives the bread and fish to the disciples to distribute to the crowd. This not only suggests that anybody can deliver the message of God's love, but also teaches the importance of faith in God. It is implied that unless the disciples have faith in Jesus and God, the bread and fish will run out. It is not simply enough to ask for something and to be grateful in receiving it: one must have total faith that God wants to and will provide for His people.

Five loaves of bread

Numbers often carry a symbolic significance in the Bible, and this miracle is no exception. Not only are there 12 baskets of leftover food, recalling the 12 tribes of Israel in the Old Testament and the 12

disciples in the New Testament. The five pieces of bread that Jesus is handed could represent the Pentateuch of the Torah: Genesis, Exodus, Leviticus, Numbers, and Deuteronomy. Jesus takes these five loaves and multiplies them into something more, in the same way that He takes the Mosaic Law from the Torah and builds upon it.

This is not the only way in which the feeding of the 5,000 refers back to the Old Testament. In John 6, Jesus explains the miracle of the multiplication of the loaves with a sermon that draws direct parallels between God providing for the multitudes at Bethsaida and His provisions for the Israelites during their time in the wilderness. Jesus closes this sermon with a difficult teaching that foreshadows the Last Supper: "I am the living bread that came down from heaven. Whoever eats this bread will live forever" (6:51).

Feeding the Gentiles

This is not the only miracle recorded in which Jesus and His disciples feed the multitudes. Both Matthew and Mark describe two versions of what is seemingly the same miracle. While Matthew 14 tells the story of the feeding of the 5,000, which occurs after the death of John the

The Lord Almighty will prepare a feast of rich food for all peoples.
Isaiah 25:6

> I [the Lord] will bless
> [Israel] with abundant
> provisions; her poor I
> will satisfy with food.
> **Psalms 132:13–15**

Baptist, Matthew 15 goes on to describe Jesus and the disciples feeding a crowd in a region of the Gerasenes, near the Decapolis, a cluster of ten allied cities east of the Sea of Galilee. The narrative is similar to that in Matthew 14, except for two key details: the numbers and the type of people who were fed.

Some Bible scholars have questioned why the Gospel writers would include two such similar miracles so close together in their accounts of Jesus's life. However,

both the numbers cited and the audiences are important. While the crowd at Bethsaida was predominantly Jewish, scholars suggest that those gathered in the "feeding of the 4,000" were more likely to be Gentiles. This feeding of the multitudes, therefore, was proof that God would provide for all people, Jews and Gentiles.

Doubting disciples

It is notable that when Jesus tells His disciples in the Gerasenes that He plans to feed the multitude, they express doubts. They ask Him "where could we get enough bread in this remote place to feed such a crowd?" (Matthew 15:33). They either do not quite believe He will work in this "remote place" or they have forgotten how Jesus recently performed this very miracle for the 5,000 gathered at Bethsaida. Some scholars have taken this skepticism to show that the disciples are, at this point, still learning: they do not yet possess an unwavering faith in the power of God to do what, to humans, seems impossible. ■

Jesus as the king of the Jews

Since the prophet Isaiah, the Jewish people had waited for a king from the line of David to deliver them from their enemies and preside over an era of economic prosperity and international influence.

Throughout His ministry, Jesus, a descendant of David, proves Himself to be this very savior. He preaches the word of God to the multitudes, heals the sick, and provides them with food. Not concerned with earthly kingdoms, Jesus performs acts that show Him to be divine, leading many who hear Him to accept Him as the promised Messiah. The crowds that gather to listen to Him speak are testament to His growing support among both Jews and Gentiles. Jesus's following, of course, eventually becomes so great that enemies of His decide that He poses too much of a threat. As Jesus undergoes questioning at His trial, it is no wonder that Pilate refers to Him as the "king of the Jews," a title that also appears on the cross on which He is crucified.

	Feeding of the 5,000	**Feeding of the 4,000**
Featured in Matthew/Mark	Yes	Yes
Featured in Luke/John	Yes	No
Location	Bethsaida	Near the Decapolis, in the Gerasenes
The people being fed	Jews	Gentiles
Number of loaves/ fish before miracle	Five loaves and two fish	Seven loaves and several fish
Remaining food after miracle	Twelve baskets' worth	Seven baskets' worth

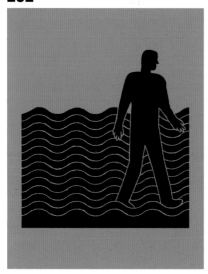

TAKE COURAGE! IT IS I. DON'T BE AFRAID
MATTHEW 14:27, JESUS WALKS ON WATER

IN BRIEF

PASSAGE
Matthew 14:27

THEME
God's sovereignty over all things

SETTING
c.26–27 CE The Sea of Galilee.

KEY FIGURES
Jesus The Messiah and Son of God during His ministry in Galilee and Judea.

Peter One of Jesus's inner circle of disciples, who later denies knowing Him. Peter was one of several disciples who were originally fishermen.

Disciples Jesus's close group of 12 followers, who often witness His miracles.

J esus walking on the waters of the Sea of Galilee is one of the most significant miracles recorded in the New Testament. It follows on from another miracle—feeding 5,000 people with five loaves of bread and two fish—and is succeeded by Jesus's retreat up a mountain to pray. The sight of Jesus walking on water astounds

the disciples and, for the first time in the Bible, they begin to worship Jesus, exclaiming, "Truly you are the Son of God" (Matthew 14:33).

A stormy sea
The scene takes place in the Sea of Galilee in the lower part of the Jordan valley. At 13 miles (21km) long and 8 miles (13km) wide, it is Israel's largest freshwater lake. It is also prone to sudden storms, as the disciples discover to their cost.

One evening, the disciples go down to the lake, get into their boat, and set off for Capernaum. They soon find themselves struggling to make headway against a powerful headwind. Even though most are experienced fishermen, they become exhausted after hours of straining on their oars in the face of the gathering storm.

It is at this moment—probably in the early hours of the morning—that Jesus comes to the disciples' rescue. He approaches them in a totally unexpected way, by walking on the turbulent waters as if they are as stable as solid rock.

The disciples are confused. They see something or someone coming toward them, but they do not realize who or what it is. Rather,

Jesus and the Sea of Galilee

Key
1. The Sermon on the Mount
2. Calming the Storm
3. Demons and the Herd of Pigs
4. Feeding the 5,000
5. Jesus Walks on Water
6. Feeding the 4,000

See also: Demons and the Herd of Pigs 224–25 ▪ Feeding the 5,000 228–31 ▪ Peter's Denial 256–57 ▪ The Empty Tomb 268–69

they are terrified, because they believe the figure is an apparition. Jesus calls out to them to calm them down, but Peter asks Jesus to command him to come. When Jesus calls for Peter, Peter climbs out of the boat and starts walking on the water toward Jesus. When Peter's faith wavers, he begins to sink, but Jesus rescues him.

Immediately Jesus reached out his hand and caught him. "You of little faith," He said, "why did you doubt?"
Matthew 14:31

Jesus walks on the water toward the helpless disciples. Despite Peter questioning Jesus's identity and betraying his faith in the process, Jesus saves His servants.

The Gospel writers vary slightly in the way they tell the story of this particular miracle. According to Matthew 14, Peter walks on the water in response to Jesus's one-word command, "Come," before his faith fails him. The focus of the story as told in Mark 6:47–51 and John 6:16–21 differs from that of Matthew: in those Gospels, only Jesus is shown to walk on water.

Messages in the miracle

There are two important points to note in this particular miracle. One is the lesson the disciples learn when Jesus comes to save them from the stormy waters. The message is universal: Jesus will always be there for His followers at the times when He is needed the

Flawed faith

Although Peter steps out onto the water, his faith is not strong enough to overcome his fear. This is not the only time Peter loses faith in Jesus. As Jesus accurately predicts on the Mount of Olives immediately after the Last Supper, "this night, before the rooster crows, you will disown Me three times" (Matthew 26:69–75). Fear and frailty usurp Peter's faith—but he learns from these moments to go on to become a pillar of the early Christian Church. His three denials of Christ are counterbalanced by his three declarations of love after Jesus's resurrection.

There are many examples of flawed faith in the Bible. The prophet Jonah fails to go to the Ninevites and tell them to repent. Instead, he flees through fear and because he does not think they deserve to be forgiven (Jonah 1:1–3). Just as Jesus rescues Peter, Jonah is forgiven by God.

In renewed faith there is redemption—these stories show that it is never too late to return to God.

most. Jesus helps the disciples to go safely to their destination, and they hail Him as the Son of God.

It is also significant that Jesus is shown as having the power to walk on water. In the Old Testament, this ability is described as being unique to God. Genesis 6–7 and 9 and Exodus 14:21 and 15:8 all state clearly that only God has power over the seas. This fact is also confirmed by Job 9:8, which states: "He alone … treads on the waves of the sea." Jesus's ability to walk on water is therefore proof of His close relationship to God. ▪

HIS FACE SHONE LIKE THE SUN, AND HIS CLOTHES BECAME AS WHITE AS LIGHT
MATTHEW 17:2, THE TRANSFIGURATION

IN BRIEF

PASSAGE
Matthew 17:1–13; Mark 9:2–13; Luke 9:28–36

THEME
Jesus is affirmed by God

SETTING
c.27–29 CE Mount Tabor.

KEY FIGURES
Jesus The Messiah and Son of God during His ministry.

Peter Together with James and John, a member of Jesus's inner circle of three disciples.

James and John Sons of Zebedee. Originally fishermen on the Sea of Galilee.

Moses Israel's liberator and lawgiver, who led the people out of slavery in Egypt.

Elijah A prophet active in the reign of King Ahab of Israel in the 9th century BCE.

Mark, Matthew, and Luke—the so-called Synoptic Gospels—all tell the story of the Transfiguration. This event follows two outbursts by Peter, one of Jesus's favored disciples. In the first, Peter makes a bold statement about Jesus's identity: "You are the Christ, the son of the living God" (Matthew 16:15). After the second, in which Peter objects to Jesus's intimations that He will suffer rejection and be killed, Jesus issues the stinging reply: "Get behind me, Satan!"—"Satan" here meaning simply an adversary of the Lord— "Your thoughts are not thoughts from God but from men" (Mark 8:33).

Shining glory
Six days after Jesus's rebuke, according to Mark and Matthew, or eight days in Luke, Jesus takes His closest disciples—Peter and the brothers James and John—up a high mountain. A tradition dating from the 4th century CE identifies it as Mount Tabor in Lower Galilee, but mounts Carmel and Horeb are other candidates. There, the astonished disciples witness an extraordinary metamorphosis. Jesus's clothes become dazzling white—"no one on earth could clean them so white" (Mark 9:3)— while His face shines like the sun.

With Him are two other figures, whom the disciples identify as Moses and Elijah. The disciples are terrified and, as ever, it is Peter who speaks. He suggests erecting three

The Transfiguration of Christ
(1516–1520), by Raphael, sets the transfiguration against a story of the Apostles, who, unlike Christ, are only human, failing to rid a boy of demons.

See also: The Baptism of Jesus 194–97 ■ The Crucifixion 258–65 ■
The Empty Tomb 268–71 ■ The Great Commission 274–77

The Five Milestones of Jesus's Ministry

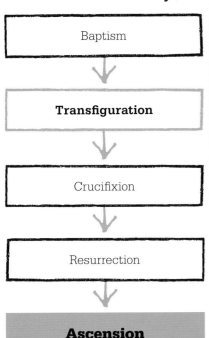

Baptism

↓

Transfiguration

↓

Crucifixion

↓

Resurrection

↓

Ascension

shelters to worship in: one each for Jesus, Moses, and Elijah. However, as he speaks, a cloud envelops them and the voice of God comes forth: "This is my much loved Son. Listen to Him!" (Mark 9:7). After this, everything returns to normal. When the disciples look around, there is no one there but Jesus.

Divine revelation

The Transfiguration has been seen by some theologians as a blueprint for how to respond to the glory of God. While the disciples' first response is to fear it, they learn to listen and believe, reassured by the touch of their friend, Jesus, who says, "Do not be afraid." For a moment, it seems, some kind of partition is drawn back between the heavenly and earthly realms, allowing the disciples to glimpse Jesus in His glory as the Christ, the son of the living God.

In the Hebrew Bible, Yahweh reveals himself in a cloud on a mountaintop to both Moses and Elijah. The cloud that descends upon this mountain conveys the same divine presence, known in rabbinic literature as the *Skekinah*. The words uttered by God from the cloud are similar to those spoken at Jesus's baptism: "This is my Son, whom I love" (Matthew 3:17).

God now adds a command: "Listen to Him!" Luke's Gospel tells us more about what this refers to. In Luke's version of events, Jesus, Moses, and Elijah speak with Jesus concerning His "departure, which He is about to bring to fulfillment at Jerusalem." In other words, they are discussing the suffering and death Jesus had recently warned His disciples about. The use of the word "departure"—*exodus* in Greek—draws a deliberate parallel to the Old Testament. Just as Moses had freed the Israelites from Egypt, the suffering of Jesus would deliver the people from their sins. ■

We did not follow cleverly devised stories … we were eyewitnesses of His majesty.
2 Peter 1:16–18

The new Elijah

According to the Hebrew Bible, the prophet Elijah did not die in the usual sense. Instead, he was taken up into heaven in a blazing chariot of fire. This gave rise to a belief that he would come back one day to prepare the way for the Messiah. Indeed, the very last verses of the Old Testament make this prediction. "See, I will send you the prophet Elijah before that great and dreadful day of the Lord comes," the prophet Malachi proclaims in Yahweh's name.

Descending the mountain after the Transfiguration, the three disciples ask Jesus about this prophecy. His reply is that it has already been fulfilled in the person of John the Baptist: "But I tell you, Elijah has already come, and they did not recognize him … In the same way, the Son of Man is going to suffer at their hands" (Matthew 17:12). John the Baptist suffered and died at the hands of Herod Antipas, and Jesus says again that He will suffer the same fate. In fulfilling God's plans for redemption and restoration, the way of glory and the way of suffering are inseparable.

FOR GOD SO LOVED THE WORLD, THAT HE GAVE HIS ONE AND ONLY SON

JOHN 3:16, THE NATURE OF FAITH

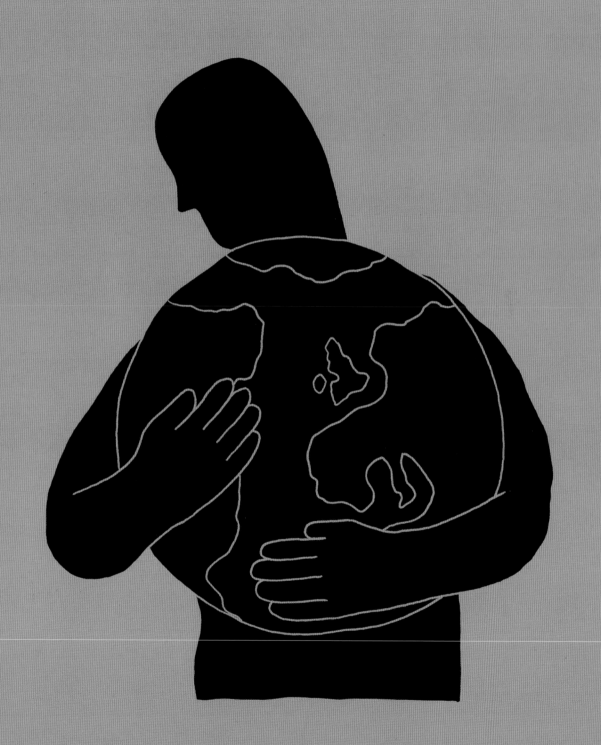

IN BRIEF

PASSAGE
John 3:3–21

THEME
The nature of faith

SETTING
c.27–29 CE Roman Palestine.

KEY FIGURES
Jesus The Messiah and Son of God, who requires that people believe in Him in order to be saved.

Nicodemus A Jewish leader and teacher who came to question Jesus. After Jesus's death, he brings myrrh and aloes to embalm His body with strips of linen.

The Brazen Serpent, a sculpture by Giovanni Fantoni, in Madaba, Jordan, commemorates the bronze snake erected by Moses, which Jesus draws on to illustrate His teaching on faith.

Different religious leaders come to test Jesus as He grows in popularity as a teacher. Some listen to His public preaching; others examine Him in more private settings. One leader, a Pharisee named Nicodemus, comes to Jesus with questions. A member of the Sanhedrin, the ruling religious council, Nicodemus is an important teacher in his own right.

Nicodemus does not understand what Jesus means when He says that people must be born again to see the kingdom of God, and Jesus tells him he should not be surprised by the statement, if he is truly a teacher of Israel. Jesus says, "I have spoken to you of earthly things and you do not believe; how then will you believe if I speak of heavenly things?" (John 3:12). Jesus then refers to an event that happened during the wilderness wanderings of the Israelites; He describes how God judged the Israelites' bitter attitude toward Him by sending venomous snakes into their camp. When Moses cried out to God, he was instructed to make a bronze serpent and lift it up where the people could see it. The snakebites of those who gazed upon the snake were healed. Jesus compares Himself to the snake, saying that He must also be lifted up (a reference to the crucifixion), so that whoever believes would have eternal life in Him (3:14–15).

Faith in Christ

Having acknowledged the promise of eternal life, Jesus begins to broach the topic of faith, which is the major precondition for salvation. In what is perhaps the most famous statement in the Bible (John 3:16), Jesus tells Nicodemus that God loved the world so much, "He gave His one and only Son, that whoever believes in Him shall not perish but have eternal life." John's Gospel goes on to say that God's love is for everyone, but can only be experienced through faith in Jesus. Although Jesus had come to save the world, not condemn it, escaping God's Final Judgment depends upon having faith in Jesus first. According to John, those who do not believe in Jesus stand condemned already (3:17–18).

The result of believing in Jesus is to enjoy eternal life instead of divine judgment. Such faith involves trust in Jesus and belief that His death and resurrection is sufficient for salvation. Paul teaches that when a person has such faith, affirmation through words and deeds should be the result. Writing in Romans 10:9–10, Paul states, "If you declare with your mouth, 'Jesus is Lord,' and believe in your heart

See also: Ruth and Naomi 108–09 ■ The Empty Tomb 268–71 ■ Fruits of the Spirit 300 ■ Salvation Through Faith 301 ■ Faith and Works 312

that God raised him from the dead, you will be saved. For it is with your heart that you believe and are justified, and it is with your mouth that you profess your faith and are saved."

Walking by faith

Christianity is defined by the tenet that those who believe in Jesus's crucifixion and resurrection receive life, and those who do not face condemnation. Though this idea may serve to alienate non-Christians, its purpose is to convey the gravity of the call to faith and the urgency of believing in Jesus.

This faith in Christ initiates the Christian life, but also drives it forward. In his second letter to the Corinthians, Paul writes that Christians should live by faith, not by sight (2 Corinthians 5:7). This did not mean that Paul understood faith as being irrational or contrary to evidence, or that the contrast between faith and sight should mean that faith is blind. Some versions of the Bible translate the phrase as "walk by faith, not by sight," which may illuminate Paul's

Faith is a living, daring confidence in God's grace, so sure and certain that a man could stake his life on it a thousand times.
Martin Luther

Ask God … and it will be given to you … but when you ask, you must believe and not doubt, because the one who doubts is like a wave of the sea, blown and tossed by the wind.
James 1:6

meaning: a Christian's life should be guided by trusting God's judgment, not by one's own.

The source of faith

The Bible most often uses the word "faith" to describe people believing some assertion or trusting in God or Jesus. People are commanded to believe statements and to believe that Jesus has done or said things. For this reason, it would be easy to conclude that faith is a purely human response to propositions or persons. Yet the Bible speaks of God as the One who produces faith in people. It is not an instrument of human will, adapted to accomplish human purposes. Instead, it is a gift of God that accomplishes God's purposes in those who receive it. Paul held that belief in Christ was something that God granted to people (Philippians 1:29).

The idea of faith as God's gift also appears in Ephesians 2:8–9, where people are saved through faith that is "not from yourselves, it is the gift of God." The gift of »

St. Augustine

Augustine (396–430 CE), the Bishop of Hippo, an ancient port on the coast of Roman North Africa, advised that in studying the Bible, one ought not seek to understand in order to believe, but rather believe in order to understand. Augustine's counsel was intended to produce humility. It is too easy, he seemed to say, to dismiss the parts of the Bible that are difficult to understand as incoherent or to say that the logic is fatally flawed. Belief, on the other hand, perseveres in study and often finds flashes of insight.

Augustine, who had previously studied the Bible as a pagan teacher of rhetoric and a student of Platonic philosophy, argued that there was a connection between faith and reason. He came to believe that even the best thinkers in the world made mistakes, due to their human nature. Faith, he argued, was illuminating, and allowed a philosopher to see the truth of scripture more clearly.

Augustine was an important scholar in the early Church and a contemporary of St. Jerome. This painting (c.1480) by Sandro Botticelli shows him in his study.

Fra Angelico's *Entombment* (c.1438–1443) shows Nicodemus (behind), the Virgin Mary, and John attending the dead Christ. Belief in His death and resurrection are cornerstones of faith.

describes faith as being more than merely an affirmation that something is true. Faith is also about entrusting oneself to God or Jesus. Here there is a personal aspect to faith: one has "faith in" or "believes in" Jesus.

Trust or entrusting one's self to God is perhaps the most essential characteristic of faith in the Bible. One acknowledges the truth of what God has said because one trusts the God who said it. The biblical words for faith, such as *aman* (Hebrew for "believe, trust, be faithful"), *emunah* (Hebrew for "certainty, faithfulness, trust"), and *pistis* (Greek for "believe, trust, be faithful"), also convey the idea of fidelity, which points to persistent adherence to God or God's will over time. Christians, therefore, must not only trust in God, but continue to trust in Him even when their faith is tested. The wavering of a person or people's faith in God can have dire consequences, as the

faith is understood to come by hearing the Word of God, which summons forth faith in a person's heart, just as God's first words in the Bible, "Let there be light," summoned light into existence at the beginning of creation.

Understanding God as the creator of faith in human beings means that there is not an insurmountable barrier to the production of faith in flawed people. Indeed, some of the least likely

people in the Bible became some of its most powerful examples of faith—for example, in the Old Testament story of Ruth, who demonstrates faithfulness to both God and Naomi; or in the conversion of Paul, a Pharisee who had previously and zealously persecuted Christians, in the New Testament.

Characteristics of faith
Hebrews 11 defines faith as "confidence in what we hope for and assurance about what we do not see"; this definition summarizes the cumulative examples of faith in the Old Testament. However, faith is more complicated than this. According to the Bible, faith has many characteristics.

One of the most obvious is that it gives assent to the truth of a statement. The New Testament speaks of having "faith that …" and exhorts people to "believe that …" more than 20 times, with most examples relating to statements about Jesus. Yet the Bible

Never be afraid to trust an unknown future to a known God.
Corrie ten Boom
Holocaust rescuer (1892–1993)

I believe in Christianity as I believe that the sun has risen: not only because I see it, but because by it I see everything else.
C. S. Lewis
Author, Oxford professor (1898–1963)

Israelites find in the example given by Jesus: God sends snakes into the camp of the Israelites because they do not have faith that God and Moses are guiding them on the best path through the desert.

Active faith

The Bible therefore stresses the importance of an enduring and obedient faith. Having faith that God knows best—because He is all-knowing and all-loving—is key to ensuring obedience to His laws, and throughout the Bible a lack of adherence to God's will usually correlates with a loss of faith.

While assenting to true statements, and even trusting in God are salient features of faith in the Bible, the active nature of faith (faithfulness) is significant. The epistle of James, in particular, deals with the question of whether or not the faith in God that saves is mere assent or is naturally active, producing good works. James writes "Show me your faith without deeds, and I will show you my faith by my deeds. You believe that there is one God … Even the demons believe that—and shudder" (James 2:18–19). James writes that it is not enough for Christians to believe in God, but they should also show this belief through their actions—just as, in the Old Testament, Abraham showed his faith through his willingness to sacrifice his son, Isaac.

Paul takes the idea of active faith even further in his letter to the Romans, when he tells them that "whoever has doubts is condemned if they eat, because their eating is not from faith; and everything that does not come from faith is sin" (Romans 14:23).

While reason and experience can challenge a Christian's faith, they can also vindicate it. Faith produces the good, loving deeds that comprise a life lived in Christ, standing with hope and charity as one of the three theological virtues identified by Paul in his letter to the Thessalonians (1 Thessalonians 1:3). ∎

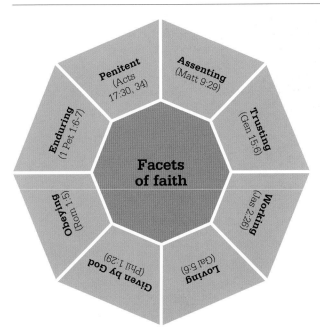

Facets of faith
Protestants identify eight characteristics of faith that come up again and again in the Old and New Testaments, from the stories of the patriarchs to the teachings of the Apostles.

Facets of faith diagram labels:
- Penitent (Acts 17:30, 34)
- Assenting (Matt 9:29)
- Enduring (1 Pet 1:6–7)
- Trusting (Gen 15:6)
- **Facets of faith**
- Obeying (Rom 1:5)
- Working (Jas 2:26)
- Given by God (Phil 1:29)
- Loving (Gal 5:6)

Darkness and light

In John 3, Nicodemus comes to Jesus in the night. This otherwise minor detail is part of a larger theme in John's Gospel and one that originates at the very start of the Bible: "Let there be light" (Genesis 1:3). John describes Jesus as the Light, and those who do not believe in Him as being in darkness. Although the light of faith was available to all who encountered Jesus or His teaching, people still rejected the light. They loved the darkness that hid and enabled their wicked deeds, while hating the light that exposed them.

Jesus identified Himself as the "light of the world" and commanded His followers not to walk in darkness. The imagery of light and dark is also present in the miracle of healing the man who had been blind from birth, and the betrayal, arrest, and crucifixion of Jesus, when foreboding shadow prevails. Yet the triumph of the light was also evident on the morning of the resurrection, and in each person who came to have faith in Jesus.

FOR THE SON OF MAN CAME TO SEEK AND TO SAVE THE LOST

LUKE 19:10, JESUS EMBRACES A TAX COLLECTOR

IN BRIEF

PASSAGE
Luke 19:1–10

THEME
God's kingdom is for all

SETTING
c.27–29 CE Jericho.

KEY FIGURES
Jesus The Messiah and
Son of God at the height
of His ministry.

Zacchaeus A rich tax
collector, whose salvation
is proclaimed by Jesus after
he gives up half of his riches
to the poor and defrauded.

Throughout the Gospels, Jesus is the obvious protagonist. However, in the Gospel of Luke, there are several other figures who become unexpected heroes: notably those who were previously considered "unclean," sinners, or otherwise socially unacceptable.

Luke 19 describes one such outcast by the name of Zacchaeus. He is a chief tax collector in Jericho, viewed by many in the Judean community as a traitorous enemy, seizing money from his own people to fill the Roman coffers. Zacchaeus is also a *rich* tax collector, which suggests to the people of Jericho that he extorts additional funds for personal gain. They therefore deem him a sinner.

A second chance

Zacchaeus makes up for in riches what he lacks in stature—he is so short that he cannot see Jesus above the crowds when He comes into town. Consequently, Zacchaeus climbs a sycamore-fig tree to get a better view. Of all the people assembled, Jesus notices Zacchaeus. He calls to him by name, beckons him down from the tree, and proclaims "I must stay at your house today" (Luke 19:5).

While the people of Jericho complain that Jesus has chosen to be the guest of a sinner, Zacchaeus eagerly welcomes Jesus into his home. Zacchaeus then says he will give half of his possessions to the poor, and that, if he has ever cheated anyone, he will pay them back fourfold. His newfound generosity toward the poor is

Jesus spies Zacchaeus (in red) watching from a sycamore tree as He enters the city of Jericho in this 1908 illustration by English artist William Brassey Hole.

See also: The Temple Tax 222 ▪ Workers in the Vineyard 223 ▪ Cleansing the Temple 244–45 ▪ Faith and Works 312–13 ▪ Holiness 314–15

evidence of his salvation—as Jesus says, "the Son of Man came to seek and to save the lost" (19:10).

Unlikely redemption

Zacchaeus's story is particularly noteworthy because of another tale that precedes it. In Luke 18, a rich ruler queries Jesus about what he must do to gain eternal life. Despite the man's adherence to Jewish teachings, he does not meet the final criteria that Jesus requires— that he give the proceeds from the sale of his belongings to the poor and follow Him. Jesus tells him that it is extremely difficult for the wealthy to enter the kingdom of God: it is harder for a camel to go through the eye of a needle than for a rich person to enter the kingdom.

However, Zacchaeus's example shows it is not impossible: he gives up more than half of his total wealth because he has been made righteous by Jesus. This turn of events exemplifies the power of Jesus's ministry: He transforms the sinner, loves the rejected, and saves the lost—showing that no one is ever fully "lost." ▪

The Pharisee and the tax collector

The **Pharisee** and the **tax collector** go to the Temple to pray.

The **Pharisee** pridefully thanks God that he is not "like this **tax collector**" (Luke 18:11).

The **tax collector** humbly says "God, have mercy on me, a **sinner**" (18:13).

Jesus says "I tell you that [**the tax collector**], rather than the other, went home **justified** before God" (18:14).

Those who exalt themselves will be humbled, and those who humble themselves will be exalted.

Roman taxation

The Roman Empire, like all empires, levied taxes so it could grow and thrive—its subsumed nations bore the financial weight of Rome's imperialism. Judeans who lived in Palestine had a particular distaste for new Roman taxes, because they already paid local and religious taxes. While Roman taxes brought roads, aqueducts, and other societal needs to the area, political and religious tensions still rose. Some Jewish factions resisted Roman occupation and taxation, which led to revolts and subsequent military interventions. Eventually, in 70 CE, the Romans invaded Jerusalem and destroyed the Temple, resulting in the displacement of many Jews into other parts of the empire. These events would resonate with readers of New Testament stories of Jesus's interactions with tax collectors (Luke 19) and others who question Him about His opinions on the empire and its compulsory tributes (Luke 20).

This 2nd century CE relief from a Roman mausoleum depicts a tax collector making an entry in a ledger.

HE SCATTERED THE COINS OF THE MONEY CHANGERS AND OVERTURNED THEIR TABLES
JOHN 2:15, CLEANSING THE TEMPLE

IN BRIEF

PASSAGE
Matthew 21:12–17; Mark 11:15–19; Luke 19:45–48; John 2:13–16

THEME
Challenging corruption in the old religion

SETTING
c.27–29 CE The Temple courtyard in Jerusalem, before Jesus is crucified.

KEY FIGURES
Jesus The Messiah and Son of God, who is filled with anger at the corruption He finds in His Father's Temple.

Temple merchants Priests who sold offerings to Jewish pilgrims visiting the Temple, capitalizing on the fact that they could not enter the Temple's innermost altars.

Jesus chasing money changers and merchant priests from the Temple in Jerusalem is described in all four Gospels. Often referred to as the cleansing of the Temple because Jesus expelled corrupt, "impure" priests, the event shows Jesus fulfilling prophecies of Isaiah (56:7) and Zechariah (14:21).

When Jesus arrives in Jerusalem, it is the height of the Passover pilgrimage season, a time when Jews would travel en masse to the city to visit the Temple. Priests would often sell offerings to the pilgrims to be sacrificed in their name, as only priests could approach the Temple's innermost altars. Such transactions typically took place outside the Temple walls. However, when Jesus goes inside, He sees money changers, as well as priests selling sheep, cattle, and doves.

Anger of Jesus
Jesus sees this as corruption. The priests are profiting from the faithful and not allowing them clear access to God. He proceeds to overturn the priests' tables and call them a den of robbers. He tells them: "Stop turning my Father's

house into a market!" (John 2:16). Many people remember only the compassionate, "turn the other cheek" descriptions of Jesus; however, Jesus is angry here. John's narrative states that Jesus "made a whip out of cords and drove all from the Temple courts, both sheep and cattle" (2:15).

This and other accounts describe Jesus "driving out" the priests and money lenders—in the Greek, the same word is used for Jesus cleansing the Temple as

Jesus drives out the corrupt in this 19th-century oil painting by Danish artist Carl Heinrich Bloch. Jesus is shown holding the whip above His head, ready to strike.

See also: A Child in the Temple 188 ■ The Temple Tax 222 ■
Betrayal in the Garden 254–55 ■ The Crucifixion 258–65

is used elsewhere in the Gospel when He expels demons. The power of Jesus's command alone is enough to force the corrupt to leave His Father's Temple.

Jesus's motives

In the 1st century CE, there were a number of sectarian groups unhappy with the administration of the Temple. One such group was the Essenes, some of whom had exiled themselves to the Dead Sea. Jesus's anger in the Temple has led some to suggest that He may have been a member of the Essenes, but there is little evidence of this. Some historians believe Jesus was crucified by the Romans for trying to incite a riot and that His actions in the Temple would have been viewed as those of a rebellious Jewish leader.

Some Christians see Jesus's actions as evidence of Him looking toward a reformation and split from traditional Judaism. Others see His actions as working to fulfill Mosaic Law and institute a new covenant. According to this interpretation, Jesus is not a rebel: He is exercising responsibility and authority as an heir to King David to order the service of the priests and ensure the purity of their obedience to the Mosaic Law. ■

Palm Sunday

Jesus enters Jerusalem on a day now known as Palm Sunday, and does so by humble means, on the back of a donkey. This fulfills the prophecy of Zechariah, that the king would come in riding a donkey. As Jesus enters the city, people gather to greet Him. The crowds spread their cloaks and branches from palm trees to cover the ground, and proclaim *Hosanna*—the imperative form of the Hebrew word meaning "save"—as a form of praise. The crowd also quotes Psalm 118, proclaiming that Jesus is the Son of David coming in the name of the Lord.

Although it takes place at a different time of year, Palm Sunday is reminiscent of the Jewish holiday of Sukkot. During this festival, Jews weave together pieces of palms and wave them in each of the four cardinal directions. The palm frond is also a symbol of life and resurrection, and a symbol for the Assyrian Tree of Life. Some scholars believe that the palm fronds of Palm Sunday could therefore signify that Jesus will die in Jerusalem, but soon also be resurrected.

Solomon builds the Temple (10th century BCE) as a house of prayer **for all nations** (1 Kings 6–7) …

⬇

… **Babylon destroys** the Temple (587 BCE), which had become a focus of **Israelite pride** …

⬇

… **Ezra rebuilds** the Temple (c.520–15 BCE), evoking **humble worship** from the people …

⬇

… After **Herod's renovation** (19 BCE–63 CE), the Temple again becomes a focus of **nationalistic pride** …

⬇

Jesus cleanses the Temple for all nations.

SHE HAS DONE A BEAUTIFUL THING TO ME

MARK 14:6, JESUS ANOINTED AT BETHANY

IN BRIEF

PASSAGE
Matthew 26:6–13; Mark 14:3–9; John 12:1–8

THEME
Foretelling Jesus's death

SETTING
c.29 CE The village of Bethany, near Jerusalem.

KEY FIGURES
Jesus The Son of God, in the last days of His earthly life.

The woman Possibly Mary of Bethany, who anoints Jesus.

Judas The disciple who later betrays Jesus.

A woman anoints Jesus with nard as He dines with friends in Bethany, in this illumination from the *Codex de Predis* by 15th-century Italian miniaturist Cristoforo de Predis.

In the last week of His life, Jesus has a moving encounter in Bethany. Two days before Passover, He is reclining at the table in the home of Simon the Leper in Bethany, near Jerusalem, where He is staying. Unexpectedly, a woman enters Simon's home. Uninvited, and unprompted, she comes to Jesus and pours perfume onto His head from an alabaster jar. The perfume is nard—an expensive oil imported from India. Following its use in this symbolic act of anointing, Jesus foretells His coming death to His disciples and to the other guests that are assembled in the house.

Afterward, the woman is rebuked by some of those present—disciples and others—who accuse her of wasting perfume that could have been sold "for more than a year's wages" (Mark 14:5), raising money to be given to the poor. However, Jesus immediately defends the woman and tells her accusers to leave her alone. He argues that the poor will always be there, and the disciples can help them at any time.

Jesus then adds that He will not be with His discipes for much longer and explains this to the assembled company: "She poured perfume on My body beforehand

See also: The Raising of Lazarus 226–27 ▪ The Last Supper 248–53 ▪ Betrayal in the Garden 254–55 ▪
The Crucifixion 258–65 ▪ The Empty Tomb 268–71

to prepare for My burial" (Mark 14:8). None of the Gospel authors tell us how the disciples responded to Jesus's claim.

Mary of Bethany

In the version of this scene in John's Gospel, the anointing takes place at a dinner held in Jesus's honor in Bethany. Here, Mary, the sister of Lazarus, whom Jesus had previously resurrected from the dead (John 11:1), anoints Jesus. According to John, she pours oil over His feet and then wipes them with her hair (John 12:3), filling the house with perfume. This action would have been doubly shocking, given that it was against custom for Jewish women to let down their hair when in public.

John's description echoes another Gospel event (Luke 7:36–50), in which a "sinful woman" weeps at Jesus's feet, before drying His feet with her hair and anointing them. While Mary of Bethany is sometimes incorrectly confused with this sinful woman, in all the biblical accounts that

reference Mary she is generally portrayed as a good and devoted servant of Jesus.

Jesus portrays Mary's actions as a sign that she knows what is coming: she, unlike the disciples, accepts His imminent death. The Gospels give no other clues to her motives, although some scholars propose it was to show gratitude to Jesus for raising her brother from the dead. Whatever Mary's reasons, Jesus asks the disciples to remember her act: "wherever this gospel is preached … what she has done will also be told, in memory of her" (Matthew 26:13).

Preface to betrayal

When Mary anoints Jesus, the disciples are taken aback, not by the scale of her devotion, but rather her extravagance. As John notes, the nard cost 300 denarii, or a year's wages (a laborer at the time would earn one denarius per day). John's Gospel attributes the objection about wasting money to just one disciple—Judas Iscariot, the group's treasurer, who, it is

> The poor you will always have with you, and you can help them any time you want. But you will not always have me. She did what she could.
> **Mark 14:7**

implied, wanted the money for himself (John 12:6). The story closes with Judas going to the chief priests, who offer him money in exchange for handing Jesus to them. Scholars have long debated the correlation between the events at Bethany and Judas's subsequent betrayal. It is not clear if Jesus's foretelling of His own demise is a trigger for Judas's actions. ▪

Anointing for burial

In the ancient world, anointing corpses for burial was a common practice. This symbolic act consisted of pouring aromatic oil over a person's head, feet, or entire body. The effect of the ritual was to designate its object as belonging to God. It did not matter whether the consecration took place when the person—or creature— was alive, or after their death. Sometimes, even inanimate objects were anointed in the Bible—Jacob, for example,

anointed a rock in Genesis 28:18, to designate a place, Bethel, as the house of God.

These oils were also used as a form of medicine for centuries by many different cultures. They were thought to have special properties that could drive out demons that were believed to cause disease. To this day, European kings and queens are sanctified with oil in ceremonies involving a divine blessing. When Jesus is anointed in Bethany, this simple act represents a symbolic preparation for His death and an affirmation of His holiness.

A pharaoh is anointed by gods Horus and Thoth in this bas relief from the Temple of Horus and Sobek in Kom Ombo, Upper Egypt.

THIS IS MY BODY, WHICH IS GIVEN FOR YOU

LUKE 22:19, THE LAST SUPPER

IN BRIEF

PASSAGE
Luke 22:7–38

THEME
**New symbolism
of Passover**

SETTING
c.29 CE An upper room of
a house in Jerusalem on the
night of the Passover feast.

KEY FIGURES
Jesus The Messiah and Son
of God in the period leading
up to His crucifixion.

Peter and John Two of
Jesus's disciples, who are
sent by Jesus to prepare the
Passover meal in Jerusalem.

Judas Iscariot The disciple
who goes on to betray Jesus
in the Garden of Gethsemane.

A Flemish miniature by Simon
Bening (c.1525–30) shows Jesus
preparing to wash the feet of His
disciple Peter, an act normally
performed by a servant.

A s opposition mounts to
Jesus's ministry, Jesus
decides to spend time
privately with His closest disciples,
sharing with them the most
important occasion of the Jewish
year, the Passover supper. During
this meal, they remember God's
rescue of their ancestors from
slavery in Egypt. Like many
other Jews, they have traveled
to Jerusalem so that they can
share the Passover meal within
the walls of their holy city, in
proximity to the Temple, the
focus of their worship of God.

Since they are staying at Bethany,
just outside the city, they need
to find a room in which to share
the meal. Jesus sends Peter and
John, two of His disciples, to
make the arrangements for the
feast. "Where do you want us to
prepare for it?" they ask (Luke 22:9).
Jesus tells them that as they enter
the city, they will find a man
carrying a jar of water, quite an
unusual sight in an age when this
was considered to be a woman's
task. They are to follow him back
to the house and say to the owner:
"The Teacher asks: 'Where is the

guest room, where I may eat the
Passover with my disciples?'" (Luke
22:11). Jesus tells the two disciples
that they will then be shown to a
large upper room, where they can
prepare for the meal.

Peter and John go to the city,
and find everything just as Jesus
has said. They buy all the elements
that make the meal a reminder of

See also: Covenants 44–47 ▪ The Passover 72–73 ▪ The Baptism of Jesus 194–97 ▪ The Crucifixion 258–65 ▪ The Day of Pentecost 282–83

their ancestors' escape from Egypt: unleavened bread, roasted lamb, bitter herbs, and wine.

The table is set

Later that day, Jesus and the rest of the disciples arrive at the room to share the meal. A low table is set, and Jesus and the disciples recline around it, in the customary way. Stone jars filled with water stand by the door, so that guests can wash their dusty feet before sitting down. Usually, this task is done for them by a servant, but to their surprise, the disciples watch as Jesus strips off His robe, ties a towel around His waist, and begins to wash their feet.

Peter is horrified: "Lord, are you going to wash my feet?" he asks (John 13:6). In answer, Jesus tells the disciple that unless he allows his feet to be washed by Him, Peter will not be able to share the meal with Jesus, or all it symbolizes. Jesus is setting His disciples an example here, turning the usual expectations of greatness on their head. Jesus, their honored leader, is humbly serving them by washing their feet, an act that symbolizes

Very truly I tell you, no servant is greater than his master, nor is a messenger greater than the one who sent him.
John 13:16

For whenever you eat this bread and drink this cup, you proclaim the Lord's death until He comes.
1 Corinthians 11:26

a spiritual cleansing. All that Jesus is about to face in the next 24 hours can be understood as Him serving them in the ultimate way—His sacrifice will cleanse the stain of sin from their lives.

Preparing the disciples

As they eat bitter herbs and roasted lamb and remember God's deliverance of the Israelites from Egypt, Jesus alludes to the significance of the occasion. "I have eagerly desired to eat the Passover with you before I suffer," He says (Luke 22:15), knowing that this will be the last meal with His disciples before His opponents lay hands on Him. As they share one of the traditional cups of wine around the table, Jesus notes with foreboding that He will not eat this meal with them again "until the kingdom of God comes" (Luke 22:18). Just as the Israelites have shared a last meal in Egypt before their divinely ordained rescue and journey to freedom, so this is Jesus's last meal before the events that will bring about a new freedom for the world in the kingdom of God. »

Herod's Jerusalem

Seeking to establish his reputation as Israel's ruler despite his association with the Roman overlords, Herod the Great, King of Judea (37–4 BCE), decided to refurbish the Second Temple. He aimed to nearly double its overall footprint with a vast paved court, and this work was still ongoing during the time of Jesus. According to historian Flavius Josephus (c.37–100 CE), the Temple was "like a snow-clad mountain for all that was not gold was gleaming white." Situated alongside the Temple walls was the Antonia Fortress, which Herod built to house the occupying armies. Other major sites included his palace, the Praetorium, and the home of the Roman governor.

Jerusalem's population around this time is estimated at 40,000, though at festival times, pilgrims coming into the city to worship could increase that number to about 250,000. However, many of these visitors would not find accommodation in the city; instead, they would look for rooms in nearby villages— such as Bethany, where Jesus and His disciples stayed.

A model of Herod's Temple shows what it might have looked like. The Temple was 164 feet (50m) high and stood on the highest hill in Jerusalem.

In a **Catholic** mass, the priest acts *in persona Christi*—in the **person of Christ**.

During the **sacrament**, he says: "**Take this**, all of you, and **eat of it**: for this is my body which will be given up for you."

Catholic dogma teaches that when this phrase is spoken by the **priest**, transubstantiation occurs.

This means that although the **bread remains unchanged** in appearance …

… Catholics believe that the essence of the bread has become the body of Christ.

This is my body; this is my blood

The words that Jesus instructs His disciples to use when they re-enact this meal together have provoked controversy through the centuries. Known as the words of institution, the phrases "this is my body" and "this is my blood" announce the special significance of the elements of this special meal, now celebrated in the Eucharist.

Churches have differing views about the force of the word "is." For some Christians, it means that Jesus becomes physically present in the elements, an understanding known as "transubstantiation."

In the 13th century, the great theologian St. Thomas Aquinas explained this concept: while the physical characteristics of the bread and wine stay the same, the "substance" of them is transformed into the very being of God. Other Christians understand the words to be purely symbolic, inviting them simply to remember Jesus's suffering and sacrifice. In between these two views, a third understanding suggests that Jesus is spiritually present "along with" the bread and the wine when Christians today celebrate the Eucharist.

Taking the unleavened bread, Jesus lifts it up and thanks God for it, tears it apart, and then passes it to each of His disciples. "This is my body," He says, "given for you; do this in remembrance of me" (Luke 22:19). Then, pouring out another cup of wine, He raises it in blessing, and gives it to them to share around: "This cup is the new covenant in my blood, which is poured out for you" (Luke 22:20).

Foretelling His death

With the words, "This is my body" and "This is my blood," Jesus brings a deeper significance to the Passover meal. He foretells that He will soon give Himself up for others, and during this last meal with His disciples, He warns them about the events that are about to unfold: Jesus's arrest and trial, His crucifixion, and, after three days, His resurrection. The Gospels make it clear that these are not events that will befall Jesus unexpectedly; rather, they are part of God's plan. They are integral to His new covenant with humanity, which will be sealed by the sacrifice of His only son.

Jesus has used the familiar Passover meal to teach His disciples about His impending death. Since Moses's day, the lamb at the Passover meal had been a reminder of the blood of the lamb that the Israelites painted on the doorposts of their houses so that God's angel would "pass over" their homes and only bring destruction to the Egyptian overlords. Now Jesus is offering Himself up as a new Passover lamb, a perfect lamb in accordance with God's instructions to Moses. The goblet of wine symbolizing the blood of His sacrifice introduces the New Covenant—the promise of eternal life through Christ—foretold by Jeremiah (31:31–34).

Judas leaves

During the Passover meal, Jesus also explains to His disciples that one of them will betray Him to the authorities and trigger the events that will lead to His crucifixion.

According to John, this too has been foretold: "This is to fulfill this passage of Scripture: 'He who shared my bread has turned against me'" (John 13:18).

As the evening goes on, one disciple fulfills this prophecy. Judas Iscariot makes his excuses and leaves, because he has made arrangements to betray Jesus later that night. The remaining disciples continue with their evening of food, drink, prayer, and storytelling, until, after a final hymn, they make their way to the Garden of Gethsemane on the Mount of Olives.

Everlasting sacrament

Importantly, Jesus does not envisage His last supper as being a one-off occasion for His disciples. Just like the Passover meal, it will serve as a reminder to Jesus's followers of the significance of His life and death. As the first Christians gather in the days following Jesus's resurrection and ascension to heaven, they share this meal together, joyfully remembering that Jesus's death has brought them life. Unlike

I am the living bread that came down from heaven. Whoever eats this bread will live forever. This bread is my flesh, which I will give for the life of the world.
John 6:51

Passover, which is celebrated once a year, the Last Supper will be shared more frequently, even weekly in some church traditions.

Today, the Last Supper remains a vital part of the life of the Church and is one of its "sacraments"—special activities that convey God's profound truth through physical actions. There are many ways of celebrating the Last Supper; some are highly formal, while others are

intimate and informal. In some traditions, the ritual is called "communion," because it is a sharing with Jesus; in Catholicism, it is called "mass," from the Latin words *Ite, missa est*, the dismissal, the concluding rite of the Eucharist during the medieval period.

What all forms of the Eucharist share is their connection to the meal that Jesus shared with His disciples that final night before His betrayal, arrest, and crucifixion. The Last Supper reveals the deeper significance of Jesus's crucifixion and shows that He was well aware of His impending confrontation with the forces of evil and death. As Jesus says in John 10:18, He gives His life freely: "No one takes it from me, but I lay it down of my own accord. I have authority to lay it down and authority to take it up again. This command I received from my Father." ∎

Judas Iscariot (fifth from left) leans back in shadow, his face turned away, in Leonardo da Vinci's *The Last Supper*. This 19th-century copy of the painting is by Michael Kock.

THE HOUR HAS COME, AND THE SON OF MAN IS DELIVERED INTO THE HANDS OF SINNERS
MATTHEW 26:45, BETRAYAL IN THE GARDEN

IN BRIEF

PASSAGE
Matthew 26:46–56; Mark 14:42–52; Luke 22:47–53; John 18:1-11

THEME
Betrayal of Jesus

SETTING
c.29 CE The Garden of Gethsemane, Jerusalem, in the last week of the life of Jesus.

KEY FIGURES
Jesus The Messiah and Son of God at the end of His time on earth, as He prepares to be crucified in Jerusalem.

Judas Iscariot One of Jesus's 12 disciples, who betrays Him by leading the authorities to the Garden of Gethsemane.

After the Last Supper, Jesus retires to the Garden of Gethsemane to pray, in an event which is often called the "Agony of Jesus." There He is "deeply distressed and troubled," and tells His disciples: "My soul is overwhelmed with sorrow to the point of death" (Mark 14:34). Jesus knows that the end is near, and indeed, the Garden of Gethsemane is the place where Jesus is betrayed by one of His own followers.

This story is within the Gospel narratives called the Passion: the cycle of Jesus's arrest, crucifixion, and resurrection. For the most part, all four Gospels agree in their depiction of the betrayal, albeit with different emphases. Judas, one of the 12 disciples, leads the Temple guards to Jesus in the garden. The three Synoptic Gospels (Matthew, Mark, and Luke) write that Judas betrays Jesus with a kiss, which identifies Him to the guards. A kiss was a significant gesture at the time, often given by a student to a teacher as a sign of honor and respect. It is notable that Judas calls Jesus "rabbi" and performs this gesture of respect in the very moment he hands Him to those who would kill Him.

Necessary betrayal
John is the only Gospel not to mention the kiss. Instead, he focuses on a fight that breaks out between the disciples and the guards, and one of the 12 (John says it is Peter) cuts the ear off a soldier. Jesus stops the violence and goes willingly—according to Luke, He even heals the soldier's ear. He tells Peter "Put your sword away! Shall I not drink the cup the Father has given me?" (John 18:11). His "cup" here is a metaphor for His destiny. According to John 13, Jesus

Judas kisses Jesus in this scene from the Santa Croce Altarpiece (1328) by Italian painter Ugolino di Nerio. The panel sat at the altar's predella (base) beside an image of the Last Supper.

See also: The Last Supper 248–53 ▪ Peter's Denial 256–57 ▪
The Crucifixion 258–65 ▪ The Empty Tomb 268–71

Jerusalem at the time of Jesus

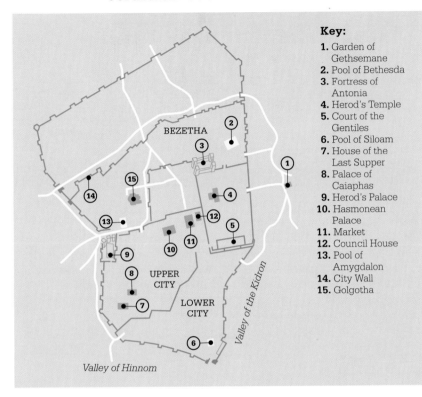

BEZETHA

UPPER
CITY

LOWER
CITY

Valley of the Kidron

Valley of Hinnom

Key:
1. Garden of Gethsemane
2. Pool of Bethesda
3. Fortress of Antonia
4. Herod's Temple
5. Court of the Gentiles
6. Pool of Siloam
7. House of the Last Supper
8. Palace of Caiaphas
9. Herod's Palace
10. Hasmonean Palace
11. Market
12. Council House
13. Pool of Amygdalon
14. City Wall
15. Golgotha

Judas Iscariot

The Greek version of the Hebrew name Hudahudas, Judas means "the one who praises." No one knows what "Iscariot" truly means: some believe that it is the now-unknown place Judas came from, while others have suggested that the name might relate to a group of Zealots called the Sicarii.

Scholars have long debated Judas's motives in betraying Jesus. A popular theory was that Judas wanted to bring about a war between Romans and Jews, and when Jesus did not make this happen, Judas turned Him in to the officials. In the so-called "Gospel of Judas"—a 2nd-century CE text composed by a Gnostic writer, comprised of conversations between Judas and Jesus—Jesus Himself tells Judas to betray Him.

The betrayal ends with not one death, but two. Matthew 27 states that after Jesus is condemned, Judas returns the money and hangs himself in remorse. Acts 1:18 has a gory alternative: Judas buys a field with his blood money and, falling down in it, dies, his body bursting open and his intestines spilling out.

already knew that He would be betrayed, and He knew that He was going to die. In fact, Jesus's death and resurrection is a fundamental pillar of Christian theology, which makes Judas's betrayal a crucial act: Matthew 26:56 states that the betrayal is necessary so that the writings of the prophets are fulfilled.

Judas, however, had his own motives. Despite numerous theories, no one knows why he decided to betray Jesus. According to Matthew 26:14–16, Judas betrays Jesus for money and he receives 30 pieces of silver for leading the guards to the garden. Luke agrees that Judas received money, but declines to inform the reader of the amount; according to Luke, Judas only goes to the chief priests in the first place because he is possessed by Satan (Luke 22:3).

Garden motif

Whether it is the Hanging Gardens of Babylon or the Garden of Eden, the garden is seen as a special place in the ancient Near East. Gardens—especially those in the desert—were understood as places where the divine can interact with the earthly. While the Garden of Gethsemane is not the Garden of Eden, the story of Jesus's betrayal is related to that in Genesis. Adam and Eve's betrayal of God leads to death entering the world, while Judas's betrayal of Jesus leads to Him conquering death. ▪

I DON'T KNOW THIS MAN YOU'RE TALKING ABOUT

MARK 14:71, PETER'S DENIAL

IN BRIEF

PASSAGE
Matthew 26:31–35, 69–75; Mark 14:27–31, 66–72; Luke 22:31–34, 54–65; John 13:38, 18:25–27

THEME
Peter denies Christ

SETTING
c.29 CE Jerusalem, the courtyard of the High Priest right before the crucifixion of Jesus.

KEY FIGURES
Jesus The Messiah and Son of God, in His final days before His crucifixion.

Peter Also called Simon Peter, one of Jesus's inner circle and seemingly the leader of the disciples. Despite this, he still fears the officials.

Predicted by the prophets of the Old Testament, the disciples' abandonment of Jesus in the period leading up to the crucifixion has long been a conflicting issue for many readers of the New Testament. During the Last Supper, Jesus quotes Zechariah 13:7, which foretold how: "This very night you will all fall away on account of me, for it is written: 'I will strike the shepherd, and the sheep of the flock will be scattered'" (Matthew 26:31).

Hearing this prophecy, the disciples protest. Jesus tells them that once He—the figurative shepherd—is captured, His disciples, the sheep, will flee. Peter

is especially upset by this claim and argues that this will never happen: "even if all fall away on account of you, I never will" (26:33). At this, Jesus sets him right; He tells Peter that before the rooster crows, he will deny Him three times. Peter, however, remains adamant—he says he would rather die alongside Jesus than disown Him.

The denials

Jesus's words come to fruition immediately after Judas betrays Him in the Garden of Gethsemane. Guards take Jesus to the high priest's house to stand trial. Peter follows, waits in the courtyard, and is approached by three people (John mentions two) who ask if he knows Jesus. Just as Jesus has predicted, when questioned, Peter denies knowing Jesus, even after he is identified as a Galilean by his speech—and is recognized as a disciple by a relative of the high priest's servant (Luke 22:59).

Peter denies Christ in a miniature by 15th-century Italian artist Cristoforo de Predis. All four Gospels agree that Peter's first denial is to a servant girl who accuses him of being with Jesus.

See also: The Last Supper 248–53 ▪ Betrayal in the Garden 254–55 ▪
The Crucifixion 258–65 ▪ The Empty Tomb 268–71

Peter's three denials, according to Mark's Gospel

Accuser	Peter
"You also were with that Nazarene, **Jesus**."	"**I don't know** or **understand** what you're talking about."
"This fellow is **one of them**."	"Again he **denied** it."
"Surely you are one of them, for you are a **Galilean**."	"**I don't know** this man you're talking about."

The third time Peter denies knowing Jesus, the rooster crows. Luke's Gospel also says that at that Jesus turns to look at Peter through an open window, as if acknowledging His words coming to pass; all accounts, however, describe how Peter weeps once he realizes what he has done.

Symbolic dawn
The crowing of the dawn rooster signifies not only the breaking of dawn, but also that Jesus's fate has been decided upon. Dawn signifies the new life that Jesus will bring about through His death, as does the rooster itself, a symbol of fertility. However, the coming of dawn is significant for another reason: at the time, trials were required to take place after daybreak if the Sanhedrin were to sentence the defendant to death.

Disciples forgiven
The Gospels give no reasons for the betrayal. Peter and the disciples are human, and may be afraid that they, too, will be arrested. The Gospels frequently describe the disciples as vulnerable and even dimwitted: they constantly question Jesus and have difficulty understanding His parables. Some appear to be in denial that Jesus will die. Their fallibility, however, shows that one does not have to be perfect to be a servant of Christ. Peter denies Jesus, yet he is the one who will eventually hold the keys to heaven. ∎

The Sanhedrin

Described in all four Gospels, the Sanhedrin was a body of elders and priests that met to discuss religious and political matters. According to Acts, it convened several times a year.

The term Sanhedrin comes from a Greek word meaning "assembly." There were lesser Sanhedrins that could form in any town or province, but the Great Sanhedrin was a large body of more than 70 elders that met in Jerusalem. It gathered to discuss the Law and acted as a judiciary body.

When Jesus met with the high priest elders, it is generally assumed that He is meeting with the Great Sanhedrin, whose members will determine whether He has committed blasphemy. However, they are portrayed in the Gospels as corrupt: Matthew writes that "the whole Sanhedrin were looking for false evidence against Jesus so that they could put Him to death" (26:59), an accusation that is repeated in Mark's Gospel (14:55).

Christ Before the High Priest (c.1617), a painting by Gerrit van Honthorst, illuminates a book containing the Mosaic Law, which Jesus is accused of breaking.

SURELY THIS MAN WAS THE SON OF GOD

MARK 15:39, THE CRUCIFIXION

IN BRIEF

PASSAGE
Matthew 27; Mark 15; Luke 23; John 18:28–19:42

THEME
Jesus dies for the sins of many

SETTING
c. 29 CE The Antonia Fortress, Herod's Palace, and Golgotha, in Jerusalem.

KEY FIGURES
Jesus The Messiah and Son of God, accused of blasphemy and treason.

Pontius Pilate Roman governor who tries Jesus.

Herod Antipas Son of Herod the Great, who rules the regions of Galilee and Perea as client king for the Romans.

Joseph of Arimathea
A member of the Jewish ruling council, the Sanhedrin, who is sympathetic to Jesus.

onsidering the short length of each of the four Gospels, it is remarkable how much space the authors give to the build-up to Jesus's crucifixion, known as the "passion narrative"—passion meaning suffering. While the Gospels (which differ in the level of detail but largely correspond) are the accounts of the event drawn on by Christians, various historical sources also mention Christ's trial and crucifixion, including *Annals* by the Roman historian Tacitus (56–120 CE) and Flavius Josephus's *Antiquities of the Jews* of c.94 CE.

In the eyes of the Sanhedrin, the Jewish court that first tries Jesus, He is guilty of blasphemy, for which the penalty is death. However, they cannot enforce this: under the rules of the Roman occupation, they do not have the authority to execute anyone, so, early in the morning, after Jesus's arrest and trial, they take Him to the palace of Pontius Pilate, the Roman governor, which is situated beside the Temple in the Antonia Fortress. As it is the Passover festival, the Jewish leaders are careful not to set foot inside Pontius Pilate's residence

In Hieronymus Bosch's *Mocking of Christ* (c.1500), the gauntlet of the man crowning Him with thorns and the spiked collar worn by the figure on the right symbolize the mockers' brutality.

themselves, since doing so would render them unclean and unable to participate in the religious ceremonies later that day. Staying outside the palace, they send Jesus in with their charges against Him: "We have found this man subverting our nation. He opposes payment of taxes to Caesar and claims to be Messiah, a king" (Luke 23:2).

See also: The Suffering Servant 154–55 ■ The Nature of Faith 236–41 ■ The Last Supper 248–53 ■ Betrayal in the Garden 254–55 ■ The Empty Tomb 268–71

Foreseeing that Pilate would not consider the charge of blasphemy to be sufficiently serious to merit execution, they tell him that Jesus is a threat to security and guilty of treason against Caesar. They know this will force Pilate to take action.

All four Gospels record Pilate asking Jesus: "Are you the king of the Jews?" Jesus asserts that He is, but points out that He is not the kind of king who will cause a military threat to Rome. He says, "My kingdom is not of this world" (John 18:36). Impressed by the authenticity of Jesus's words, Pilate realizes that Jesus does not pose a direct threat to Caesar. He then goes back to the Jewish authorities and tells them that Jesus is innocent of the charges they have brought against Him.

Brought before Herod

Pilate's verdict is not the one the Sanhedrin want. They insist again that Jesus has been inciting rebellion, beginning in the region of Galilee and spreading to Jerusalem itself. In Luke's Gospel (23:6), on hearing of Jesus's link with Galilee, Pilate sends Him

You disowned the Holy and Righteous One and asked that a murderer be released to you.
Acts 3:14

"Don't you hear the testimony they are bringing against you?" But Jesus made no reply.
Matthew 27:13

under guard to Herod Antipas, the Jewish king appointed by Rome, who has jurisdiction in the region.

Herod is delighted to see Jesus, because he has heard the stories about Him and hopes to see some of the miracles for which He is famous. When Jesus simply stands in silence before Herod, saying and doing nothing, Herod is frustrated. He orders his soldiers to dress Jesus in a royal robe to mock the claim that He is a king. After they have had their fun, Jesus is escorted back to Pilate.

By this time, a crowd has gathered at the palace. Pilate, who must now decide Jesus's fate, considers a way to let Him go free. It is his custom during Passover to release a prisoner (invariably one of the Jews' popular leaders) to please the crowds who arrive in Jerusalem for the festival. Pilate says to the crowd, "There is no basis for your charges against Jesus. Therefore, I will punish Him and then release him." To his surprise, the crowd cries out, "Away with this man! Release Barabbas to us" (Luke 23:18). Pilate is unable to believe his »

Pontius Pilate

Appointed by the Emperor Tiberius, Pontius Pilate was the prefect (or governor) of Judea and the neighboring regions of Samaria and Idumea from 26 to 36 CE. He had a residence in the provincial capital of Caesarea and the use of the Antonia Fortress in Jerusalem.

Pilate's responsibilities included taxation, public spending, and law and order. His relationship with the Jewish people was fragile, particularly because he repeatedly disregarded their religious and social customs. He minted coins bearing pagan religious symbols and hung worship images of the emperor in Jerusalem.

In 36 CE, Pilate was forced back to Rome after the Samaritans (an offshoot of Judaism) lodged an official complaint about him with the legate (in charge of provincial governors) in Syria. Pilate died shortly after his term of office in Palestine. According to the Christian bishop and historian Eusebius of Caesarea, in *Ecclesiastical History*, Pilate killed himself on the orders of the Emperor Caligula in 39 CE.

The route of the crucifixion taken by pilgrims

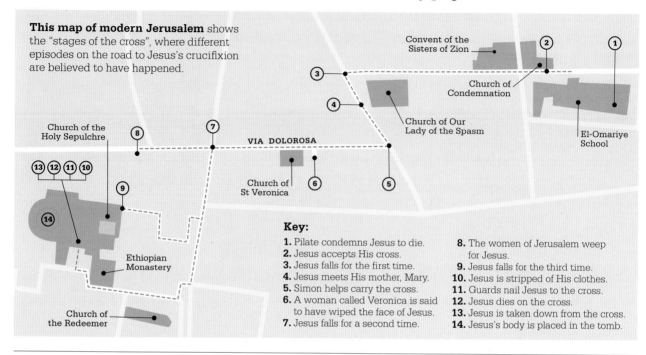

This map of modern Jerusalem shows the "stages of the cross", where different episodes on the road to Jesus's crucifixion are believed to have happened.

Convent of the Sisters of Zion

Church of Condemnation

Church of Our Lady of the Spasm

El-Omariye School

Church of the Holy Sepulchre

VIA DOLOROSA

Church of St Veronica

Church of the Redeemer

Ethiopian Monastery

Key:
1. Pilate condemns Jesus to die.
2. Jesus accepts His cross.
3. Jesus falls for the first time.
4. Jesus meets His mother, Mary.
5. Simon helps carry the cross.
6. A woman called Veronica is said to have wiped the face of Jesus.
7. Jesus falls for a second time.
8. The women of Jerusalem weep for Jesus.
9. Jesus falls for the third time.
10. Jesus is stripped of His clothes.
11. Guards nail Jesus to the cross.
12. Jesus dies on the cross.
13. Jesus is taken down from the cross.
14. Jesus's body is placed in the tomb.

Day of Preparation

Friday, the day before the Sabbath, was known as the Day of Preparation, when Jews would prepare themselves to keep the Sabbath "holy," as instructed by the fourth of the Ten Commandments. Food would be prepared and cooked, and errands completed so that the Sabbath would be free for the worship of God. As Jesus was crucified on the Day of Preparation, the Jewish authorities requested that His body be taken down from the cross and buried. This was a break from Roman custom, which was to leave the body on view as a deterrent. With the Sabbath starting at sunset (around 6 pm), Jesus's body was taken down after He died (around 3 pm).

ears—Barabbas is a hardened criminal, imprisoned for murder— but the Jewish authorities had been weaving through the crowd, inciting them to ask for Barabbas (Mark 15:11).

Sentenced by the mob

According to Matthew's Gospel, Pilate's wife, who had a disturbed night's sleep, then sends her husband a message. "Don't have anything to do with that innocent man," she says, worried by a dream she has had (27:19). Once again, Pilate asks the crowd: "Jesus or Barabbas," and together they reply, "Barabbas." Asking what he should do with Jesus, the people shout "Crucify him! Crucify him!" Pilate realizes there would be a riot if he didn't give the crowd what they wanted, so, taking a bowl of water, he washes his hands in full view, saying, "I am innocent of this man's blood" (Matthew 27:24).

Jesus is handed to the Roman guards to be crucified. They know the process, and are practiced at inflicting suffering on their prisoners. First, Jesus is flogged, then they dress Him in another royal robe, twisting thorny branches together to make a crown. "Hail, King of the Jews!" they cry in mockery. Some spit, others prod Him with sticks, and still others hit Him across the head (Matthew 27:30). Humiliated and beaten, Jesus then begins His painful journey to the place where He will be crucified, a publicly visible hill called Golgotha ("place of the skull"), also known by the Latin translation Calvary, just outside the city wall. Crucifixions serve as prominent reminders to the Jews that the Romans are in charge.

A heavy wooden beam, which will become the cross on which He is crucified, is then thrust upon Jesus. Weakened from the flogging,

He stumbles under the weight, prompting the soldiers who are escorting Him to haul out of the crowd an unsuspecting pilgrim called Simon to help Jesus carry the cross. While many look on, jeering and shouting, others follow, including women, who weep and wail. The mournful procession makes its way out to the hill.

Three crosses

Along with Jesus, two criminals are brought to be crucified. When they arrive, the soldiers set to work, nailing Jesus to the wooden crossbeams by His wrists and to the wooden upright through His ankles, fulfilling a prophecy in Zechariah 12:10: "They will look on me, the one they have pierced." The three crosses are then hoisted into position, with Jesus in the center. The charge against Jesus is nailed to the cross: "This is the King of the Jews" (Matthew 27:37 and Luke 23:38). The chief priests protest against the sign, saying it implied that Pilate thought Jesus was a king. It should say, they said, "this man claimed to be the King of the Jews" (John 19:21). By retaining his description of Jesus, Pilate implies that those who demanded His death are the ones truly guilty of treason.

The Way to Calvary, by Marco Palmezzano (c.1460–1539) shows Jesus carrying His cross. Victims of crucifixion were required to carry their own cross to the place of execution.

Twelve hours after His arrest, Jesus looks down upon the crowd, who are mocking Him and baying for His blood. "Father, forgive them, for they do not know what they are doing," He says (Luke 23:34). Taking no notice, the soldiers gamble for the clothes of the crucified men, again fulfilling a prophecy in Psalm 22: "They divide my clothes among them and cast lots for my garment." A crowd gathers to watch, and the Jewish authorities begin to hurl insults at Jesus: "He saved others; let Him save Himself if He God's Messiah, the Chosen One" (Luke 23:35).

Darkest hours

At midday, the sky grows dark, the sun blotted out of sight. In the darkness, Jesus calls to the few followers who have remained with Him to the end: a small huddle of women and His disciple John.

"Come down from the cross, if you are the Son of God!" **Matthew 27:40**

Speaking to His mother Mary, Jesus says "Dear woman, here is your son," indicating John. And in turn, He says to John, "Here is your mother." Even in His own pain, Jesus makes arrangements for John to care for His grief-stricken mother.

The darkness lasts for three hours, until the ninth hour of the Jewish day, around 3 pm. As the »

Michele da Verona's *Crucifixion* (c.1501) combines several scenes from the event, including the centurion's conversion and the proffering of a sponge soaked in vinegar.

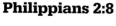

> And being found
> in appearance as
> a man, He humbled
> Himself by becoming
> obedient to death—
> even death on a cross!
> **Philippians 2:8**

life drains from His body, Jesus grows weaker, but then He calls out in a loud voice: *"Eloi, Eloi, lama sabachthani,"* Aramaic for "My God, my God, why have you forsaken me?" (Matthew 27:46). Again, the words draw directly on Psalm 22, the ancient Hebrew poem written by David. Having memorized the psalm as a young boy, Jesus now recognizes that it describes His present experience: "All who see me mock me. ... all my bones are out of joint" (Psalm 22:7–14). Some of those around the cross mishear Jesus, thinking He is calling for the prophet Elijah to come and save Him.

In the heat of the afternoon sun, with pain taking its toll on His body, Jesus cries out "I thirst." Some of those nearby find a jar of sour wine—a vinegarlike liquid considered to be a thirst-quenching drink for the poor—and offer it to Jesus on a sponge at the end of a stick. The Israelites had often been likened to a vineyard, charged with producing fine wine of holy lives for God. Here, Jesus tastes the best they can offer, and it is sour.

Last breath

Just as Jesus had told His disciples during His last supper with them the night before, He had now given His life for them. Speaking with a loud voice, Jesus cries out, "It is finished" (John 19:30). With a final prayer of trust in God, quoting from Psalm 31, Jesus takes His last breath and dies: "Father, into your hands I commit my spirit" (Luke 23:46). Matthew's Gospel goes on to record how the ground then shakes, tombs split open, and the curtain of the Temple in Jerusalem is rent in two. Matthew, Mark, and Luke record one of the Roman guards, who has witnessed many frantic last moments of the crucified, being astonished at Jesus's dignified death, trusting in God as His Father right to the end. The centurion unwittingly blurts out the truth: "Surely this man was the Son of God" (Mark 15:39).

As Jesus hangs dead on the cross, the Jewish authorities ask the soldiers to finish off the crucifixions and take down the bodies before nightfall, since the next day would be the Sabbath. One of the soldiers pierces Jesus's side with a spear, proving beyond doubt that Jesus is dead.

Two Jewish noblemen and scholars, Joseph of Arimathea and Nicodemus, then get Pilate's permission to take Jesus's body for burial in Joseph's garden tomb. Anointed in sweet spices and wrapped in linen, Jesus's body is sealed in the tomb by a stone.

Why Jesus died

The fact that Jesus died was central to early Christian belief. Crucially, Jesus is innocent of

Deposition from the Cross, by Antonio Allegri, c.1525, shows Mary swooning over the dead Christ, a detail that became a popular embellishment of the story in the Middle Ages.

The symbol of the cross

For Christians today, the cross is a symbol of God's love and forgiveness. Yet, when Jesus died, it was clearly a symbol of Roman power and oppression and of violence and torture. Many early Christians were also crucified for their belief in Him.

As early Christian believers shared the message that God had set up His kingdom on Earth through Jesus, God's true Son and king, they explained that Jesus's death on the cross was not an embarrassing end to Jesus's life's work, but rather the means through which He fulfilled His greatest task of triumphing over sin and offering forgiveness. This turned the symbolism of the cross on its head. As the Apostle Paul put it, "the message of the cross is foolishness to those who are perishing, but to us who are being saved it is the power of God" (1 Corinthians 1:18). The cross became the universal sign of Christian faith after the Christian conversion of the Roman Emperor Constantine in the early 4th century.

Crosses still represent death and sacrifice, as at the Auckland War Memorial Museum, New Zealand, remembering soldiers killed in war.

the charges that are brought against Him. Although He is convicted and condemned to death in an alarmingly short space of time, both Pilate and Herod are unable to find any grounds for capital punishment. Jesus does not die because He presents a military threat against the Roman Empire. His ministry has been filled with miracles of healing and teaching to "love your enemies" (Matthew 5:44), not with criminal behavior or political revolution. Even the Sanhedrin's charge that Jesus had blasphemed against God by claiming to be God's special representative, the Messiah, is false, since Jesus is, in fact, who He claims to be.

This lays the foundations for the Church's teaching about Jesus's death: He did not die because of His own wrongdoings, but because of those of humankind. By trying to protect their own positions of authority by getting rid of Jesus as a troublemaker, and condemning an innocent man to death, the opponents of Jesus represent the pride and self-centeredness that characterize the whole of humanity.

Even though Jesus is innocent, the crucifixion narrative does not present Him as a passive victim. All through His suffering, Jesus is in control and not at the mercy of His circumstances. As Jesus had taught earlier, "No one takes my life from me, but I lay it down of my own accord" (John 10:18). The sinless Jesus took humanity's sin onto Himself, willingly drinking the world's cup of suffering (Matthew 26:39) in order to save others from doing so. On the cross, Jesus was not a victim, but a savior.

Dying to save sinners

Jesus's cross is seen as the culmination of His life's work, rather than an unfortunate ending. When Jesus declares, "It is finished," Christians believe He means that the mission He had been sent to achieve is now complete: the kingdom of God has been set up as Jesus's cross was raised into the air. This kingdom, in which Jesus is the king, is not a military state that uses violence to coerce people into obedience, but rather a kingdom of love, in which King Jesus lays down His life so people can be free from the sin that would otherwise drag them into eternal death. By dying, the sinless for the sinful, Jesus clears the way for a new relationship with God to which all people are invited.

Yet, as Jesus's body is sealed in the tomb for the Sabbath day, no one has yet understood how Jesus's death is, in fact, good news. That life-transforming awareness would only be possible after the Sabbath had passed, as the story continues on the morning of Easter Day. ■

Fixing our eyes on Jesus, the pioneer and perfecter of faith. For the joy set before Him He endured the cross, scorning its shame, and sat down at the right hand of the throne of God.
Hebrews 12:2

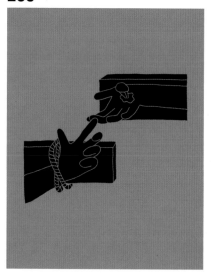

REMEMBER ME WHEN YOU COME INTO YOUR KINGDOM

LUKE 23:42, THE REPENTANT THIEF

IN BRIEF

PASSAGE
Luke 23:39–43

THEME
**It is never too late
for salvation**

SETTING
c.29 CE Golgotha, a hill
outside the walls of Jerusalem,
during Jesus's crucifixion.

KEY FIGURES
Jesus The Messiah and Son
of God, who is crucified by
the Roman authorities in place
of the criminal, Barabbas.

The repentant thief The
criminal to Jesus's right:
although unnamed in the
Gospels, later Christian
tradition calls him "Dismas"
or "Demas."

The unrepentant thief
A fellow revolutionary who
taunts Jesus; later tradition
named him "Gestas."

Jesus is crucified between two criminals on the hill of Golgotha, overlooking one of the roads into Jerusalem. The two men on either side of Him are "robbers" (Matthew 27:38) who may well have been comrades of Barabbas, a resistance fighter against Roman occupation of Judea. Jesus, who is Himself being crucified on the charge of rebellion, has taken Barabbas's place in execution, and occupies the central of the three crosses.

As Jesus hangs on the cross, the crowds taunt Him and tell Him to come down if He really is God's chosen king. The criminal on Jesus's left joins in: "Aren't you the Messiah?" he asks. "Save yourself and us!" (Luke 23:39). As far as the thief is concerned, Jesus cannot be the savior if He is unable to put an end to their suffering.

The thief calls out

However, the second condemned man realizes Jesus really is the savior. He sees now that the violent attempts of Barabbas and his comrades to resist Roman occupation had been misguided, and that God desires something far deeper than political nationalism: a kingdom of people who follow Him through humility and service.

Calling over to the first man, the repentant thief tells him to stop mocking Jesus: while the two of them are hanging on their crosses for real offenses, Jesus—despite dying in the place of a criminal—

The penitent thief's soul is carried into paradise by angels in James Tissot's 1897 illustration. Tissot aimed to portray the people and setting of the Gospels as faithfully as possible.

See also: The Divinity of Jesus 190–93 ▪ The Crucifixion 258–65 ▪ Salvation Through Faith 301 ▪
The Power of the Resurrection 304

"has done nothing wrong" (23:41). The thief then asks Jesus to "remember me when You come into Your kingdom" (23:42). The Jewish faith had long spoken about a kingdom beyond death, in which God's faithful people would enjoy everlasting life. This, he realizes, is the kingdom of which Jesus is king. Jesus replies with assurance: "Truly I tell you, today you will be with me in paradise" (23:43).

Deathbed salvation

The repentant thief illustrates a vital aspect of the Christian faith. Acceptance into God's kingdom is not dependent upon good works or a blameless life, since the thief clearly had no time to amend his ways. Instead, Jesus freely gives places in His kingdom to those who recognize that He is their only hope. Jesus's promise to the thief, just moments before his death, is also part of the rationale for the later practice of deathbed confession and absolution, or last rites. In this, a dying person is given assurance in their final moments that their sins have been forgiven by God; it is never too late to repent. ▪

Jesus forgives many types of sins

The sinful woman
"Her many sins have been forgiven … whoever has been forgiven little loves little."
Luke 7:47

The tax collector
"Today salvation has come to this house, because this man, too, is a son of Abraham."
Luke 19:9

The repentant thief
"Truly I tell you, today you will be with me in paradise."
Luke 23:43

Romans and Jews at His crucifixion
"Father, forgive them, for they do not know what they are doing."
Luke 23:34

Crime and punishment in the time of Jesus

Like any society, Jesus's world had a complex system of law and punishments. In Jewish law, the practice of reparation—giving back what was taken with interest—was typical. Stoning to death was the form of capital punishment favored by the Jews for serious offenses.

However, the Romans—the occupying overlords—routinely used crucifixion to execute criminals who were not Roman citizens, especially those who resisted their authority or slaves found guilty of wrongdoing. Crucifixion was a humiliating death, in which the victim was stripped, flogged, and then nailed to a horizontal beam of wood through the wrists, and an upright beam through the ankles. Jews detested it because of one of their laws, which said "anyone … hung on a pole is under God's curse" (Deuteronomy 21:23).

Dressed as a Roman soldier, a man carries a replica of a Roman whip in a Good Friday procession in San Miguel de Allende, Mexico.

BLESSED ARE THOSE WHO HAVE NOT SEEN AND YET HAVE BELIEVED

JOHN 20:29, THE EMPTY TOMB

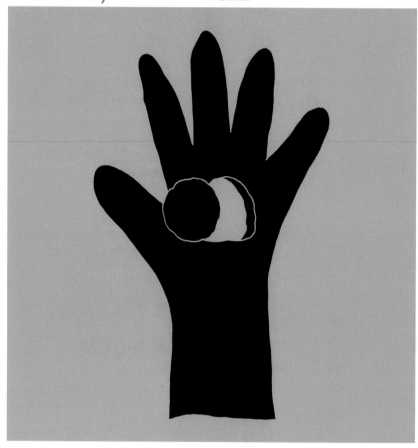

IN BRIEF

PASSAGES
Matthew 28:1–10; Mark 16:1–8; Luke 24:1–12; John 20:1–18

THEME
The resurrection of Jesus

SETTING
Spring c.29 CE, during Passover The garden tomb of Joseph of Arimathea in Jerusalem.

KEY FIGURES
Mary Magdalene A prominent disciple of Jesus.

Mary, the mother of the Apostle James A follower of Jesus in her own right.

Salome Another follower, and probably the wife of Zebedee and the mother of the Apostles James and John.

Jesus This story tells of the first encounters with Jesus after His resurrection.

T he events of the first Easter morning are foundational for the whole of Christianity. One of the primary messages of Christian faith is that Jesus could not be held by the power of death.

The Gospels give varying accounts of the dramatic events of that Sunday morning. Matthew, Luke, and Mark generally agree that Jesus was buried in haste late on Good Friday afternoon, with only the minimum of preparation, so that His body would be in the

See also: The Divinity of Jesus 190–93 ▪ The Crucifixion 258–65 ▪ The Road to Emmaus 272–73 ▪ The Word Spreads 288–89

Turin Shroud

In Jesus's day, it was customary for families to embalm a dead body in sweet-smelling spices, wrap it in linen cloth, and leave it until only the bones remained. From there, the skeletal remains would be gathered up into an ossuary—a bone box, or chest—which would then be placed in the family vault.

After His crucifixion, Jesus had been hastily wrapped in linen cloth and placed in the tomb of Joseph of Arimathea. When the tomb was discovered empty on the Sunday morning, the linen cloths were found neatly folded where Jesus's body had been (John 20:6–7).

The Turin Shroud is a large linen cloth kept in the cathedral in Turin, Italy. The cloth bears the faint image of a body, and a bearded man's face. It is claimed to be Jesus's burial cloth, His image having been impressed on it when it was wound tightly around Him after death. This claim has been contested since the Middle Ages, and carbon dating tests strongly suggest the cloth is not old enough.

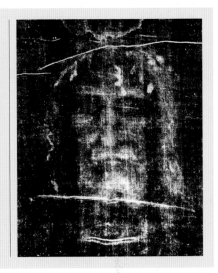

grave by sunset, the start of the Jewish Sabbath day. The morning after Jesus's grief-stricken friends observe the Saturday Sabbath, Mary Magdalene, Mary, the mother of the Apostle James, and another woman called Salome visit the tomb to embalm Jesus's body, according to Jewish custom. The women stumble to the tomb in the half light of dawn, clutching bags of spices, which they will use to anoint Jesus's body and counteract the anticipated odor of decay.

The empty tomb

As the women approach the tomb, however, the ground shakes violently. Out of their sight, an angel of God appears at the tomb's entrance and rolls back the stone sealing it. The guards that the Roman authorities had posted to prevent the disciples from stealing Jesus's body had fainted with fear on seeing the angel and run off.

When the women arrive at the tomb, they are astonished to see that it is already open. Wondering who has arrived before them, they look inside—but there is no one there. The rocky ledge, where Jesus had been carefully laid down before sunset on Friday, no longer holds His body. Instead, the women see a few strips of linen cloth, carefully folded on the spot where His body had previously been.

In the Gospels of Matthew and Mark, the women then meet God's angel at the tomb (Luke reports the presence of a second angel). The message the women receive is one of reassurance: "Do not be afraid, for I know that you are looking for Jesus, who was crucified" (Matthew 28:5); "Why »

In three Gospel accounts, an angel (or angels), shown here in Gustave Doré's illustrated Bible of 1865, appears to Mary, the mother of James, and Mary Magdalene at the tomb's entrance.

Some of our women … went to the tomb early this morning but didn't find His body.
Luke 24:22–23

do you look for the living among the dead?" (Luke 24:5); and an explanation for the empty tomb: "He has risen! He is not here!" (Mark 16:6).

The women struggle to comprehend what the angel has told them. Jesus's body has not been stolen—He is a living, breathing human being again. The women then hear the angel give them a task. "Go quickly and tell His disciples: 'He has risen from the dead and is going ahead of you into Galilee. There you will see Him'" (Matthew 28:7). Galilee was a significant place for the disciples, since it was where much of Jesus's ministry had taken place.

The resurrected Jesus

The women, "afraid yet filled with joy" (Matthew 28:8), turn from the tomb and head away to relate these incredible events to the other disciples. On the path, the women suddenly come across a man. It is Jesus, who utters one simple word: "Greetings" (Matthew 28:9). Falling to the ground, the women cling to His feet, realizing what the angel had said was true—Jesus is really alive—and they begin to worship Him. Stooping, Jesus encourages them to their feet and tells them to go and pass on their joyful news.

Women were not normally asked to give testimony in Jesus's day, since they were considered to be incapable of presenting the truth. Here was a clear signal that God's kingdom is turning expectations upside down, as women become the first to meet and then share news of the risen Jesus.

The Gospel of John

John's Gospel focuses on Mary Magdalene's experience that morning. Upon seeing the empty chamber, she immediately rushes back to tell the other disciples that "they have taken the Lord out of the tomb, and we don't know where they have put Him!" (John 20:2). Peter and John race to the tomb and look inside, seeing for themselves that Jesus's body is gone. Peter and John leave, but Mary, overcome with emotion, stays by the tomb. She sees a man near her and, presuming it to be the gardener, says, "Sir, if you have carried Him away, tell me where you have put Him, and I will get Him" (20:15). It isn't the gardener, however; it is Jesus. Through her tears, Mary does not recognize Jesus until He speaks her name. When Mary realizes who it is, she turns and clings to Him, crying "Rabboni!," the Aramaic word

Raphael's *The Resurrection of Christ* (c.1501–1502) imagines the reaction of the Roman guards. Mathew's Gospel says they "shook and became like dead men" (28:4).

for "teacher" (20:16). Jesus gently tells her to return to the other disciples to share the news of His resurrection. Back at the house where they were gathered, Mary bursts in on the others, shouting, "I have seen the Lord!" (20:18).

Mary's mistake, thinking Jesus was the gardener, is a profound discovery: just as God planted the Garden of Eden at the beginning of the Bible, now, through Jesus, God is restoring that garden.

As Peter put it in his sermon a few weeks later, human authorities may have killed Jesus, but God raised Him to life (Acts 2:23–24).

God has raised this Jesus to life, and we are all witnesses of it.
Acts 2:32

Thomas the Apostle doubts the man before him is the risen Jesus until he touches His wounds. Jesus says, "Blessed are those who have not seen and yet have believed" (John 20:29).

Jesus's disciples begin to understand the logic of what had happened: if Jesus is alive, that means death is not all-powerful and that sin—understood to be the inevitable human tendency to turn away from God, leading to death— does not have to mar human life forever, but can be forgiven.

Faith and reason
All that Christianity believes about God—forgiveness, salvation, and transformation—depends on Jesus's resurrection. As Paul puts it in 1 Corinthians 15:14, "if Christ has not been raised, our preaching is useless and so is your faith."

Still, the accounts of Jesus's resurrection raise many questions and demands for events to be explained in terms of natural causes. In place of the Gospel's explanation, some have suggested that the disciples experienced mass-hallucination or that local leaders hid Jesus's body to prevent His disciples from removing it themselves and then proclaiming His resurrection. These theories do not explain why the disciples would later allow themselves to be martyred for preaching a message they knew to be false.

If the Gospels are to be taken literally, the women discovered an empty tomb; Jesus's body was never found, there or anywhere else; and the women and other disciples met Jesus, not just as a memory but as a living person. Discovering what the resurrection of Jesus means is the concern of the rest of the New Testament, and the ongoing task of the Church today. ∎

Mary Magdalene

One of Jesus's closest followers, Mary Magdalene is remembered particularly for being one of the early witnesses to Jesus's resurrection. Mary's name indicates she was from the town of Magdala Nunaya on the shore of the Sea of Galilee. Luke 8:2 records that she received healing from Jesus when He cast seven demons out of her. Grateful for the wholeness that Jesus had given her, she became a prominent disciple, accompanying Jesus on His final trip to Jerusalem and bearing witness to both His crucifixion and burial (Matthew: 27:56–61). Later tradition associated Mary Magdalene with Mary of Bethany, the prostitute who anointed Jesus's feet with expensive perfume while He was in the house of Simon the Pharisee (Luke 7:36–50), although most modern biblical scholars believe that this association is apocryphal.

It is noteworthy that several of Jesus's most faithful followers were women (Acts 1:14) and that they continued to play key roles in the life of the early Church.

WERE NOT OUR HEARTS BURNING WITHIN US WHILE HE TALKED WITH US ON THE ROAD?

LUKE 24:32, ROAD TO EMMAUS

IN BRIEF

PASSAGE
Luke 24:13–35

THEME
Witnessing Jesus's resurrection

SETTING
c.29 CE Jerusalem, at the end of Jesus's ministry.

KEY FIGURES
Jesus The Son of God, crucified by the Romans but resurrected days later.

Jesus's disciples A group of men and women who followed Jesus. They traveled with Him during His ministry and preached about Him and His teachings after His death.

Peter Also called Simon Peter; one of Jesus's closest disciples, to whom Jesus appeared after the resurrection.

The good news of Jesus's resurrection is first told to female disciples by angels, who appear to them at Jesus's empty tomb. The angels remind the women that Jesus had already foretold His death and resurrection, and the women subsequently report the miracle to the other disciples. However, the disciples do not believe them.

Later that same day, two of Jesus's disciples make their way to a village called Emmaus, about 7 miles (11km) from the city of Jerusalem. The two disciples, one of whom is named Cleopas, are reflecting on recent events when Jesus starts traveling alongside them. The disciples, however, do not recognize Him. He probes them about their conversation and they

Jesus takes supper at Emmaus with the disciples. Like other Renaissance depictions of the event, Caravaggio's 1601 version includes an innkeeper not mentioned in Luke's account.

See also: The Last Supper 248–53 ▪ The Crucifixion 258–65 ▪ The Empty Tomb 268–71 ▪ The Great Commission 274–77

explain the cause of their grief to the "stranger": the prophet and miracle worker, Jesus, had died on the cross three days before.

They tell Him the story of the women at the tomb and, finally, acknowledge their sorrow because they had formerly believed Jesus was the Messiah. As they recount recent events and admit to feeling disillusioned, they reveal their denial of the truth of Jesus's resurrection—while, unbeknown to them, He stands right before their eyes. Jesus then declares them ignorant of the scriptures and proceeds to explain how Jesus is, indeed, the Messiah. Still, the disciples do not comprehend who the man is or what He is saying.

Jesus is recognized

The disciples finally become aware of their companion's identity when they stop for the evening and share a meal. Jesus takes the bread, and after blessing and breaking it, He gives it to the disciples—an action reminiscent of the Last Supper in Luke 22. With that action, they recognize Him as Jesus.

Luke highlights this moment with an inversion of a metaphor from the beginning of the story: at first, the disciples did not recognize Jesus (24:16), but now, "their eyes were opened and they recognized Him" (24:31). Before the disciples can even blink, however, Jesus disappears. Dumbfounded and embarrassed, they remark that they had felt their hearts burn while Jesus spoke to them on the road.

Soon after their conversation, the disciples return to Jerusalem, find the other disciples, and share the good news—also known as the Gospel—that Jesus has risen from

Why are you troubled, and why do doubts rise in your minds? Look at My hands and My feet. It is I Myself! Touch me and see; a ghost does not have flesh and bones, as you see I have.
Luke 24:38

the dead. Unlike when the women first reported the news, the others believe their story, and tell them that "it is true! The Lord has risen and has appeared to Simon" (24:34). Shortly before He joined Cleopas and the other disciple on the road, Jesus had appeared to Simon Peter in John 21.

Witnesses of Christ

Jesus appears on several other occasions in the New Testament. In 1 Corinthians 15:5–8, Paul provides a list of those who have witnessed Him, including: Peter; the 12 disciples; 500 men and women "at the same time"; James; the apostles; and Paul, the letter-writer himself. Other famous Gospel accounts include Jesus appearing to Mary Magdalene (Mark 16; John 20) and Thomas (John 20). These stories function as proof for Christians that Jesus died and rose again; they also point to a deeper theological belief that Jesus conquered death and offers everlasting life to others. ▪

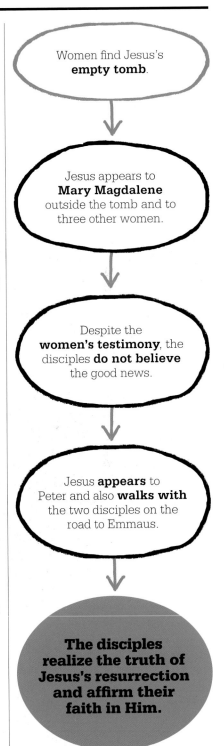

Women find Jesus's **empty tomb**.

Jesus appears to **Mary Magdalene** outside the tomb and to three other women.

Despite the **women's testimony**, the disciples **do not believe** the good news.

Jesus **appears** to Peter and also **walks with** the two disciples on the road to Emmaus.

The disciples realize the truth of Jesus's resurrection and affirm their faith in Him.

GO AND MAKE DISCIPLES OF ALL NATIONS

MATTHEW 28:19, THE GREAT COMMISSION

IN BRIEF

PASSAGE
Matthew 28:16–20

THEME
Spreading the good news

SETTING
c.29 CE Around Galilee
and Judea, during the
40 days following Jesus's
resurrection.

KEY FIGURES
Jesus The risen Jesus,
who is both familiar and
unfamiliar to His disciples.
He is often recognized by
His actions or His words, or
when He performs miracles.

Peter A member of Jesus's
inner circle of disciples and
often a spokesman for the
other disciples.

The other disciples The
remaining 10 disciples.

For the 40 days following His resurrection, Jesus spends time with His disciples, teaching them about the significance of His death and resurrection, and preparing them for the future. On the evening of His resurrection, He had told them, "As the Father has sent me, I am sending you" (John 20:21). Although they have spent three years traveling with Jesus, only now do they begin to appreciate what He is asking them to do. In the past, He had sent them out to neighboring villages and towns to tell people about the kingdom of God that would soon be arriving through Jesus (Luke 9:1–6). Now,

See also: The Calling of the Disciples 200–03 ▪ Peter's Denial 256–57 ▪ The Road to Emmaus 272–73 ▪ The Word Spreads 288–89

Chriſtus apparet xi apoſtoliſ

however, He is sending them out on a permanent mission that would last the rest of their lives. Jesus understands that it will take some persuasion to transform the fearful disciples into bold ambassadors for His message and tells them that the Holy Spirit will support them.

The risen Christ appearing to His disciples in the 40 days before His ascension is depicted on a colorful, carved wooden frieze in the Cathedral of Notre Dame, Paris, France.

Inspiration at Galilee

At the end of the Passover festival, the disciples return to Galilee, where they had first met Jesus, and had been called to follow Him. Peter decides to go fishing and several disciples accompany him. They catch nothing all night, but as morning breaks, they turn toward the shore and see a man on the beach. He calls out to them, "Friends, haven't you any fish?" "No," they reply. He tells them to throw the net out to the right of the boat. Miraculously, when they do

so, the net fills with so many fish that it nearly breaks. One of the disciples exclaims, "It is the Lord!" Peter immediately jumps out of the boat and wades to the shore, and the other disciples follow in the vessel, towing the net full of fish. On the shore, Jesus has already prepared a "fire of burning coals" with fish and bread on it. He asks them to bring a few more fish and they all sit down to eat breakfast together.

After breakfast, Jesus turns to Peter and asks him, "Do you truly love me?" Peter says that he does. Then Jesus says, "Feed my lambs." Twice more, Jesus repeats the »

The Ascension

Forty days after Jesus's resurrection, He summons His disciples to a hillside near Bethany, just outside Jerusalem. As He blesses and commissions them, He is "taken up before their very eyes" and hidden from sight by a cloud (Acts 1:9). His ascension is the end of His earthly ministry; Christians understand that He now ministers in God's presence, praying for His disciples to receive His Spirit and go out and gather more followers. Aspects of the ascension are familiar. The hill is a reminder of the mountain where Moses received God's Law, the cloud is a visible image of God's presence during the Exodus journey from Egypt, and Heaven was long perceived as a physical realm above the Earth. Theologically, the significance of such imagery is to emphasize Jesus's divinity.

The Ascension of Christ (1884) painted by the Polish artist Jan Matejko shows Christ in a cloud known as an "aureola," often used by artists to depict God or Christ.

The number 12

Throughout the Bible, the number 12 recurs often, and signifies the complete people of God. Early on, Abraham's grandson Jacob has 12 sons. They become the fathers of the 12 tribes of Israel, God's special people and a sign of His presence in the world. For this reason, Jesus chooses 12 disciples to be the foundation of a renewed family of God, marked out by faith. After his betrayal of Jesus, the disciples have to find a replacement for Judas in order to restore their number to 12. The criteria for apostleship was personal knowledge of Jesus's ministry, so that the apostle could provide witness to the fact and significance of Jesus's life, death, resurrection, and ascension. The disciples chose Matthias. The number 12 also appears frequently in the Book of Revelation, referring to the final completeness of God's worldwide family.

The Tree of Life bore 12 crops of fruit in John of Patmos's vision of Eden restored (Revelation 22:2), one for every month.

question, and both times Peter replies that he does. Both times, Jesus also instructs Peter to take care of His sheep—a reference to the family of believers. Peter, who had denied that he knew Jesus three times in the high priest's courtyard during Jesus's trial, is now restored as a faithful disciple of Christ and instructed to take care of the community of believers that would soon grow.

Telling the world

During this period, Jesus often meets the disciples as they eat together. On one occasion, He tells them to "wait for the gift my Father promised, which you have heard me speak about" (Acts 1:4). The gift is God's Holy Spirit, whom He has told them is "power from on high" (Luke 24:49) that will strengthen them in their mission. God's power will be essential, because Jesus is sending them to take His message not just to Judea and Galilee, but also to Samaria (a region often avoided because of longstanding political tension) and "to the ends of the earth'" (Acts 1:8).

At the end of the 40 days, in His last moments with the disciples, Jesus sums up all He has taught them in words that have become

Declare His glory among the nations, His marvelous deeds among all peoples.
Psalm 96:3

A 5th-century Roman mosaic from an eastern Mediterranean church has the cross as a central image, testimony to the spread of Christianity at the time. It is now in the Louvre, Paris.

known as "the Great Commission." First, He reminds the disciples of the significance of His resurrection from the dead: "All authority in heaven and on Earth has been given to me" (Matthew 28:18). By defeating death, Jesus proves that God has validated His life and teaching, and has granted Him divine authority over all things. He then commissions the disciples to bring others into His kingdom: "Therefore go and make disciples of all nations, baptizing them in the name of the Father and of the Son and of the Holy Spirit, and teaching them to obey everything I have commanded you" (Matthew 28:19–20). Jesus will be with the disciples, but is now entrusting His divine mission to human hands and feet.

From disciples to apostles

Jesus's Great Commission signals a change in the identity of His closest followers. Throughout His ministry, the 12 have been called "disciples," which comes from a Greek word meaning "learners'" or "followers." Now, the 11 disciples remaining—

after Judas's betrayal and suicide—have become "Apostles," from the Greek word meaning "sent." For three years, Jesus has drawn them closer to Him, demonstrating the reality of God's kingdom through stories, teaching, and miracles. Now, His "inner circle" can no longer stay by His side, but must go and announce the good news of Jesus and His resurrection to all the world.

A blessing for all

The Great Commission must have been both daunting and exciting for a group of ordinary men from Galilee and Judea. For a long time, the Jewish people had thought that the appeal of their God would bring people of all nations streaming to the Temple of Jerusalem. Converts, or proselytes, would then have to commit to Jewish customs of life

and faith. The Great Commission subverts this idea. Rather than people converging on Jerusalem, the apostles must go from the city to the four corners of the world, even to those Gentiles who have no regard for Jewish faith at all. Baptism in the name of the Father, Son, and Holy Spirit becomes the initiation ritual for new believers. Those who are baptized must center their lives, not on the Temple in Jerusalem, but on Jesus and His presence in their lives through the Holy Spirit. The Great Commission thus fulfills an older promise given to Abraham that through his descendants "all people on earth will be blessed".

After two millennia, the Great Commission remains a regular impetus of the Christian faith. The teachings of Jesus reached the

Therefore I want you to know that God's salvation has been sent to the Gentiles, and they will listen!
Acts 28:28

ends of the known earth within the first two centuries CE. Today, the mission is as focused on sharing the message of the resurrection as it is about journeying to the other side of the world. ■

Spread of early Christianity

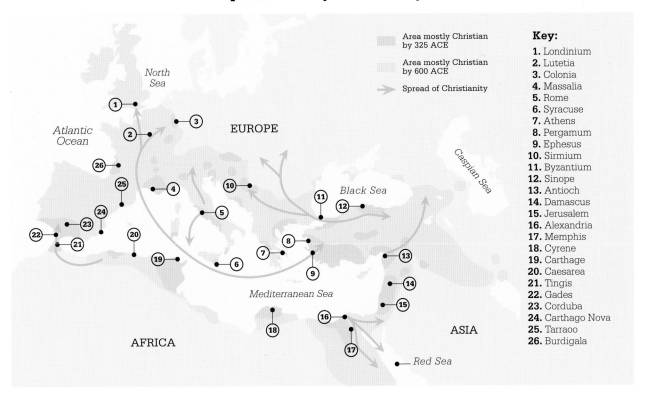

ACTS,
EPISTLE
REVELA

S, AND
TION

The Apostles receive the **Holy Spirit** on the feast of **Pentecost** in Jerusalem.

Philip converts an official of the Queen of Ethiopia on the road to Gaza.

Paul is **arrested** in Jerusalem and is **imprisoned** for two years, after which he is taken to Rome.

ACTS 2:1–47

ACTS 8:26–38

ACTS 21:17–26:32

ACTS 3:1–10

ACTS 9:1–30

1 CORINTHIANS 12:27

Peter performs the Apostles' first miracle when he **heals a beggar** outside the Temple in Jerusalem.

Saul, a persecutor of Christians, is **miraculously converted** on the **road to Damascus**.

Paul tells the Corinthians they are the **body of Christ** and each one of them is a part of it.

The Acts of the Apostles is the first Christian work to trace the dissemination of the Gospel message. Written by the author of the Gospel of Luke, the book presents key events and speeches in support of the mission that Jesus gave His followers: "You will receive power when the Holy Spirit comes on you; and you will be my witnesses in Jerusalem, and in all Judea and Samaria, and to the ends of the Earth" (Acts 1:8). It describes the coming of the Holy Spirit at Pentecost, the witness of the disciples in Jerusalem and Judea, and the persecution that drives the Apostles through the Roman Empire. A pivotal point is the conversion of the zealous persecutor Saul into the missionary Paul, the most influential leader in the early Church.

Acts demonstrates the struggles of the early Christians to deal with persecution, hypocrisy, old jealousies, and the cultural divide between Jews and Gentiles. It also narrates the spread of the Gospel through the eastern Roman Empire by means of the preaching and church-founding efforts of Paul. Descriptions of Paul's ministry in Corinth, and the churches of Galatia, Ephesus, Philippi, and Thessalonica, provide valuable contextual material for the New Testament Epistles.

The Epistles
Part of a larger tradition of letter-writing in the Greco-Roman world, the Epistles comprises 20 of the 27 books of the New Testament. Letters were taken to be a way for the author to be "present" and

"speak" with the reader when face-to-face conversation was impossible. They often followed the same basic structure: an introduction of the author and the recipients, a short prayer before the main text of the letter, concluding greetings to mutual acquaintances, and a brief blessing.

Thirteen of the New Testament letters name Paul as their author. Most of them address churches or groups of churches with which Paul had contact. Others (1–2 Timothy, Titus, and Philemon) address specific individuals, but with the apparent intention of being read in the recipient's churches. The remaining letters (James, 1–2 Peter, 1–3 John, and Jude) are known collectively as the "general" or "catholic" (meaning "universal") epistles. This designation indicates

Paul **asserts the Trinity** in a blessing at the end of a letter he writes to the Corinthians.

2 CORINTHIANS

Paul warns against "false teachers" in his letter to the Philippians and urges **belief in the resurrection**.

PHILIPPIANS 3

John of Patmos receives a series of dramatic and terrifying visions of the **apocalypse**.

REVELATION 1–20

EPHESIANS 2:1–10

Paul tells the Ephesians that **personal salvation** can only happen through **faith**, not good deeds.

JAMES 2:14–26

James rejects passive faith and praises **active faith** that honors God through good deeds.

REVELATION 21–22

After the Final Judgment, John's vision shows heaven and Earth renewed in the **New Jerusalem**.

that they were written to churches scattered over a wide geographical range, or to all Christians wherever they might be found. The Book of Revelation, while not a letter in its entirety, begins with seven brief letters to churches in Asia Minor. Its apocalyptic message describing Christ as the Final Judge of the wicked and vindicator of believers was partly an encouragement to those experiencing persecution.

Academic debates

Given their nature as letters, the Epistles give readers access to one side of a conversation. Readers can "overhear" the authors speak to congregations and individuals. The situation being addressed, however, must be inferred from the letters themselves. This has led modern scholars to speculate about the

nature of the societies in which the recipients lived. One important area of discussion focuses on opponents called "false teachers," which are mentioned and/or rebutted several times in the Epistles. The false teachers included practices and philosophies, such as Jewish legalism and mysticism, popular Greek philosophical and religious ideas, speculation about angels and spiritual powers, and ascetic and ritual practices.

Fierce debate also rages about the authorship of several Epistles. Since the 2nd century CE, scholars have speculated about the authorship of Hebrews. An early tradition attributed Hebrews to Paul, but others credited Peter's companion Silvanus, the early preacher Apollos, or one of Paul's companions—Barnabas, Priscilla,

or Luke. Some modern scholars have also challenged authorship of certain Pauline epistles (especially Ephesians) and 1–2 Peter.

A new beginning

Taken together, the Book of Acts and the New Testament Epistles demonstrate that the resurrection of the crucified Jesus was not the end of God's work in the world, but a new beginning through the Holy Spirit. The Epistles, while written by men, are included in the canon because they are seen as divinely inspired. They unpack the significance of the Gospel message of faith in Christ, in the service of "teaching, rebuking, correcting, and training in righteousness, so that the servant of God may be equipped for every good work" (2 Timothy 3:16–17). ∎

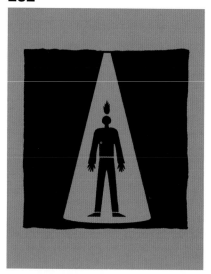

EVERYONE WAS FILLED WITH AWE AT THE MANY WONDERS AND SIGNS
ACTS 2:43, THE DAY OF PENTECOST

IN BRIEF

PASSAGE
Acts 2:1–47

THEME
The day of Pentecost

SETTING
c.29 CE Jerusalem. The city is full of Jewish pilgrims, who converge there annually for the feast of Pentecost (Shavu'ot), seven weeks after Passover.

KEY FIGURE
Peter Despite his denial of Jesus following Christ's arrest, Peter is again leader among the core disciples.

Other disciples According to Acts, the male disciples number about 120. Alongside them are Jesus's mother Mary and the other female disciples.

Just as thunder, lightning, and dense cloud accompany the giving of the Torah in Exodus, so dramatic phenomena accompany the giving of God's Spirit at the beginning of Acts. This happens during the feast of Pentecost, or Shavu'ot—one of three great pilgrimage festivals that each year brought throngs of Jews from across the known world to Jerusalem. Also in Jerusalem, according to Acts, is the core group of Jesus's disciples, who have met to pray, as they have done regularly since His ascension, ten days previously. Suddenly, a noise like that of a strong wind fills the house where the disciples are meeting and tongues of fire come to rest on their heads. Impelled by a strange inner power, the disciples find themselves speaking in languages they do not know.

A great confusion

The disciples make so much noise that a crowd gathers, including many of the pilgrims who have come to Jerusalem from other parts of the world. These foreigners are astonished because the disciples, who by now appear to have spilled out onto the street, are miraculously speaking to them in their native languages, telling them about the "wonders of God."

In response to these strange happenings, some of the onlookers are skeptical and dismissive, accusing the disciples of being

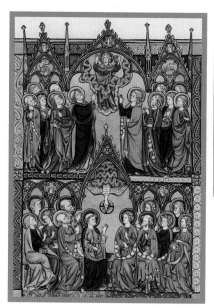

Celebrating the ascension (top) and Pentecost, this miniature is from *La Somme le Roi*, an illuminated manuscript produced in France between 1290 and 1300 and now held in the British Museum.

See also: The Calling of the Disciples 200–03 ▪ The Crucifixion 258–65 ▪ The Empty Tomb 268–71 ▪ The Great Commission 274–77

drunk. At this point, Peter, the leader of the disciples, stands up and addresses the crowd. The strange phenomena they are witnessing, he announces, are not the result of drunkenness, but they are the work of God—as foretold by the Prophet Joel in the Hebrew scriptures. He reminds his listeners of Jesus, who was God's prophet and Messiah and whom the people of Jerusalem have recently killed. This same Jesus, God has now raised from the dead.

Peter's speech has an electrifying effect on the crowd, many of whom are "cut to the heart" and beg to know what they can do in an attempt to make things right. Peter exhorts them to repent and become baptized. According to the Book of Acts, some 3,000 pilgrims follow his command, creating a massive increase in the number of believers.

The Pentecost event

Acts presents Peter's speech as a work of the Holy Spirit. At His ascension, Jesus promises that the Spirit would empower His disciples

All of them were filled with the Holy Spirit and began to speak in other tongues as the Spirit enabled them.
Acts 2:4

to be witnesses to His resurrection, beginning in Jerusalem (Acts 1:8). At Pentecost, God gives His Spirit—dramatically and emphatically—to the disciples. Just as the Spirit enabled the disciples to speak in other languages, so He inspires Peter's speech to the people of Jerusalem. Some scholars, however, think that Luke—the author of Acts—employed a literary device, common among ancient Greek historians, in which speeches are

put into the mouths of leading figures in order to comment upon the events they describe.

Peter's speech begins with the words of the Prophet Joel, who said the Spirit would be poured out on God's people at a critical point in history: "Even on my servants, both men and women, I will pour out my Spirit in those days, and they will prophesy. … And everyone who calls on the name of the Lord will be saved" (Joel 2:18–32). Peter goes on to argue that God had empowered Jesus's life and ministry, leading to His crucifixion. He quotes David's words that God would not abandon His holy one to death (Psalm 16:8–11), noting that while David's body was still in its tomb, God had raised Jesus and poured out His Spirit as promised. Jesus had then risen into heaven in fulfillment of God's command that the Messiah sit at His right hand until God defeated all the Messiah's enemies (Psalm 110:1). Luke reports that 3,000 of the assembled people of Jerusalem, convinced by Peter's words, repent their sins and receive forgiveness and the Holy Spirit. ▪

The early Christian community

Luke's account of the events of Pentecost concludes with a brief description of the community that emerged in Jerusalem as a result of that day's conversions. This is marked, says Acts, by four elements: teaching by the Apostles; fellowship; the breaking of bread; and prayer. The fellowship is radical: the believers are said to have owned everything in common, selling their possessions and distributing the money that they raised according to people's needs—all in a spirit of gladness and generosity.

All four elements were no doubt present in the early Christian community of Jerusalem, but later in Acts, Luke reveals tensions among them as well. Attempting to win unwarranted regard, some lie about their generosity and are judged by the Holy Spirit (Acts 5:3–5). For Christians since, it has remained an inspiration and a challenge.

The Apostles Going Forth to Preach, a 15th-century miniature by the Limbourg brothers, shows the Christian community at work.

IN THE NAME OF JESUS CHRIST OF NAZARETH, WALK

ACTS 3:6, THE HEALING OF THE BEGGAR

IN BRIEF

PASSAGE
Acts 3:1–5:42

THEME
**The disciples work
in Jesus's name**

SETTING
c.29–31 CE Jerusalem.

KEY FIGURES
Peter A leader among the
believers, twice imprisoned by
the Sanhedrin but defiantly
loyal to God. Peter was in
Jesus's inner circle of disciples.

John Brother of James, son
of Zebedee. He is with Peter
when they heal the beggar.

Sanhedrin A supreme court
in Jerusalem presided over by
the high priest.

Acts 3 tells the story of one of the first holy works performed by Jesus's disciples in the wake of His death, resurrection, and ascension. Peter and John approach a gate of the Temple in Jerusalem. It is a time of prayer, and they have come to pray, but they stop at the gate when they come across a beggar.

Crippled from birth, this beggar is a familiar figure at the Temple; he is carried there each day by friends or family to beg for money from the worshippers who stream by. On this day, the beggar is being carried to what was referred to as

See also: The Raising of Lazarus 226–27 ▪ Peter's Denial 256–57 ▪ The Great Commission 274–77 ▪ The Day of Pentecost 282–83 ▪ The Word Spreads 288–89

Peter (right) heals the lame man in this detail from Renaissance master Raphael's depiction of the miracle. It is one of a set of tapestries by the artist depicting the works of Peter and Paul.

the Beautiful Gate—possibly the bronze-clad Nicanor Gate, between the court of the Gentiles and the court of the women.

The beggar asks the disciples for money, and both of them look him directly in the eyes. "Look at us!" Peter says, and so the beggar looks. "Silver or gold I do not have, but what I do have I give you. In the name of Jesus Christ of Nazareth, walk" (Acts 3:4–6). Peter then takes the beggar by the hand and the

beggar's feet and ankles heal in an instant. He jumps up and walks for the first time in his life. Peter has just performed an astonishing, awe-inspiring miracle—the very kind, in fact, that Jesus used to perform before He was killed.

Powerful proof

Following Pentecost, Jesus's disciples continue to preach and perform great works. Luke, the author of Acts, gives many examples of signs and wonders that the disciples perform. As Jesus had promised them, His believers start to do even greater things in His name than He himself did during His three-year ministry.

The healing of the beggar is, as it were, the inaugural miracle of the post-Pentecost order. According to Luke, the beggar goes with Peter and John into the Temple, "walking

and jumping, and praising God" (3:8)—a triumphant sight that draws a large crowd. This gives Peter an opportunity to make a speech similar to the one he made at Pentecost: he reminds his listeners of their guilt in handing Jesus over to be killed, telling them to "repent … and turn to God" (3:19).

Disciples on trial

Some 5,000 people are converted that day, although some scholars suggest that this figure given by Luke is not meant to be taken literally—it simply suggests a large number. However, while ordinary people react with jubilation and awe to the healing of the beggar, it also attracts negative attention from the authorities, who are greatly disturbed by the events.

That same evening, the Temple guards arrest the two Apostles and throw them into prison overnight, before bringing them before the high priest and Sanhedrin the next morning. Standing before them, a Spirit-emboldened Peter speaks out yet again about Jesus, in whose »

Almsgiving

For people with disabilities— such as Bartimaeus, the blind man whom Jesus healed outside Jericho (Mark 10:46–52), and the man at the Beautiful Gate— begging was not demeaning, but simply one of the few ways they could make a living. Giving to the poor was encouraged by Jewish scripture—"I command you to be open-handed toward … the poor and needy in your land" (Deuteronomy 15:11)—and by Jesus. In the Sermon on the Mount, He names almsgiving

(giving to the poor) as one of the three prime works of piety, along with prayer and fasting (Matthew 6:1–4). From the point of view of beggars hoping to receive alms, location was key. Bartimaeus positioned himself by one of the gates into Jericho, to benefit from the constant flow of people into and out of the city; the man at the Beautiful Gate relied on the visiting pilgrims who were especially aware, as they entered or left the Temple, of their religious duty to give.

It is by the name of Jesus Christ of Nazareth, whom you crucified but whom God raised from the dead, that this man stands before you healed.
Acts 4:10

name the beggar has been healed. Baffled at such eloquence in the mouth of these two "unschooled, ordinary men" (4:13)—and by the undeniable fact that a great miracle has taken place—the council commands the Apostles to keep silent from now on.

Peter and John's reply is simple: "Which is right in God's eyes: to listen to you, or to Him? You be the judges! As for us, we cannot help speaking about what we have seen and heard" (4:19–20). The council members threaten them further, but with so much excitement at the miracle, the Sanhedrin has no option but to let the men go free.

The second Pentecost

Peter and John return to their community. What follows is sometimes called the "second Pentecost." Aware of the growing opposition they face from the authorities, the believers pray to God for renewed boldness in telling the world about Jesus. They ask, "Lord, consider their threats and enable your servants to speak your word with great boldness" (4:29). The Greek word that Luke uses for this boldness is *parrhesia*, also meaning "free speech," "frankness," even "plain speaking." As a sign of divine approval, the building where the believers are meeting shakes.

Thereafter, the community of believers in Jerusalem prospers: "all the believers were one in heart and mind" and they shared their possessions among each other (4:32). Most but not all of the believers are willing to take part in this. Acts 5 tells the story of Ananias and Sapphira, a couple who suddenly fall down and die after Peter reveals that they have

After they prayed, the place where they were meeting was shaken.
Acts 4:31

lied—wanting to receive praise, they pretend to hand over all their property while keeping some back for themselves.

The community thrives, as many more signs and miracles lead to an impressive growth in numbers. Inevitably, however, such success brings further jealousy and

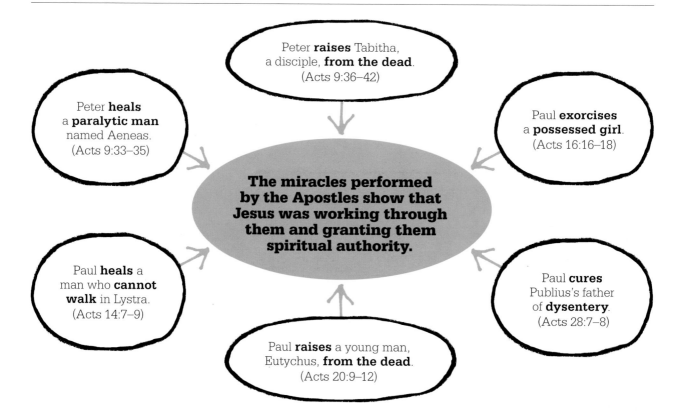

Peter **raises** Tabitha, a disciple, **from the dead**. (Acts 9:36–42)

Peter **heals** a **paralytic man** named Aeneas. (Acts 9:33–35)

Paul **exorcises** a **possessed girl**. (Acts 16:16–18)

The miracles performed by the Apostles show that Jesus was working through them and granting them spiritual authority.

Paul **heals** a man who **cannot walk** in Lystra. (Acts 14:7–9)

Paul **cures** Publius's father of **dysentery**. (Acts 28:7–8)

Paul **raises** a young man, Eutychus, **from the dead**. (Acts 20:9–12)

persecution from the authorities, at which point Luke's narrative borders on comedy. Once more the Apostles are arrested and thrown into prison, but during the night an angel comes and opens the prison doors, allowing them to go free. The angel tells them to go back to the Temple and preach as they usually do. When morning comes, the Sanhedrin meets and sends for the prisoners. Shocked officers return empty-handed with this report: "We found the jail securely locked, with the guards standing at the doors; but when we opened them, we found no one inside" (5:23).

Outwitting the council

Baffled once more, the Sanhedrin then receive a report from the Temple: the men imprisoned last night are there teaching the people. Yet again the Apostles are arrested. When upbraided for continuing to teach about Jesus, they reply: "We must obey God rather than human beings!" (5:29). Infuriated, many of the Sanhedrin want to put them to death and are only dissuaded by the more cautious counsels of a Pharisee named Gamaliel. In the

> People brought the sick into the streets and laid them on beds and mats so that at least Peter's shadow might fall on some of them as he passed by.
> **Acts 5:15**

end, the Apostles are flogged, once more told not to speak in Jesus's name, and allowed to go free. Yet again they ignore the Sanhedrin's orders. They continue, Luke writes, joyfully "teaching and proclaiming the good news that Jesus is the Messiah" (Acts 5:42).

Inherited leadership

Throughout this narrative, Luke makes important theological points. With their bold Spirit-empowered preaching, confirmed by God in signs and wonders, the Apostles have established that they stand in a clear line of continuity reaching back as far as Abraham, Moses, and the prophets of the Hebrew scriptures. God has been faithful: the great covenants He made with Abraham and the Hebrew patriarchs have found fulfillment in Jesus, the promised Messiah, whom God affirmed with miraculous works—notably, the supreme miracle of His resurrection. Now though, the traditional leaders of the Jews, the Sanhedrin refuse to accept Jesus as the Son of God, and so the leadership of God's people passes out of their hands and to the Apostles. The believers are portrayed by Luke as the "new Israel," true heirs of the covenant promises of the Old Testament.

In this context, the fact that Peter and John heal the beggar in the name of Jesus is important. Peter's speech acknowledges that not only are the disciples following in the tradition of Jesus's ministry, the power they are exercising is not their own: Jesus now works through them. Peter, John, and their fellow disciples have been empowered by the Holy Spirit to continue Jesus's work on Earth, and have been given the authority to carry out this task because of their faith in Him. ∎

Simon Peter

One of Jesus's closest disciples Simon Peter became a leading member of the early Church. His real name was Simon, but Jesus called him "Rock": "Peter" in Greek, "Cephas" in Aramaic. He and his brother Andrew were both fishermen, and worked with another pair of brothers, James and John. John's Gospel says Peter met Jesus through Andrew, who was a disciple of John the Baptist. However, the Gospels of Mark and Luke report that Peter and Andrew were working as fishermen when Jesus called them to be His disciples.

During the ministry of Jesus, Peter was one of the inner circle of three disciples, along with James and John, but when Jesus was arrested, Peter denied Him three times. This failure marked a turning point in Peter's life; he was forgiven by Jesus and soon emerged as a dauntless leader in the early Church. He was also the first to share the Christian message and baptism with non-Jews. Peter was famously crucified upside-down during the persecution unleashed by Emperor Nero in 64–68 CE.

HE TOLD HIM THE GOOD NEWS ABOUT JESUS

ACTS 8:35, THE WORD SPREADS

IN BRIEF

PASSAGE
Acts 7:54–8:40

THEME
God's word is for everyone

SETTING
c.32–35 CE The countryside around Jerusalem.

KEY FIGURES
Saul of Tarsus A Hellenistic (Greek-speaking) Jew later known as Paul. At this stage, he is a diehard persecutor of the fledgling Church.

Philip One of the "Seven" appointed to oversee the distribution of food to widows in Jerusalem. He spreads the word of God.

Ethiopian official Chief treasurer to the Queen of Ethiopia; a eunuch who is baptized by Philip.

L ife for most of the believers in Jerusalem is relatively peaceful in the period after Pentecost, despite some conflicts between the Sanhedrin and the Apostles. However, this changes when the Sanhedrin, alarmed by the evangelical success of a Hellenistic Christian called Stephen, sentences him to death by stoning. Stephen's execution begins "a great persecution" against the Jerusalem Church, masterminded by a young man called Saul, at whose feet Stephen's killers had laid their outer garments. Luke's Gospel describes Saul going from house to house, dragging off men and women and throwing them into prison.

From curse to blessing

The Apostles stay in Jerusalem to face the persecution, while the rest of the community scatter across Judea and Samaria to escape the violence. However, what at first seems like a setback leads to the fulfillment of Jesus's prophecy at His ascension: "You will be my witnesses in Jerusalem, and … to the ends of the Earth" (Acts 1:8).

Proselytes and God-fearers

In the period after Jerusalem's Temple was rebuilt in the 6th century BCE, there was a growth in the number of "proselytes"— those who went through the full rites of conversion to Judaism, including circumcision—and "God-fearers," who followed many Jewish religious practices without full conversion. This growth resulted partly from increased contact between Jews and non-Jews, and partly because of the missionary zeal of the Pharisees. Later, many proselytes and God-fearers were drawn to the teaching of Jesus and His disciples.

In Matthew's and Luke's Gospels, a Roman centurion whose servant Jesus heals may well be a God-fearer, as may the Ethiopian official in Acts. Two converts in Acts—the centurion Cornelius, and Lydia, a cloth dealer in Philippi—are described as God-fearers. Cornelius and his household are baptized after hearing Peter preach, Lydia and hers after hearing Paul.

See also: Ruth and Naomi 108–09 ▪ The Suffering Servant 154–55 ▪ The Great Commission 274–77 ▪ The Day of Pentecost 282–83 ▪ The Road to Damascus 290–91

Wherever the believers go, they "preach the word" to the great joy of those who hear and accept it.

The Ethiopian

In Samaria, Philip, a former associate of the martyred Stephen, makes an impact. He was one of seven men appointed to oversee the distribution of food to widows in Jerusalem. Now in Samaria, he preaches to large crowds and performs dramatic healings.

Luke describes two aspects of the events that follow. On one level is the persecution that scatters the believers, who then set out to preach the word. On the other is the direct intervention of God, whose influence becomes clear when He sets Philip a new task. As Philip returns to Jerusalem from Samaria, an angel tells him to take the road to Gaza. He sets out and sees a chariot ahead. God's Spirit tells Philip to catch up with it, and there he finds a high official of the Queen of Ethiopia, a eunuch who has been to Jerusalem to worship. The man is reading one

They all paid close attention to what He said. For with shrieks, impure spirits came out of many, and many who were paralyzed or lame were healed.
Acts 8:6–7

of the Suffering Servant Songs from the Book of Isaiah, which speaks of the arrival and suffering of the Messiah. Philip asks the eunuch if he understands what he is reading. The eunuch replies that he does not and invites Philip to sit with him to explain the passage. Philip agrees and tells the man "the good news about Jesus," as predicted by Isaiah. Later, when they pass a stretch of water, the eunuch asks Philip to baptize him. Philip does so, and then the "Spirit of the Lord" miraculously takes Philip away, depositing him on the coast near Caesarea. The eunuch, meanwhile, continues on his way, rejoicing.

Joy thus marks the spreading of the Gospel—a process that Saul's persecution has only, in the end, promoted. As Jesus foretold,

The Ethiopian eunuch is baptized by Philip the Evangelist, in a stained-glass window in Brackley, England. This act symbolized the start of the Ethiopian Church.

the "good news" has spread from Jerusalem into Judea and Samaria. Now, with the conversion of the Ethiopian, it pushes farther afield.

God of all

The conversion of the eunuch shows a key difference between Judaism and Christianity. For Jews, castration was unlawful, so, as a eunuch, the Ethiopian would not have been allowed to worship in the Temple. God, however, prompts Philip to baptize the man. The episode is seen as proof that the word of God was meant for the whole world—not just the Jews. ■

I AM JESUS, WHOM YOU'ARE PERSECUTING

ACTS 9:5, THE ROAD TO DAMASCUS

IN BRIEF

PASSAGE
Acts 9:1–19

THEME
Miraculous conversions

SETTING
c.33–36 CE The road to Damascus, Syria, where many Jews have become Christians.

KEY FIGURES
Saul Better known by his Latin name Paul, Saul is initially a fanatical persecutor of Christian believers.

Ananias A Christian believer in Damascus who was a former disciple of Jesus. Described as a "devout observer of the Law," he was sent to heal Paul and bring him the Gospel.

The conversion of Paul on the road to Damascus is one of the most dramatic episodes in the Book of Acts. The most fanatical persecutor of the early Christians has an overwhelming experience with the risen Jesus and becomes a member of the very community he has previously attacked. Within a short space of time, Paul became one of his new community's most eloquent preachers, earning him many converts but also the enmity of his former allies. Not once but twice he has to flee for his life. The arch-persecutor thus joins the ranks of the persecuted.

Saul's vision

The story in Acts begins with Paul, who is then known by his Hebrew name, Saul, "breathing out murderous threats against the Lord's disciples" (Acts 9:1). Armed with warrants from the high priest, he is on his way to Damascus to hunt down believers and bring them back to Jerusalem as prisoners. Just outside the city, however, he has an extraordinary encounter. A "light from heaven" flashes around him, and a voice says, "Saul, Saul, why do you persecute me?" (9:3–4).

Saul, who has fallen to the ground, asks who is speaking. The voice replies, "I am Jesus, whom you are persecuting. Now get up and go into the city, and you will be told what you must do" (9:5–6).

Finding himself blinded, Saul is taken into Damascus by his traveling companions. After three days, the Lord appears to a local believer named Ananias and tells him to visit Saul. Ananias does as the Lord says and baptizes Saul, who receives the Holy Spirit and the return of his sight.

According to Luke, Saul is soon preaching about Jesus in the Damascus synagogues, arousing the animosity of local Jews, who conspire to murder him.

Lowered in a basket from the city wall by his disciples, Saul escapes the conspirators and goes to Jerusalem, where he makes contact with the initially suspicious Apostles. Once again, his preaching earns him the hostility of certain Jews—probably the very group of diaspora Jews with whom he had previously associated—and he has to flee, this time to his home city of Tarsus. The conversion of Saul is so fundamental to the evolution of the early Church that Luke tells the

See also: The Word Spreads 288–89 ▪ The Council of Jerusalem 292–93 ▪
Paul's Arrest 294–95 ▪ The Power of the Resurrection 304–05

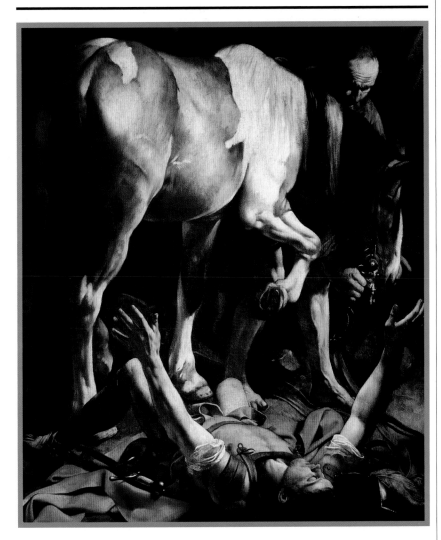

Paul, Apostle to the Gentiles

Paul was born in the city of Tarsus, in today's Turkey, to a family of Hellenistic (Greek-speaking) Jews. The well-educated young man had a knowledge of Greek thought and studied under the famous Pharisee Rabbi Gamaliel in Jerusalem.

Paul makes reference to his conversion in his letters to the Galatians and Corinthians. Paul adds to Luke's account in Acts, saying he traveled from Damascus to Arabia after his conversion and that it was three years before he went to Jerusalem to meet Peter and the other Apostles.

In the years that followed, Paul traveled around the eastern Mediterranean, preaching the Gospel and establishing communities of Christians in the major cities. The hostility of Jewish opponents led to his eventual arrest in Jerusalem and then transportation to Rome for trial. The New Testament gives no account of his death, but an early tradition asserts that he died by beheading during the persecution unleashed in 64 CE by the Roman Emperor Nero.

story three times (Acts 9, 22, and 26). His aim is clear: to establish Paul as an apostolic and prophetic figure, who was called, revealed, and confirmed as such by God.

God's prophet

As in the rest of the Bible, God works through signs and wonders, but also through suffering. The fact that Paul is now persecuted affirms both the power of God and the status of Paul as God's prophet, suffering with Jesus and the

The drama of Paul's experience is captured by Caravaggio's *Conversion on the Way to Damascus* (1601), in which the blinded Saul is thrown into a pool of light.

Hebrew prophets who came before Him. As God reveals to Ananias, He has selected the former enemy of His people to become His "chosen instrument to proclaim My name to the Gentiles. … I will show him how much he must suffer for my name" (9:15–16). ▪

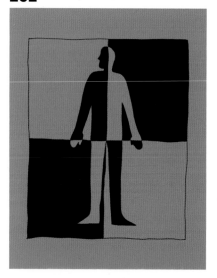

HE PURIFIED THEIR HEARTS BY FAITH

ACTS 15:9, THE COUNCIL OF JERUSALEM

IN BRIEF

PASSAGE
ACTS 15:1–35

THEME
Accommodating Gentiles

SETTING
c.49 CE Antioch and Jerusalem.

KEY FIGURES
Paul The Apostle argues in both Antioch and Jerusalem against an insistence on Gentile circumcision.

Barnabas Paul's longtime friend accompanies him on his journey to Jerusalem.

Peter The Apostle speaks decisively at the Council of Jerusalem against the need for circumcision.

James A leader of the Jerusalem church, James sums up the Council's findings.

The growing influx of Gentile believers posed problems for the early Church. Questions arose as to whether they should be regarded as full members of the Church, or have to meet further requirements to put them on an equal footing with Jewish followers of Christ.

According to Acts, these burning questions come to a head in Antioch after Paul's return to the city at the end of his first missionary journey. Jewish believers, having recently arrived from Judea, are teaching that all believers must be circumcised, according to the Law of Moses. Paul and his long-standing ally

Barnabas deny this, insisting that circumcision is not necessary for Gentile believers. The debate becomes so heated that the Antioch church sends a delegation, led by Paul and Barnabas, to consult the elders of the founding church in a meeting that became known as the Council of Jerusalem.

The Council meets

In Jerusalem, much like in Antioch, the debate becomes vigorous. Peter speaks first, insisting that faith alone is necessary for salvation. He cites the recent conversion of the Roman centurion Cornelius and his household, who heard the Gospel from Peter and believed. God confirmed their salvation by filling them with the Holy Spirit, just as He did with Jewish believers. God, Peter says, "did not discriminate between us and them, for He purified their hearts by faith" (Acts 15:9). As a result, no extra yoke, such as circumcision, should be placed on their necks. Following further testimony from

A Bible study card (c.1900) illustrates Acts 15:22–33, in which the Gentile believers of Antioch are told which of Moses's Laws they must keep.

See also: The Nature of Faith 236–41 ▪ The Word Spreads 288–89 ▪ Salvation Through Faith 301 ▪ The Power of the Resurrection 304–05

Paul and Barnabas, James, an increasingly influential leader in the Jerusalem church, cites the prophet Amos to show that it was always God's intention that people from other nations would "seek the Lord" (15:17). Like Peter, he concludes that "we should not make it difficult for the Gentiles who are turning to God" (15:19).

A compromise

James proposes a compromise: there will be no circumcision for Gentile believers, but they will be required to observe certain Jewish dietary and cleanliness laws, chiefly to ensure that Jewish and Gentile believers can eat together. James's proposal is accepted, and so believers from Jerusalem are chosen to go back to Antioch with Paul and Barnabas, bearing a letter confirming the Council's resolutions.

The Council of Jerusalem is a watershed. It stresses above all the importance of understanding that God wants to reach out to Gentiles, as He did with Cornelius and his household, and the Gentile converts Paul and Barnabas made in their travels. This creates a consensus

> The rest of mankind may seek the Lord, even all the Gentiles who bear my name.
> **Acts 15:17**

between God and His people, as reflected in a famous clause from the letter the Council sends to the believers in Antioch: "It seemed good to the Holy Spirit and to us not to burden you" (15:28). In the new "kingdom" that is therefore established, Gentile believers enjoy full and equal citizenship with Jewish ones. Faith alone gives entry. With these truths firmly established, the rest of Acts is dominated at the human level by Paul, God's "chosen instrument" (9:15), for bringing the message of the Gospel to the Gentiles. ▪

The elders of the **Church** meet in Jerusalem.

Some argue that because Christianity is the fulfillment of promises made in the **Pentateuch** …

… **Gentiles** converting to Christianity should be circumcised, according to Mosaic Law.

But the Council decides that **salvation** does not require adherence to the Law …

… and makes no faith distinction between Gentile and Jew.

This decision preserves the unity of the Church and takes its reach beyond that of **Judaism**.

Paul and Peter's fight at Antioch

In his letter to the Galatians, Paul describes a combative encounter in Antioch with the Apostle Peter over Jewish dietary laws. Paul publicly accuses Peter of inconsistency and hypocrisy because Peter sometimes eats with Gentile believers, but at other times refrains from doing so for fear of offending Jewish visitors from Jerusalem (Galatians 2:11–12). Paul argues, "You are a Jew, yet you live like a Gentile … How is it, then, that you force Gentiles to follow Jewish customs?" (2:14).

These were difficult issues for leaders of the early Church. As shown at the Council of Jerusalem, Peter and other Church leaders eventually agree that outreach to the Gentiles was God's initiative through Christ and could not be ignored by the Church.

I ADMIT THAT I WORSHIP THE GOD OF OUR ANCESTORS AS A FOLLOWER OF THE WAY
ACTS 24:14, PAUL'S ARREST

IN BRIEF

PASSAGE
Acts 21:17–28:31

THEME
Faith under trial

SETTING
c.57–60 CE Jerusalem and Caesarea Maritima.

KEY FIGURES
Paul An Apostle of Christ.

Claudius Lysias A tribune (high-ranking military officer) in command of the Roman garrison in Jerusalem.

Roman procurators Governors of Judea, first Marcus Antonius Felix c.52–60 CE, then Porcius Festus c.60–62 CE.

Agrippa II Great-grandson of Herod the Great. A Roman-appointed king whose realms include Galilee.

Despite it leading to his arrest and near lynching at the hands of a mob, the Apostle Paul's decision to return to Jerusalem from Rome is made for a simple and virtuous reason: he wants to hand over money that has been collected among Gentile churches to relieve the poor of the Judean Church. The intent is generous, yet, as Luke makes clear, by traveling to the Jewish capital, Paul is entering dangerous territory. The Apostle is only too aware of this. "I am going to Jerusalem," he tells friends, "not knowing what will happen to me there. I only know that in every city the Holy Spirit warns me that … hardships are facing me" (Acts 20:22–23).

Pain and trials

It is not long until Paul must face these hardships. His first act upon arriving in Jerusalem is to meet with James, the leader of the Judean Church, who warns him that many believers in Judea think Paul is subverting the Law of Moses because of a rumor that Paul has been teaching Jews to abandon their obedience to that law. To prove them wrong, he suggests that Paul join four local believers who are about to undergo a Jewish purification rite. Paul agrees and reaches the last day of the rite before he is spotted in the Temple by Jews from Asia. He has also been seen in the company of a Greek from Ephesus, and the Jews assume he has sacrilegiously taken

The arrest of Paul is a popular subject in religious artwork, such as this fresco from the Papal Basilica of St. Paul Outside the Walls, which was built on the site of Paul's burial.

See also: Peter's Denial 256–57 ▪ The Crucifixion 258–65 ▪ The Word Spreads 288–89 ▪ The Road to Damascus 290–91

the Greek into parts of the Temple forbidden to Gentiles. A riot ensues in which, according to Acts, the Asian Jews drag Paul from the Temple and try to kill him. He is saved only by the intervention of a Roman commander who takes him into protective custody and, after discovering a plot within the Jewish Sanhedrin to murder Paul, sends him to the headquarters of the Roman governor, Felix.

Paul remains a prisoner there for two years until Felix is replaced by another Roman governor, Festus, who reviews the case alongside the Herodian King Agrippa. He proposes another meeting with the Sanhedrin, but Paul, revealing that he is a Roman citizen, insists on his case being referred to Rome.

While imprisoned, Paul tells the story of his conversion outside Damascus twice and portrays the risen Jesus he encountered there as the fulfillment of all that God has promised the Jewish people. In the end, Festus and Agrippa can find no just cause to sentence Paul to

I am saying nothing beyond what the prophets and Moses said would happen—that the Messiah would … bring the message of light to his own people and to the Gentiles.
Acts 26:22–23

My brothers … I stand on trial because of the hope of the resurrection of the dead.
Acts 23:6

death, and he is sent on to Rome to live under house arrest for a further two years, before he eventually gains his freedom.

Gospel parallels

Throughout the trials of Paul, there are parallels with the account in Luke's Gospel of the trial of Jesus, who, like Paul, strived to spread the word of God amid often barbaric opposition. Unlike his portrayal of Jesus, who remained largely silent during His torments and judgment, in Acts Luke records three major speeches in which Paul defends himself and his record. Moreover, Paul advocates for his own holiness with a vehemence that Jesus does not display, arguing that he is not merely a Jew, but a Pharisee, and thus, like all Pharisees, fully believes in bodily resurrection, like that experienced by Jesus.

Although the trajectories of Jesus and Paul are not identical— after all, within biblical scripture Paul escapes his mission alive— both men represent devout teachers of the word of God who, despite suffering, choose to persist under the burden of their holy mission. ▪

Persecution and martyrdom

For prophets in the Bible, faithfulness to God draws hostility. Jeremiah speaks for many when he begs God to "think of how I suffer reproach for your sake" (Jeremiah 15:15). Likewise, Jesus makes clear in the New Testament that just as He will suffer, so will the disciples that spread His message: "they will seize you and persecute you … all on account of my name" (Luke 21:12).

The changing meaning of the Greek word transliterated as "martyr" reflects this close link between preaching and suffering. In the New Testament, the word occurs often, meaning "witness"— someone who bears witness to Christ. By the end of the 1st century CE, as witnessing increasingly began to lead to persecution and death, the word took on its modern meaning of one who suffers and dies for the sake of their religious beliefs. Paul himself was beheaded on the orders of Emperor Nero.

LOVE IS PATIENT, LOVE IS KIND. IT DOES NOT ENVY, IT DOES NOT BOAST, IT IS NOT PROUD.

1 CORINTHIANS 13:4, THE WAY OF LOVE

IN BRIEF

PASSAGE
1 Corinthians 13:1–13

THEME
Love is everlasting

SETTING
54 CE Ephesus, a province in modern-day Turkey.

KEY FIGURES
Paul Apostle who became a Christian after Jesus's death. One of the leading figures in the early Church, he travels extensively, preaching the word of God.

Corinthian believers The community in Corinth, who are prone to factionalism and cliquishness.

The Apostle Paul's letters to the Corinthians are his response to various questions the Corinthian believers have sent him on topics ranging from marriage and divorce to the use of spiritual gifts, such as speaking in tongues. In his first letter, he describes seven things that love is and does—love is patient; is kind; rejoices with truth; protects; trusts; hopes; and perseveres; and, eight that it is not or does not do—does not envy or boast; is not proud, rude, self-seeking, or easily angered; keeps no record of wrongs; and does not delight in evil. This is the core of

Paul's extended "hymn" to love, which itself forms the heart of a discourse by Paul on how believers should behave and relate when they meet for worship.

For Paul, as for all other New Testament writers, love is the touchstone of the Christian faith; this begins with God's love. In the words of John's Gospel: "God so loved the world" (3:16) that He sent His own son to die for the sins of man. That son, Jesus, shows that same love with acts of mercy, healing, and forgiveness, and tells His followers that love is the greatest commandment of all: love your neighbor, and "love the Lord your God with all your heart … with all your soul and with all your mind" (Matthew 22:37).

Above all else

Writing to the Romans, Paul says: "you shall not commit adultery," "you shall not murder," "you shall not steal," "you shall not covet," which are summed up in one

The martyrs Spes, Caritas, and Fides, or Hope, Love (a modern translation for Caritas), and Faith, named after the three virtues, depicted in the Church of St. Martin, Cumbria, England.

Types of love in the Bible

Agape—Divine love
Love found between God and Jesus, Jesus and His disciples, believers and God, and also among believers.

Eros—Romantic love
The "erotic" or romantic love between two lovers (spouses), as depicted in Song of Songs.

Philia—Brotherly love
Love found in close friendships, such as that between Jonathan and David in the Old Testament.

Storge—Familial love
The love between family members, as shown in the Bible between Jacob and Isaac, or Mary, Martha, and Lazarus.

command: "Love your neighbor as yourself" (Romans 13:9). Writing to the Corinthians, Paul applies this "royal law" in a particular context. The Corinthians, he believes, are far too individualistic. They pride themselves on spiritual gifts, such as speaking in tongues or prophecy, in a way that causes division. Love is missing, and Paul highlights the emptiness this causes in the first part of his hymn: "if I speak in the tongues of … angels, but do not have love, I am only a resounding gong or a clanging cymbal" (1 Corinthians 13:1).

The last section of Paul's letter begins with the declaration, "love never fails" (13:8). In a world of constant change, he says, just three things last: faith, hope, and love. Of these three, Paul writes, the greatest is love. Love is produced by God's Spirit and should guide the use of the Spirit's gifts. While tongues and other gifts may fade and cease, love brings humility, unity, and peace.

Apostle of love
Some describe Paul as the "Apostle of love." As he writes in his letter to the Galatians—where the issue is "Judaising" believers trying to impose circumcision on Gentile believers—"neither circumcision nor uncircumcision has any value. The only thing that counts is faith expressing itself through love" (Galatians 5:6). ▪

Corinth

The believers in Corinth were citizens of a rich, culturally diverse metropolis. Much of its prosperity was because of its location on the isthmus connecting the Peloponnese with the rest of mainland Greece, commanding not one but two trade routes: from the south to the north between the Peloponnese and the rest of the mainland, and west to east between the Adriatic and Aegean seas. The capital of the Roman province of Achaea, Corinth had sizable foreign communities, which included Egyptians and Jews, as well as many native Greeks.

According to Acts 18:1–11, Paul arrived in Corinth for the first time around 50 CE during his second missionary journey, and stayed for 18 months with a Jew, Aquila, and his wife, Priscilla. The couple had fled from Rome the year before, after the Jews were expelled from the city.

The fractious church Paul helped to establish in Corinth remained close to his heart, and was the recipient of a number of the Apostle's letters and appeals. Two of these letters became part of the New Testament as the books of 1 and 2 Corinthians.

THE GRACE OF THE LORD JESUS CHRIST AND THE LOVE OF GOD AND THE FELLOWSHIP OF THE HOLY SPIRIT
2 CORINTHIANS 13:14, THE HOLY TRINITY

IN BRIEF

PASSAGE
2 Corinthians 13:1–14

THEME
The Trinity

SETTING
54–55 CE Corinth, a major city in Greece and the provincial capital of the Roman province of Achaea. It was occupied by Rome until around 521 CE.

KEY FIGURES
Paul The Apostle who founded the church at Corinth in around 50 CE during his ministry in the Aegean.

The Corinthians Christians in the troubled church of Corinth, who have been led astray by teachers opposed to Paul.

The church in Corinth, which the Apostle Paul had founded and led for several years, faced many difficulties after Paul left to continue his missionary work, mainly arising from the arrival of teachers opposed to Paul. These problems prompted two letters from the Apostle to correct and redeem the wayward church.

Writing from Ephesus in Asia Minor, Paul takes a sharp tone in 2 Corinthians, but ends on a gentle note. In the final paragraph (13:11–14), he exhorts his readers to become spiritually mature and to come together, reminding them that God is hard at work among them to this end. Paul then ends by blessing the entire congregation, concluding, "May the grace of the Lord Jesus Christ, and the love of God, and the fellowship of the Holy Spirit be with you all" (13:14).

In this blessing, Paul combines three ideas about the relationship of God, Christ, and the Holy Spirit to Christians, affirming the equal dignity of the three persons. It is thus one of the most complete references in the New Testament to the concept of the Trinity.

Three in one
The New Testament affirms that there is only one true God, yet also asserts that the Father is God,

The Holy Trinity (1440) by the Master of the Darmstadt, an anonymous artist from Germany, shows God holding the body of His Son, and the Holy Spirit represented by a dove.

See also: The Divinity of Jesus 190–93 ▪ The Nature of Faith 236–41 ▪ The Council of Jerusalem 292–93 ▪ Salvation Through Faith 301

Holy Trinity

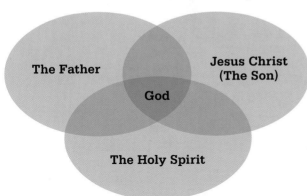

The Trinity refers to the existence of God as three consubstantial persons. These three persons are distinct— The Father, Christ, and Holy Spirit—yet share one nature.

Jesus is God (John 5:22–23), and the Holy Spirit is God (Matthew 12:32). Christians have therefore concluded that the Bible teaches its readers that, while there is only one divine being, there are three divine persons within that being. Reinforcing this idea are texts in which each Person is present but distinct, such as in the baptismal formula in Matthew 28:19; and the "confessions" of faith in Ephesians 4:4–6 and 1 Peter 1:1–2.

The Nicene Creed
In 325 CE, centuries after Paul's death, Church leaders met at Nicaea (modern Iznik, Turkey) to address the teachings of Arius. His followers defended the uniqueness of God and the personal distinction between the Father and Son by denying the godhood of Jesus, arguing that the Son merely had a nature "similar" to the Father's. The Council of Nicaea developed the ideas essential to the doctrine of the Trinity: the uniqueness of God, the divinity of the Father and Son, and the personal distinction between them. Christians argued over these concepts extensively,

but most eventually agreed that to deny the deity of Jesus was to render dependence upon Jesus for salvation and that worship of Him was a form of idolatry. While Arians affirmed that Jesus had a nature that was homoiousios (similar) to that of God the Father, defenders of the Nicene Creed insisted that Jesus's nature was homoousious (same). In English, the latter idea is expressed by the word "consubstantial" or "being of one substance with the Father." ▪

I believe in the Holy Spirit, the Lord, the giver of life, who proceeds from the Father and the Son, who with the Father and the Son is adored and glorified.
The Nicene Creed

Council of Nicaea

Constantine the Great's Council of Nicaea was the first of seven ecumenical councils held between 325 and 787 CE. The purpose of each of these meetings was to address some of the heresies that were arising within the Church and answer difficult questions raised by Christian skeptics. Constantine realized that by establishing universal doctrines that could be widely shared and promulgated, the Church, and his empire, would strengthen and expand. Prior to the Council of Nicaea, doctrine had been decided at the local level, such as at the Council of Jerusalem in 50 CE.

Constantine himself presided over the council meeting, even though he was a Catechumen (the name given to an adherent of Christianity who had not been baptized). The rest of the council was made up of representatives drawn from across Christendom.

Constantine the Great presides at the Council of Nicaea, in 325 CE, in a 12th-century fresco in the Bachkovo Monastery in Bulgaria. The figure below him is Arius.

BUT THE FRUIT OF THE SPIRIT IS LOVE, JOY, PEACE, FORBEARANCE, AND KINDNESS
GALATIANS 5:22–23, FRUITS OF THE SPIRIT

IN BRIEF

PASSAGE
Galatians 5:13–26

THEME
Living by the Spirit

SETTING
48–55 CE Galatia, a province in modern-day Turkey.

KEY FIGURES
Paul An Apostle of Christ who acted as a missionary in the early Christian Church, later writing letters to the churches he founded. Many of these epistles became books of the New Testament.

Galatians Lapsed followers of Christ from Galatia, a Roman province founded in the 3rd century BCE.

In his letter to the Galatians—new churches in a province in present-day Turkey—Paul delivers an impassioned affirmation of the importance of having faith in Christ, as he implores the people not to return to a sinful life.

In Galatians 5, in particular, Paul uses two lists in order to compare the vices produced by human effort to the virtues that are "the fruit of the Spirit" (5:22). The first list outlines "acts of the flesh," listing qualities such as "sexual immorality … hatred" and "selfish ambition" (5:19–20) among the vices of sinful humanity. For Paul, these sins dominate a society that has become focused purely on its selfish impulses.

The second list establishes the virtuous alternative to sin as the "fruit of the Spirit"—love, joy, peace, forbearance, kindness, gentleness, and self-control. For Paul, those who have embraced these "have crucified the flesh" (5:24) within themselves and have been freed from their egotism, enabling them to better serve God.

Although Greek and Roman philosophers often made lists of vices and virtues, Paul's primary intention in Galatians is to draw attention to the inevitable choice between the sins of the self-righteous and living by the Spirit.

Paul focuses on vices that cause dissent among communities, such as jealousy, factions, and envy. The "fruit of the Spirit," in contrast, emphasizes principles centered on healing communities; such as love, patience, and gentleness. ■

So, I say, walk by the Spirit, and you will not gratify the desires of the sinful nature.
Galatians 5:16

See also: Council of Jerusalem 292–93 ■ The Way of Love 296–97 ■ The Power of the Resurrection 304–05

FOR IT IS BY GRACE YOU HAVE BEEN SAVED, THROUGH FAITH ... NOT BY WORKS
EPHESIANS 2:8–9, SALVATION THROUGH FAITH

IN BRIEF

PASSAGE
Ephesians 2:1–10

THEME
Faith and salvation

SETTING
61–62 CE Ephesus, a province in modern-day Turkey.

KEY FIGURES
Paul An Apostle of Christ who acted as a missionary in the early Christian Church. He wrote letters to the churches he founded, such as the church in Ephesus. Many of these epistles became books of the New Testament.

Saints in Ephesus Jewish and Gentile Christians in the church in Ephesus.

After he is arrested, and while he awaits trial in Rome, Paul writes letters of encouragement to churches he has founded around the Aegean Sea. In one such letter, to the people of Ephesus, Paul discusses the importance of having faith in God, compared to the significance of performing "works"—that is, good deeds and actions. Despite stating that "we were created ... to do good works" (Ephesians 2:10), Paul repeatedly writes that personal salvation—being welcomed into the kingdom of heaven—can only happen through faith in Jesus.

A gift from God
According to Paul, the Ephesians were "dead in [their] transgressions and sins" (2:1), yet because God is loving and merciful, He made them alive with Christ. By this, Paul means that the people's actions were previously of a sinful nature, not good works in the name of God. However, when the Ephesians were converted, they were saved through God's favor, His grace (2:8–9).

Protestant reformer Martin Luther was a firm proponent of the doctrine of *sola fide*—salvation through faith alone. This view was fundamental to the Protestant Reformation.

Crucially, Paul tells the Ephesians that even their faith is a gift from God, rather than a virtue they have cultivated themselves. According to Paul, God alone may take credit for the salvation of the Ephesians: the people have been saved not because they have done good deeds, but because God, in His grace, gave them faith. ■

See also: Fruits of the Spirit 300 ▪ The Power of the Resurrection 304–05 ▪ Faith and Works 312–13

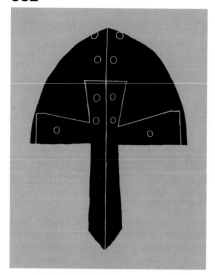

PUT ON THE FULL ARMOR OF GOD

EPHESIANS 6:11, ARMOR OF GOD

IN BRIEF

PASSAGE
Ephesians 6:10–20

THEME
The protection of God

SETTING
c.61–62 CE Ephesus The Ephesian letter was probably written for churches in western Asia Minor, of which the church in Ephesus was the largest and most important.

KEY FIGURES
Author of Ephesians Early Christians believed this to be Paul. Some modern scholars argue that it is more likely to be one of his disciples.

Readers The recipients of the letter were mostly Gentile converts to Christianity.

The author of Ephesians uses fierce military imagery to convey his view that believers face all-out warfare in the fight against evil. It is a struggle populated not with human foes at the earthly level, but with powerful and malevolent supernatural beings—the scheming devil and the hierarchy of "spiritual forces of evil in the heavenly realms" (Ephesians 6:12).

For believers, however, God's power is greater. Drawing on the Old Testament prophet Isaiah, who depicts God putting on

"righteousness as His breastplate, and the helmet of salvation on His head" (Isaiah 59:17), Ephesians describes the "full armor of God" (Ephesians 6:11) that believers, too, can and must adorn to take their stand "against the rulers, against the authorities, against the powers of this dark world" (Ephesians 6:12).

The Ephesian audience
As with all New Testament writings, Ephesians is addressing believers in a particular context. The Ephesians live in a region of Asia Minor whose chief city, Ephesus, is famous for magical practices associated with the goddess Artemis. For them, as for the area's Jewish converts, the world has two dimensions—earthly and heavenly—and the heavenly realm includes fearsome forces of evil as well as of good. Ephesians in no way denies this vision of things—it simply puts this idea into a wider perspective by asserting the supreme power

St. Michael the Archangel dons full armor in his victorious battle against Satan in the book of Revelation. This painting, composed in the early 16th century, is by an unknown artist.

See also: The Nature of Faith 236–41 ▪ The Crucifixion 258–65 ▪ The Road to Emmaus 272–73 ▪ The Power of the Resurrection 304–05 ▪ The Final Judgment 316–21

of God and the authority of the risen Christ seated "at His right hand in the heavenly realms, far above all rule and authority, power, and dominion" (Ephesians 1:20–21).

Standing firm

Just as God's power has raised Christ from the dead, so it has also raised believers from their pagan practices. Even so, Ephesians says, the world and believers are in an interim state. There is a fullness yet to come—a further, definitive stage in history "when the times reach their fulfillment" and unity will be brought to "all things in heaven and on earth under Christ" (Ephesians 1:10).

Until this happens, believers are still vulnerable to the ever-active forces of spiritual evil. For this reason, they need to "be strong in the Lord" (6:10), emphasizing their complete reliance on God when cultivating courage. Believers are instructed to put on the "full armor" of God and stand firm— a command that is repeated in Ephesians three times.

The full armor of God is stated as including truthfulness, righteousness, salvation, peace, and faith. Ultimately, Ephesians is about resisting the assaults of temptation—originating in both the individual's sinful nature and the spiritual forces of evil—and living one's daily life in a truly Christian way by being moral, honorable, and loving. ▪

Stand firm then, with the belt of truth buckled around your waist, with the breastplate of righteousness in place, and with your feet fitted with … peace.
Ephesians 6:14–15

The Armor of God

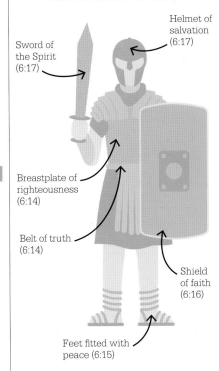

Helmet of salvation (6:17)

Sword of the Spirit (6:17)

Breastplate of righteousness (6:14)

Belt of truth (6:14)

Shield of faith (6:16)

Feet fitted with peace (6:15)

According to Ephesians, the conflict with Satan is a spiritual one. Thus, one requires a full complement of spiritual weapons to use against him and other evils.

Ephesus

Standing on the Aegean coast of Asia Minor (roughly modern Turkey), Ephesus was an intellectual and cultural hub of up to 250,000 people and capital of the Roman province of Asia. The city was also an important religious center renowned for magical practices, mystery cults, and, above all, the worship of Artemis, Greek goddess of woods and hunting and the most venerated deity of Asia Minor. Her temple at Ephesus was one of the seven wonders of the ancient world and the largest Greek temple ever built.

According to the Book of Acts, Paul visited Ephesus twice. He most likely founded the community of Christian believers there on a brief visit during his second missionary journey. Later, during his third mission, Paul spent more than two years in the city before he and his companions were forced to leave—their ministry success triggered a riot among silversmiths, who saw them as a threat to their livelihood, which depended on making devotional offerings to the goddess Artemis.

I WANT TO KNOW CHRIST

PHILIPPIANS 3:10, THE POWER OF THE RESURRECTION

IN BRIEF

PASSAGE
Philippians 3:1–14

THEME
The power of Christ's resurrection

SETTING
c.50 CE Philippi, a Roman colony in Macedonia.

KEY FIGURES
Paul The Apostle, who founded the church in Philippi. According to the letter, he is a prisoner at the time of writing—most likely in Rome.

The Philippians Christians in Philippi, most of whom are Gentile converts.

St. Paul holding the sword of the Spirit. This painting is attributed to the Italian Renaissance artist Macrino d'Alba, 1490–1527.

Paul wrote his letter to the Christians in Philippi while imprisoned, preparing his defense in rebuttal of charges of treason against the Emperor Nero. The charge arose because early Christians affirmed that "Jesus is Lord," refusing Roman oaths of loyalty, because they considered them blasphemous. To their enemies, however, their refusal suggested subversive intent.

A critical part of Paul's defense would have been that loyalty to Jesus did not foster rebellion, but instead produced virtuous citizens. Philippi, a military colony, was mainly populated by retired Roman soldiers or their descendants—an outpost of loyalists with a duty to secure the province of Macedonia. Demonstrating that Christians were exemplary citizens in a city unquestionably loyal to the Empire would persuade the Romans to tolerate the new religion.

Paul seemed to have this in mind when he urged the people to "conduct yourselves"—literally, live out your citizenship—"in a matter worthy of … Christ" (Philippians 1:27). The key to Paul's defense was the moral behavior of the Christians in Philippi. Yet he

See also: The Empty Tomb 268–71 ▪ The Road to Damascus 290–91 ▪ Paul's Arrest 294–95 ▪ Armor of God 302–03

notes that their good character had been threatened by "false teachers," who claimed that righteousness depended on keeping the Mosaic Law of circumcision. Paul was writing to the Christians in Philippi to testify against this belief, and argue that Christians received their righteousness from God.

Alive in Christ

Christians believe they become righteous when faith leads them to experience "the power of [Christ's] resurrection" (3:10). This means the power of God that raised Jesus from the dead similarly transforms the spiritually "dead" (sinners) into "living" saints. Indeed, Paul saw any person's conversion to faith in Jesus as a manifestation of the power of the resurrection.

In a letter to the Colossians, Paul writes that although believers once lived in sin, their sins have been buried, and they have been reborn through Jesus. By coming to know God, they now share in his resurrecting power. In Colossians 3:3–4, for example, Paul writes

"for you died, and your life is now hidden with Christ in God. When Christ, who is your life, appears, then you also will appear with Him in glory."

Paul teaches that the power of the resurrection drives the entire Christian way of living: Jesus's resurrection enables His people thereafter to live new, transformed lives, characterized by obeying God's laws in all that they do. Peter's teaching echoes this idea: "His divine power has given us everything we need for a godly life" (2 Peter 1:3). Even in difficult times, such as those faced by the early Christians, belief in Christ's resurrection would transform the character of the converts to make them exemplary citizens in Philippi—justifying the claim that "Jesus is Lord" (Philippians 2:11).

The final resurrection

Paul concludes that ultimate experience of "the power of His resurrection" will come in the future, at the Second Coming of Christ from heaven—which

> At the name of Jesus every knee [shall] bow … and every tongue acknowledge that Jesus Christ is Lord, to the glory of God the Father.
> **Philippians 2:10–11**

is the true place of Christian citizenship. At that time, the dead will rise, and the living will be brought up to meet Christ in the air, in physical bodies like that of the resurrected Lord. In that moment, Paul writes, the appearance of the resurrected savior will complete the process of eliminating sin and perfecting righteousness in Christians. ▪

An illustration of the preaching of the first missionary Apostles, after a 15th-century Arras tapestry in Tournai Cathedral, Belgium.

Paul's influence on Christianity

Paul molded Christianity more than any other Apostle, paving the way for it to become a major world religion. Although Peter and Philip converted the first Gentiles, it was Paul's tireless missionary journeys that brought the Gospel to thousands across the eastern Roman Empire and finally in Rome itself. Crucial in this quest was Paul's insistence, against considerable opposition, that all believers—Gentile and Jewish—had equal status and that Gentile converts should not be made to submit to the rite of circumcision and Jewish dietary laws. This helped Christianity to spread throughout the Greek and Roman worlds, rather than merely remaining the faith of a small Jewish sect.

Paul's other legacy was his letters. Thirteen of the 27 books of the New Testament are attributed to him. These letters elaborate much of the New Testament's theology and, for Christians, act as a guide for the application of its teaching in a practical context.

AND HE IS THE HEAD OF THE BODY, THE CHURCH
COLOSSIANS 1:18, THE BODY OF CHRIST

IN BRIEF

PASSAGES
**Colossians 1:15–23,
1 Corinthians 12:12–31,
Ephesians 4:1–16**

THEME
**The body of Christ as
a metaphor for the
Christian Church**

SETTING
c.54 CE Letters written to
the churches of Asia Minor
by Paul and his disciples.

KEY FIGURES
Paul An Apostle of Christ,
writing to the churches in
Corinth and Asia Minor.

Author of Colossians Early
Christians believed this to be
Paul. Some modern scholars
argue that it is more likely to
have been one of his disciples.

The image of the community of believers as a discrete entity unfolds and develops in the Pauline writings of the New Testament. It was by no means a new idea. The concept of the "body politic"—an understanding of a nation of peoples as one body—was commonplace among Greek and Roman philosophers. Plato had used it, as had Aristotle, Cicero, Seneca, and many others.

For his part, Paul takes hold of the idea and begins to develop it in earnest in his first letter to the Corinthians. Writing to the fractious people and chastising them, Paul employs the image to press home a message about unity despite diversity. "Just as a body, though one, has many parts … all its many parts form one body," he tells his readers. Then, he continues: "So it is with Christ" (1 Corinthians 12:12).

A united body

Despite coming from diverse backgrounds, the Corinthian believers must remember the basic unity they have through God's Spirit. "For we were all baptized by one Spirit so as to form one body—whether Jews or Gentiles, slave or free—and we were all given the one Spirit to drink" (12:13).

Continuing with the image of the body, Paul reminds the different cliques among the Corinthians of their inescapable need for one another: "The eye cannot say to the hand, 'I don't need you!' And the head cannot say to the feet, 'I don't need you!'" (12:21).

St. Ignatius, painted in oils by Giuseppe Franchi (1565–1628), was an early Christian writer and Bishop of Antioch. He was the first to employ the term "Catholic Church" in writing.

See also: The Word Spreads 288–89 ▪ The Way of Love 296–97 ▪ The Holy Trinity 298–99 ▪
The Power of the Resurrection 304–05

Pope Francis, the 266th head of the Roman Catholic Church, rides through the crowds of the faithful in September 2015, as he attends mass at the Vatican.

Nor is there any room for one group of members to regard itself as better than the others: "God has put the body together, giving greater honor to the parts that lacked it, so that there should be no division in the body, but that its parts should have equal concern for each other" (12:24–25).

In several letters, Paul refers to certain "gifts," such as wisdom or faith, that Christians receive by believing in Jesus. The analogy of the body as a united entity is a way of ensuring that none of these gifts is viewed as superior to others. If more visible "gifts" are held in too great esteem, they will promote pride, with one exception—love—as there is no greater gift that one can possess or give in return. Paul ends his exhortation with a simple metaphor: "Now you are the body of Christ, and each one of you is a part of it" (12:27).

Instead, speaking the truth in love, we will grow to become in every respect the mature body of Him who is the head, that is, Christ.
Ephesians 4:15

This is the first mention of "the body of Christ" in the Bible and, in 1 Corinthians, the concept has a relatively narrow focus. It is about living out the Christian message of love and service in the context of a local place of worship.

Developing the image

Two later writings of the New Testament—the letters to the Colossians and the Ephesians— are regarded by some scholars as the work of two of Paul's disciples, and add to the image of the united body. Jesus Christ "is before all things, and in Him all things hold together" (Colossians 1:17).

The author of Ephesians expounds on this idea: "We will grow to become in every respect the mature body of Him who is the head, that is, Christ. From Him the whole body, joined and held together by every supporting ligament, grows and builds itself up in love, as each part does its work" (Ephesians 4:15–16). This vivid depiction presents the body of Christ as a living, breathing organism. Built on love, the body of Christ depends and thrives on the faith of its members. ▪

The concept of the Church

In Greek, the word *ekklesia*, usually translated in the New Testament as "church," simply refers to an assembly called together for, say, a political purpose. The Greek version of the Hebrew Bible, the Septuagint, uses the term in this sense to describe various assemblies of the people of Israel. It is later—in Acts and the Pauline writings, above all—that the word starts to acquire the meaning of "church" as we know it today.

Generally, in the Pauline writings, the term refers to an assembly of believers in a particular city or region— as when Paul refers to the Galatians, for example, as the "churches in Galatia." In the later New Testament books of Colossians and Ephesians, the use of the term "church" (*ekklesia*) further develops the more transcendent meaning of the body of all believers, united as the body of Christ and the Holy Spirit.

SCRIPTURE IS GOD-BREATHED

2 TIMOTHY 3:16, THE BIBLE AS GOD'S WORD

IN BRIEF

PASSAGE
2 Timothy 3:14–17

THEME
Authorship of scripture

SETTING
c.64–67 CE Letter written by Paul in Rome.

KEY FIGURES
Paul The Apostle, who is imprisoned in Rome awaiting trial. He writes letters to various churches and disciples, including Timothy.

Timothy A disciple and former representative of the Apostle Paul. Timothy serves as the pastor of the church Paul founded in Ephesus.

Jesus The Messiah and Son of God, whose proclamations are divine. Jesus's teaching highlighted the divine authority of scripture.

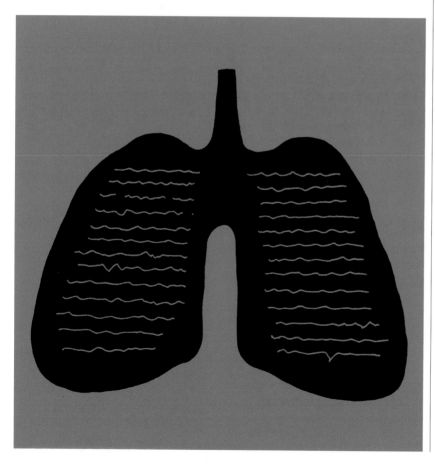

Near the end of his life, Paul was imprisoned in Rome, awaiting trial before the emperor for charges related to his faith. During this time, the Apostle wrote several letters to colleagues and friends, including to his young disciple, Timothy. He had become a trusted aide to Paul as the two men traveled to Greek cities on both sides of the Aegean Sea.

In his second letter to Timothy, Paul encouraged him to deal with false teachers and remain committed to what he had been taught. As a child, Timothy's mother and grandmother had taught him the Hebrew scriptures,

> [Scripture] is useful for teaching … and training in righteousness, so that the servant of God may be thoroughly equipped.
> **2 Timothy 3:16**

which had prepared him to hear and understand Paul's message that Jesus was the fulfillment of the Old Testament prophecies of a messiah who would redeem God's chosen people.

These scriptures, Paul wrote, were "God-breathed" (2 Timothy 3:16). This phrase indicates that Paul himself understood the Hebrew scriptures to be God's Word. It is little surprise that Paul,

Illustrated manuscripts of the Bible, such as this page from the Book of Kells, an Irish manuscript of the Gospels from c.800, both glorified God's word and aided understanding.

who had been trained among the Pharisees as a rabbi, would see the Old Testament as coming directly from the Lord. Since Moses, the prophets had introduced their pronouncements with the phrase, "This is what the Lord says …" more than 400 times, while "the word of the Lord came" appears 245 times in the Bible.

Prophecies of old

At roughly the same time as Paul, the Apostle Peter writes that the prophets of the Old Testament never came by their prophecies based on their own interpretations: "For prophecy never had its origin in the human will, but prophets, though human, spoke from God as they were carried along by the Holy Spirit" (2 Peter 1:21). These writings were not considered to be the prophets' personal opinions about what was happing or what they wanted to see happen in the future. The prophets were mere agents; they spoke from God, and they had as much control over the content of their writings as sailors on a small boat in a storm. God's Spirit was the wind that carried them along and determined their course.

Jesus speaks in ways similar to the Old Testament prophets, but with a unique development. Like the prophets, Jesus says that He speaks from God (John 12:49). Unlike the prophets, however, Jesus does not preface His sermons with "This is what God says." Instead, »

Timothy

Timothy was a colleague of the Apostle Paul during several of Paul's missionary journeys and his imprisonment in Rome. The son of a Jewish-Christian mother and a Greek father, Timothy had been taught the Hebrew scriptures (the Old Testament) from an early age. Paul used Timothy as either a coauthor or the recording secretary for his letters to the Philippians, Colossians, and to Philemon. During Paul's life, Timothy served as his representative to churches in Thessalonica, Corinth, and Philippi, before he eventually took up the role of pastor in Ephesus. Paul wrote two letters directly to Timothy in Ephesus; these became the books of 1 and 2 Timothy. The latter, written from prison in the last days of his life, is considered to have been Paul's spiritual last will and testament.

One Christian author in the eighth century claimed Timothy was present with Mary, the mother of Jesus, at the end of her life. According to *Foxe's Book of Martyrs*, Timothy was beaten to death by a mob in Ephesus in 97 CE.

The Bible in its entirety has been translated into 363 languages, and the New Testament into 1,442. These pilgrims in Lalibela, Ethiopia, hear the word of God in their native Amharic.

Apocrypha

The apocryphal books are an additional set of writings associated with the Old Testament. Mostly written in Greek, all were completed between 300–100 BCE, and came into use by Christians due to their inclusion in some Greek translations of the Old Testament (the Septuagint).

While many early Christian bishops did not accept the apocryphal books, recognition of them grew among Roman Catholic bishops in the late Middle Ages. They were formally adopted as scripture by the Council of Trent in 1546. Of the 18 apocryphal texts, Roman Catholics accept seven as scripture, plus the expanded versions of the books of Daniel and Esther. They can be found in the Old Testament of the Roman Catholic Bible.

He prefaces His pronouncements with "I tell you," and uses this phrase nearly 140 times throughout the Bible. Paul indicates that he sees Jesus's teachings as the Word of God when he introduces a combined quote of Deuteronomy and Jesus with the words, "Scripture says …" Interestingly, this expanded understanding of the divinity of scripture also encompasses the writings of Paul himself. Peter says that Paul writes with God-given wisdom and warns that false teachers will attempt to distort Paul's writings, "as they do the other Scriptures" (2 Peter 3:16).

Dual authorship

The Bible's words on its divine origin stand alongside clear acknowledgment of its human authorship. Jesus attributes the Pentateuch of the Old Testament to Moses. The Psalms are attributed to King David, while David's son, Solomon, is identified as the author of many of the

proverbs. The prophetic books of the Old Testament (from Isaiah to Malachi) identify human authors, as do each of the New Testament epistles, except for the mysterious Epistle to the Hebrews.

The human authors of the Bible each display vast differences in background, language, and style, as well as geographical, cultural, and historical location. They wrote in ancient Hebrew, Aramaic, and the common Greek spoken in the first century CE. Some authors were highly educated (for example, Moses, Isaiah, and Paul), while others were farmers and fishermen (Amos and Peter), producing a wide variety of literary genres ranging from narratives and histories to genealogical records. Other biblical writings take the form of poetry, proverb, and apocalyptic vision.

The concept of dual authorship addresses the question of how to reconcile the interaction between divine and human in the scriptures. The Bible depicts authors as recording messages that they had

Prophets, though human, spoke from God as they were carried along by the Holy Spirit.
2 Peter 1:21

God's role in producing the scriptures is interpreted in three major ways.

The theory of **Limited Inspiration** argues God **guided** the authors of the Bible but did not preserve them from making **errors**.

The theory of **Verbal Plenary Inspiration** maintains that every word of the Bible has been directly **"God-breathed"** and preserved by God (2 Timothy 3:16).

Neo-orthodoxy teaches that the Bible was written by fallible humans and only **becomes** the word of God when He reveals Himself through it.

been given by God; describing visions; explaining and applying already-written scripture; and even conducting investigations before making a written account of the findings (Luke 1:3). For the most part, the Bible describes no fixed process by which the authors were "moved by God," but Peter teaches that the writing process was superintended by God, so what they wrote was God's word.

Divine authority

The belief that the scriptures were God's own words carried several significant implications in the minds of biblical figures. One was the total trust of, and belief in, scripture. The truthfulness of God's word therefore became a proverb: "Every word of God is flawless" (Proverbs 30:5).

Divine authorship implies divine authority. To disregard the message of the prophets was to disbelieve or disobey God. Even the writings of the Apostles were to be treated as God's commandments. When tempted by Satan, Jesus quoted scripture to rebut him. Jesus also appealed to scripture to answer

the challenges of the religious leaders of His day. This pattern of appeal to, and explanation of, Old Testament scripture was followed by the authors of the New Testament. Old Testament quotations or allusions are present in 26 of the 27 books of the New Testament—absent only in the Book of Philemon—making up about a third of its content.

For Paul, the divine authorship of the Bible is closely linked to its transformative power. The Apostle reminds Timothy that the "God-breathed" nature of the Bible makes it a fit instrument for addressing issues of faith and behavior, writing that the scriptures "make you wise for salvation through faith" (2 Timothy 3:15). Paul teaches that the faith that unites people to Christ comes by hearing the word of God. Delivering "what the Lord says," the prophet Isaiah wrote, "My word that goes out from my mouth, will not return to me empty, but will … achieve the purpose for which I sent it" (Isaiah 55:11).

The concept of the divinity of scripture has also influenced which writings are included in the

Bible by different Christian groups. Jews believed that divine prophecy, the basis for the scriptures, had ceased by 400 BCE, and Jesus Himself only acknowledged "the Law and the Prophets" of the Hebrew Old Testament as Israel's scripture. In spite of this, some Christians, such as those in the Eastern Orthodox Church, accept the so-called "apocryphal books," written centuries later—including Ecclesiasticus (also known as Sirach), 1 and 2 Maccabees, and Judith—as scripture. ∎

England has two books; the Bible and Shakespeare. England made Shakespeare, but the Bible made England.
Victor Hugo

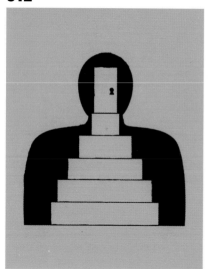

KNOW THAT THE TESTING OF YOUR FAITH PRODUCES PERSEVERANCE

JAMES 1:3, FAITH AND WORKS

The Epistle of James is addressed to Jewish Christians scattered across the Roman Empire. This one letter, written in Greek, takes the form of a series of miniature sermons.

James begins with a reflection on how God tests faith in order to refine it (1:2–12), and later returns to the subject of faith in relation to good works (2:14–26). Good deeds, especially obedience to the Law of Moses, were part of the first Christians' Jewish heritage. The Gospel message of salvation through faith in Jesus, however, made the relationship between faith and the good deeds that demonstrate faith a pressing question for Jewish believers.

Even demons believe

James rejects faith that is passive, asking, "Can such faith save them?" (James 2:14). He goes on to describe his opponents who claim that faith in Jesus relieves believers of the duty to live in a righteous way. These false teachers attempt to prove their faith simply by affirming the Shema, "the Lord is One," the statement of monotheism central to Old Testament teaching. Dismissing this less than adequate show of faith, James says, "Even the demons believe that—and shudder!" He goes on to cite Abraham as the paradigm of living, active faith. When God promises Abraham a son, he says, Abraham "believed the Lord, and He credited it to him as righteousness" (Genesis 15:6).

Adherence to the Torah, the Law of Moses, was seen by James as an important aspect of faith. Other church fathers, such as Paul, believed that faith alone was the key to salvation.

See also: Entering the Promised Land 96–97 ▪ The Nature of Faith 236–41 ▪
Salvation Through Faith 301

Later, when God commanded Abraham to sacrifice his son, Isaac (Genesis 22), Abraham placed him on an altar, believing that God could bring his son back to life (Hebrews 11:19). For James, that obedience fulfills the claim that God had reckoned Abraham righteous. James then cites Rahab, a Jericho prostitute, who showed the same kind of faith when she sheltered two Israelite spies (Joshua 2). Both Abraham and Rahab demonstrated and grew their faith through honoring God with their actions under difficult circumstances.

The faith that saves

The conclusion that people are justified—worthy of salvation—by their works, or actions, seems to contradict Paul's views. When false teachers in Galatia taught Christians that obedience to the Law of Moses is an essential addition to faith in Jesus, Paul insisted that such works cannot justify (Galatians 2:16). The apparent conflict arises because the two authors use the word "justify" differently. While James sees works as the visible evidence of faith, Paul speaks of justification as righteousness before God. Paul and James agree that the faith that saves is active, not passive. In Romans, Paul writes of "the obedience of faith" and he reminds the Galatians that what matters is "faith working through love."

The relationship between faith and works is a key point of debate between Roman Catholics and Protestants. Catholics see works as a necessary addition to faith. Protestants see them as the result of genuine faith, and therefore affirm that salvation is *sola fide* (by faith alone). ▪

Rahab demonstrates faith through action by helping two Israelite spies escape the clutches of her fellow Canaanites, in an image from a 12th-century French manuscript.

James the Just

There were several figures in the New Testament who bore the name "James." Two were disciples of Jesus, but the third was one of Jesus's four brothers, later known as James the Just. This James did not believe in Jesus as the Messiah during His lifetime, but came to have faith in Jesus after the resurrection, possibly because the risen Christ appeared to him in person (1 Corinthians 15:7).

There is debate about which James wrote the New Testament Epistle of James, although the most likely author is James the Just. Tradition holds that James was martyred in Jerusalem for his faith in Jesus.

James came to be called "the Just" (meaning "the righteous") because of his fidelity to the Law of Moses. Although he voiced the consensus of the Council of Jerusalem (Acts 15), which recognized that Gentiles did not need to observe the Law of Moses—specifically circumcision—to become Christians, he did believe that they should adhere to other Jewish practices.

JUST AS HE WHO CALLED YOU IS HOLY, SO BE HOLY IN ALL YOU DO

1 PETER 1:15, HOLINESS

IN BRIEF

PASSAGE
1 Peter 1:3–2:25

THEME
Holiness

SETTING
c.60–65 CE 1 Peter is addressed to believers scattered throughout Roman provinces in northwestern Asia Minor.

KEY FIGURES
Peter Although the letter is written in the name of the Apostle Peter, scholars are divided about whether or not he was the actual author.

The readers The recipients of the letter are mostly Gentile Christians experiencing persecution because of their faith.

In his letter to Christians scattered throughout Asia Minor (modern Turkey), Peter praises God for the salvation secured by Christ's resurrection. Although his audience is facing various troubles, Peter is confident of God's purpose in allowing their suffering, and of their future joy.

For the New Testament, salvation through faith in Jesus is not merely a release from the eternal consequences of sin. Salvation also liberates believers from sin's tyranny in their daily lives. One of God's primary tools for accomplishing this, Peter says, is suffering. In Peter 1:7, he uses imagery suggesting that God is

I am the Lord your God; consecrate yourselves and be holy because I am holy.
Leviticus 11:44

like a goldsmith, working on the precious metal of the believer's faith. The divine smith heats it so that impurities rise and can be skimmed off, until the smith can see His reflection without blemish in the purified gold. Enduring troubles righteously serves to refine the believer's faith and bring their character into conformity with God's holiness.

Divine holiness

Holiness is the most frequently mentioned attribute of God in the Bible. At its core, "holy" indicates separation. For God, holiness refers to His transcendence over all created things and to His alienation from unrighteousness and sin. These qualities are reflected in the description of things, places, and even people as "holy" in the Old Testament. Such things could be called "holy" insofar as they were separated from common use for the service of God, and as they were preserved from contamination by sin or ritual impurity. Israel was to be "a holy nation" (Exodus 19:6), and the construction of a "Holy of Holies" in the Tabernacle and Temple set that area apart as a place for God's presence.

Just as you used to offer yourselves as slaves to impurity and to … wickedness, so now offer yourselves as slaves to righteousness leading to holiness.
Romans 6:19

The holiness of God, and its representation in ritual aspects of the Mosaic Laws of piety, highlights a central tension in the biblical narrative: how sinful humanity can come into the presence of God when God's holiness separates Him from sin. The Bible tells how only the High Priest could enter the Holy of Holies, and then only once a year after ritual cleansing. Those who entered unworthily would be struck down by the holiness of God. Laws concerning ritual uncleanliness illustrated the separation of unclean people from God and others; they could not worship in the Temple, nor could they enjoy human contact without spreading uncleanliness.

Cleansing sinners

Although Jesus claimed to be the Final Judge, who would condemn unrepentant sinners to hell, He demonstrated that holiness did not make God unloving or unmerciful. Through His miraculous healings of, and fellowship with, sinners—those who did not comply with Mosaic Law—He welcomed sinners into God's kingdom. Rather than approving their sins, He cleansed them. Those He healed became fit to worship God under Mosaic Law.

The Apostles taught that after His death, Jesus sent the Holy Spirit to remove sin and "sanctify" sinners (make them holy). Believers, they said, were already holy in the sense of being set apart by God

In Revelation 12, a star-crowned woman represents the Church born through Christ. Edward Robert Hughes draws on this symbolism in his painting *Star of Heaven*.

and called "saints" (holy ones). Yet, Peter says, believers should also demonstrate holiness through their character and deeds. That way, their persecutors could level no legitimate charge against them. ▪

The ritual washing of feet on Maundy Thursday replicates Jesus washing the disciples' feet at the Last Supper. It is an act of humility.

Key rituals of the Church

Worship in the early Church focused on two key rituals. The first was baptism, which initiated new believers and brought them together spiritually, bound by the symbolic purification and holiness of following Jesus. The other was a meal, the Lord's Supper, celebrated during weekly gatherings of believers, which involved the ritual sharing of bread and wine. A forerunner of the Eucharist, this ceremonial meal recalled Jesus's "last supper" with His disciples before His crucifixion and symbolized the believers' holy unity with Jesus and each other in the "body of Christ." It also was the setting for Church discipline, preserving the holiness of the Church by removing those who persisted in sin. Restoration and readmittance to the fellowship of the table was accomplished through repentance. For early Christians, the Lord's Supper anticipated the banquet that awaited them in heaven at the end of time.

THE DEAD WERE JUDGED ACCORDING TO WHAT THEY HAD DONE

REVELATION 20:12, THE FINAL JUDGMENT

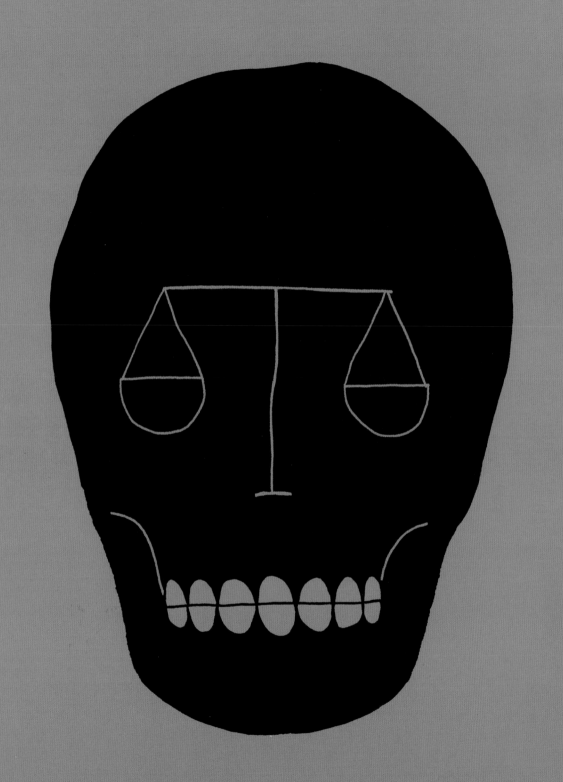

IN BRIEF

PASSAGE
Revelation 1:1–20:15

THEME
Justice for all

SETTING
God's heavenly throne room. An unspecified future time.

KEY FIGURES
Jesus The key figure in the Final Judgment, described alternately as "the Son of Man," "the lamb on the throne," and "the First and the Last."

All humanity All people, who ever lived, from all nations and all times.

John the Seer The author of Revelation, who sees the events described in a vision.

The Greek word used in the book of Revelation for judgment originally meant "to sift," and from there it came to mean choosing right from wrong. It essentially means that each human life will be examined according to God's standards and sorted into what is acceptable and what is not. However, unlike today's conception of judgment, which calls for justice here and now, in the first century CE people believed in an impending judgment. For many in the Greek and Roman worlds, this was at the end of their earthly life, at the point of death. Christians, however, building on Jewish beliefs, looked toward a future, Final Judgment in which all people of all places and times would need to give an account of their lives before God.

In the Old Testament, this future judgment is called "the Day of the Lord." In one of the prophet Daniel's visions, he sees a picture of God's throne room, where God sits ready to judge the world. Many beasts try to establish their rule over the world, but then, at the

> Therefore keep watch, because you do not know on what day your Lord will come.
> **Matthew 24:42**

climax of the vision, Daniel sees "one like a Son of Man"—a clear reference to the name Jesus takes throughout His ministry—approach God's throne. God then gives Jesus the authority and power to bring the Final Judgment to the world.

Royal return

At Jesus's ascension, the Apostles were told that "this same Jesus … will come back in the same way you have seen him go into heaven" (Acts 1:11), which is thought to mean that Jesus will return bodily on earth one day. The image of a king arriving to bring judgment was familiar in the Roman world, where an emperor occasionally visited key cities to hold court— he would punish his enemies and reward his friends. The Greek word for this is *parousia*, which means "coming," and early Christians understood Jesus's return as the coming of God's appointed king.

Jesus says that the criteria for the Final Judgment will henceforth be whether people trust Him as

The Whore of Babylon is introduced in Revelation 17 riding a beast with seven heads. An angel tells John that the heads represent the sinners Christ will defeat in the battle at Armageddon.

Beliefs matching John's visions in Revelation

	Judaism	Christianity	Islam
A day of judgment	✗	✓	✓
Resurrection of the dead	✓	✓	✓
Separation of the righteous and the wicked	✓	✓	✓
Book of Life	✓	✓	✗
Book of Deeds	✗	✓	✓
New Jerusalem	✓	✓	✗

John the Seer

The author of Revelation identifies himself as Jesus's "servant John" (Revelation 1:1). Since the second century, it has been suggested that this John is the same as Jesus's disciple John, brother of James and author of the Gospel and three epistles that bear his name. However, even from the third century CE, Bible scholars have argued that there is such a difference in style between Revelation and the other writings that it is unlikely they could have come from the same author.

Whoever he was, this "servant John" wrote down his visions toward the end of the first century CE while on the island of Patmos, off the coast of present-day Turkey. John writes that he is on the island "because of the word of God and the testimony of Jesus"; scholars therefore believe that he was living in exile, and see this as further proof that authorities were already starting to persecute Christians as troublemakers.

a savior: "If anyone is ashamed of me and my words … the Son of Man will be ashamed of him when He comes in His Father's glory with the holy angels" (Mark 8:38).

Many of Jesus's parables speak about a coming Final Judgment. He explains in one parable that the weeds will be burned by fire, while the good crop will be harvested into God's barn. Whereas the crops and the weeds grow side by side in the present, one day each will become distinct when Jesus makes His judgment (Matthew 13:24–30). In another parable, Jesus speaks of His role in the coming Final Judgment as being like that of a shepherd separating sheep from goats (Matthew 25:31–46).

Signs and symbols

John's visions, recounted in the book of Revelation, paint a dramatic picture of the Final Judgment. They begin in the throne room of heaven, where all the heavenly creatures are preparing for the scroll containing God's final order for the world to be opened. At first, the creatures cannot find anyone who is worthy to open the seven seals that keep the scroll rolled. Then, however, John sees a lamb that looks like it has been sacrificed, standing alive on the throne: a clear reference to Jesus. As this lamb takes the scroll, all of heaven sings with joy, "You are worthy to take the scroll and to open its seals" (Revelation 5:9).

Out of the first four seals ride the "horsemen of the apocalypse," one of Revelation's most enduring »

He will judge the world … by the man He has appointed. He has given proof … by raising [Jesus] from the dead.
Acts 17:31

images. The riders are atop a white horse, a red horse, a black horse, and a pale horse, representing conquest, war, famine, and death (6:1–8). The four horsemen are traditionally viewed as harbingers of the imminent Final Judgment.

Evil destroyed

The events described after this are complex—John's intention does not seem to be to describe his visions in a logical order, but rather to remind Christians of the finality of the approaching judgment.

Revelation 6–18 cover a series of vignettes in which John witnesses different symbolic judgments. One of the most well-known scenes in John's account is the Battle of Armageddon, "the Day of the Lord." The word "Armageddon" is used

> You know very well that the day of the Lord will come like a thief in the night.
> **1 Thessalonians 5:2**

only once in the Bible, and it is thought to come from the word *har*, meaning mountain, and *Megiddo*. Mount Megiddo was the site of Old Testament battles, such as Deborah and Barak's victory against the Canaanites. Whether this location

is intended to be literal or symbolic, it ties the final battle of humanity to early wars fought by the Israelites.

In the final battle, all the "kings of the whole world" (Revelation 16:14) gather at Armageddon. They are influenced by Satan, and bring their armies to fight with God for control of the earth. God, on the other hand, calls on Jesus to return. There, the Son of God strikes back at those willing to go to war with Him. John describes how "Coming out of His mouth is a sharp sword with which to strike down the nations" (Revelation 19:15); Jesus thus destroys the evil enemies of God, leaving only good behind. With evil vanquished, God appoints Jesus to replace existing systems of governance and rule over the newly established Kingdom of God.

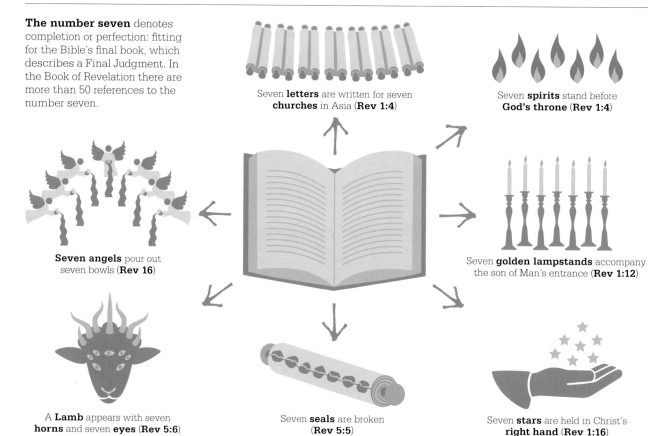

The number seven denotes completion or perfection: fitting for the Bible's final book, which describes a Final Judgment. In the Book of Revelation there are more than 50 references to the number seven.

Seven **letters** are written for seven **churches** in Asia (**Rev 1:4**)

Seven **spirits** stand before **God's throne** (**Rev 1:4**)

Seven **angels** pour out seven bowls (**Rev 16**)

Seven **golden lampstands** accompany the son of Man's entrance (**Rev 1:12**)

A **Lamb** appears with seven **horns** and seven **eyes** (**Rev 5:6**)

Seven **seals** are broken (**Rev 5:5**)

Seven **stars** are held in Christ's **right hand** (**Rev 1:16**)

This sets the scene for the Final Judgment itself. As the climax of John's vision draws near, in Revelation 19–20, he sees a great white throne, in front of which is a vast crowd of all of the people who have ever lived. Jesus then opens the "book of life," and every person is judged "according to what they [have] done" (20:12). Those whose names are in the book of life are welcomed into God's new creation; those whose names are absent are thrown into a lake of fire, the final hell, where "death and Hades" (the underground world of the dead) are also thrown (20:14–15).

Humanity on trial

The Final Judgment is a crucial motivation for the holiness and mission of Christians. Although Christians are assured that they will be considered acceptable by God on the "Day of the Lord" simply because of their trust in Jesus—this is called "justification," meaning that they are judged to be righteous because Jesus has

The Angel of Revelation, painted by William Blake between 1803–05, shows St. John on the island of Patmos gazing up at a mighty angel "robed in a cloud," as described in Revelation 10:1.

died for their sins and has cleaned their record before God—they will still be exposed to God's judgment of their deeds. Paul writes that on "the day" fire will test each person's "foundation," which will reveal its quality, whether it was made from "gold, silver, costly stones, wood, hay, or straw." When this fire comes, if "what he has built survives," Paul writes, "he will receive his reward" (1 Corinthians 3:12–14). Paul thus teaches that some will pass through judgment with nothing, while others will be rewarded for their faithful lives.

This impending judgment also promotes urgency in the missionary task. Jesus tells His disciples to be ready: His *parousia* may occur at any moment (Mark 13:33). As Peter says, "the Day of the Lord will come like a thief" (2 Peter 3:10). Because of this, Jesus's great commission to His disciples is all the more urgent. God does not want anyone to go to hell, but wants all to have the chance of eternal salvation. ◼

God is just: He will pay back trouble to those who trouble you and give relief to you who are troubled.
2 Thessalonians 1:6-7

Revelation as a letter to early Christians

The book of Revelation was written to a number of early Christian congregations who were facing the threat of persecution. Although seven churches are mentioned in the early chapters—those in Ephesus, Smyrna, Pergamum, Thyatira, Sardis, Philadelphia, and Laodicea—the book of Revelation became important in encouraging all Christians.

The language of the book relies heavily on symbolism, and the recurring mentions of "Babylon," Israel's ancient enemy, are a veiled reference to the Roman Empire, which was putting increasing pressure on early Christians, because of their refusal to worship the emperor. Through its colorful language and dramatic visions, the Book of Revelation is a pastoral letter that seeks to encourage Christians to keep faith in the face of persecution, for regardless of the horrors of history, the risen Jesus remains the world's ultimate King, and faith in Him as savior and Lord is the sole criteria for salvation from eternal condemnation at the Final Judgment.

The seven churches are guarded by God's angels. At the start of Revelation, Jesus appears to John and instructs him to write to them recounting the coming vision.

THERE WILL BE NO MORE DEATH OR MOURNING

REVELATION 21:4, THE NEW JERUSALEM

IN BRIEF

PASSAGE
Revelation 21–22

THEME
Eschatology (the end of all things)

SETTING
Future time Heaven and Earth.

KEY FIGURES
Jesus At the center of the vision, God's chosen King rules with peace from the New Jerusalem.

The saints God's people who are welcomed to the marriage feast of heaven and Earth.

John of Patmos The narrator of Revelation (sometimes identified as Jesus's disciple John), who received the vision described while in exile on the island of Patmos.

In the final pages of the Bible, the story of God and the world, which began with the first words of Genesis, concludes with an extraordinary vision of a glorious city where God reigns supreme. Despite recording many human failings and frequent rebellions against God, in its last chapters the Bible returns to the universal subject matter with which it began: the creation of perfection. Heaven

New Jerusalem is depicted in a fresco from the Rila Monastery in Bulgaria. It was painted in the 1840s after reconstruction of the ancient building following a devastating fire.

and Earth are renewed and the stage is set for God to manifest His loving relationship with the people He has made and saved.

John receives his vision of "a new heaven and a new Earth" after the judgment of the dead and the banishment to the lake of fire of those whose evil deeds and unbelief made them unworthy of inclusion in the Book of Life (Revelation 20:12–15). We are told that "the first Heaven and the first Earth had passed away" (21:1). The heavens and elements having been destroyed by fire, the way is cleared for God's new creative work.

John adds a specific detail to this passing: "and there was no longer any sea." For the Israelites, the sea was always a symbol of chaos and danger. During the Exodus, for example, the sea stood between them and safety

Apocalyptic language

The Book of Revelation is one of a number of biblical passages that can be categorized as "apocalyptic." The term comes from the Greek *apokaluptó* ("to uncover"). Apocalyptic literature foretells cataclysmic events that will occur when the world ends; sometimes, as in the book of Daniel, apocalyptic symbols such as supernatural beasts represent contemporary persecutors. Such literature also typically presents a fantastical picture of God's throne room

and those who serve in heaven. Trying to evoke what cannot be put into words, apocalyptic language uses vivid imagery and driving narrative to tell the story of God's ultimate triumph. Although such language may be difficult to understand, clues link certain passages to their historical context. For instance, "Babylon" here is understood to refer to the Roman Empire. Christians through the ages have reinterpreted this language to proclaim the victory of God's Kingdom and the expectation of God's City of Peace.

Characteristics of New Jerusalem

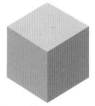

It shines with the brilliance of a very precious **jewel**, "clear as crystal," which reflects the glory of God.

It has **12 gates** inscribed with "the names of the 12 tribes of Israel," indicating the restored Israel.

The city is a **perfect cube**, "12,000 stadia in length, and as wide and high," with room for all of God's people.

Its **walls** are 144 cubits **thick** and "made of jasper," sturdy enough to exclude the wicked.

There is **no temple**, because **God and the Lamb** (Jesus) live among His people. Heaven has come to earth.

There is **no sun or moon**, "for the glory of God gives it **light**, and the Lamb is its **lamp**."

from Pharaoh, and in the New Testament, Jesus calms "a furious storm" that terrifies His disciples as they sail on the Sea of Galilee (Matthew 8:23–27). In John's vision, all that threatens the life of God's people has been banished from the new creation.

The new City of Peace

John then sees "the Holy City, the New Jerusalem, coming down out of heaven from God" (Revelation 21:2). Jerusalem, which means "City of Peace," had been a focus of life for the Israelites since it became King David's capital city. Despite its name, it had also been a place of conflict from David's time onward. Human efforts to bring about lasting peace had always dissolved into strife. Following the violent warfare of the previous

chapters of Revelation, John now sees a City of Peace, prepared by God Himself, being established on Earth. This signals the fulfillment of repeated promises throughout the Bible that one day God will end all world conflicts by asserting His peaceful rule. God's chosen King, now known to be His Son Jesus, is the "Prince of Peace" and "Of the greatness of His government and peace there will be no end. He will reign on David's throne and over His kingdom … from that time on and forever" (Isaiah 9:6–7).

God with His people

The arrival of God's home on Earth also satisfies the pledge that He had made to His people long ago, when He said, "I will take you as my own people, and I will be your God" (Exodus 6:7). There have been

moments throughout the Bible when this promise has seemed in doubt, when God's people have strayed from His path, and when God has seemed distant and even hidden while His people suffer. But now, God is at home among His people, sharing the same space, »

See, I will create new Heavens and a new Earth.
Isaiah 65:17

The prophet Abraham (center) sits with other biblical figures in the New Jerusalem sculpted above the western entrance to the Abbey Church of Saint Foy in Conques, France.

and all the suffering of the past is wiped away. "There will be no more death or mourning or crying or pain, for the old order of things has passed away" (Revelation 21:4). John hears a loud voice from God's throne announcing, "I am making everything new!" (21:5).

The shining city

John now gets a further glimpse of the New Jerusalem, as one of God's angels takes him around the city, which shines with the glory of God. Jerusalem's outer wall is made of jasper, a precious stone that is usually opaque, but here it is transparent; light passes through the wall, revealing what is within the city. Everything is exquisite: the enormous city gates are each made of a single pearl, and the city's great street is pure gold.

In the Bible, the number 12, often symbolizing perfection, signifies the completeness of the nation of Israel. The walls around the New Jerusalem have 12 gates—three on each of its four sides—and an angel standing by every gate. The gates bear the names of the 12 tribes of Israel,

reassuring John that none of God's faithful people will be excluded. The wall has 12 foundations, inscribed with the names of the 12 apostles, and decorated with 12 kinds of precious stone. When the angel measures the city, its length, breadth, and height are each 12,000 stadia (1,400 miles/2,200km) and the walls are 144 cubits (about 200 ft/65 meters) thick.

Most striking of all, John notices that the Temple is missing from the New Jerusalem. The Temple had

For the Lord Himself will come down from Heaven, with a loud command … and with the trumpet call of God, and the dead in Christ will rise first.
1 Thessalonians 4:16

been the greatest building in the Old Jerusalem, being the focus of Jewish worship and the meeting point between heaven and Earth. Now, no such meeting point is needed, because God Himself lives in the city—heaven has come to Earth. The light of God's presence shines from the city into the whole world, and all the people from every nation whose names are in the Book of Life stream through the gates, guided by God's light, to bring their worship and devotion into God's presence.

A vision to be shared

The angel brings John into the city, where he sees a mighty river flowing from God's throne down the golden street. The Tree of Life, last seen in the Garden of Eden, is growing on the banks of the river. It is so large that it straddles both sides of the river, and so fruitful that it bears a significant 12 crops every year. Its leaves bring healing to the nations and finally do away with the pain and suffering that have marred humanity's existence since Creation (22:1–3). God's people joyfully serve Him here, and their new life goes on forever.

After receiving the dazzling vision of God's promised future, John is so overwhelmed that he falls down at the feet of the angel who has been guiding him. But the angel lifts him up and reminds him that he is just a messenger. John should not be overawed by the image of the New Jerusalem, but rather by the goodness and glory of God the Father, His Son, and the Holy Spirit, who alone can bring it

Let us rejoice and be glad and give Him glory! For the wedding of the Lamb has come, and His bride has made herself ready.
Revelation 19:7

to pass. John is told to share his vision to motivate God's people to do good. In the words of God, the angel says, "Let the one who does wrong continue to do wrong; let the vile person continue to be vile; let the one who does right continue to do right; and let the holy person continue to be holy" but warns, "I will give to each person according to what they have done" (22:11–12).

In the final verses of Revelation, John returns to an image that emphasizes the relationship of love that God longs to have with all people. When John first saw the New Jerusalem, he described it as "a bride beautifully dressed for her husband" (21:2). Now, at the end of the vision, this "bride"—God's people, collectively cleansed from sin and dressed in the robes of righteousness—awaits the groom, Jesus, God's Son, the true king of all. The marriage and celebrations will signal the beginning of the new life of eternity, where heaven and Earth are wedded together, God's home is among His creation, and all of God's people, that is "everyone who does right," will be released from sin and death to live in holy freedom forever. The vision ends with a longing cry for this future, "Come, Lord Jesus" (22:20).

Interpreting the vision

John's vision in Revelation is the basis for Christian eschatology, a word that means "the study of last things" and is an attempt to describe the indescribable. His words depict the end of evil and the beginning of God's reign of peace in awe-inspiring detail. Over the centuries, some people have tried to fit the visions of Revelation into a chronology, using them to predict

A stained-glass window depicts the alpha and omega, the first and last letters of the Greek alphabet, symbolizing God as "the Beginning and the End" (Revelation 22:13).

when the world will end. Given Jesus's warning that "You do not know when that time will come" (Mark 13:33), it seems better to focus on what God's future looks like rather than when it will occur.

One key theme of eschatology is recapitulation, which means that the end is a summary of all that has gone before, and a return to »

The Kingdom of Heaven

The terms "kingdom of Heaven" and "kingdom of God'" are used extensively by Jesus in His teaching to refer to God's righteous reign on Earth. The arrival of Heaven's kingdom on Earth is the purpose of Jesus's ministry. He says, for instance, "Repent, for the kingdom of Heaven is near" (Matthew 4:17), and uses it as the motivation for prayer, "Your kingdom come, Your will be done, on Earth as it is in heaven" (Matthew 6:10). In popular imagination, heaven is often thought of as a spiritual, non-physical realm. The early Christians, however, building on the convictions of Jewish faith, understood heaven as the reality of living under God's order, as directed by Him.

While some might perceive heaven as existing elsewhere, the Christian hope is for heaven to come to Earth, so that God's rule is established in the physical world. Such a hope reassures Christians that the injustices of this life will be made right in God's future, and that death is not the end, but rather—for those with faith—a gateway into God's kingdom.

LA NOUVELLE JÉRUSALEM.

Si tu hais le péché, de la croix charge toi,
Marche avec courage, soutenu par ta foi,
Suis moi sur le chemin pierreux, plein d'épines,
Qui te conduit au Ciel, aux délices divines.

Si tu crains ici-bas, les soucis, la fatigue,
Et te ris des conseils, que ton Dieu te prodigue,
Prends le chemin facile des plaisirs matériels,
Qui te mène à l'Enfer, aux tourments éternels.

its original purpose. The Bible begins in Genesis with a picture of God in harmony with His good creation, and ends in Revelation with evil destroyed forever and that harmony restored. The reality of the long, hard history of sin and suffering that lies between is not simply denied, however. In Genesis, creation is good simply by virtue of its origin in God, but in Revelation, the future is good, both because of its origin in God and because it has been set free from sin by the death and resurrection of Jesus. From the earliest days of Christianity, believers looked forward to when

God would gather up those with faith in Him from the four corners of the world to celebrate God's glory. This picture, which appears in many of Jesus's parables, is stated by Paul the Apostle. God's purpose—"to be put into effect when the times reach their fulfillment"—is "to bring unity to all things in Heaven and on Earth under Christ" (Ephesians 1:10).

The promise of new life

Central to this "recapitulation" is the expectation that all God's people who have ever lived will be physically present. Throughout

A popular French print dating from around 1900 shows Christ waiting above the entrance to New Jerusalem to welcome those who have been redeemed.

the Bible, there is a growing understanding that death is not the end for those who have a place in God's family. Since justice is often not received in the present life, Old Testament prophets look forward to a future time when the wrongdoers will be punished and God's faithful dead will be raised (Isaiah 26:19). Jesus affirms this expectation and extends it when

He himself is raised from the grave to a new life. Christian logic sees a correlation between Jesus's resurrection and ours. Jesus is resurrected because He has defeated sin and death, and the grave could not hold Him. Jesus has ascended to heaven and is waiting for the moment when the present creation has "passed away" and God's new creation is revealed.

Jesus is described by Paul the Apostle as the "first fruits of those who have fallen asleep" (1 Corinthians 15:20). The words "first fruits" and "fallen asleep" are believed to indicate that what happened to Jesus will happen to those who die in faith, "that God will bring with Jesus those who have fallen asleep in Him" (1 Thessalonians 4:14). At the new creation, Christians believe that they, too, will share a new life as all things return to their original purpose of worshipping and service to God in a relationship of love.

Heaven on Earth

For centuries, an image of the afterlife as a vague, heavenly realm where people float around playing angelic harps has captured popular imagination. The eschatology of the Bible has little to do with this

> The perishable must clothe itself with the imperishable, and the mortal with immortality.
> **1 Corinthians 15:53**

> Creation itself will be liberated … and brought into the freedom and glory of the children of God.
> **Romans 8:21**

idea. Christians look forward to the coming of heaven on Earth. This means that every part of the world we know will be transformed by the rule of Jesus, the King of the City of Peace, the New Jerusalem. Evil will have been destroyed, the old will disappear to be replaced by the new, providing a fresh start for all who believe. At death, Christians who have "fallen asleep," secure in God's presence, await resurrection in the new creation. Christian eschatology reaches a grand finale: at some unspecified moment, a sumptuous wedding feast will celebrate the marriage between heaven and Earth, God's home and ours.

However, eschatology, "the last things," is not only found in the future in the Bible. Another strong theme in the New Testament is that Jesus brings some of God's future into the present. His core message is, "The kingdom of God has come near. Repent and believe the good news!" (Mark 1:15). By placing all their trust in Jesus, Christians bring that kingdom into their lives. The "last things" begin now—through their prayers and deeds, empowered by God's Holy Spirit—and continue forever. ∎

Hell and purgatory

"Nothing impure" will ever enter New Jerusalem, nor "anyone who does what is shameful or deceitful" (Revelation 21:27), which raises questions about the fates of the people who are excluded. Images of tortuous destruction by fire are often associated with hell. In Revelation 21:8, God warns that evildoers will be put in "the fiery lake of burning sulphur" and will suffer "the second death." The description of hell is another example of apocalyptic language and serves as a warning about being separated from God for eternity. Roman Catholics also affirm belief in purgatory, a place where God's people are purged of remaining sin through refining fire (1 Corinthians 3:11–15). By the Middle Ages, purgatory was believed to be a physical place where people were held after death to be made pure before entering Heaven.

Freed from purgatory, souls are welcomed by the Virgin Mary, God the Father, His Son, and the Holy Ghost (as a dove) in a 19th-century print by François Georgin.

DIRECTO

RY

DIRECTORY

Central to both Judaism and Christianity, the Bible has shaped the development of the world and human thought more than any other single work. Its influence is so great that, from ancient times to the modern day, many Bible stories have become inextricably intertwined with art, culture, philosophy, and society. The Bible is often deemed a single, cohesive work, but a more accurate view of it would be as an anthology of the writings of many authors that has developed through several iterations. In addition to foundational narratives, such as creation, the Ten Commandments, and the crucifixion and resurrection detailed in the main part of this book, many less well-known stories have also been woven into this tapestry of Jewish and Christian thought.

THE CURSE OF CANAAN
Genesis 9:20–11:26

Noah is the first person to plant crops after the Flood. Drinking wine from his vineyard, he falls asleep naked. His youngest son Ham sees him and tells his brothers, Shem and Jephthah. Shocked, they walk backward into the tent, so they cannot see their naked father as they cover him with a coat. When Noah wakes and hears that Ham has seen him naked, he puts a curse on Ham's son, Canaan, and his offspring, saying they will be "servants of servants" while Shem and Jephthah's offspring will be blessed. This story acted as justification for the Israelites' subjugation of the Canaanites.
See also: The Flood 40–41 ▪ Covenants 44–47

A BRIDE FOR ISAAC
Genesis 24

Growing old in Canaan, Abraham sends a servant with 10 camels to his native lands to find a suitable wife for his son Isaac. The servant prophesies that if any woman he meets at a local well not only responds to his request for water, but also offers pitchers of water for his camels, she will be the chosen bride. The young woman who does these things is Abraham's great niece, Rebekah. Her marriage to Isaac ensures the continuation of Abraham's lineage and fulfills his covenant with God.
See also: Covenants 44–47 ▪ The Testing of Abraham 50–53 ▪ Esau and Jacob 54–55

ISAAC FOUNDS BEERSHEBA
Genesis 26:12–33

Blessed by God, Isaac becomes a rich farmer, making the Philistines so jealous that they block up his wells, and King Abimelech asks him to leave the country. Isaac goes into the Negev desert where his servants dig fresh wells, and he prospers once more. Seeing this, Abimelech seeks out Isaac to apologize, saying that he now realizes that God is with Isaac. They make an oath of peace. After a feast, Isaac's servants discover another well, so the place is called Beersheba, meaning "Well of the Oath."
See also: The Testing of Abraham 50–53 ▪ Esau and Jacob 54–55 ▪ David and Bathsheba 118–19

MOSES'S FLIGHT FROM EGYPT
Exodus 2:11–22; 4:24–26

When Moses's murder of an Egyptian for beating a Hebrew slave becomes known to Pharaoh, Moses flees Egypt. Arriving in the desert of Midian, where he will spend the next 40 years, Moses defends seven women from some shepherds who want to drive them from a well. Their father, the priest Jethro, invites Moses to stay, and he marries Zipporah, one of Jethro's seven daughters, who bears him two sons. This begins Moses's transformation into one of the most important prophets.
See also: Moses and the Burning Bush 66–69 ▪ The Exodus 74–77 ▪ The Ten Commandments 78–83

THE LAST DAYS OF MOSES
**Numbers 27:12–23;
Deuteronomy 34**

On Mount Abarim, Moses looks over the land God has given to the children of Israel. God tells him to make Joshua his successor, presenting him to the priests and the people. At the age of 120, Moses takes his leave of the people, giving instructions on how they should live. God then gives him a last look at the lands promised to Abraham and his descendants, so as to reaffirm the importance of Moses's mission and celebrate his faithfulness. When Moses dies, the Israelites weep for 30 days.
See also: Covenants 44–47 ▪ The Ten Commandments 78–83 ▪ Entering the Promised Land 96–97

ACHAN'S SIN
Joshua 7

After the fall of Jericho, an Israelite named Achan secretly pillages gold, silver, and a Babylonian garment from the city. In the subsequent Israelite attack on the city of Ai ordered by Joshua, 36 Israelites are killed and the rest are chased from the city gate, fleeing in terror. Later, tearing his clothes before the Ark of the Lord, Joshua appeals to God to save His people. God tells Joshua that one of the Israelites has broken His covenant, and will be punished. The next day, God identifies Achan as the culprit. After Joshua's encouragement, Achan admits to his crimes. As punishment, Achan, his family, and livestock are stoned to death.
See also: The Ark and the Tabernacle 86–87 ▪ The Fall of Jericho 98–99

THE BATTLE OF AI
Joshua 8

Following the death of Achan, God commands Joshua and the entire Israelite army to attack Ai once again—this time, with an ambush from behind the city. Approaching from the north with 5,000 men, Joshua lures the army out of Ai, allowing his forces to enter the city from the west. Unopposed, they burn it to the ground. The Israelites then go on to defeat Ai's army and kill all of its citizens.
See also: Entering the Promised Land 96–97 ▪ The Fall of Jericho 98–99

JEPHTHAH'S VOW
Judges 10:6–11:40

Jephthah, a great warrior, leads the people into battle against the Ammonites, vowing to God that he will sacrifice to Him the first thing he sees coming out of his house if he returns victorious. Fatefully, it is his daughter who runs out to greet him. He is struck with grief, but she accepts her fate. This brutal tale of human sacrifice has puzzled commentators. Some note that God does not explicitly endorse Jephthah's fulfillment of his vow and that the sacrifice itself is not confirmed.
See also: The Testing of Abraham 50–53 ▪ Herod's Infanticide 187

ARK OF GOD RETURNED TO ISRAEL
1 Samuel 5:1–6:21

After defeating the Israelites in battle and taking the Ark of the Covenant, the Philistines are afflicted with a plague of tumors in every city the Ark enters. After suffering seven months of plagues, the Philistines finally agree to return the Ark in a cart laden with golden treasure in order to appease the God of the Israelites.
See also: The Ten Plagues 70–71 ▪ The Ark and the Tabernacle 86–87

THE MEETING OF SAUL AND SAMUEL
1 Samuel 9–10

Kish, a man from the small tribe of Benjamin, sends his son Saul to look for his stray donkey. Frustrated by the search, Saul's servant suggests they ask the seer of a nearby town for help. This seer is the Prophet Samuel, who anoints Saul and tells him God has chosen him to rule over the Israelites. The blessing sanctifies Saul's new role, preparing the way for him to become the first king of Israel.
See also: Jacob Wrestles with God 56–57 ▪ Moses and the Burning Bush 66–69 ▪ The Prophet Samuel 110–15

SAUL, KING OF ISRAEL
1 Samuel 11

When Saul hears that the Ammonites have threatened the people of Jabesh, he rushes to their defense, rallying the people of Israel by cutting up two oxen and telling them that the oxen of anyone who did not join him in battle would be similarly butchered. The Israelites are victorious and Saul is declared king, having earned the respect of his people with his leadership.
See also: The Ark and the Tabernacle 86–87 ▪ The Prophet Samuel 110–15

SAUL'S FALL FROM FAVOR
1 Samuel 18

After slaying Goliath, David becomes a close friend of Saul's son, Jonathan. Jealous of the popularity and success of David, Saul realizes that God favors David above him. He therefore hopes to eliminate David by setting him the impossible task of killing 100 Philistines as a precondition of marrying his daughter Michal. When David accomplishes this feat, Saul grows more fearful of the young man's power. Saul's malice toward David is cruel and unwarranted, showing a turning away from God.
See also: David and Goliath 116–17 ▪ David and Bathsheba 118–19

THE JEALOUS KING
1 Samuel 20

David suspects that the jealous Saul will kill him at a New Moon feast. He therefore asks Jonathan to tell his father that he has given David permission to absent himself from the feast. Saul's fury at this news confirms his murderous intentions. He tells Jonathan to fetch David, who must pay for this insult with his life, but Jonathan engineers David's escape. Here, loyalty to family proves secondary to aiding David, God's chosen king of Israel.
See also: David and Goliath 116–17 ▪ David and Bathsheba 118–19

SAUL'S ROBE
1 Samuel 24

In pursuit of David, Saul and his 3,000-strong army go into the wilderness where they stop by a cave, unaware that David and his army are sheltering inside. David quietly approaches Saul and cuts a corner off his robe. When David presents the corner of the robe to Saul—to show that he could have killed Saul but chose not to—Saul realizes that David is the chosen king of Israel, and the two make their peace. Although Saul has wronged David in the past, his show of mercy disarms Saul and demonstrates his virtuous nature.
See also: Esau and Jacob 54–55 ▪ David and Goliath 116–17

THE WITCH OF ENDOR
1 Samuel 28

Saul has banished soothsayers from his kingdom, but when an army of Philistines threatens and God fails to answer his call, he turns to the Witch of Endor to summon the spirit of Samuel. From beyond the grave, Samuel refuses to help, telling Saul that God has chosen David to become king and that Saul and his sons will soon be dead. In the ensuing battle, Saul kills himself to avoid capture. This episode demonstrates that God's judgment is absolute and unavoidable.
See also: The Prophet Samuel 110–15 ▪ David and Goliath 116–17

THE ARK IN JERUSALEM
2 Samuel 6

Under King David's leadership, the Ark is removed from Abinadab's house in Kiriath-jearim and transported to Jerusalem. When a driving ox stumbles on the journey, Abinadab's son Uzzah steadies the Ark with his hand and is promptly struck dead by God. David, in fear, sets the Ark aside in the house of Obed-edom before finally taking it to Jerusalem three months later. By killing Uzzah, God emphasizes a tenet established in the Book of Numbers—that only the Kohathites should be permitted to carry the Ark, and, more broadly, that anyone who touches it will die.
See also: The Ark and Tabernacle 86–87 ▪ Entering the Promised Land 96–97 ▪ Rebuilding Jerusalem 133

ABSALOM'S REBELLION
2 Samuel 15

Under the pretense of going to Hebron to give sacrifices to God, Absalom, David's third son, rallies support for a revolt against his father. David, who is now elderly, flees Jerusalem, but his forces later confront Absalom at the Battle of Ephraim's Wood, where Absalom is killed in revenge by his cousin Joab. Absalom's unnatural rebellion, motivated by greed, is thus punished by a just God.
See also: Cain and Abel 36–37 ▪ David and Bathsheba 118–19

NABOTH'S VINEYARD
1 Kings 21

When a Jezreelite called Naboth refuses to sell his family vineyard to King Ahab of Samaria, Queen Jezebel successfully conspires to have Naboth stoned to death for insulting God. After the king takes possession of the vineyard, Elijah visits him to tell him that his sin was so great that he will suffer Naboth's fate, that Jezebel will be eaten by dogs, and that his descendants will be outcasts. Seeing Ahab is truly repentant,

God relents and says he would not bring down these curses on Ahab and his family until after his death. In this way, while the deception and greed of Ahab and Jezebel bring dire consequences for his descendants, they allow for God to display His justness and mercy.

See also: A Prophet Hiding 124 ▪ Elijah and the Prophets of Baal 125

SOLOMON BECOMES KING
1 Kings 1:28–53

In poor health in his old age, King David needs to name a successor. Adonijah, his oldest son, proclaims himself king. Solomon, his younger son, is supported by his mother Bathsheba, the priest Zadok, Nathan the prophet, and the army chief Benaiah. David has Solomon crowned, and after David's death Solomon consolidates power by executing Adonijah.

See also: David and Bathsheba 118–19 ▪ The Wisdom of Solomon 120–23 ▪ Proverbs 148–51

JEROBOAM AND REHOBOAM
1 Kings 12–2 Kings 25

As predicted by the prophet Ahijah, Solomon turns away from God. Consequently, when he dies, God gives the lands in the north to Jeroboam, one of Solomon's officials, and 10 tribes of Israel, while Judah and Benjamin in the south fall to Solomon's son Rehoboam. Rehoboam imposes harsh working conditions on his people, and many flee north to join Jeroboam. Rehoboam's attempts to reunite the country fail.

See also: The Wisdom of Solomon 120–23 ▪ The Prophet Jeremiah 156–59

ELISHA'S MIRACLES
2 Kings 4:1–7, 38–44; 6:1–7

The Prophet Elisha exemplifies the divine principles of compassion and charity in four simple yet miraculous acts of kindness. First, a widow who owes money to her dead husband's associate asks Elisha for help. He tells her to pour her valuable oil into as many containers as she has. As she pours the oil, she realizes that its quantity has increased vastly, and she sells it to pay off the debt. Second, a servant unwittingly poisons a large stew with deadly berries. Using flour, Elisha removes the poison. In another miracle, there are only 20 loaves of bread to feed 100 men but when Elisha hands it out, there is plenty to go around, with some to spare. Last, cutting a beam, a man drops his axe head in the river. Elisha throws a stick, which brings the axe head to the surface, so that the building work can continue.

See also: The Raising of Lazarus 226–27 ▪ Feeding the 5,000 228–31

ELISHA AND THE CHILDLESS COUPLE
2 Kings 4:8–37

In repayment for bread and lodging offered freely by an elderly, childless couple in Shunem, Elisha promises they will have a baby within the year. This comes true and they have a son. However, when the child is a few years old, he dies. The woman lays him on the bed that the prophet used, before going to tell him of the reason for her grief. Consoling her, Elisha agrees to help the child. He goes to the woman's house and shuts himself in the room with the child, who is miraculously restored to life. By giving Elisha power to bring the dead back to life, God shows that through Him, all things are possible.

See also: The Prophet Samuel 110–15 ▪ The Raising of Lazarus 226–27 ▪ The Empty Tomb 268–71

ELISHA'S SKIN CURE
2 Kings 5:1–14

Naaman, commander of the Syrian army, is advised by an Israelite girl captive to seek a cure for his leprosy from Elisha. The prophet tells him to wash seven times in the River Jordan. Believing the Jordan to be an unworthy river, Naaman at first refuses, but then relents and washes himself. His body becomes as unblemished as a child's, showing that even if temporarily obstructed by pride, faith results in great transformation.

See also: Baptism of Jesus 194–97 ▪ The Raising of Lazarus 226–27 ▪ The Healing of the Beggar 284–87

ELISHA'S TEARS FOR A KING
2 Kings 8:7–15

In Damascus, Ben-Hadad II, King of Syria, is sick, so he sends his servant Hazael to ask Elijah if he will ever recover. In tears, the prophet tells Hazael that not only will the king die, but Hazael will replace him and commit terrible crimes against the children of Israel. The following day Hazael suffocates the king and seizes the throne. Later, following the death of Hazael, he is succeeded by his son, Ben-Hadad III.

See also: The Prophet Jeremiah 156–59 ▪ Herod's Infanticide 187

JOASH, KING OF JUDAH
**2 Kings 12:1–21;
2 Chronicles 24:1–27**

At the age of 7, with the help of the high priest Jehoiada, Joash begins his 40-year rule of Judah. On the death of Jehoiada, the king and his people stop worshipping in the Temple. When his son Zechariah complains, Joash orders him to be stoned to death. In retribution, God allows a small Syrian army to conquer the army of Judah and raid Jerusalem.
See also: The Wisdom of Solomon 120–23 ▪ The Prophet Jeremiah 156–59

DEATH OF ELISHA
2 Kings 13:14–20

On his deathbed, Elisha instructs King Joash to fire an arrow out of the window. This, he said, was "the Lord's arrow of victory." He tells Joash to fire the remaining arrows, but when Joash does so only three times, Elisha asks why he has not shot five or six arrows, as this would have completely defeated the Syrians. Now they will be defeated only three times. After issuing this warning, Elisha dies.
See also: A Prophet in Hiding 124 ▪ Elijah and the Prophets of Baal 125 ▪ The Chariot of Fire 126–27

HEZEKIAH'S REFORMS
2 Kings 18

At the age of 25, Hezekiah becomes King of Judah. His religious reforms demand the destruction of images, including Nehushtan, the bronze serpent said to have been made by Moses. He purges the priesthood and centralizes the worship of God at the Temple in Jerusalem. This act represents an emphatic denunciation of impure gods and false idols.
See also: The Golden Calf 84–85 ▪ Daniel in Babylon 164–65

DANIEL IMPRESSES NEBUCHADNEZZAR
Daniel 1:1–21

Four noble Israelites are selected to serve Nebuchadnezzar's royal palace in Babylon. They are to be trained for three years and given the best food and wine. Daniel does not want to eat or drink anything against God's Law, and he asks the chief official if they may eat only vegetables and drink water. After ten days, Daniel and his compatriots look much healthier than the king's men, showing Daniel's wisdom and virtue, and they become the most respected wise men in the kingdom.
See also: Joseph the Dreamer 58–61 ▪ Daniel in Babylon 164–65

DEFYING THE KING'S FIERY FURNACE
Daniel 3

When Shadrach, Meshach, and Abednego fail to take part in the worship of a huge new golden image which Nebuchadnezzar has created, he orders them to be burned to death. The furnace is built and the fire is so intense that the soldiers in charge of the victims are burned, but the three Israelites remain completely unharmed by the flames. Seeing this miracle, Nebuchadnezzar is converted, and says anybody offending God would be cut to pieces. This story reflects the moral imperative to avoid worshipping false idols, while the conversion of the tyrannical Nebuchadnezzar reflects the might and reach of God's influence.
See also: Daniel in Babylon 164–65 ▪ The Road to Damascus 290–91

BECOMING A WILD ANIMAL
Daniel 4

Nebuchadnezzar dreams of a giant tree reaching to the sky being cut down, dispersing the animals sheltering beneath it, though the stump of the tree remains. Daniel interprets the dream as the king being driven into the wilderness to live like the animals, although the remaining stump implies that he will return to power when he acknowledges the Kingdom of Heaven. Daniel's interpretation of Nebuchadnezzar's dream introduces his ability to explain the significance of visions.
See also: Joseph the Dreamer 58–61 ▪ Daniel in Babylon 164–65

BELSHAZZAR'S FEAST
Daniel 5

King Belshazzar of Babylon hosts a banquet for 1,000 nobles, who drink wine from golden goblets taken from the Temple of Jerusalem. When a finger appears and writes a message across a wall, the king promises riches for anyone who can interpret the sign. Daniel is summoned and offered riches and status in exchange for deciphering the message. Refusing the offer, he explains to King Belshazzar that God is displeased with his lack of faith and his days are numbered. The king rewards him with high office, recognizing Daniel as God's loyal servant.

See also: Joseph the Dreamer 58–61 ▪ Daniel in Babylon 164–65

WATER INTO WINE
John 2:1–11

Jesus, Mary, and His disciples attend a wedding at Cana in Galilee. When the entire supply of wine has been consumed by the wedding guests, Mary comes to Jesus and tells Him what has happened. Jesus instructs the servants to pour water into jars and take it to the master of the banquet, who, upon tasting it, discovers it has been transformed into wine. Despite performing the miracle, Jesus initially showed reluctance when Mary approached Him, saying, "Why do you involve me? My time has not yet come." Jesus makes multiple references to His "time" or "hour" throughout the Gospels, alluding to His crucifixion and resurrection, when His blood, often symbolized by wine, will cleanse humanity of all sin.

See also: The Raising of Lazarus 226–27 ▪ Feeding the 5,000 228–31 ▪ The Healing of the Beggar 284–87

WOMAN AT THE WELL
John 4:1–42

Jesus meets a woman drawing water from Jacob's well. Although Samaritans are not meant to speak with Jews, Jesus talks to her, revealing Himself as the Messiah, saying, "Everyone who drinks this water will be thirsty again, but whoever drinks the water I give

them will never thirst." Many in the town come to believe in Him and they urge Him to stay. Jesus's interactions with the Samaritan woman and surrounding crowd are imbued with clear metaphorical connotations, as He demonstrates to those present that the water of life will provide sustenance to any who will follow Him, regardless of their nationality or origin.

See also: The Calling of the Disciples 200–03 ▪ The Good Samaritan 216–17 ▪ Road to Emmaus 272–73

THE WISE AND FOOLISH BUILDERS
Matthew 7:24–27

During the Sermon on the Mount, Jesus tells a parable in order to demonstrate the importance of following His teachings in daily life. He describes a man who faithfully practices the word of God as one "who built his house on the rock." Jesus explains that after the house is built, and when the rains come, the streams rise, and the winds beat against the house, it stays standing because of its solid foundation.

By contrast, those who do not practice the word of God are compared to "a foolish man who built his house on sand." For him, when the rains come, the streams rise, and the winds beat against the house, it crashes to the ground. Through this parable, Jesus signifies that through times of affliction, practicing faith in God will give believers the strength they need to persevere.

See also: The Raising of Lazarus 226–27 ▪ Feeding the 5,000 228–31 ▪ The Healing of the Beggar 284–87

BEHEADING OF JOHN THE BAPTIST
Mark 6:16–29

Following the death of her husband, Philip, Princess Herodias marries Philip's brother, King Herod. When John the Baptist insists that this union is unlawful and immoral, Herodias nurses a grudge against him. At a banquet, Herod asks the daughter of Herodias, Salome, to dance, before promising her any gift she chooses. At Herodias's suggestion, the girl asks for the head of John the Baptist. Although Herod has no quarrel with John, he carries out his promise. John the Baptist is executed, and his head is brought to Herodias on a platter. This story demonstrates the vicious and brutal nature of Herod's rule.

See also: Baptism of Jesus 194–97 ▪ The Crucifixion 258–65 ▪ Paul's Arrest 294–95

A GIRL POSSESSED
Matthew 15:2–28; Mark 7:24–30

A Gentile in the region of Tyre and Sidon begs Jesus to cure her daughter, who is possessed by a demon. At first, He refuses, saying He has been sent to help the children of Israel, and that it was not right to take their bread and toss it to the dogs (meaning Gentiles). She replies that even the dogs eat the crumbs that fall from their master's table. For her faith in Him, He tells her to go home where she will find her daughter cured. In doing so, Jesus rewards all those who show their faith in Him.

See also: Demons and the Herd of Pigs 224–25 ▪ The Raising of Lazarus 226–27 ▪ The Nature of Faith 236–41

FEEDING 4,000
Matthew 15:29–32; Mark 8:1–13

After feeding the 5,000, a crowd of 4,000 follow Jesus into the mountains. Many are lame, blind, or dumb and hope to be cured. After three days, in which He cures many people, Jesus does not want to send them away hungry. The disciples bring seven loaves and a few fishes, and with this amount of food, Jesus feeds the multitude.
See also: Feeding the 5,000 228–31 ▪ The Healing of the Beggar 284–87

WOMAN CAUGHT IN ADULTERY
John 8:1–12

An adulterous woman is brought before Jesus by the scribes and Pharisees, who ask Him why the Law of Moses, which calls for death for adulterers by stoning, should not be carried out. Jesus says to the people, "Let he who is without sin throw the first stone." The crowd disperses and Jesus tells the woman to go and sin no more. With this act, Jesus successfully evades the trap of those wishing to force Him to choose between holiness and mercy.
See also: The Golden Rule 210–11 ▪ Jesus Anointed at Bethany 246–47

THE MAN WITH THE SHRIVELED HAND
Matthew 12:10–13; Mark 3:1–5; Luke 6:6–10

Angry that Jesus has been defying their rules about the Sabbath, and looking for reasons to bring charges against Him, some Pharisees in a synagogue ask Jesus if it is lawful to heal on a Sabbath. Seeing a man with a shriveled hand in the synagogue, Jesus heals him. He then asks the Pharisees, "If any of you has a sheep and it falls into a pit on the Sabbath, will you not take hold of it and lift it out? How much more valuable is a person than a sheep! Therefore it is lawful to do good on the Sabbath." After this, the Pharisees plot how they might kill Jesus.
See also: Jesus Embraces a Tax Collector 242–43 ▪ The Healing of the Beggar 284–87

A MAN BORN BLIND
John 9:1–38

Meeting a man who is born blind, the disciples ask Jesus if his blindness is due to his parents' sins or his own sins. Jesus says that he is blind so that the work of God can be shown in him. "I am the light of the world," Jesus says, and He restores the man to sight by pressing clay into his eyes and sending him to wash it off in the Pool of Siloam. The man, now healed, reflects God's ability to work through people in order to show His love and power.
See also: Jesus Embraces a Tax Collector 242–43 ▪ The Healing of the Beggar 284–87

LAZARUS AND A RICH MAN
Luke 16:19–31

Jesus tells the parable of a rich man who lives in luxury, and Lazarus, who is full of sores and lives in poverty at his gate. When they die, Lazarus is taken up to heaven by Abraham; the rich man is sent to hell. Abraham denies the rich man any comfort, and refuses his request to send Lazarus to his five living brothers to warn them of their likely similar fate. Abraham says they have already been warned by the prophets. The message is clear—judgment will be fair, as we have all heard God's message.
See also: The Testing of Abraham 50–53 ▪ The Ten Commandments 78–83 ▪ The Raising of Lazarus 226–27

THE EXTENT OF FORGIVENESS
Matthew 18:21–35

Asked by His disciple Peter how many times he should forgive somebody who has wronged him, Jesus says seventy times seven, and He tells the parable of the servant who owes a king money. When the servant pleads with him, the king relents and cancels the debt. The servant then finds a fellow servant who owes him money and has him thrown into prison when he cannot pay. When the king hears this, he berates the servant for not treating his debtor as he has been treated himself and orders for him to be imprisoned and tortured. The parable affirms the Golden Rule, and suggests that forgiveness is not a finite resource.
See also: The Golden Rule 210–11 ▪ Parables of Jesus 214–15 ▪ The Prodigal Son 218–21 ▪ The Temple Tax 222

TEN CURED, ONLY ONE GRATEFUL
Luke 17:11–17

On His way to Jerusalem, Jesus is passing through a village when ten men with leprosy walk toward Him,

calling out for mercy. Jesus tells them to go to see the priests, and as they do so, they are healed. One of them, a Samaritan, returns to give thanks, and Jesus expresses His disappointment that only one man has done so, showing the importance of expressing gratitude.
See also: The Good Samaritan 216–17 ▪ The Healing of the Beggar 284–87

A BANQUET FOR THE POOR
Luke 14:1–24

On the Sabbath, Jesus heals a man in the house of a Pharisee. Afterward He tells a parable about a large banquet, where all invited guests make excuses and do not attend. In anger, the host tells his servants to go into the streets and invite the poor, the crippled, and the blind to come and eat with him, until the house is so crowded that there will be no room for any other guests. This parable emphasizes that, having been rejected by the religious people, God would ensure the salvation of all kinds of social outcasts.
See also: The Golden Rule 210–11 ▪ Parables of Jesus 214–15 ▪ Feeding the 5,000 228–31

THE TWO SONS
Matthew 21:28–32

In this parable, Jesus describes a man with two sons. The man asks both of them to work in his vineyard for the day. The first son refuses, but later changes his mind and begins working. The second son agrees to work in the field, but, ultimately, does not fulfill his promise. Jesus asks the crowd, "Which of the two did what his

father wanted?" They reply the first son. Jesus confirms this, and tells them that the prostitutes and tax collectors who repented to John the Baptist will enter heaven before them. Jesus explains that these sinners, despite their past actions, believed in God and repented. The crowd, however, with their hollow professions of faith, will not enter God's kingdom.
See also: The Raising of Lazarus 226–27 ▪ Feeding the 5,000 228–31 ▪ The Healing of the Beggar 284–87

STEPHEN, THE FIRST CHRISTIAN MARTYR
Acts 6:8–7:60

Stephen, a deacon of the early church, is Christianity's first martyr. He is a Greek speaker and a powerful debater, and the speech he delivers at his trial before the Sanhedrin in Jerusalem is recorded in the Acts of the Apostles. His last words before he is stoned to death for blasphemy are a plea to God not to hold the sin of his executioners against them. The cloaks of those who step forward to stone him are guarded by a Roman citizen named Saul, who is yet to convert to Christianity and change his name to Paul. Saul's sins in his early life are thus framed against the piety of early Christian martyrs.
See also: Road to Damascus 290–91 ▪ Paul's Arrest 294–95 ▪ The Power of the Resurrection 304–05

THE HEALING OF TABITHA
Acts 9:32–43

Tabitha (known as Dorcas in Greek), a well-loved Christian woman in Joppa, dies and her

body is placed in an upstairs room. The Apostle Peter, who has recently cured a paralyzed man in the town of Lydda, is sent for. Peter is taken into the upstairs room where Tabitha's body has been washed and placed. Grieving women show him clothes that Tabitha had made for them. After sending the women out of the room, Peter kneels and prays. He then commands Tabitha to get up, and she rises from the bed, returned to life. Through the miracle of resurrection, the status of Peter as one of God's primary miracle workers is reaffirmed, and Tabitha is rewarded for living a good and virtuous life.
See also: The Raising of Lazarus 226–27 ▪ The Empty Tomb 268–71

PETER IN THE HOUSE OF A GENTILE
Acts 10:1–11:18

An angel appears to the Roman centurion Cornelius in Caesarea and tells him to send men to find the Apostle Peter and bring him to him. Meanwhile, Peter has a vision from God telling him that he may eat "unclean" food as it is not unclean when God says it is not. A servant takes Peter to Cornelius's house even though religious laws prevent Peter from entering the house of a Gentile. Peter realizes that God is telling him that He has no favorites and will accept all those who believe in Him and he baptizes everyone there. God's treatment of Cornelius allows for a transnational approach to salvation, as Peter demonstrates that the Kingdom of God is open to all who have faith.
See also: The Word Spreads 288–89 ▪ The Council of Jerusalem 292–93

GLOSSARY

Amen An affirmation meaning "trustworthy" or "surely" that is often used to end prayers or religious statements.

Annunciation The announcement by the angel Gabriel to the Virgin Mary that she would conceive the Son of God by the Holy Spirit.

Anoint To apply oil or ointment to a person or object to mark their dedication to God.

Apocrypha (or apocryphal) Books of the Bible added to the Hebrew Old Testament by Catholic and Orthodox churches. Jews and Protestants do not accept the Apocrypha as part of the canon.

Apostles Special messengers commissioned by Jesus to preach with authority in His name. These included 11 of the 12 original disciples and Paul.

Ark of the Covenant A wooden box overlaid with gold that God instructed the Israelites to build to contain the Ten Commandments.

Armageddon The place of God's ultimate victory over evil. It is mentioned only once in the Bible, in the Book of Revelation.

Ascension Jesus's ascent to heaven on the 40th day after His resurrection.

Baal The storm god of the Canaanites and the most important (though not chief) god in the Canaanite pantheon.

Baptism A Christian ceremony in which the "washing away" of sins with water symbolizes rebirth and admission to the Church.

Beatitudes, The A series of blessings that Jesus bestows on those with special qualities in His Sermon on the Mount. These blessings echo His teachings.

Birthright The right of a firstborn son to inherit a larger share of his father's property than his siblings.

Blasphemy The offense of misusing or desecrating God's name in action, speech, or writing.

Burnt offering A type of sacrifice common in the Old Testament— in which an entire animal is consumed by fire. Such offerings were either thanksgivings for God's goodness or atonements for sin.

Canaan The land between the River Jordan, the Dead Sea, and the Mediterranean Sea. It is sometimes referred to as the Promised Land.

Canon, The From Greek for "rule." It refers to the list of books accepted as part of the Bible.

Cherub (plural cherubim) An angelic being with a human face and wings that serves God.

Chief Priests The men in charge of Temple worship in Jerusalem.

Christ From *Christos*, Greek for "messiah," the anointed one. In the New Testament, this is Jesus.

Circumcision The removal of the foreskin done when a Jewish boy is 8 days old as a sign of membership in God's Covenant.

Codex A handwritten manuscript with writing on both sides of the page that can be made into a book.

Council of Jerusalem Possibly the first assembly of the Christian Church, in 49 CE. It affirmed that Gentiles did not need to adopt the custom of circumcision for entry into the community of believers.

Covenant A binding agreement, based on faithful loyalty, between God and His people.

Cubit An ancient measure, both of length and distance, of about 18 inches (0.5m)—the distance from the fingertips to the elbow.

Cult A system of religious worship. In the Hebrew Bible, the Temple cult was a system of sacrifices and rituals.

Cuneiform A writing system developed by the Sumerians that used wedge-shaped characters.

Denarius A Roman coin and the standard pay for a day's work during the time of Jesus.

Diaspora, The The dispersal or scattering of large groups of people throughout the world.

Disciple A follower who serves Jesus Christ. In the Gospels, the term refers to Christ's inner circle.

Elder A local community leader. In the New Testament, elders are senior members of the Church.

Epistle A letter. Twenty-one of the New Testament's books are epistles.

Evangelist One who preaches the Gospel of Jesus Christ to those who are not believers, aiming to bring people to recognize Jesus as Lord and Messiah.

Exiles, The The name given to expelled inhabitants of Israel after the Assyrian conquest of the northern kingdom in 722 BCE and also to those forced from the southern kingdom of Judah after the Babylonian conquest a century later.

Exodus, The The Israelites' release from slavery in Egypt and their journey to Canaan, the Promised Land, under the leadership of Moses.

Fall, The The disobedience of Adam and Eve that led to judgment of mankind. In Christian doctrine, this is when sin enters the world and pervades all humanity.

Gentile A non-Jewish person.

Gnosticism A general term for 2nd-century heretical sects that sought to live a purely spiritual life by way of a secret knowledge (*gnosis*).

Gospel The teaching that God offers redemption to humanity through the salvation Jesus Christ brought by His life, death, and resurrection. When written with an initial capital, it refers to the first four books of the New Testament.

Grace Abundant love freely given to humanity by God through Christ.

Hanukkah A Jewish religious festival lasting eight days that commemorates the victory of the Maccabees in 160 BCE and the rededication of the Temple.

Hebrew Bible The name used by some non-Jews to refer to the Jewish Scriptures. The Hebrew term is Tanakh.

Hellenism The characteristics and spirit of Alexander the Great's empire and its successors. Additionally, the attempt by those empires to impose Greek language, culture, and religion on the peoples they had conquered.

Herodian Of, or concerning, Herod the Great, king of Judea (37–4 BCE), or members of his family.

High place A raised place used for religious worship, hence a sanctuary. Often used in relation to shrines for Canaanite gods.

High priest The senior Jewish leader responsible for the nation's spiritual well-being.

Idol An image, often carved and made of wood, metal, or stone, which is worshipped as a god.

Israel and Judah The northern and southern Jewish kingdoms, respectively, created after the United Monarchy was divided in c.930 BCE.

Jehovah A name for God related to the Hebrew term *Yahweh*.

Jews The tribespeople of Israel and their descendants.

Judgment Day The day when Jesus returns to Earth. Some believe it is also the end of the world, when God will assess every human being by identifying and condemning sin and absolving and rewarding believers.

Judges Leaders who governed the tribes of Israel from the death of Joshua to the time of Samuel; and the name of the Old Testament book concerning that same period.

Kingdom of God The teaching that the entire world will come to accept sovereign rule of God; the Kingdom of God comes wherever God's authority is recognized.

Law, The Mosaic Law given to the Israelites by God, aimed at creating a society based on their obligations to each other, to the land, and to God under the Covenant.

Leprosy An infectious skin disease. In the Bible, leprosy denotes a wider range of ailments than just the modern definition.

Living God Term denoting God as a living, active, and powerful deity in contrast to the idols of nations opposed to Israel.

Lots, casting of A traditional Israelite method of discerning the will of God in conflicts or disputes.

Manna Food provided by God for the Israelites on their journey from Egypt to the Promised Land, with the appearance of coriander seed and the taste of honey.

Martyr Initially used to refer to one who spread the word of Jesus, it is later used to refer specifically to those who die for their faith.

Menorah A sacred candelabrum with seven branches used in the Temple in Jerusalem. It became an emblem of Israel and Judaism.

Mesopotamia Land between the Tigris and Euphrates rivers that included such cities as Babylon, Ur, and Nineveh.

Messiah Hebrew term meaning "the anointed one."

Midrash A Jewish commentary on the Hebrew Bible.

Ministry The Old Testament associates the term with the work of the Temple priests. The New Testament cites Jesus as the model for Christian ministry.

Miracle An event defying natural laws that is usually attributed to divine powers.

Mishnah Jewish teachings, compiled in the late 2nd century CE, which forms the earlier portion of the Talmud.

Most Holy Place (also known as Holy of Holies) The most sacred part of the Temple in Jerusalem. It originally contained the Ark of the Covenant.

Ordination A ceremony in which someone is officially appointed into a religious leadership role.

Pagan From Latin *paganus,* meaning rural or of the countryside, the word came to refer to one who did not follow the one true God.

Parable A short story that uses everyday language and events to convey moral and spiritual truths.

Paradise A blessed place in which the righteous live. Paradise can refer to heaven or to the Garden of Eden prior to the Fall.

Passover The annual Jewish holiday commemorating the Israelites' escape from slavery in Egypt.

Pentateuch A Greek word used by Christians to describe the first five books of the Bible that comprise the original Torah.

Pentecost A feast, celebrated 50 days after Passover, when harvest fruits were offered at the Temple. In the New Testament, the Holy Spirit descended on believers at Pentecost.

Pharaoh The title of the ancient Egyptian rulers.

Pharisees One of the main Jewish religious groups of the New Testament, known for their strict adherence to the Law.

Philistines Descendants of a people who possibly came from Crete, the Philistines infiltrated the eastern Mediterranean. Arriving in Canaan around the same time as the Israelites, they are their most notorious enemies.

Polytheistic Of, or concerning, the belief that there are many gods.

Praetorium Originally used to refer to a general's tent in a camp or a military headquarters; also, the governor's official residence in Jerusalem.

Prefect A title given to a local military or civil official of the Roman Empire.

Promised Land Canaan, the homeland God promised to the Israelites upon their escape from Egypt in Exodus.

Prophecy A message concerning the past, present, or future that is inspired and/or revealed by God and delivered by a prophet.

Prophets People who spoke words of prophecy. In the Old Testament, they are often called by God to explain the responsibilities and privileges of God's Covenant.

Proverb A short popular saying that conveys a lesson about how to live wisely, often based on observations of everyday life.

Psalm A song, often used in worship to demonstrate praise and thanksgiving.

Rabbi From Hebrew for "teacher," a title of honor given to a qualified Jewish religious teacher.

Repentance A complete change of heart leading to a change of action, involving confession of, deep regret for, and sincere turning away from sin to God.

Resurrection The giving of new life to a dead person, especially in relation to the raising of Jesus Christ by God after His death on the cross.

Revelation The disclosure of God's will, nature, and purpose through the scriptures.

Righteous, The Especially in the Old Testament, the designation of people who lead lives that have spiritual and moral integrity according to God's commands.

Sabbath The seventh day of the week, set aside as a day of rest and for the worship of God. It originally began on Friday evening for both Jews and Christians, but as Christ's resurrection took place on Sunday, this displaced the Sabbath for Christians.

Sacrifice In the Hebrew Bible, an offering made to God, often involving slaughtering an animal. For Christians, the death of Jesus Christ is the one sacrifice that secures forgiveness by God.

Sadducees A Hellenized aristocracy of Jewish priests in the New Testament who dominated both temple worship and also the Sanhedrin. They opposed the Pharisees and Jesus.

Sanhedrin A Jewish council, either local or, in Jerusalem, the supreme council that was directed by the high priest. Members included teachers of the Law, elders, and chief priests.

Scripture The biblical writings received as the word of God; for example, the Hebrew Bible and/or the New Testament.

Septuagint The name of the Greek translation of the Hebrew Bible. The Bible of the early Church, the books of the New Testament were added as they became accepted.

Seraph (plural seraphim) Celestial being with two or three sets of wings that is a guardian of God's throne.

Sheol Used in the Hebrew Bible to refer to a grave, pit, or tomb, cut off from God.

Showbread "Bread of the presence," made from the finest ingredients, which was placed on a table in the Tabernacle and, later, in the Temple of Jerusalem.

Speaking in tongues A phenomenon in which people speak in languages unknown to them to praise God or to deliver a message from God.

Spirit The innermost nonmaterial part of a human being—one's soul. The Old Testament sometimes describes the "Spirit of God." In the New Testament, the Holy Spirit is the third person of the Trinity.

Synoptic From Greek for "seeing things together." The Gospels of Matthew, Mark, and Luke are known as the Synoptic Gospels, because they share much material and have similar frameworks.

Tabernacle The large portable tent that formed the sanctuary in which the Israelites carried the Ark of the Covenant during their journey from Egypt to Canaan.

Talent A unit of weight equivalent to about 75 pounds (34kg) in Old Testament times. In the New Testament, it was a unit of value worth the wages of a laborer for 20 years.

Talmud A Jewish work containing interpretation of, and commentary on, the Torah, and the primary source of Jewish religious law.

Tanakh An acronym comprising the initial letters of the three sections of the Hebrew Bible: the Torah (the Teaching/Law), Nev'im (the Prophets), and Kethuvim (the Writings), combined in one work.

Temple, The In Jerusalem, the place where sacrifices could be made. The First Temple was built by King Solomon. The Second was built after the exile and was the one known to Jesus.

Teraphim Household gods or images venerated by ancient Semitic peoples.

Torah A term that used to refer solely to the Pentateuch, but in Jewish tradition came to mean the whole Hebrew Bible.

Transfiguration The revelation of Christ's glory, witnessed by His closest disciples.

Transubstantiation The Catholic belief in the conversion of the wine and bread given at communion into the blood and body of Christ.

Typology The interpretation of figures or events in the Old Testament as foreshadowing those in the New Testament, particularly in relation to Christ.

Yahweh The name for God given by God to Moses. Yahweh stems from the letters "YHWH."

Zealots Jewish rebels who fought against the Roman occupation of Judea at the time of Jesus Christ.

Ziggurat An Assyrian or Babylonian tower in which each successive story is smaller than the one beneath it.

Zion Synonym for Jerusalem. The Temple was also known as Mount Zion. Zion is also used to refer to Israel, the Church, and heaven and is often represented as a peak extending into the heavens.

INDEX

Page numbers in **bold** refer to main entries; those in *italics* refer to captions

N

O

P

Q

R

S

ACKNOWLEDGMENTS

Dorling Kindersley would like to thank Anukriti Arora, Jomin Johny, and Meenal Goel for design assistance; Tina Jindal for editorial assistance; Rajesh Kumar Mishra and Zafar-ul-Islam Khan for cartographic assistance; and Ankita Sharma for illustrations.

PICTURE CREDITS

The publisher would like to thank the following for their kind permission to reproduce their photographs:

(Key: a-above; b-below/bottom; c-center; f-far; l-left; r-right; t-top)

22 Alamy Stock Photo: Science History Images. **23 Bridgeman Images:** Bible Society, London, UK. **24 Getty Images:** DEA / G. DAGLI ORTI. **25 Alamy Stock Photo:** Oksana Mitiukhina. **27 123RF.com:** Cosmin-Constantin Sava (tl). **Alamy Stock Photo:** Granger Historical Picture Archive (br). **28 Alamy Stock Photo:** SuperStock. **29 Alamy Stock Photo:** Eyal Bartov. **32 Alamy Stock Photo:** Peter Horree. **33 Getty Images:** Godong / Universal Images Group. **34 akg-images. 36 Getty Images:** Vincenzo Fontana. **38 Getty Images:** Wathiq Khuzaie / Stringer. **41 Alamy Stock Photo:** Heritage Image Partnership Ltd. **43 Alamy Stock Photo:** Granger Historical Picture Archive (br). **Getty Images:** DEA / G. DAGLI ORTI (bl). **45 Alamy Stock Photo:** Science History Images (tr). **Rex Shutterstock:** Gianni Dagli Orti (cb). **46 Rijksmuseum, Amsterdam:** Gift of A. Bredius, The Hague. **49 Alamy Stock Photo:** Niday Picture Library. **51 akg-images. 52 Getty Images:** CM Dixon / Print Collector. **54 Alamy Stock Photo:** Louise Batalla Duran. **55 Alamy Stock Photo:** Jim Gibson (bl). **Getty Images:** Buyenlarge (tr). **56 Getty Images:** SuperStock. **57 Alamy Stock Photo:** Godong. **59 Alamy Stock Photo:** Granger Historical Picture Archive. **60 Alamy Stock Photo:** Lebrecht Music and Arts Photo Library. **61 Bridgeman Images:** Private Collection / Photo © Christie's Images. **67 Alamy Stock Photo:** classicpaintings (tl); Stan Pritchard (tr). **68 Alamy Stock Photo:** Greg Balfour Evans. **69 Getty Images:** DEA PICTURE LIBRARY. **70 Alamy Stock Photo:** Heritage Image Partnership Ltd. **73 Alamy Stock Photo:** Rafael Ben-Ari (tr). **Rijksmuseum, Amsterdam:** (bl). **75 Alamy Stock Photo:** Heritage Image Partnership Ltd (tl). **iStockphoto.com:** Konoplytska (bl). **76 akg-images:** Tristan Lafranchis. **77 Getty Images:** bildagentur-online / uig. **80 Alamy Stock Photo:** Heritage Image Partnership Ltd. **81 Alamy Stock Photo:** MuseoPics—Paul Williams. **82 Alamy Stock Photo:** Kevin Lang (br); www.BibleLandPictures.com (tl). **84 Getty Images:** Fine Art Images / Heritage Images. **87 Alamy Stock Photo:** Chronicle. **89 Alamy Stock Photo:** Art Collection 2. **90 Alamy Stock Photo:** Granger Historical Picture Archive. **96 Getty Images:** DEA / A. DAGLI ORTI. **97 Alamy Stock Photo:** www.BibleLandPictures.com. **98 Alamy Stock Photo:** Duby Tal / Albatross. **99 Alamy Stock Photo:** Granger Historical Picture Archive (tr); Colin Underhill (tr). **102 Alamy Stock Photo:** 505 collection. **105 Alamy Stock Photo:** Paul Fearn (crb); Lebrecht Music and Arts Photo Library (tr). **106 Alamy Stock Photo:** Lanmas. **107 Rex Shutterstock:** Paramount / Kobal. **108 Getty Images:** DEA / A. DAGLI ORTI. **109 Alamy Stock Photo:** Boris Diakovsky. **112 Alamy Stock Photo:** ART Collection. **113 Alamy Stock Photo:** Heritage Image Partnership Ltd. **114 Getty Images:** Bettmann. **116 Alamy Stock Photo:** Archivart. **119 Alamy Stock Photo:** Heritage Image Partnership Ltd. **121 Alamy Stock Photo:** Granger Historical Picture Archive. **122 Alamy Stock Photo:** age fotostock. **124 Getty Images:** Fine Art Images / Heritage Images. **127 Getty Images:** Fine Art Images / Heritage Images. **129 Alamy Stock Photo:** www.BibleLandPictures.com. **130 Alamy Stock Photo:** Artokoloro Quint Lox Limited. **131 Alamy Stock Photo:** Artokoloro Quint Lox Limited. **133 Getty Images:** Culture Club. **140 Getty Images:** Imagno. **142 Alamy Stock Photo:** robertharding. **143 Getty Images:** Luis Castaneda Inc. **144 Alamy Stock Photo:** Jan Wlodarczyk. **145 Getty Images:** Walter Sanders / The LIFE Images Collection. **146 Alamy Stock Photo:** ART Collection. **147 Alamy Stock Photo:** Science History Images. **149 Getty Images:** SeM / UIG. **150 Alamy Stock Photo:** Ivan Vdovin. **153 Alamy Stock Photo:** Lin Pernille Kristensen. **154 Alamy Stock Photo:** Art Collection 2. **155 Alamy Stock Photo:** Photononstop. **157 Getty Images:** Fine Art Images / Heritage Images. **158 Alamy Stock Photo:** Lebrecht Music and Arts Photo Library. **159 Getty Images:** Mondadori Portfolio. **160 Alamy Stock Photo:** Art Collection 3. **161 Alamy Stock Photo:** Chronicle. **162 Getty Images:** Leemage / Corbis. **163 Getty Images:** Godong / UIG. **164 Alamy Stock Photo:** World History Archive. **165 Alamy Stock Photo:** Paul Fearn. **166 Getty Images:** DEA / G. DAGLI ORTI. **167 Rex Shutterstock:** Alfredo Dagli Orti. **169 Alamy Stock Photo:** Timewatch Images. **170 Alamy Stock Photo:** www.BibleLandPictures.com. **171 Alamy Stock Photo:** INTERFOTO. **173 Alamy Stock Photo:** Peter Horree. **178 Alamy Stock Photo:** World History Archive. **179 Alamy Stock Photo:** migstock. **182 Alamy Stock Photo:** PRISMA ARCHIVO. **183 Getty Images:** Fine Art Images / Heritage Images. **184 Alamy Stock Photo:** Ian Dagnall. **185 Alamy Stock Photo:** Kerstin Land. **186 Alamy Stock Photo:** Science History Images. **188 Alamy Stock Photo:** The Artchives. **191 Getty Images:** DEA / S. VANNINI. **192 Getty Images:** DEA / G. DAGLI ORTI. **193 Alamy Stock Photo:** betty finney. **195 Alamy Stock Photo:** ACTIVE MUSEUM (tr); Heritage Image Partnership Ltd (bl). **196 Getty Images:** Alinari Archives. **197 Alamy Stock Photo:** Andrey Kekyalyaynen. **198 Getty Images:** Fine Art. **199 Alamy Stock Photo:** Norman Barrett. **201 Alamy Stock Photo:** Heritage Image Partnership Ltd. **202 Alamy Stock Photo:** V&A Images. **203 iStockphoto.com:** BMPix. **206 Alamy Stock Photo:** Duby Tal / Albatross. **207 Alamy Stock Photo:** Granger Historical Picture Archive. **209 The Metropolitan Museum of Art:** Rogers Fund, 1991. **210 Alamy Stock Photo:** ASP Religion. **211 Alamy Stock Photo:** Finnbarr Webster. **213 Getty Images:** Paul Popper / Popperfoto. **214 Alamy Stock Photo:** Art Collection 2. **216 Alamy Stock Photo:** Peter Barritt. **217 Getty Images:** Richard T. Nowitz. **219 Alamy Stock Photo:** Artokoloro Quint Lox Limited. **220 Alamy Stock Photo:** Ian Dagnall. **221 Getty Images:** SuperStock. **222 Alamy Stock Photo:** Artokoloro Quint Lox Limited. **224 Rex Shutterstock:** Alfredo Dagli Orti. **225 Getty Images:** Granger Historical Picture Archive. **226 Alamy Stock Photo:** Peter Horree. **229 Bridgeman Images:** Monasterio de El Escorial, Spain. **230 Alamy Stock Photo:** Dan Porges. **231 Alamy Stock Photo:** Steve Skjold. **233 Alamy Stock Photo:** PRISMA ARCHIVO. **234 Alamy Stock Photo:** Heritage Image Partnership Ltd. **235 Alamy Stock Photo:** World History Archive. **238 Alamy Stock Photo:** Hemis. **239 Alamy Stock Photo:** World History Archive. **240 Alamy Stock Photo:** SuperStock. **241 Alamy Stock Photo:** PjrTravel. **242 Alamy Stock Photo:** Chronicle. **243 Getty Images:** DEA / G. DAGLI ORTI. **244 Getty Images:** Rischgitz. **245 Getty Images:** Jeremy Horner. **246 Getty Images:** Alinari Archives. **247 Alamy Stock Photo:** Kumar Sriskandan. **250 Alamy Stock Photo:** PAINTING. **251 Alamy Stock Photo:** www.BibleLandPictures.com. **253 Alamy Stock Photo:** World History Archive. **254 Alamy Stock Photo:** Art Collection 2. **255 Alamy Stock Photo:** ASP Religion. **256 Alamy Stock Photo:** PRISMA ARCHIVO. **257 Getty Images:** Fine Art Images / Heritage Images. **260 Alamy Stock Photo:** Heritage Image Partnership Ltd. **261 Alamy Stock Photo:** Heritage Image Partnership Ltd. **263 Alamy Stock Photo:** Godong (br). **Getty Images:** De Agostini / V. Pirozzi (tl). **264 Getty Images:** Mondadori Portfolio. **265 Alamy Stock Photo:** Rafael Ben-Ari. **266 Alamy Stock Photo:** The Print Collector. **267 Alamy Stock Photo:** Don Paulson / Jaynes Gallery / DanitaDelimont.com. **268 Dreamstime.com:** Camptoloma (tr). **269 Alamy Stock Photo:** World History Archive (bl). **270 Getty Images:** DEA / G. DAGLI ORTI. **271 Getty Images:** DEA PICTURE LIBRARY (tl, tr). **272 Getty Images:** Fine Art. **275 Alamy Stock Photo:** ART Collection (tr); Juha Remes (tl). **276 Alamy Stock Photo:** Lanmas (tr). **Library of Congress, Washington, D.C.:** LC-DIG-pga-03638 (clb). **282 Getty Images:** Print Collector. **283 Alamy Stock Photo:** ART Collection. **285 Alamy Stock Photo:** Granger Historical Picture Archive. **287 Getty Images:** Fine Art Images / Heritage Images. **289 Alamy Stock Photo:** Colin Underhill. **291 Alamy Stock Photo:** INTERFOTO (tr). **Getty Images:** DEA PICTURE LIBRARY (tl). **292 Getty Images:** Donaldson Collection / Michael Ochs Archives. **294 Alamy Stock Photo:** Zvonimir Atletic. **295 Alamy Stock Photo:** Azoor Photo. **296 Alamy Stock Photo:** Stan Pritchard. **297 Alamy Stock Photo:** imageBROKER. **298 Alamy Stock Photo:** Peter Horree. **299 Alamy Stock Photo:** INTERFOTO. **301 Getty Images:** National Galleries Of Scotland. **302 Getty Images:** Fine Art Images / Heritage Images. **303 Alamy Stock Photo:** Funky Stock—Paul Williams. **304 Rijksmuseum, Amsterdam:** Legislature of Mr. P. Formijne, Amsterdam. **305 Alamy Stock Photo:** North Wind Picture Archives. **306 Getty Images:** DEA / VENERANDA BIBLIOTECA AMBROSIANA. **307 Alamy Stock Photo:** PACIFIC PRESS. **309 Alamy Stock Photo:** Paul Fearn (tr); World History Archive **310 Alamy Stock Photo:** dave stamboulis. **312 Alamy Stock Photo:** Itsik Marom. **313 Alamy Stock Photo:** Paul Fearn (bl); Heritage Image Partnership L (tr). **315 Alamy Stock Photo:** Godong (bl). **Getty Images:** Fine Art Photographic (tr). **318 Alamy Stock Photo:** Art Collection 4. **319 Alamy Stock Photo:** Masterpics. **321 Alamy Stock Photo:** ART Collection (tl); Paul Fearn (br). **324 Getty Images:** Paul Almasy / Corbis / VCG. **326 Alamy Stock Photo:** Godong. **327 Alamy Stock Photo:** ClassicStock (tr). **Getty Images:** DEA PICTURE LIBRARY (br). **328 Alamy Stock Photo:** The Print Collector. **329 Alamy Stock Photo:** World History Archive

All other images © Dorling Kindersley
For further information see:
www.dkimages.com

3 1333 04715 0600